Texts and Monographs in Computer Science

F. L. Bauer
David Gries
editors

The Design of Well-Structured and Correct Programs

Suad Alagić
Michael A. Arbib

Springer-Verlag
New York Heidelberg Berlin

Suad Alagić
Department of Informatics
Faculty of Electrical Engineering
University of Sarajevo
Sarajevo
Yugoslavia

Michael A. Arbib
Department of Computer and
  Information Science
University of Massachusetts
Amherst, MA 01003
USA

editors

F. L. Bauer
Mathematisches Institut der
  Technischen Hochschule
8000 München
Arcisstrasse 21
West Germany

David Gries
Department of Computer Science
Cornell University
Upson Hall
Ithaca, NY 14859
USA

AMS Subject Classifications: 02B10, 02E15, 68A05, 68A40
(C.R.) Computer Classifications: 4.22, 4.34, 4.6, 5.21, 5.24

Library of Congress Cataloging in Publication Data
Alagić, Suad, 1946–
    The design of well-structured and correct
programs.

    (Texts and monographs in computer science)
    "Portions of the material, in rather different form,
appeared in Alagić's Serbo-Croatian text Principi
programiranja."
    Bibliography: p.
    Includes indexes.
    1. Electronic digital computers—Programming.
2. PASCAL (Computer program language) I. Arbib,
Michael A., joint author. II. Title.
    QA76.6.A44   001.6'42   77-27087

33, 111

Second, corrected printing

ISBN 0-387-90299-6   Springer-Verlag New York
ISBN 3-540-90299-6   Springer-Verlag Berlin Heidelberg

Preface

The major goal of this book is to present the techniques of top-down program design and verification of program correctness hand-in-hand. It thus aims to give readers a new way of looking at algorithms and their design, synthesizing ten years of research in the process. It provides many examples of program and proof development with the aid of a formal and informal treatment of Hoare's method of invariants. Modern widely accepted control structures and data structures are explained in detail, together with their formal definitions, as a basis for their use in the design of correct algorithms. We provide and apply proof rules for a wide range of program structures, including conditionals, loops, procedures and recursion. We analyze situations in which the restricted use of gotos can be justified, providing a new approach to proof rules for such situations. We study several important techniques of data structuring, including arrays, files, records and linked structures.

The secondary goal of this book is to teach the reader how to use the programming language Pascal. This is the first text to teach Pascal programming in a fashion which not only includes advanced algorithms which operate on advanced data structures, but also provides the full axiomatic definition of Pascal due to Wirth and Hoare. Our approach to the language is very different from that of a conventional programming text. Certain details crucial to "getting on the machine"—such as the format of a program—are not treated until Chapter 5. Instead, the reader is first taught how to break a program into pieces, and how Pascal control structures can put those pieces together again. Then the reader is taught how to design structured data types which provide the appropriate representation of the information involved in problem solution. In this way, the reader develops a full understanding of the conceptual role of Pascal in algorithm design.

We believe that by combining the study of Pascal with that of the tools of top-down design and correctness, the reader will emerge with a far deeper knowledge of Pascal than that offered by an informal introductory Pascal text. We teach the reader to think carefully about the design of his algorithm before producing a program and submitting it for execution. In the appendices, we offer a complete syntax of Pascal keyed to the sections in which we present the material, as well as a summary of Pascal proof rules.

One of the main features of the book is an extensive, carefully chosen sample of the algorithms that we believe should be included in every modern programming curriculum. We also include some typical examples from business data processsing. This collection is supplemented by an extensive set of exercises.

This book is written for a reader who has already had an introductory course in programming. The book assumes no particular mathematical background, but does require that the reader understand what it means to prove a theorem—for without that, how can you understand a proof of correctness? All the mathematics beyond that of a few simple properties of numbers (e.g., "what is a divisor?", "what is a prime?") is spelled out in the text itself. However, a student with little experience in formal mathematical reasoning will need a few supplementary lectures from the instructor to get through the first few proofs. The instructor of a course which uses this text should devote several lectures to aspects of the local Pascal implementation and the conventions involved in running Pascal programs. We suggest that this occur during the teaching of Chapter 3. A one-semester course should cover the basic material provided by Chapters 1 through 5 (with the exception of some of the more advanced examples). Just how much of Chapters 6 and 7 can be covered will depend on the degree of preparation of the students.

The book was written while the authors were together in Edinburgh from January to May of 1977 and completed the following August. Portions of the material, in rather different form, appeared in Alagić's Serbo-Croatian text *Principi programiranja*. Suad Alagić acknowledges the support from the British Council and Zajednica za naucni rad SR Bosne i Hercegovine, and the hospitality of the Department of Computer Science of the University of Edinburgh, Sidney Michaelson in particular. Michael Arbib expresses his appreciation to the National Science Foundation for support under Grant No. DCR72-03733 A01 and to Jimmy Thorne of the School of Epistemics of Edinburgh University. The authors would also like to thank Rod Burstall, Robin Milner, David McQueen, Gordon Plotkin, John Reynolds, and Christopher Wadsworth for many discussions on topics related to this book. Special thanks are due to Rolf Braae, Frank

Friedman, Stephen Hegner, Radovan Jović, Gary Levin, and Robert Melville, who carefully read the complete manuscript and suggested a number of improvements.

Vyvienne Hosie and Gwyn Mitchell did a superb job of typing the manuscript.

August 1977
Suad Alagić
Michael A. Arbib

Contents

1
Introducing Top-down Design

1.1 The Idea of Top-down Design

If we want a computer to solve a problem for us, we must develop an
algorithm—a recipe which spells out explicitly and unambiguously the steps
which must be carried out on the problem *data* to obtain *a correct solution*
(where one exists) *within a finite time*. We must specify this algorithm so
precisely that its instructions can be followed automatically by a computer.
In other words, the algorithm must be written as a *program* in a *programming
language*—a specially chosen notation in which we specify algorithms to a
level of detail suitable for mechanical interpretation. We shall say more
about programming languages in Section 1.3, and we shall devote many
pages to showing the reader how to program in Pascal, a programming
language which is particularly well suited for the specification of algorithms.
However, the thrust of our book is that, although the final product of the
programmer's task is expressed in a programming language, the specific
properties of the language should *not* enter into the early stages of algorithm
development.

For too long, people have tried to formulate algorithms directly in a
programming language, rather than carefully decomposing the problem
into simpler problems and checking the relationship between them before
proceeding to a more detailed specification. This book develops the second
approach—we call it *top-down design*—because experience has shown that
it allows one to generate clean algorithms with far fewer mistakes than by
the old line-by-line method. Once an algorithm is elaborated to the level of
detail of a program, the question is whether the process of performing the
action specified in it by a computer terminates within a finite time, and yields

the correct results. When a program is produced line by line, the only way of checking this is to have the program executed by the computer for various arguments and see whether the results of execution will be as expected. This is known as *program testing*, and the process of changing the program to correct for errors is known as *debugging*. If the program performs correctly for a judiciously chosen set of arguments, the confidence with which we can assert that our program will perform correctly for *all* arguments may be reasonably high. But this method can never guarantee correct performance of the program in all cases. The only way to do this is through a careful top-down design process of the kind presented in this book, which includes a convincing demonstration that *all* the computations which the program represents meet the desired specifications by yielding the correct results within a finite time.

The method of top-down design, then, is simply this: decompose the over-all problem into precisely specified subproblems, and prove that if each subproblem is solved correctly, and these solutions are fitted together in a specified way, then the original problem will be solved correctly. Repeat this process of "decompose and prove correctness of the decomposition" for the subproblems; and keep repeating this process until reaching subproblems so simple that their solution can be expressed in a few lines of a programming language.

We make this process more vivid for the reader by immediately turning to the examples of the next section.

1.2 An Example: The Greatest Common Divisor

To give the reader an intuitive feeling for concepts which will be developed at length in later chapters, we now look at the top-down design of an algo-rithm to solve the following problem.

> *Given integers a and b, find their greatest common divisor.*   (1)

Before we attempt to solve the problem posed in (1), let us define the notion of the greatest common divisor and its basic properties.

If x and y are integers, not both zero, then their greatest common divisor, denoted by $gcd(x,y)$, is the largest integer which divides both of them (that is, without remainder). For example, $gcd(7,11) = 1$, $gcd(16,28) = 4$ and $gcd(90,135) = 45$. Observe that the gcd always exists. Indeed, if $y \neq 0$, then no integer greater than $|y|$ (the absolute value of y) can divide y. On the other hand, the integer 1 divides both x and y, and so there must be a largest integer which divides them both. When both x and y are zero, the above definition does not apply, since every integer divides 0. We shall set

$$gcd(0,0) = 0. \tag{2}$$

It is obvious that the following properties follow from the above definitions:

$$gcd(u,v) = gcd(v,u) \tag{3}$$

$$gcd(u,v) = gcd(-u,v) \tag{4}$$

$$gcd(u,0) = |u|. \tag{5}$$

Looking back at the problem (1), we realize that, because of the properties (3) and (4), we can actually concentrate on the following problem:

Given non-negative integers a and b, find their greatest common divisor. (6)

Indeed, if we know how to solve the problem (6), then in order to find the greatest common divisor of arbitrary integers a and b, we just apply the method used for solving (6) to $|a|$ and $|b|$. So let us now tackle the problem (6).

In order to solve the task posed in (6), we will decompose it into a number of simpler subtasks and specify the order in which these subtasks are to be solved to obtain the solution to the whole problem (6). The decomposition of any problem can usually be done in many different ways, and we shall see several such ways later in the book. For the present, we shall develop what seems to us the simplest decomposition for problem (6).

Remember that we are now dealing with nonnegative numbers. Suppose that we could reduce the problem of finding $gcd(a,b)$ for $b > 0$ to that of finding $gcd(x,y)$, where x and y are still nonnegative and $y < b$. Then after performing this reduction only a finite number of times we must reach the stage where $y = 0$, and then (5) will assure us that $gcd(a,b) = x$, for the x in $gcd(a,b) = gcd(x,0)$. An observant reader will notice that the decomposition outlined above requires the introduction of auxiliary variables x and y, and that it can be defined as follows:

  i. *Set x to a and y to b* (7)
 ii. *If $y \neq 0$ then*:
      a. *Decrease y and change x in such a way that they remain nonnegative and that the value $gcd(x,y)$ remains the same*
      b. *Repeat step* ii
iii. *If $y = 0$ set $gcd(a,b)$ to x.*

We have just been through an argument which says that the number of reduction steps in (7) is finite.

Since steps i. and iii. in (7) are simple enough, we now try to decompose step ii. further. This decomposition is not at all trivial, and requires a mathematical invention, which is attributed to Euclid. The problem is to spell out 'decrease y' and 'change x' in greater detail.

If we denote the quotient obtained on dividing x by y by x **div** y, and the remainder by x **mod** y, then we have the following familiar relation

$$x = (x \text{ div } y) * y + x \text{ mod } y \tag{8}$$

where $*$ denotes the usual operation of integer multiplication. For example, 20 **div** 7 = 2, 20 **mod** 7 = 6, and we do indeed have 20 = 2 * 7 + 6.

If we rewrite the relation (8) as follows:

$$x \text{ mod } y = x - (x \text{ div } y) * y \tag{9}$$

we can draw the following conclusions, which will help us decompose step ii. (a) in (7).

Any common divisor of x and y is a divisor of both y and $x - (x \text{ div } y) * y$, and conversely any common divisor of y and $x - (x \text{ div } y) * y$ must divide both x and y. In particular, the greatest common divisor of x and y must be the same as the greatest common divisor of y and $x - (x \text{ div } y) * y$, i.e., the following holds:

$$gcd(x, y) = gcd(y, x \text{ mod } y). \tag{10}$$

Since $x \text{ mod } y < y$, the relation (10) tells us how to decrease the value of y (and change the value of x) without affecting the value of $gcd(x, y)$. We simply have to compute the remainder $x \text{ mod } y$, denote it by r, and then set first x to y and then y to r. So we obtain the following decomposition of step ii. (a) in (7)

> i. *Set r to x **mod** y* (11)
> ii. *Set x to y*
> iii. *Set y to r.*

This decomposition does indeed have the property that it decreases the value of y and changes the value of x, but in such a way that both x and y remain nonnegative. Moreover, the value of $gcd(x, y)$ is preserved. Thus, the overall decomposition developed so far has the form:

> i. *Set x to a and y to b* (12)
> ii. *If y $\neq$ 0 then:*
>   a. *Set r to x **mod** y*
>   b. *Set x to y*
>   c. *Set y to r*
>   d. *Repeat the step* ii.
> iii. *If y = 0 set gcd(a,b) to x.*

An *algorithm* consists of a number of actions to be performed upon objects called *data*, in a specified order, with possible repetitions under specified conditions. If we assume that the steps in (12) are simple and well understood then we have developed an algorithm for computing the greatest common divisor of nonnegative integers a and b. We now examine the components of this algorithm more closely to introduce a number of concepts which will play an important role throughout the book.

The symbols x, y and r in (12) denote *variables* in the sense that the value of a variable can change as a result of some action of an algorithm. However, the set of values which that variable may possibly assume is fixed as part of the specification of the algorithm, and we speak of each variable as belonging to a particular *data type*. Specifying the data type restricts the values a variable may take and—as we shall see in Chapter 3—specifies some of the basic operations which can be carried out on the variable.

The variables x, y, and r in (12) all have the set of nonnegative integers as their data type. The *constants* a and b—the *input data*—also have the nonnegative integers as their data type.

Actions to be performed in an algorithm are described by *statements*. An example of a statement is *Set x to y*. This statement is called an *assignment statement*. It specifies the action which assigns the current value of the variable y as the new value of the variable x. With the exception of the *test* for whether $y \neq 0$, the whole algorithm (12) is expressed in terms of assignment statements which are to be performed in a certain order.

A careful analysis of the way in which the assignment statements are composed in the algorithm (12) shows the following: The assignments a, b and c are to be performed one after the other, that is *sequentially*. This ordering is essential for obtaining the correct answer. For example, if we perform first the assignment c and then the assignment b, we would violate the requirements under which we decomposed ii. (a) in (7). The values of x and y would remain nonnegative, and the value of y would be reduced, but not in such a way that the value of $gcd(x,y)$ can be guaranteed to remain unaffected. Consequently, the result of the algorithm, represented as the final value of the variable x, would not be equal to $gcd(a,b)$, i.e., it would be wrong. The other example of sequential composition of actions in the algorithm (12) is given by the statements i. and ii. The action described by the statement i. must be performed first, and then it is followed by the action described by the statement ii.

If we now look carefully into the statement i., we realise that it itself consists of two assignment statements, *set x to a*, and *set y to b*. However, the order in which these two assignments should be performed is immaterial, one can be performed after the other in either order, and in fact, the quickest way may be to perform them in parallel, if we have a computer which can do that sort of thing. But we shall not use concurrent operations in this book, and express the statement i. as a sequential composition of two assignments, as follows:

$$\text{i. a. } \textit{Set x to a} \hspace{4cm} (13)$$
$$\text{b. } \textit{Set y to b.}$$

Consider the statement ii. in more detail. If we denote by S the sequential composition of the assignments a, b and c, then we can say that the action defined by ii. consists of repeating the action S while the value of the variable y is different from zero. If initially the value of y equals zero, S will not be performed at all. The repetition process terminates when the value of y equals zero. This type of composition of actions is particularly important. It is called *repetitive* (sometimes also *iterative*) *composition*. We also say that in such a case the statements constitute a *loop*.

By now we have a much more precisely defined algorithm for computing the greatest common divisor of two nonnegative integers. We learned that apart from the operations of testing whether the value of y is different from zero, and computing the remainder of integer division, we need the assignment statements and two types of composition: sequential composition and repetitive composition. These two types of composition are represented in the form of diagrams as explained below.

If S_1 and S_2 are statements, then their sequential composition is represented as:

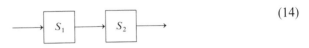

(14)

If the statement S is to be repeated while the condition B is true, then we represent this repetitive action as:

(15)

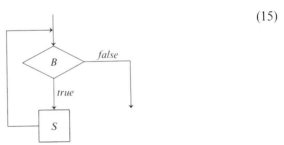

In both these cases, it is the shape of the boxes and the direction of the arrows that matters, not the position of the boxes on the page. With these conventions in mind we can represent the process of development of the algorithm for computing $gcd(a,b)$ in Figure 1.1.

Observe that the diagrams are annotated with relations which should hold before and after specific statements. In particular, our analysis shows that if a and b are nonnegative integers, then at the completion of the actions specified by the developed algorithm, x will be equal to the greatest common divisor of a and b. Note that the diagrams are incomplete in one important respect—they do not specify the data types of the variables.

Our decomposition process may be regarded as completed only if we assume that particular actions in terms of which it is composed are simple and well-understood. So, for example, although the computation of the remainder obtained on integer division may be regarded as a simple and

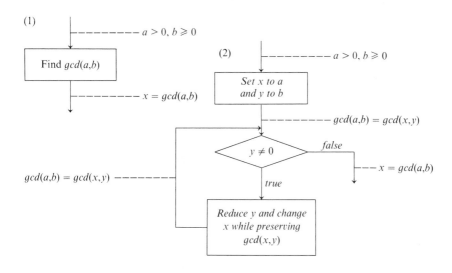

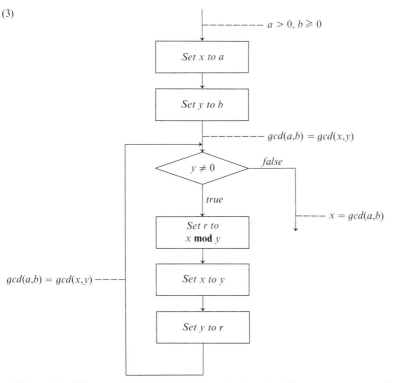

Figure 1.1   Three stages in the development of an algorithm to compute $gcd(a,b)$

well-understood operation, we can also decompose it in the usual way, reducing the operation of division to simpler operations of addition and subtraction. In order to demonstrate that the strategy which we used in obtaining the decomposition of Figure 1.1 will work just as well for further reduction, we now discuss the further decomposition of the statement

Set r to x **mod** *y.*

Computing just the remainder x **mod** y is certainly simpler than computing both the quotient x **div** y and the remainder x **mod** y. But we will develop the full division algorithm, since this provides another valuable exercise in the top-down design of algorithms.

Remember that the values of x and y just before the statement *Set r to x* **mod** y is performed are such that $x \geqslant 0$ and $y > 0$. There thus exists a unique pair of integers q and r such that the following relations hold:

$$\begin{align} \text{i. } & x = q * y + r \tag{16} \\ \text{ii. } & 0 \leqslant r < y. \end{align}$$

In order to compute q and r, we start with $q = 0$ and $r = x$, and then repeatedly subtract y from r and increase q by 1, until we reach the state when $r < y$. Apart from the familiar intuitive reasons for this decomposition, we observe that initially setting q to 0 and r to x will ensure that the relation (16)i. will hold, and that subtracting y from r and increasing q by 1 does not affect this relation, since we have

$$(q + 1) * y + r - y = q * y + r. \tag{17}$$

That, of course, is exactly what we want, since it means that upon completion of the repetition process (16)i. will hold. The repetition process is performed while $r \geqslant y$, which means that before every subtraction of y from r, $r \geqslant y$, or $r - y \geqslant 0$, holds. Since $r - y \geqslant 0$ holds before r is set to $r - y$, we conclude that throughout the process of subtracting y from r the value of the variable r remains nonnegative, and it thus has that property upon completion of the repetition process, which accounts for the $0 \leqslant r$ part of (16)ii. The repetition process terminates when $r < y$ (the right part in (16)ii.), and so upon completion of the algorithm, (16) holds, i.e. the desired result is obtained.

It only remains to check that this process will terminate after only a finite number of the repetition steps. Our analysis just showed that r remains nonnegative throughout the process. Its initial value is x, so if initially $x < y$ the remainder algorithm terminates immediately with the remainder x and the quotient 0. If $x \geqslant y$ initially, then since the value of r is always nonnegative, we can subtract $y(y > 0)$ from it only a finite number of times before we reduce its value below y. So the repetition process will actually terminate after only a finite number of steps.

The above reasoning thus leads to the algorithm which is represented in the diagram in Figure 1.2.

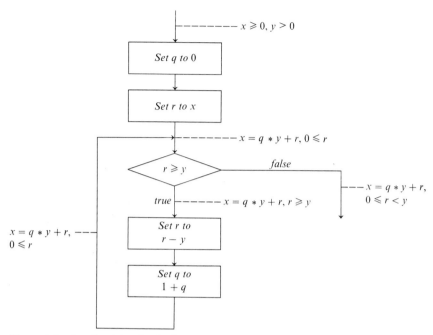

Figure 1.2   An algorithm for finding q and r so that $x = q * y + r$ and $0 \leqslant r < y$ both hold. Thus, on exit—following the arrow that leads out of the flow diagram—we have $q = x \,\mathbf{div}\, y$ and $r = x \,\mathbf{mod}\, y$.

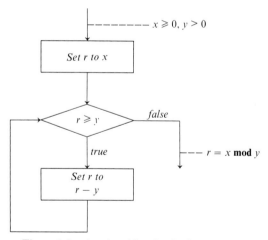

Figure 1.3   An algorithm for finding $x \,\mathbf{mod}\, y$.

It is easy to see that if we want to compute just the remainder, and not both the quotient and the remainder, then we just have to simplify Figure 1.2 to yield Figure 1.3.

1.3 Programming Language and Machine Language

Figure 1.1 of Section 1.2 traces the result of two successive decompositions of the problem of finding the greatest common divisor of two nonnegative integers. As most readers know, the algorithm of Figure 1.1(3) must be reexpressed as a program in some programming language before it can be presented to a computer, and the computer will need a translator unless the program is already in machine language. This section simply spells out these ideas in more detail, and introduces a few basic features of the programming language Pascal.

A modern computer is a machine which, under normal circumstances, would not accept Figure 1.1(1) as a sufficiently precise and detailed specification of the algorithm it is to perform. Figure 1.1(2), and even Figure 1.1(3), are still in a general and imprecise form, and because of that they are called abstract algorithms. In order to obtain from Figure 1.1(3) an acceptable description of the desired algorithm for a computer, specification of data and statements must be further decomposed to a lower level of detail. An important goal of this transformation is to make explicit and precise those portions of the algorithm description which are implicit and rely on the intuition, common sense, or technical knowledge of the reader. The reason for this is that computers are, in most cases, devoid of these virtues.

The level by level transformation represented in Figure 1.1 must thus continue until the algorithm is specified in the form of a *programming language*—a specially chosen notation which, as we have already seen in Section 1.1, allows specification of algorithms in an unambiguous manner, to the level of detail where they can be mechanically interpreted. Such a specification of the developed algorithms of Figure 1.1(3) and Figure 1.2 in the programming language Pascal, which is going to be used in this book, is given below in (1) and (2) respectively. The programming language Pascal is a result of years of development in programming languages and programming methodology. It grew from efforts to find a successor to the programming language Algol 60. Pascal was designed by Niklaus Wirth. The design was completed in 1970—Wirth's revised report on the language is conveniently published in Jensen and Wirth (1974). The major novelties introduced in Pascal in comparison with Algol 60 are a variety of structuring methods for data, programmer definable data types (both treated in detail in Chapter 3) and better composition methods for statements (discussed carefully in Chapter 2). But all the features of Pascal are introduced with one important consideration in mind—that they can be efficiently implemented on modern computers. Pascal is thus a language of relatively moderate complexity and size, available on many types of computers.

$$\begin{aligned}
&\textbf{begin } \{a > 0, b \geqslant 0\} \qquad\qquad\qquad\qquad\qquad (1)\\
&\quad x := a; y := b;\\
&\quad \textbf{while } y \neq 0 \textbf{ do } \{gcd(a,b) = gcd(x,y)\}\\
&\quad \textbf{begin } r := x \textbf{ mod } y;\\
&\qquad\quad x := y;\\
&\qquad\quad y := r\\
&\quad \textbf{end}\\
&\quad \{x = gcd(a,b)\}\\
&\textbf{end}
\end{aligned}$$

$$\begin{aligned}
&\textbf{begin } \{x \geqslant 0, y > 0\} \qquad\qquad\qquad\qquad\qquad (2)\\
&\quad q := 0; r := x;\\
&\quad \textbf{while } r \geqslant y \textbf{ do } \{x = q * y + r, r \geqslant y\}\\
&\quad \textbf{begin } r := r - y;\\
&\qquad\quad q := 1 + q\\
&\quad \textbf{end}\\
&\quad \{x = q * y + r, 0 \leqslant r < y\}\\
&\textbf{end}
\end{aligned}$$

The reader is not yet expected to understand all of this notation since it will be introduced gradually as we progress through the book. Some aspects of this notation will be briefly discussed here.

Sequences of symbols which in (1) and (2) occur in curly brackets { and } are called *comments*. They do not describe any action and are used to explain the program to the human reader.

Every language, and a programming language in particular, is based on an *alphabet*. An alphabet is just a finite set of symbols. Sentences, which in the case of a programming language are called *programs*, are composed by concatenating basic symbols from the alphabet according to what are called the *syntactic rules* of the language (corresponding to the rules of grammar for a natural language like English).

The alphabet of a programming language usually consists of letters, digits and special symbols such as $+, -, *, ;, :=$, etc. Note that the assignment is denoted by the special symbol $:=$.

The set of special symbols in an alphabet of a typical programming language is fairly large. As a result, specially chosen English words in boldface type are often used to denote these special symbols. Examples of such words are **begin, end, while, do**, etc. The boldface type is used to indicate that, although these words are sequences of letters, they stand for single symbols of the programming language alphabet. The choice of these words is made in such a way that they make programs easier to understand. For example, the sequential composition of statements S_1 and S_2

(3)

is denoted with **begin** S_1; S_2 **end**, where **begin** and **end** play the role of bracketing a composite statement, which consists of sequential composition (denoted by ;) of two statements. So **begin** $r := r - y$; $q := 1 + q$ **end** in (2) is regarded as a single (although composite) statement delimited by the brackets **begin** and **end**, and this statement gets repeatedly performed in the loop in (2).

The loop

(4)

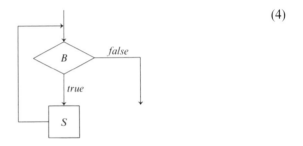

is expressed in Pascal as **while** B **do** S, which conveys the meaning of this statement, i.e., it says that it describes the action which consists of repeating the action described by S while the condition B is true.

Variables are denoted in a Pascal program by finite sequences of letters and digits called *identifiers*, which are such that the first symbol in each sequence is a letter.

In the programs (1) and (2) all the identifiers are of length one, but it follows from the above definitions that perfectly correct identifiers are also: *quotient, remainder, root1, root2*, whereas the sequences *1root, 2root, first-root, x* **div** *y, x* **mod** *y* do not conform to the rule which determines the syntax of identifiers.

As we stressed in Section 1.1, the top-down design of an algorithm starts from the formulation of the problem and proceeds through levels of decomposition which lead to the final specification of the desired algorithm in the notation of the chosen programming language. We have illustrated this design process by developing a program for computing the greatest common divisor of two nonnegative integers. In spite of the fact that extreme care must be exercised in the final stages of expressing the program according to the conventions of the chosen programming language, this last phase is relatively simple from the conceptual viewpoint. The major intellectual effort is required in the first stages of program development, i.e., in the development of a sufficiently detailed abstract algorithm. For example, the passages in Section 1.2 from (6) to (7) and from (7) to (12) were not trivial at all. They required a detailed analysis of the problem, knowledge of some properties of integers, and certainly a lot of creativity. When the desired algorithm is decomposed to a sufficient level of detail, its specification in the chosen programming language is a relatively simple task—so long as the language is appropriate to this class of problems. Although the final goal of program development is a specification of the desired algorithm in the chosen programming language, the decomposition process should not be guided by the facilitites of this language until the final stages of this process. In fact, decisions regarding specific details of the chosen representation should be postponed as far as possible. For example, the intellectual effort required to design the abstract algorithm (12) would be the same no matter whether we choose to represent (12) in Pascal or in some other language such as Algol, PL/I etc. So the design process should not be burdened by specific features of a particular programming language. However, it is not true that all languages are equally suitable for expressing algorithms. The programming language notation should allow the representation of abstract algorithms in a natural, elegant, and easily understood way, and with regard to that (and not only that) Pascal is a good choice.

Clearly then, for a programming language to be 'comfortable', it must not only allow the precise specification of algorithms, but must also allow this specification to be expressed in a fashion understandable to a human reader, who constructs it, modifies it, and proves that it really satisfies the problem requirements. By contrast, the processor within a computer requires a quite different representation of a program, written in what is called *machine language*, which is unsuitable for a human reader.

The alphabet of machine language is binary, i.e., it consists of two symbols, usually denoted by 0 and 1. Thus a statement of a machine language, which is called an *instruction*, is specified as a sequence of binary digits (bits) according to certain format conventions (syntax). Data are represented in the same way, i.e., as finite sequences of bits. In order to illustrate this, recall that in the usual decimal positional representation a sequence of decimal digits

$$a_n a_{n-1} \cdots a_0, \text{ where } a_i \in \{0,1, \ldots ,9\} \text{ for } i = 0,1, \ldots ,n,$$

denotes the number

$$a_n * 10^n + a_{n-1} * 10^{n-1} + \cdots + a_0 * 10^0.$$

Likewise, a sequence of binary digits

$$b_n b_{n-1} \cdots b_0, \text{ where } b_i \in \{0,1\} \text{ for } i = 0, 1, \ldots ,n,$$

can be interpreted as the number

$$b_n * 2^n + b_{n-1} * 2^{n-1} + \cdots + b_0 * 2^0.$$

In any case, we see that one further transformation of a program is necessary in order to get it executed by a computer. We consider the case in

which the program is translated from the programming language notation
to the machine language notation by a program called a *compiler*. The result
of compiling a program is a program in machine language, which enables the
original abstract algorithm to be executed by the processor of the machine.

While the notation of programming languages is independent of a particular computer, machine language is not, and reflects closely the characteristics of a particular machine on which programs written in that language
can be executed. Thus expressing an algorithm in a programming language
allows us to abstract from most of the particular characteristics of a computer, and concentrate on the intellectually more challenging problems of the
design of the desired algorithm. Furthermore, it makes the product of the
programming process transferable (or portable) from one machine to another
with at worst minor modifications. We can say that the existence of a
compiler makes it possible to write programs for an idealised, hypothetical
computer which is designed not according to the limitations of current
technology, but according to the capabilities of humans to express their
thoughts. In spite of this, the programmer should be constantly aware of
the inherent limitations of the physical machines on which actual programs
will be executed—especially limitations of speed and memory.

Although the processor of a computer performs the actions specified by
a program with incredible speed and accuracy, this speed is finite and varies
from one machine to another. The programmer should thus always be concerned not only with the design of a correct algorithm, but, simultaneously,
with the design of an efficient algorithm, i.e, one which does not take too long
to execute. It is possible to estimate the efficiency of a program and perform
certain structural alterations to the program under invariance of correctness
which can improve program efficiency to a great extent.

The other fundamental limitation of real computers is the size of their
memory which limits the number of instructions, data, and intermediate
results which can be stored within the machine. Even though the memory
of modern computers is enormously large by earlier standards, it is still
limited, and these size limitations must be taken into account when specifying
the length of a program and the number of variables that will be active during
its execution. While the stress in this book will be on top-down design for
correctness, we shall repeatedly draw the reader's attention to considerations
which improve efficiency in both speed and the use of memory.

2
Basic Compositions of Actions and Their Proof Rules

2.1 Relations for Program Correctness

In Chapter 1, we established the following method of *top-down design of an algorithm to solve a given problem*:

> "Decompose the overall problem into precisely specified subproblems, and prove that if each subproblem is solved correctly *and these solutions are fitted together in a specified way* then the original problem will be solved correctly. Repeat the process of "decompose and prove correctness of the decomposition" for the subproblems; and keep repeating this process until reaching subproblems so simple that their solution can be expressed in a few lines of a programming language."

Each algorithm has both a *static structure* and a *dynamic structure*. The static structure is represented by the text—whether in the form of a flow diagram, or in a program in a language like Pascal—which represents the actions to be performed and the tests to be carried out in solving a given problem. As a text, it has no dependence on the values of the input data. By contrast, the dynamic structure depends strongly on the choice of input data, for different branches will be taken in the execution of the algorithm dependent on the values given to the input variables. The dynamic structure is the process of computation, and consists of a sequence of *computation states*. The state of computation at any time comprises the values of all program variables at that time—and thus depends on the initial values of those variables, and the steps of the algorithm that have been followed so far. We then have that the current instruction either changes the computation state (alters the values of some variables) and transfers control to the next instruction in sequence; or conducts a test on the computation state (compares the values of certain variables) and transfers control to another instruction on the basis of the outcome of that test.

A programming language provides both *simple statements* and *composition methods* which allow us to form *structured statements* from other statements, which may themselves be simple or compound. Our job in this chapter is twofold:

a. To specify certain kinds of simple statements used in Pascal, and to specify several frequently used ways in which solutions to subproblems can be fitted together. For example, in Section 1.3, we met both sequential composition (3) and **while-do** composition (4).

b. To provide *proof rules* which allow us to *formally prove* that a simple statement affects the computation state in some way, and that certain properties of a compound statement follow from properties of the constituent pieces.

To motivate the work in this chapter, consider Figure 2.1, which reproduces the algorithm we designed in Section 1.2 to determine x **div** y and x **mod** y. Note that the computation state associated with the entry point comprises the values of the input variables x and y; but that, after execution of the first two statements, the computation state has been expanded to include the values of four variables, x, y, q and r. (The values of x and y may vary from use to use of the algorithm, but remain constant throughout a single run through the algorithm.) Clearly, the transfer of control following the test $r \geqslant y$ will depend on the current computation state.

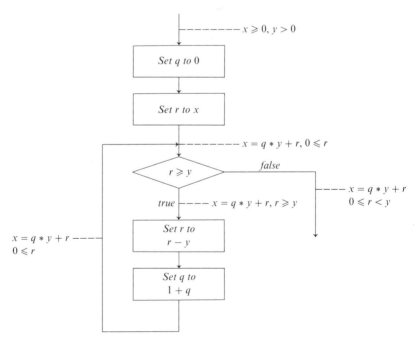

Figure 2.1   An algorithm for finding q and r so that $x = q * y + r$ and $0 \leqslant r < y$ both hold. Thus, on exit, $q = x$ **div** y and $r = x$ **mod** y.

The fundamental property of the sequential composition and the **while-do**—and of all the other forms of composition we shall describe in this chapter—is that they combine one or more diagrams each having a single entry point and a single exit point to yield a composite diagram which also has just one entry point and one exit point. As Figure 2.1 makes very clear, our design procedure attaches relations to these points. These relations describe the essential aspects of the states of computation that correspond to those points. Thus each such diagram has the form

(1)

where S may correspond to a single computer action, or may—as we repeat the top-down design process—itself become a composite diagram. To express (1) in a more concise form, we use the notation:

$$\{P\}\ S\ \{Q\}. \tag{2}$$

This is a *program specification* with the following meaning: If the relation P is true before S is executed, then Q will hold upon completion of execution of S. In other words, if P holds when the entry point in (1) is reached, then Q will hold when the exit point of (1) is reached.

A word of caution about our notation—where we use $\{P\}\ S\ \{Q\}$, many other authors write $P\{S\}Q$. But the reason for our choice is a simple one. When we document Pascal programs in this book, we enclose *comments*—remarks, intended to help the human reader understand the program, which are not for execution by the computer—in curly brackets { } to mark them off from the actual program for the machine. So we write $\{P\}$ and $\{Q\}$ in (2) because the relations P and Q behave like comments—they tell the human checking the program's correctness what properties of the state of the computation are meant to hold each time the computer comes to the corresponding point in the program.

If S is a program whose correctness we want to establish, then (2)—with the meaning we have specified—is what we want to prove, where P is the relation which the initial values of variables should satisfy and Q is the relation which the final values of variables must satisfy. For example, if S is the algorithm in Figure 2.1—or, what is the same thing, Figure 2.2(d)—then what we want to prove is

$$\{(x \geqslant 0) \wedge (y > 0)\}\ S\ \{(x = q * y + r) \wedge (0 \leqslant r < y)\} \tag{3}$$

where we use $\wedge$ as formal notation for 'and'. (We explain this notation in more detail in Section 2.2).

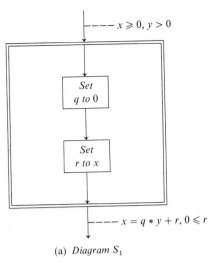

(a) *Diagram* S_1

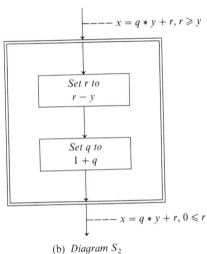

(b) *Diagram* S_2

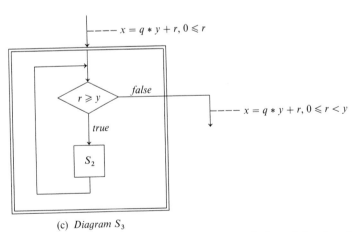

(c) *Diagram* S_3

Figure 2.2   The explicit decomposition of the diagram of Figure 2.1, using diagrams with one entry point and one exit point.

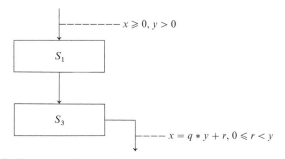

(d) *The complete Diagram S*

Figure 2.2   (*Continued*)

We said that $\{P\}\ S\ \{Q\}$ means that if P is true before S is executed, then Q must hold *upon completion* of S. This tells us that $\{P\}\ S\ \{Q\}$ is trivially true if S does not terminate, i.e., if in (1) the exit point is never reached. In other words, (2) expresses only the partial correctness of S, where a *partially correct program* is one which is guaranteed to deliver the desired result *if it terminates*. (To be more precise, we should say that the *program specification* $\{P\}\ S\ \{Q\}$ is (partially) correct, rather than that the program S is (partially) correct.) But whether it will actually terminate for some input values is another matter. If we can show, in addition, that the program terminates for all input values satisfying the relation P, then we say that the program is *totally correct*. To prove termination for a program obtained by the composition rules introduced so far will require analysis of loops, i.e., repetitive statements. That analysis was easy enough for the examples of Section 1.2, and we shall find that this continues to be so for the wide range of programs designed in this book.

We may summarize our approach to program design as follows:

(a) Our design must start with a complete program specification $\{P\}\ S\ \{Q\}$ which the program we are designing is to satisfy. We start, then, by specifying clearly and unambiguously when the program is to be used (the *precondition P*) and the outcome of using it (the *postcondition Q*) in those circumstances.

(b) The process of top-down design yields a program specification $\{P_i\}\ S_i\ \{Q_i\}$ for the pieces S_i from which the program is built.

(c) The design of the program goes hand in hand with the proofs of correctness of these various specifications.

Our process of top-down design yields diagrams (or an equivalent text) like that of Figure 2.1 with points labelled by relations which describe essential aspects of the states of computation that correspond to those points. To check that the program is correct, we must verify that the pieces—such as those in Figure 2.2—do indeed fit together in the way that the relations specify. Starting in Section 2.3, we shall introduce the *proof rules* which allow us to prove—more formally than we did in building up Figure 2.1 via the decompositions indicated in Figure 2.2—that certain properties $\{P\}\ S\ \{Q\}$

follow from properties $\{P_i\}\ S_i\ \{Q_i\}$ of the constituent pieces S_i. But first we devote Section 2.2 to a brief review of the logical formulas we use in building up the Ps and Qs which describe computational states.

2.2 Logical Formulas and Pascal Expressions

In Section 1.2, we briefly mentioned that each variable occurring in a specific program must have a specified *data type*: a set of values large enough to include all possible values which the variable may take in any computation using the algorithm, no matter what the initial data may be; together with the basic operations and tests defined upon these values. In all the algorithms that we discuss in Chapters 1 and 2, variables such as x, y, q, r, w, and n all have the set of nonnegative integers as their data type. Basic operations include the ability to add, subtract, multiply and divide numbers, and to test for equality or inequality of a pair of numbers. Because of this, we can postpone a more general dicussion of basic data types and ways of combining data types to form new data types until Chapter 3. However, once we start writing

$$r \geqslant y$$

or

$$x = q * y + r$$

we have expressions which are either *true* or *false*, depending on the particular nonnegative integers which replace the variables x, y, q and r. Since such expressions play a crucial role in our study of proof rules, we can proceed no further without introducing a new data type, *Boolean*, which comprises just two values

$$Boolean = (\textit{false}, \textit{true}) \tag{1}$$

which correspond to the two logical truth values. We shall see the basic operators associated with *Boolean* in a moment. First, we note this data type might as well have been called *Logical*. However, the designers of Pascal call it *Boolean* in honor of George Boole (1815–1864) who initiated the algebraic study of truth values.

In Section 2.1, we introduced the notation

$$(x \geqslant 0) \wedge (y > 0)$$

to indicate that $x \geqslant 0$ *and* $y > 0$. In Pascal, there are three basic operators defined over the values of type *Boolean*:

conjunction, $\wedge$ ('and'): $p \wedge q$ is interpreted as $\qquad\qquad$ (2)
$\qquad\qquad$ 'p is true *and* q is true'.

disjunction, $\vee$ ('or'): $p \vee q$ is interpreted as
$\qquad\qquad$ 'p is true *or* q is true (or both are true)'.

negation, $\neg$ ('not'): $\neg p$ is interpreted as
$\qquad\qquad$ 'p is *not* true'.

We refer to these operators (and others built up in terms of them) as *Boolean operators* or (interchangeably) as *logical operators*. Given Boolean arguments p and q, the values of the expressions $p \wedge q$, $p \vee q$, and $\neg p$ are given in the *truth table* (3), which in fact defines the meaning of the standard Boolean operators in accordance with the interpretation given in (2).

$$\begin{array}{ccccc} p & q & p \vee q & p \wedge q & \neg p \end{array} \qquad (3)$$

p	q	$p \vee q$	$p \wedge q$	$\neg p$
false	*false*	*false*	*false*	*true*
true	*false*	*true*	*false*	*false*
false	*true*	*true*	*false*	*true*
true	*true*	*true*	*true*	*false*

The logical operators $\wedge$, $\vee$, and $\neg$ satisfy various familiar properties such as:

i. *Commutative laws*: $p \vee q = q \vee p$ $\qquad (4)$
$$p \wedge q = q \wedge p$$

ii. *Associative laws*: $(p \vee q) \vee r = p \vee (q \vee r)$
$$(p \wedge q) \wedge r = p \wedge (q \wedge r)$$

iii. *Distributive laws*: $(p \wedge q) \vee r = (p \vee r) \wedge (q \vee r)$
$$(p \vee q) \wedge r = (p \wedge r) \vee (q \wedge r)$$

iv. *De Morgan's laws*: $\neg(p \vee q) = (\neg p) \wedge (\neg q)$
$$\neg(p \wedge q) = (\neg p) \vee (\neg q).$$

As an example of the use of the logical operators $\wedge$, $\vee$ and $\neg$, consider how we can use them to go from the basic relation $x < y$ on an ordered set like the nonnegative integers to the further relations $\leqslant$, $=$, $>$, $\neq$ and $\geqslant$:

New Relation	Definition	$\qquad (5)$
$a \leqslant b$	$\neg(b < a)$	
$a = b$	$(a \leqslant b) \wedge (b \leqslant a)$	
$a \neq b$	$\neg(a = b)$	
$a \geqslant b$	$b \leqslant a$	
$a > b$	$b < a$	

Notice that in Pascal we define $<$ on the data type *Boolean* by setting *false* $<$ *true*—and (5) then defines $\leqslant$, $=$, $\neq$, $\geqslant$ and $>$ for *Boolean*, too.

Two logical operators which are not included in the standard repertoire $\wedge$, $\vee$, $\neg$, but which will come in handy, are *implication* ($\supset$) and *equivalence* ($\equiv$). These two operators are defined by

$p \supset q$	$(\neg p) \vee q$	$\qquad (6)$
$p \equiv q$	$(p \supset q) \wedge (q \supset p)$	$\qquad (7)$

These new operators thus satisfy the truth table below:

p	q	$p \supset q$	$p \equiv q$	(8)
false	*false*	*true*	*true*	
true	*false*	*false*	*false*	
false	*true*	*true*	*false*	
true	*true*	*true*	*true*	

It follows then from (5) (for *Boolean*) and (8) that implication and equivalence may be expressed using the *Boolean* relational operators $\leqslant$ and $=$ as follows:

$$p \supset q \qquad p \leqslant q \qquad\qquad (9)$$
$$p \equiv q \qquad p = q.$$

Quantification

Without being formal about it, we can say that a *logical formula* is an expression (built up according to certain rules) which can be evaluated to obtain a truth value. In addition to building up logical formulas using $\vee$, $\wedge$, $\neg$ (and $\supset$ and $\equiv$), we also want to be able to write formulas like

$$\forall x (\exists y (x \geqslant y))$$

which is the statement that *for all* x, *there exists* y such that $x \geqslant y$. This, in fact, is an example of a true statement because, given any value for x, we can take x itself to be the appropriate value of y which makes $x \geqslant y$ true.

Thus, given a logical formula P, we build up new formulas as follows:

$\forall x(P)$: interpreted as 'P is true for *all* values of x' $\qquad\qquad$ (10)

$\exists x(P)$: interpreted as '*there exists* a value of x for which P is true.'

We shall assume for simplicity (and—as we shall see below—without loss of generality) that neither $\forall x$ nor $\exists x$ already occurs in P in (10). For a formula of the form $\forall x(P)$ we say that the occurence of the variable x in $\forall x$ is *universally quantified* and every occurrence of x in P *is bound* by $\forall x$. The same terminology applies to a formula of the form $\exists x(P)$, except that in this case the occurrence of the variable x in $\exists x$ is said to be *existentially quantified*. Every occurrence of a variable x in a logical formula which is not bound (quantified) is said to be a *free variable* of that formula. For example, all the variables in the formula

$$\neg \exists x (\forall y (y \leqslant x))\qquad\qquad (11)$$

are bound, whereas all the variables in the formula

$$(i < j) = (j < k)\qquad\qquad (12)$$

are free.

Each logical formula yields a rule for computing a Boolean value (*true* or *false*). If values of the free variables of a formula are specified, then operations (and functions) occurring in the formula may be performed to obtain either *true* or *false*. Then as specified in (10), the value of $\forall x(P)$ is *true* if for every value of the same type as the variable x, assigned to all occurrences of x in P, the value of P is *true*; otherwise the value of $\forall x(P)$ is *false*. Similarly, the value of $\exists x(P)$ is *true* if there exists a value of the same type as the variable x which, when assigned to all occurrences of x in P, yields *true* as the value of P; otherwise the value of $\exists x(P)$ is *false*.

Substitution

Let P be a logical formula. The notation

$$P_y^x \tag{13}$$

is used for the formula which is obtained by systematically *substituting* the expression y for all *free* occurrences of variable x in P. Similarly,

$$P_{y_1 \ldots y_n}^{x_1 \ldots x_n} \tag{14}$$

denotes *simultaneous substitution* for all free occurrences of any variable x_i in P of the corresponding expression y_i. Thus occurrences of x_i within any y_i are not replaced. The variables $x_1, \ldots x_n$ must be distinct, otherwise the simultaneous substitution is not defined.

We say that P and P_y^x are *similar* if P_y^x has free occurrences of y in exactly those places where P has free occurrences of x. For example, the following two formulas are similar:

$$\exists z((x \neq z) \wedge p(z,x)) \quad \text{and} \quad \exists z((y \neq z) \wedge p(z,y)) \tag{15}$$

The following two formulas are not similar:

$$\exists z(x \neq z) \wedge \exists y(p(x,y)) \quad \text{and} \quad \exists z(y \neq z) \wedge \exists y(p(y,y)) \tag{16}$$

In (15) and (16) p denotes some known function which yields values of the type *Boolean*—for instance, $p(x,y) = (x \geq y)$ would be such a function.

Observe that the problem in (16) is that in the formula on the right the newly substituted free variable y is now identified with the bound variable y of the formula on the left.

It is easy to see that if P and P_y^x are similar, then $\forall x(P)$ and $\forall y(P_y^x)$ are equivalent, and $\exists x(P)$ and $\exists y(P_y^x)$ are equivalent—where two formulas are said to be *equivalent* if they yield the same value for any assignment of values of the required type to the free variables of these formulas. This rule is called the *alphabetic change of variables* and it explains why in the definition of a logical formula we could assume for $\exists x(P)$ and $\forall x(P)$ that neither $\exists x$ nor $\forall x$ already occurs in P. This assumption causes no loss of generality, since it can always be satisfied by applying some alphabetic change of variables, if necessary.

Going back to the problem of conflict between free variables of y and bound variables of P illustrated in (16), we remark that this conflict may be resolved by an alphabetic change of the bound variables of P prior to performing substitution of y for x in P to obtain P_y^x. Thus, for example, the formulas

$$\exists z(x \neq z) \wedge \exists y(p(x,y)) \qquad \exists z(x \neq z) \wedge \exists w(p(x,w)) \qquad (17)$$

are equivalent and performing substitution of y for all free occurrences of x in $\exists z(x \neq z) \wedge \exists w(p(x,w))$ we obtain the formula $\exists z(y \neq z) \wedge \exists w(p(y,w))$ so that no conflict arises. We will assume that this technique is used whenever, as in (16) additional (unwanted) bound occurrences of variables are introduced. Logical formulas can get very complicated. In order to improve their readability we shall use notational abbreviations wherever appropriate. For example, we write $\forall x,y,z(P)$ rather than $\forall x(\forall y(\forall z(P)))$ etc.

Pascal Expressions

The discussion so far—of how to use the Boolean operators $\wedge$, $\vee$ and $\neg$ and the quantifiers $(\forall x)$ and $(\exists x)$ to build up new formulas from old ones—is valid for formalising logical operations independently of any programming language. In the rest of the section, though, we present the specific constructions used in the programming language Pascal to build up arithmetic and other expressions.

An *identifier* is used to denote a variable or constant. In Pascal, it is a string of one or more symbols, the first of which is a letter, while the remainder are letters or numbers. Thus x, y, z, $w13$, *hello16w* and $x1x2x3$ are identifiers in Pascal, while 43, $2x$ and $173ab2w$ are not.

Factors can be identifiers of variables, unsigned constants, function applications (like $sin(y)$ below), like

$$x \qquad (18)$$

$$13$$

$$sin(y)$$

expressions of the form $\neg p$ where p is a factor, as well as expressions of the form

$$f(a) \qquad (19)$$

$$[a]$$

$$[a,b], [a,b,c], [a,b,c,d], \text{ etc.}$$

$$[a \, . \, . \, b]$$

where f is a function designator, and each a,b,c,d is an *expression* (to be defined below). To anticipate the discussion of Section 3.2, $[a,b,c]$ denotes the set whose elements are denoted by the expressions a,b,c while $[a \, . \, . \, b]$ denotes a range of values (so, for example, $[2 \, . \, . \, 6]$ denotes the set of integers n for which $2 \leqslant n \leqslant 6$). This is spelled out in more detail in Appendix 1, *The Syntax of Pascal*.

Terms are built up from factors using the so-called 'multiplying' operators, $*, /, \textbf{mod}, \textbf{div}$ and $\wedge$. Examples include

$$a * b \tag{20}$$
$$i/(i - 1)$$
$$p \wedge q \wedge r$$
$$(x \leqslant y) \vee (x \leqslant z).$$

More precisely, terms include all factors and also constructs of the form $T \otimes F$ where T is already known to be a term, F is a factor, and $\otimes$ is one of the multiplying operators.

Simple expressions are built up from terms. They include all terms, as well as constructs of the form $S \oplus T$, $+T$ and $-T$, where $\oplus$ is one of the so-called 'adding' operators: $+, -, \vee$, and where T is a term, and S is already known to be a simple expression. Examples include:

$$x + y \tag{21}$$
$$-x$$
$$first + second$$
$$(p \wedge q) \vee r$$
$$i * j - 1.$$

(Note that in actually typing programs for the compiler, one usually has to type **not**, **and** and **or** rather than $\neg$, $\wedge$ and $\vee$.)

Finally, then, an *expression* is either a simple expression, or is obtained by combining two simple expressions, S_1 and S_2 to form $S_1 \, R \, S_2$ where R is one of the 'relational operators' $<, \leqslant, =, \neq, \geqslant$, and $>$ and **in** (the Pascal symbol for set membership). Examples thus include:

$$x = 1.5 \tag{22}$$
$$p \leqslant q$$
$$(i < j) = (j < k)$$
$$x \textbf{ in } [2,3,6].$$

This completes our informal definition of how more and more complex expressions may be built up in Pascal. We give the precise difinition in Appendix 1, which depends on some of the set theory to be introduced in Section 3.2.

From the abstract viewpoint and independently from the context in which it occurs, an expression specifies a composite (derived) operation. If the values of variables which occur in the expression are specified, then the expression may be evaluated, i.e., operators occurring in the expression may be applied to their operands. Thus an expression yields a value. But we have not as yet said how the operations specified in an expression are actually composed. For example, does $2 * 3 - 4 * 5$ mean $(2 * 3) - (4 * 5)$ or $((2 * 3) - 4) * 5$ or something else? What we have to do is to specify the order in which operators occurring in an expression are applied, i.e., to define *operator precedence*.

Operators are classified into four categories according to the precedence which they have. The operator $\neg$ has the highest precedence. The next category consists of the multiplying operators. The third category consists of the adding operators, and finally, the lowest priority goes to the relational operators, amongst which we shall include the logical operators $\supset$ and $\equiv$. Sequences of operators of the same precedence are executed from left to right. Any expression within parentheses is evaluated independently of any preceding or succeeding operators. These rules are illustrated by the following examples:

$$
\begin{aligned}
&2 * 3 - 4 * 5 = (2 * 3) - (4 * 5) = -14 \\
&15 \ \mathbf{div}\ 4 * 4 = (15\ \mathbf{div}\ 4) * 4 = 12 \\
&4\ \mathbf{div}\ 2 * 3 = (4\ \mathbf{div}\ 2) * 3 = 6 \\
&3 + 5 \neq 5 + 3 = ((3 + 5) \neq (5 + 3)) = \mathit{false}.
\end{aligned} \tag{23}
$$

If we use quantification to build up complex expressions, we shall stipulate that:

Quantifier symbols have the highest priority, the same as the operator $\neg$.

For example, evaluation of the formula:

$$\forall x(\forall y(\forall z(((x = y) \wedge (y = z)) \supset (x = z)))) \tag{24}$$

in which x, y, and z are integer variables yields *true*.

The value of the formula

$$\exists x(\forall y(x \leqslant y)) \tag{25}$$

where x and y are nonnegative integer variables is *true*, since

$$\forall y(0 \leqslant y). \tag{26}$$

Note for readers familiar with Algol 60: The choice of only four levels of priority of operators in Pascal at first seems a simplification in comparison with Algol 60, where there are nine such levels. The table (27) gives the

(27)

Algol 60	Pascal
$\uparrow$	$\neg$
$\times$ / $\div$	* / **div** **mod** $\wedge$
$+$ $-$	$+$ $-$ $\vee$
$= \neq < \leqslant \geqslant >$	$= \neq < \leqslant > \geqslant$
$\neg$	
$\wedge$	
$\vee$	
$\supset$	
$\equiv$	

priorities of operators in these two languages. In Algol 60, $\uparrow$ denotes exponentiation, $\times$ multiplication and $\div$ integer division.

However, this change is in fact unfortunate for Pascal, since it leads to more complicated Boolean expressions than in Algol 60, as can be seen from the following examples:

Algol 60	Pascal	(28)
$\neg x < y$	$\neg(x < y)$	
$x < y \wedge y < z$	$(x < y) \wedge (y < z)$	
$x < y \equiv y < z$	$(x < y) = (y < z)$	
$x \leqslant y \wedge y \leqslant z \supset x \leqslant z$	$(x \leqslant y) \wedge (y \leqslant z) \leqslant (x \leqslant z)$	

It is clear that the readability of complicated Boolean expressions is much better in Algol 60 than in Pascal. It is not only that more parentheses are necessary in Pascal. Use of the operators $=$ and $\leqslant$ in lieu of $\equiv$ and $\supset$ also causes confusion. So, for example, the meaning of the expression $x < y \equiv y < z$ is much clearer than the meaning of the expression $(x < y) = (y < z)$, as is the meaning of the expression $x \leqslant y \wedge y \leqslant z \supset x \leqslant z$ as compared with $(x \leqslant y) \wedge (y \leqslant z) \leqslant (x \leqslant z)$. The consequences of this are particularly unpleasant in proofs of program correctness, which require, sometimes very complicated, manipulation of expressions. For reasons of better readability we use the symbols $\equiv$ and $\supset$ rather than $=$ and $\leqslant$ respectively when writing logical formulas.

2.3 Proof Rules for Simple Statements

Proof rules are patterns of reasoning that will allow us to prove properties of programs. In this chapter, the proof rules will have the form

$$\frac{H_1, \ldots, H_n}{H}.$$ (1)

If $H_1, \ldots, H_n$ are true assertions, then H is a true assertion.

Two of the simplest rules of inference are formulated in (2) and (4). The first states that if the execution of a program S ensures the truth of the assertion R then it also ensures the truth of every assertion implied by R, i.e.,

$$\frac{\{P\}\, S\, \{R\},\ R \supset Q}{\{P\}\, S\, \{Q\}}.$$ (2)

For example, from

$$\{(x > 0) \wedge (y > 0)\}\, S\, \{(z + u * y = x * y) \wedge (u = 0)\}$$ (3)
$$(z + u * y = x * y) \wedge (u = 0) \supset (z = x * y)$$

we conclude using (2) that

$$\{(x > 0) \wedge (y > 0)\}\, S\, \{z = x * y\}.$$

The second rule states that if R is known to be a precondition for a program S to produce the result Q after completion of execution of S, then so is any other assertion which implies R:

$$\frac{P \supset R, \; \{R\} \; S \; \{Q\}}{\{P\} \; S \; \{Q\}} \; . \qquad (4)$$

For example, suppose that the variables x, y, r and q range over nonnegative integers. Consider now

$$(x = y * q + r) \wedge (0 \leqslant r < y) \supset (x = y * (1 + q) + (r - y)) \qquad (5)$$
$$\{x = y * (1 + q) + (r - y)\} \; r := r - y \; \{x = y * (1 + q) + r\}$$

where we note that in $\{P\} \; r := r - y \; \{Q\}$, P uses the old value of r, whereas Q uses the new value of r, which is the old value of r less the current value of y. Then (4) allows us to deduce from (5) that

$$\{(x = y * q + r) \wedge (0 \leqslant r < y)\} \; r := r - y \; \{x = y * (1 + q) + r\}.$$

The rules (2) and (4) are called the *consequence rules*.

We now turn to the specific form which $\{P\} \; S \; \{Q\}$ takes when we know something about S. We shall study the effect of structured statements in later sections. Here we look at the case in which S is a simple statement. The simplest form of simple statement is the *null statement*—which has no effect upon the values of any of the program variables. For any P, we have the proof rule

$$\{P\} \; \{P\}. \qquad (6)$$

As for simple statements that affect values of program variables and thus the Boolean values of the assertions P and Q in $\{P\} \; S \; \{Q\}$, assignment is the only one introduced so far. So let $x := e$ be the *assignment statement* which sets x to the value of the expression e. Then we may conclude that for any P

$$\{P_e^x\} \; x := e \; \{P\}. \qquad (7)$$

This says that if P is true for e substituted for x before the assignment is made; then P must be true when x has been assigned its new value. This rule is best expressed by examples given below in the form of diagrams:

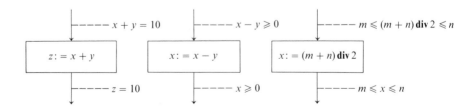

2.4 Compound and Conditional Statements

Suppose now that we want to establish that $\{P\}\ S\ \{Q\}$ holds when S is a *structured statement*. What we need is a rule for every type of composition of statements which allows us to infer the properties of the composite (structured) statement on the basis of the established properties of its components. In this section, we discuss such rules for the compound and the conditional statements.

Compound statements

The simplest form of statement structuring is to form so-called *compound statements* by *sequential* (or *serial*) *composition*, which consists of the action denoted by S_1 followed by the action denoted by S_2. This generalizes to the serial composition of an arbitrary finite number of actions $S_1, S_2, \ldots, S_n$. In Pascal, it is customary to put the serially composed statements in the brackets **begin** and **end**, which indicate that the statement obtained that way is a single, although structured, statement. Such a statement has the form

$$\textbf{begin } S_1 ; S_2 ; \ldots ; S_n \textbf{ end} \tag{1}$$

and is called a compound statement. It may be graphically represented by the following flowchart:

$$(2)$$

An example of a compound statement is

$$\textbf{begin } x := x + 1; z := x + 2; y := y + z \textbf{ end.} \tag{3}$$

The proof rule for sequential composition says that if S is **begin** $S_1 ; S_2$ **end** and if $\{P\}\ S_1\ \{R\}$ and $\{R\}\ S_2\ \{Q\}$ hold, then $\{P\}\ \textbf{begin } S_1 ; S_2 \textbf{ end}\ \{Q\}$ holds. Formally, this rule may be expressed as follows:

$$\frac{\{P\}\ S_1\ \{R\}, \{R\}\ S_2\ \{Q\}}{\{P\}\ \textbf{begin } S_1 ; S_2 \textbf{ end}\ \{Q\}} . \tag{4}$$

For example, from

$$\{x = y * (1 + q) + r - y\}\ r := r - y\ \{x = y * (1 + q) + r\}$$
$$\{x = y * (1 + q) + r\}\ q := 1 + q\ \{x = y * q + r\}$$

we conclude by (4) that

$$\{x = y * (1 + q) + r - y\}\ \textbf{begin } r := r - y; q := 1 + q \textbf{ end}\ \{x = y * q + r\}.$$

The proof rule (4) generalizes in the following obvious way:

$$\frac{\{P_{i-1}\}\ S_i\ \{P_i\}\ \text{for } i = 1, \ldots, n}{\{P_0\}\ \textbf{begin } S_1 ; S_2 ; \ldots ; S_n \textbf{ end}\ \{P_n\}} . \tag{5}$$

Conditional Statements

If S_1 and S_2 are statements and B a Boolean expression (i.e., an expression yielding a value of type *Boolean*) then

$$\textbf{if } B \textbf{ then } S_1 \textbf{ else } S_2 \tag{6}$$

is a statement which denotes the following action: B is evaluated. If it yields *true* then the action to be performed is the one described by S_1, otherwise it is the action described by S_2. (6) may be represented graphically by the diagram (7).

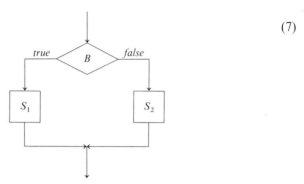

(7)

As an example, consider that the absolute value $|a|$ of an integer a (not necessarily nonnegative in this example) may be obtained as the value of b calculated by the conditional statement

$$\textbf{if } a > 0 \textbf{ then } b := a \textbf{ else } b := -a. \tag{8}$$

Ambiguity arises if we nest conditional statements, i.e., if S_1 or S_2 in (6) are conditional statements themselves. Thus the statement:

$$\textbf{if } B_1 \textbf{ then if } B_2 \textbf{ then } S_1 \textbf{ else } S_2$$

may be interpreted in the following ways:

> **if B_1 then**
> **begin if B_2 then S_1 else S_2 end**
>
> **if B_1 then begin if B_2 then S_1 end**
> **else S_2**

In order to resolve this ambiguity, we'll accept the former interpretation.

Let us now develop a proof rule for the conditional (6). If we are to establish that $\{P\}$ **if B then S_1 else S_2** $\{Q\}$ holds, then we have to prove two things.

i. If B yields *true*, then S_1 is executed. Since P holds before (6) is executed, we conclude that in this case $P \wedge B$ holds just before S_1 is executed. If Q is to hold upon execution of (6), then $\{P \wedge B\}$ S_1 $\{Q\}$ must hold. So we have to prove $\{P \wedge B\}$ S_1 $\{Q\}$.

ii. If B yields *false*, then S_2 will get executed. Since P was true just before (6) was executed, we conclude that $P \wedge \neg B$ holds before S_2 is executed.

With this precondition for S_2 we have to prove that after execution of S_2, Q will hold, i.e., we must show $\{P \wedge \neg B\}\, S_2\, \{Q\}$.

If we proved both $\{P \wedge B\}\, S_1\, \{Q\}$ and $\{P \wedge \neg B\}\, S_2\, \{Q\}$ then we can assert that if P holds before (6) is executed, then Q will hold upon completion of execution of (6), no matter which statement, S_1 or S_2, is selected for execution. So we can formulate the following proof rule:

$$\frac{\{P \wedge B\}\, S_1\, \{Q\},\ \{P \wedge \neg B\}\, S_2\, \{Q\}}{\{P\}\ \textbf{if } B \textbf{ then } S_1 \textbf{ else } S_2\ \{Q\}}. \qquad (9)$$

For example, returning to (8), we can apply (9)—with $P = true$ and $B = (a > 0)$—to

$$\{(a > 0)\}\ b := a\ \{b > 0\}$$
$$(b > 0) \supset (b \geqslant 0)$$
$$\{\neg(a > 0)\}\ b := -a\ \{b \geqslant 0\}$$

to obtain

$$\{true\}\ \textbf{if } a > 0 \textbf{ then } b := a \textbf{ else } b := -a\ \{b \geqslant 0\}$$

which guarantees that no matter what a we start with, the final b is nonnegative.

We now look at two variants of the conditional statement, and supply proof rules for each. The first is obtained by noting, in **if** B **then** S_1 **else** S_2, that S_2 may be any statement, and the empty statement in particular. The empty statement specifies the identity action, i.e., the action which does not affect values of variables. If S_2 is the empty statement, then (6) is written as:

$$\textbf{if } B \textbf{ then } S. \qquad (10)$$

The action which this specifies consists first of evaluation of B. If B is true then the action to be performed is the one specified by S, otherwise it is the identity action. (10) may be represented by the following diagram (11).

$$(11)$$

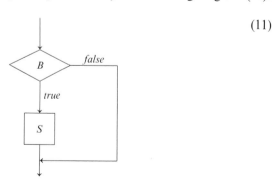

We now establish the corresponding proof rule. If we want to prove $\{P\}$ **if** B **then** S $\{Q\}$ then we have to ensure two things. The first one of them is that if S is executed, that Q will hold after its execution. Since S is selected for execution if B yields true, we conclude that $P \wedge B$ holds before S is executed, if P holds before (10) is executed. So we have to prove $\{P \wedge B\}\, S\, \{Q\}$.

The second case is when S is not executed, i.e., when B after evaluation yields *false*. So $P \wedge \neg B$ holds at this point and if Q is to hold after (10), then we must prove $P \wedge \neg B \supset Q$. An alternative of establishing the proof rule is regarding (10) as equivalent to:

$$\textbf{if } B \textbf{ then } S \textbf{ else.} \tag{12}$$

In (12) the statement after else is the null statement. But either way, the proof rule just formulated is:

$$\frac{\{P \wedge B\}\; S\; \{Q\},\; P \wedge \neg B \supset Q}{\{P\}\; \textbf{if } B \textbf{ then } S\; \{Q\}}. \tag{13}$$

Case Statement

The conditional statement **if** B **then** S_1 **else** S_2 allows selection of one of the two component actions S_1 and S_2 on the basis of the result of evaluation of the Boolean expression B. It is possible to generalize this statement in such a way that a selection is performed among a finite number of actions on the basis of the selector expression. This generalized conditional statement is called the *case statement*. It has the form:

$$\begin{aligned}
&\textbf{case } e \textbf{ of} \tag{14}\\
&\qquad L1 : S1;\\
&\qquad L2 : S2;\\
&\qquad \cdots\\
&\qquad Ln : Sn\\
&\textbf{end}
\end{aligned}$$

In (14) e is the *selector*, $S1, \ldots, Sn$ are statements, and $L1, \ldots, Ln$ are called *labels*. Labels $L1, \ldots, Ln$ are constants of the same type as the selector expression e.

The case statement (14) selects for execution that component statement whose label is equal to the current value of the selector. If no such label occurs, the effect of (14) is undefined. (14) may be represented graphically by diagram (15).

$$\tag{15}$$

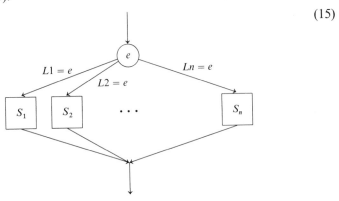

(14) may be further generalized in such a way that each component statement S_i $(i = 1, \ldots, n)$ may be preceded by a sequence of labels separated by commas. In that case S_i will be selected for execution if the current value of the selector expression is equal to some of the labels which precede S_i. An example of a case statement of that form is:

$$\textbf{case } i \textbf{ of} \qquad\qquad (16)$$
$$0, 1: i := i + 1;$$
$$2: i := 0$$
$$\textbf{end}$$

which increases i by 1 modulo 3.

Generalizing (9), it is clear that in forming a proof rule for the case statement, if we want Q to hold upon completion of execution of (14), then Q must hold no matter which S_i is selected for execution—and so we must show that $\{P \wedge (x = Li)\}\ S_i\ \{Q\}$ for $i = 1, \ldots, n$. So we obtain the following proof rule (abbreviating Li to k_i):

$$\frac{\{P \wedge (x = k_i)\}\ S_i\ \{Q\} \text{ for } i = 1, \ldots, n}{\{P \wedge (x \in [k_1, \ldots, k_n])\}\ \textbf{case } x \textbf{ of } k_1 : S_1; \ldots; k_n : S_n \textbf{ end } \{Q\}}. \qquad (17)$$

The expression $x \in [k_1, \ldots, k_n]$ means that x has one of the values $k_1, \ldots, k_n$. This condition in (17) says that we do not specify what will happen if x does not fit into any of these cases.

The above proof rule (17) applies also to the case where multiple case labels precede some S_i in (14), since $k_a, k_b, \ldots k_m : S$ in fact stands for $k_a : S$; $k_b : S$; $\ldots k_m : S$.

2.5 Repetitive Statements

In the previous section, we looked at proof rules $\{P\}\ S\ \{Q\}$ where the structured statement S was built up by serial composition or some form of conditional. In the present section, we turn to structures that involve *loops*. We first study **while-do**—which we met in Section 1.3—and then turn to **repeat-until**.

While-do Statements

If B is a Boolean expression and S is a statement then

$$\textbf{while } B \textbf{ do } S \qquad\qquad (1)$$

denotes repeated execution of the statement S as long as evaluation of B yields true. If B is false initially, S will not be executed at all. The process of repeated execution of S terminates when B yields false. This situation is shown in diagram (2).

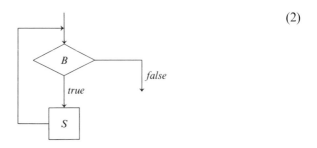

(2)

We can use this statement to compute, given any initial nonnegative integer n, the sum $1^2 + 2^2 + \cdots + n^2$ as the final value of h in the following

$$\textbf{begin } h := 0;$$ (3)
$$\textbf{while } n > 0 \textbf{ do}$$
$$\textbf{begin } h := h + n^2; n := n - 1 \textbf{ end}$$
$$\textbf{end}$$

We now want a statement $\{P\}$ **while** B **do** S $\{Q\}$. To this end, we now consider (2) in more detail as shown in (4). If P holds when we firs; enter (4), it is clear that $P \wedge B$ will hold if we get to C. Thus, if we want to be assured that P again holds when we return to A, we would want to ensure that $\{P \wedge B\}$ S $\{P\}$ was established for S.

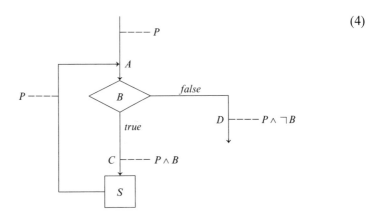

(4)

In that case it is clear that P will hold not only when the point A in (4) is reached for the first and second time, but also after an arbitrary number of cycles around the loop. Also, $P \wedge B$ holds whenever the point C is reached. When the exit point D in (4) is reached, then not only P holds, but also $\neg B$. So we obtain the following proof rule.

$$\frac{\{P \wedge B\}\ S\ \{P\}}{\{P\}\ \textbf{while}\ B\ \textbf{do}\ S\ \{P \wedge \neg B\}}. \tag{5}$$

Observe that (5) establishes an *invariant property* P of the loop in (5). If P holds of the computation state initially, then P will hold of the computation state following each loop traversal. P captures the essence of the dynamic processes which occur when (1) is executed. We also refer to P as a *loop invariant*.

Repeat-until Statements

Another form of loop statement is

$$\textbf{repeat}\ S\ \textbf{until}\ B \tag{6}$$

where S is a sequence of statements and B a Boolean expression. (6) specifies that S be executed before B is evaluated. Then, if B yields false, the process of repeated execution of S is continued, otherwise it is terminated. The structure of the repetitive statement (6) is represented by the following diagram (7).

(7)

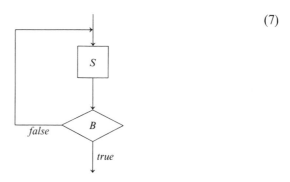

Comparing (2) and (6) we note that in (7) S must be executed at least once, whereas in (2) it may not be executed at all.

An example of the **repeat-until** statement is given in the program (8) below which computes the sum $h = 1^2 + 2^2 + \cdots + n^2$ for the initially given value of n:

$$
\begin{aligned}
&\textbf{begin}\ h := 0; \\
&\quad\ \textbf{repeat}\ h := h + n^2; \\
&\qquad\qquad\ n := n - 1 \\
&\quad\ \textbf{until}\ n = 0 \\
&\textbf{end}
\end{aligned}
\tag{8}
$$

Suppose that we allow negative values of n. Then we can use (3) and (8) to illustrate a fundamental problem with repetitive composition when we seek total rather than partial correctness. If $n \leqslant 0$, then (8) represents an infinite loop. On the other hand, the program (3) terminates even if $n \leqslant 0$. Thus we see that an improperly designed repetitive statement may in fact describe an infinite computation.

In order to establish the proof rule for

repeat S **until** B

consider the following diagram (9).

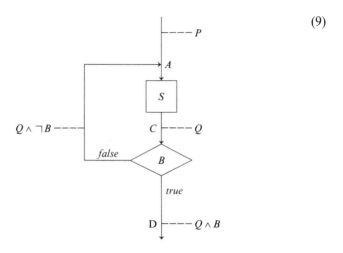

(9)

Suppose that we proved $\{P\}\ S\ \{Q\}$ and $Q \wedge \neg B \supset P$. Then if P is *true* at the entry point of (9), then Q will hold when the point C is reached for the first time. If B is *false*, then $Q \wedge \neg B$ holds and going around the loop we again reach the point A. Since $Q \wedge \neg B \supset P$, we conclude that P holds when the point A is reached for the second time (if at all). But then again because of $\{P\}\ S\ \{Q\}$, Q will hold when the point C is reached for the second time etc. So, we conclude that under the assumptions that we made, P will hold whenever A is reached and Q will hold whenever C is reached, no matter how many cycles occur around the loop. When the repetition process is terminated, i.e., when the exit point D in (9) is reached, $Q \wedge B$ must hold. This reasoning leads to the following proof rule:

$$\frac{\{P\}\ S\ \{Q\},\ Q \wedge \neg B \supset P}{\{P\}\ \textbf{repeat}\ S\ \textbf{until}\ B\ \{Q \wedge B\}} \tag{10}$$

As an exercise in the use of proof rules, we now show how to replace a **repeat-until** statement by a diagram in which the loop is given by a **while-do** statement. Remember the idea of **repeat** S **until** B—do S, then test B, then do S again if B does not hold, and keep repeating the process. In other words, do S, then keep repeating S while B holds. We thus have the equivalence:

$$\textbf{repeat}\ S\ \textbf{until}\ B \equiv \textbf{begin}\ S;\ \textbf{while}\ \neg B\ \textbf{do}\ S\ \textbf{end} \tag{11}$$

We now check that (11) allows us to deduce the **repeat-until** proof rule (10) from the **while-do** proof rule

$$\frac{\{P \wedge B\}\ S\ \{P\}}{\{P\}\ \textbf{while}\ B\ \textbf{do}\ S\ \{P \wedge \neg B\}} \tag{5}$$

and the proof rule

$$\frac{\{P\}\ S_1\ \{R\},\ \{R\}\ S_2\ \{Q\}}{\{P\}\ \textbf{begin}\ S_1\ ;\ S_2\ \textbf{end}\ \{Q\}} \tag{12}$$

which we met as 2.4(4). We shall also need the consequence rule

$$\frac{P \supset R,\ \{R\}\ S\ \{Q\}}{\{P\}\ S\ \{Q\}} \tag{13}$$

which was (4) of Section 2.3.

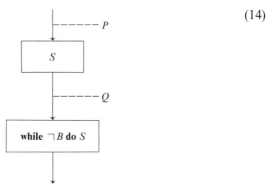

$$\tag{14}$$

If we are given that $\{P\}\ S\ \{Q\}$, then we naturally take Q as the relation at the entry point to **while** $\neg B$ **do** S, which leads us to use (5) in the modified form

$$\frac{\{Q \wedge \neg B\}\ S\ \{Q\}}{\{Q\}\ \textbf{while}\ \neg B\ \textbf{do}\ S\ \{Q \wedge B\}} \tag{15}$$

where we use the equality $\neg \neg B = B$. Now, with a suitable change of variables the consequence rule (13) tells us that

$$\frac{Q \wedge \neg B \supset P,\ \{P\}\ S\ \{Q\}}{\{Q \wedge \neg B\}\ S\ \{Q\}} \tag{16}$$

which we may combine with (15) to deduce

$$\frac{\{P\}\ S\ \{Q\},\ Q \wedge \neg B \supset P}{\{Q\}\ \textbf{while}\ \neg B\ \textbf{do}\ S\ \{Q \wedge B\}}.$$

Then, invoking (12), we have our desired result

$$\frac{\{P\}\ S\ \{Q\},\ Q \wedge \neg B \supset P}{\{P\}\ \textbf{begin}\ S;\ \textbf{while}\ \neg B\ \textbf{do}\ S\ \textbf{end}\ \{Q \wedge B\}}$$

which, given the equivalence (11), is just (10), as was to be proved.

2.6 Summary of Basic Proof Rules

At this stage, we summarize the basic proof rules developed in the previous
section. Before going further, the reader should become completely familiar
with them—not simply memorizing them, but gaining the firm understanding
of them required to "figure out" any forgotten details.

Consequence Rules

$$\frac{\{P\}\ S\ \{R\},\ R \supset Q}{\{P\}\ S\ \{Q\}}$$

$$\frac{P \supset R,\ \{R\}\ S\ \{Q\}}{\{P\}\ S\ \{Q\}}$$

Null Rule

$$\{P\}\ \{P\}$$

Assignment Rule

$$\{P_e^x\}\ x := e\ \{P\}$$

Compound Rule

$$\frac{\{P_{i-1}\}\ S_i\ \{P_i\}\ \text{for}\ i = 1, \ldots, n}{\{P_0\}\ \textbf{begin}\ S_1 ; S_2 ; \ldots ; S_n\ \textbf{end}\ \{P_n\}}$$

Conditional Rule

$$\frac{\{P \wedge B\}\ S_1\ \{Q\},\ \{P \wedge \neg B\}\ S_2\ \{Q\}}{\{P\}\ \textbf{if}\ B\ \textbf{then}\ S_1\ \textbf{else}\ S_2\ \{Q\}}$$

$$\frac{\{P \wedge B\}\ S\ \{Q\},\ P \wedge \neg B \supset Q}{\{P\}\ \textbf{if}\ B\ \textbf{then}\ S\ \{Q\}}$$

Case Rule

$$\frac{\{P \wedge (x = k_i)\}\ S_i\ \{Q\}\ \text{for}\ i = 1, \ldots, n}{\{P \wedge (x \in [k_1, \ldots, k_n])\}\ \textbf{case}\ x\ \textbf{of}\ k_1 : S_1 ; \ldots ; k_n : S_n\ \textbf{end}\ \{Q\}}$$

While-do Rule

$$\frac{\{P \wedge B\}\ S\ \{P\}}{\{P\}\ \textbf{while}\ B\ \textbf{do}\ S\ \{P \wedge \neg B\}}$$

Repeat-until Rule

$$\frac{\{P\}\ S\ \{Q\},\ Q \wedge \neg B \supset P}{\{P\}\ \textbf{repeat}\ S\ \textbf{until}\ B\ \{Q \wedge B\}}$$

When we use the proof rules in later sections, we shall refer to them by the above names, not by the numbers which marked their first appearance in the previous 3 sections. Moreover, we shall feel free to use the rules with any convenient change of variables—instead of spelling this out explicitly as we did at the end of Section 2.5.

2.7 Using the Basic Proof Rules

The Division Algorithm

As an exercise in proving the correctness of a program, let us use the proof rules we have obtained so far to verify that the program for division of nonnegative integers presented in Figure 2.1 (on page 16) is correct. The reader will now recognize that the diagram is indeed captured in the following Pascal program. Note that the relations (comments) enclosed in { } are not part of the program itself, but describe the essential aspects—as defined during our process of top-down design—of the state of computation at the corresponding points.

$$\{(x \geqslant 0) \wedge (y > 0)\} \qquad\qquad (1)$$
$$\textbf{begin}\ q := 0;$$
$$\qquad r := x;$$
$$\qquad \{(x = q * y + r) \wedge (0 \leqslant r)\}$$
$$\qquad \textbf{while}\ r \geqslant y\ \textbf{do}$$
$$\qquad \{(x = q * y + r) \wedge (0 < y \leqslant r)\}$$
$$\qquad \textbf{begin}\ r := r - y;$$
$$\qquad\qquad q := 1 + q$$
$$\qquad \textbf{end}$$
$$\textbf{end}$$
$$\{(x = q * y + r) \wedge (0 \leqslant r < y)\}$$

The correctness criterion of (1) is expressed by the relation $(x = q * y + r) \wedge (0 \leqslant r < y)$ which is required to hold upon termination of (1) if $(x \geqslant 0) \wedge (y > 0)$ holds before (1) is executed. That is what we have to prove.

Consider, first the loop in our program—which is shown as diagram S_3 in Figure 2.2(c) (on page 18):

(2)

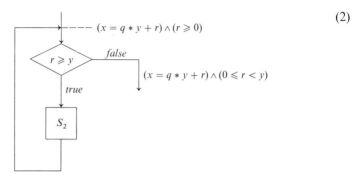

In this example, then, B takes the form $(r \geqslant y)$. If we now observe that the exit relation in (2) can be rewritten as

$$(x = q * y + r) \wedge (r \geqslant 0) \wedge \neg (r \geqslant y)$$

we see this is just $P \wedge \neg B$, where

$$P \text{ is } (x = q * y + r) \wedge (r \geqslant 0). \tag{3}$$

In other words, our job in verifying (2) is to show that

$$\{P\} \text{ while } (r \geqslant y) \text{ do } S_2 \; \{P \wedge \neg (r \geqslant y)\}$$

where the loop invariant P is given by (3). But our proof rule

$$\frac{\{P \wedge B\} \; S \; \{P\}}{\{P\} \text{ while } B \text{ do } S \; \{P \wedge \neg B\}} \tag{4}$$

assures us that this must be true as soon as we can prove

$$\{P \wedge (r \geqslant y)\} \; S_2 \; \{P\} \tag{5}$$

for the P given by (3) and the S_2 given by

$$\textbf{begin } r := r - y; \, q := 1 + q \textbf{ end}$$

(which is just the Pascal version of Figure 2.2(b) (on page 18). Now

$$(x = q * y + r) \wedge (r \geqslant 0) \wedge (r \geqslant y) \supset (x = (1 + q) * y + (r - y)) \wedge (r - y \geqslant 0).$$

Recalling the assignment proof rule, we see that

$$\{(x = (1 + q) * y + (r - y)) \wedge ((r - y) \geqslant 0)\}$$
$$r := r - y \; \{(x = (1 + q) * y + r) \wedge (r \geqslant 0)\}$$
$$\{(x = (1 + q) * y + r) \wedge (r \geqslant 0)\} \; q := 1 + q \; \{(x = q * y + r) \wedge (r \geqslant 0)\}.$$

So it follows from the compound and consequence rules that

$$\{(x = q * y + r) \wedge (r \geqslant 0) \wedge (r \geqslant y)\} \tag{6}$$
$$\textbf{begin } r := r - y; q := 1 + q \textbf{ end}$$
$$\{(x = q * y + r) \wedge (r \geqslant 0)\}$$

which is exactly the form of (5) we need in the present proof.

Thus proof rule (4) lets us conclude the desired condition

$$\{(x = q * y + r) \wedge (r \geqslant 0)\} \ S_3 \ \{(x = q * y + r) \wedge (r \geqslant 0) \wedge \neg(r \geqslant y)\}. \tag{7}$$

Our next step is to check that the desired condition

$$\{(x \geqslant 0) \wedge (y > 0)\} \textbf{ begin } q := 0; r := x \textbf{ end } \{(x = q * y + r) \wedge (r \geqslant 0)\} \tag{8}$$

holds for the diagram S_1 of Figure 2.2. Indeed observe that

$$(x \geqslant 0) \wedge (y > 0) \supset (x = 0 * y + x) \wedge (x \geqslant 0) \tag{9}$$
$$\{(x = 0 * y + x) \wedge (x \geqslant 0)\} q := 0 \ \{(x = q * y + x) \wedge (x \geqslant 0)\}$$
$$\{(x = q * y + x) \wedge (x \geqslant 0)\} r := x \ \{(x = q * y + r) \wedge (r \geqslant 0)\}.$$

So from (9) we conclude that (8) does indeed hold, on using the consequence rule and the compound statement rule.

It follows now from (7), (8) and the proof rule for the compound statement that

$$\{(x \geqslant 0) \wedge (y > 0)\}$$
$$\textbf{begin } q := 0; r := x;$$
$$\quad \textbf{while } r \geqslant y \textbf{ do}$$
$$\quad \quad \textbf{begin } r := r - y; q := 1 + q \textbf{ end}$$
$$\textbf{end}$$
$$\{(x = q * y + r) \wedge (0 \leqslant r < y)\}$$

which is what we wanted to prove. Since this was a proof of partial correctness, the condition $y > 0$ was not used in the proof. This pre-condition, however, will play an essential role in proving that the algorithm does in fact terminate. We shall see this proof in Section 2.8.

Multiplication of Numbers

Suppose that we have two positive integers x and y that we wish to multiply. Let us develop an algorithm for doing this using only addition, subtraction and tests. Our initial description of the approach is

$$\textit{Add together x copies of y.} \tag{1}$$

The usual approach to doing this is to introduce 2 new variables: z which holds the partial sum, and u which keeps track of how many copies of y have been added together. In our algorithm, we shall let the value of u denote how many copies of *y remain* to be added. We thus get our next decomposition:

i. *Set z to 0 and set u to x* (2)

ii. *Increase z by y, and reduce u by 1; repeating the process until u = 0.*

It is easy to put this into the form of a Pascal program, with entry condition $(x > 0) \wedge (y > 0)$ and exit condition $(z = x * y)$.

$$\{(x > 0) \wedge (y > 0)\} \tag{3}$$
begin $z := 0; u := x;$
    repeat $z := z + y; u := u - 1$
    until $u = 0$
end
$\{(z = x * y)\}$

We now want to give a formal proof that (3) is indeed correct. To do this, we need to insert relations internal to the program, as shown in (4).

(4)

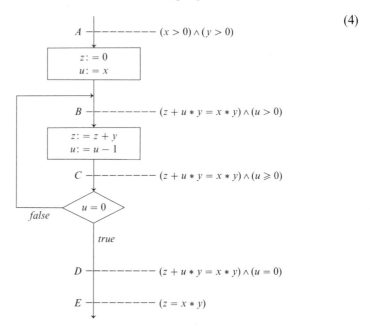

We first justify the relations informally. The relation of A is the entry condition for (3). To understand the relations at B and C, recall the idea we had in forming the decomposition (2)—z was to be the sum so far, while u tells us how many copies of y still had to be added in to obtain $x * y$. But this is precisely

$$z + u * y = x * y \tag{5}$$

which we thus take to be our loop invariant. The role of the terms $(u > 0)$ and $(u \geqslant 0)$ should be clear. Finally, the relation at E is just the exit condition specified in (3).

We now use the relations in (4) to prove formally, i.e., by rigorous use of the proof rules, that (3) holds. We first observe that

$$(x > 0) \wedge (y > 0) \supset (x * y = x * y) \wedge (x > 0)$$

and

$$\{(x * y = x * y) \wedge (x > 0)\} \ z := 0; \ u := x \ \{(z + u * y = x * y) \wedge (u > 0)\}$$

so that

$$\{(x > 0) \wedge (y > 0)\} \ z := 0; \ u := x \ \{(z + u * y = x * y) \wedge (u > 0)\}. \quad (6)$$

Furthermore, we can easily show that

$$\{(z + u * y = x * y) \wedge (u > 0)\} \ z := z + y; \quad (7)$$
$$u := u - 1 \ \{(z + u * y = x * y) \wedge (u \geqslant 0)\}$$

as well as

$$(z + u * y = x * y) \wedge (u \geqslant 0) \wedge \neg (u = 0) \supset (z + u * y = x * y) \wedge (u > 0). \quad (8)$$

Applying the **repeat-until** proof rule to (7) and (8) we conclude that

$$\{(z + u * y = x * y) \wedge (u > 0)\} \quad (9)$$
$$\textbf{repeat } z := z + y;$$
$$u := u - 1$$
$$\textbf{until} \quad u = 0$$
$$\{(z + u * y = x * y) \wedge (u \geqslant 0) \wedge (u = 0)\}$$

Now obviously

$$(z + u * y = x * y) \wedge (u \geqslant 0) \wedge (u = 0) \supset (z = x * y). \quad (10)$$

So the desired result (3) follows immediately.

Note that, for a simple program like this, it really isn't necessary to write (6)–(10) out to verify correctness—once we have labelled (4) properly, we can check that the corresponding $\{P\} \ S \ \{Q\}$ hold by direct inspection. Thus, in "real life" one often stops with a design like (4). But if the relations get at all complicated, a careful proof of the corresponding $\{P\} \ S \ \{Q\}$ will be required.

Another Division Algorithm

So far, we have verified two programs, and in each case we provided a top-down design which motivated the relations. But sometimes we will want to check the correctness of a program we did not design. Let us, then, consider the following division algorithm, which is more efficient than that given in (1). Fortunately, it is already annotated with the relations we need. In many situations of course, we shall have to work out these relations for ourselves as part of our task in proving correctness.

begin $\{(x > 0) \land (y > 0)\}$ (11)
    $r := x; q := 0; w := y;$
    $\{\exists n(w = 2^n * y) \land (x = q * w + r) \land (0 \leqslant r)\}$
    while $w \leqslant r$ **do** $w := 2 * w;$
    $\{\exists n(w = 2^n * y) \land (x = q * w + r) \land (0 \leqslant r < w)\}$
    while $w \neq y$ **do**
    begin $q := 2 * q; w := w$ **div** $2;$
       if $w \leqslant r$ **then**
         begin $r := r - w; q := 1 + q$
         end
    end
    $\{(x = q * y + r) \land (0 \leqslant r < y)\}$
end

We start by observing that after the assignments $r := x; q := 0; w := y$

$$\exists n(w = 2^n * y) \tag{12}$$

holds since $w = 2^0 * y$. Further, at that point

$$x = q * w + r \tag{13}$$

holds since $q = 0$ and $r = x$. Since $x > 0$ initially, we also have $r \geqslant 0$.

The assertions (12) and (13) remain invariant when the statement $w := 2 * w$ is executed. Invariance of (12) is clear, and the invariance of (13) follows from the fact that $q = 0$, so that increase of w has no effect on $q * w + r$. $w := 2 * w$ also leaves the relation $0 \leqslant r$ invariant. Applying now the proof rule for the **while-do** statement, we conclude that upon completion of the loop **while** $w \leqslant r$ **do** $w := 2 * w$ not only do (12) and (13) hold, but also $(r < w)$. So altogether, we have that upon completion of this loop the following statement is true:

$$\exists n(w = 2^n * y) \land (x = q * w + r) \land (0 \leqslant r < w). \tag{14}$$

We now prove the invariance of (14) over the second loop in (11). According to the proof rule for the **while-do** statement, we have to show that if (14) and $w \neq y$ hold before the body of the second loop is executed, then (14) will hold upon completion of execution of this loop body.

We start with the observation that if $\exists n(w = 2^n * y)$ and $w \neq y$, then $w = 2^n * y$ for some $n > 0$. So w is even, and if w is even the product of $q * w$ does not change if the statements $q := 2 * q; w := w$ **div** 2 are executed. So (13) remains invariant over execution of these two assignments. The assignment $q := 2 * q$ certainly does not affect (12), and since $w = 2^n * y$ for some $n > 0$, i.e., (12), holds before $w := w$ **div** 2 is executed, we conclude that upon execution of this assignment, it will still hold. These two assignments do not affect the relation $0 \leqslant r$, but, of course, the assignment $w := w$ **div** 2 may affect the relation $r < w$.

Thus our analysis shows that upon execution of the assignments $q :=$ $2 * q$; $w := w$ **div** 2 the following holds:

$$\exists n(w = 2^n * y) \wedge (x = q * w + r) \wedge (0 \leqslant r). \tag{15}$$

Now we have to deal with the conditional **if** $w \leqslant r$ **then begin** $r := r - w$; $q := 1 + q$ **end**. If $r < w$ the assignments $r := r - w$; $q := 1 + q$ are not executed at all, and thus (15) is not affected. (15) together with $r < w$ yields (14). If $w \leqslant r$, then the assignments $r := r - w$; $q := 1 + q$ get executed, but these assignments do not affect (12) and (13). Indeed, substituting $1 + q$ for q and $r - w$ for r in (13) we obtain $x = (1 + q) * (r - w) + r$ which in view of the properties of integer arithmetic is the same relation as (13). Furthermore, if $w \leqslant r$, then $r - w \geqslant 0$, and after the assignment $r := r - w$ we have that $r \geqslant 0$ holds. It still remains to be proved that $r < w$ when the assignments $r := r - w$; $q := 1 + q$ are executed. In order to do that, observe that if $r < w$ holds before $w := w$ **div** 2 is executed, then $r < 2 * w$ must hold upon execution of this assignment. But if $r < 2 * w$ (i.e., $r - w < w$) holds before the assignment $r := r - w$, then $r < w$ must hold after it.

This completes the proof that (14) holds upon completion of execution of the body of the second loop in (11) if (14) as well as $w \neq y$ hold before it. But then, according to the proof rule of the **while-do** statement, we have that (14) and $w = y$ hold when the second loop is completed. But (14) and $w = y$ imply

$$(x = q * y + r) \wedge (0 \leqslant r < y)$$

which completes our proof of partial correctness of (11). To prove complete correctness, of course, we must show that the computation will always emerge from the two loops of (11), so long as the initial relation $(x > 0) \wedge (y > 0)$ is satisfied. But this is easy to do, and will be left as an exercise to the reader following Section 2.8.

Greatest Common Divisor

We now present a new algorithm (16), designed to compute the greatest common divisor of natural numbers x and y. The result, $gcd(x,y)$, is left as the value of both of the variables a and b. In this subsection, we prove partial correctness, and then show, in the next section, how keeping track of $a + b$ allows us to prove termination—and thus total correctness.

$$\{(x > 0) \wedge (y > 0)\} \tag{16}$$
$$\textbf{begin } a := x; b := y;$$
$$\{(a > 0) \wedge (b > 0) \wedge (gcd(a,b) = gcd(x,y))\}$$
$$\qquad \textbf{repeat}$$
$$\qquad\qquad \textbf{while } a > b \textbf{ do } a := a - b;$$
$$\qquad\qquad \textbf{while } b > a \textbf{ do } b := b - a$$
$$\qquad \textbf{until } a = b$$
$$\qquad \{a = b = gcd(x,y)\}$$
$$\textbf{end}$$

The above algorithm is designed on the basis of the following properties of the function gcd:

$$(a > b) \supset (gcd(a,b) = gcd(a - b, b)) \tag{17}$$
$$gcd(a,b) = gcd(b,a)$$
$$gcd(a,a) = a.$$

And indeed, correctness of (16) may be verified easily using the relations (17). After the assignments $a := x$; $b := y$ we have that

$$gcd(a,b) = gcd(x,y) \tag{18}$$

holds, as well as

$$(a > 0) \wedge (b > 0). \tag{19}$$

We prove that (18) and (19) remain invariant over the loops

$$\textbf{while } a > b \textbf{ do } a := a - b \tag{20}$$

$$\textbf{while } b > a \textbf{ do } b := b - a. \tag{21}$$

Invariance of (19) is clear. If $a > b$ (i.e., $a - b > 0$) then $a := a - b$ is executed and the new value of a is certainly positive. Similarly, if $b > a$ (i.e., $b - a > 0$) then $b := b - a$ is executed after which $b > 0$ holds. The relation $b > 0$ is not affected by the assignment $a := a - b$ and the relation $a > 0$ is not affected by the assignment $b := b - a$.

If $a > b$ then $gcd(a,b) = gcd(a - b, b)$, so that $gcd(a - b, b) = gcd(x,y)$ holds before the assignment $a := a - b$ is executed. But then $gcd(a,b) = gcd(x,y)$ must hold after this assignment. So we conclude (according to the proof rule of the **while-do** statement) that upon completion of (20) the following holds

$$(0 < a \leqslant b) \wedge (gcd(a,b) = gcd(x,y)). \tag{22}$$

According to (17) $gcd(a,b) = gcd(b,a)$, so that if $b > a$, we have, again by (17), that $gcd(b - a, a) = gcd(x,y)$ hold before the assignment $b := b - a$ is executed. But then, after this assignment, $gcd(b,a) = gcd(x,y)$ must hold. By the proof rule for the **while-do** statement, we conclude that upon termination of the loop (21) the following holds:

$$\{(0 < b \leqslant a) \wedge (gcd(b,a) = gcd(x,y))\}. \tag{23}$$

Since $gcd(b,a) = gcd(a,b)$, we have in fact proved:

$$\{(a > 0) \wedge (b > 0) \wedge (gcd(a,b) = gcd(x,y))\} \tag{24}$$
$$\textbf{while } a > b \textbf{ do } a := a - b;$$
$$\textbf{while } b > a \textbf{ do } b := b - a$$
$$\{(0 < b \leqslant a) \wedge (gcd(a,b) = gcd(x,y))\}$$

(23) and $a \neq b$ implies (18) and (19). (23) and $a = b$ in view of (17) imply

$$a = b = gcd(x,y). \tag{25}$$

Applying the proof rule for the **repeat-until** statement to the outer (**repeat-until**) loop in (16) we conclude that (25) will hold upon completion of this loop, which completes our proof of partial correctness.

2.8 Correct Termination of Algorithms

So far we have been mainly concerned with whether any results produced at the exit point are correct, if the arguments satisfy the input assertion. But that, of course, is merely one aspect of program correctness. The other one, equally important, is that the execution process yields results after only a finite number of steps. How this aspect can be taken into account in the design process was illustrated in Section 1.2. In this section we present a more careful treatment of this problem, and show that loop invariants play a crucial role here as well.

Consider first the **while** B **do** S loop (1) and let e be an integer expression.

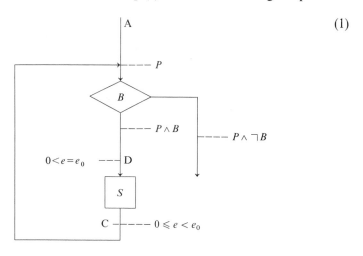

(1)

Suppose

$$P \wedge B \supset (e > 0) \tag{2}$$

and, for e_0 running over the integers (not expressions)

$$\forall e_0(\{0 < e = e_0\} \ S \ \{0 \leqslant e < e_0\}) \tag{3}$$

This means that $e \geqslant 0$ is also an invariant of the loop (1), i.e., the value of the expression e remains nonnegative during the repetition process. Furthermore, (3) says that each execution of S decreases the value of e. This is indicated in the diagram (1) by attaching the assertion $0 < e = e_0$ to the point D and the assertion $0 \leqslant e < e_0$ to the point C. Given (2), (3) and supposing that $\{P \wedge B\} \ S \ \{P\}$ was established, the immediate conclusion is that the repetition process is finite, since e cannot be decreased infinitely often and still stay positive as required by (2).

A similar analysis can be given for the **repeat** S **until** B loop (4). We have

(4)

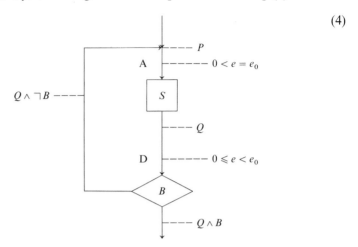

to show that the relations attached to A and D in (4) are invariants. This will follow if we can prove the following

$$P \supset (e > 0) \tag{5}$$

$$\forall e_0(\{0 < e = e_0\} \, S \, \{0 \leqslant e < e_0\}) \tag{6}$$

In addition to $\{P\} \, S \, \{Q\}$ and $Q \wedge \neg B \supset P$, which we would have to prove to verify partial correctness, we would have to prove (5) and (6). But then we can conclude that the repetition process must be finite.

The above reasoning will be illustrated in proving termination of the algorithms whose partial correctness has been verified in this chapter. Consider first the multiplication algorithm (7).

$$
\begin{aligned}
&\textbf{begin } \{(x > 0) \wedge (y > 0)\} \qquad\qquad (7)\\
&\qquad z := \ 0 \, ; u := x; \\
&\qquad \textbf{repeat } \{u + y > 0\} \\
&\qquad\qquad z := z + y; \\
&\qquad\qquad u := u - 1 \\
&\qquad\qquad \{u + y > 0\} \\
&\qquad \textbf{until } u = 0 \\
&\textbf{end}
\end{aligned}
$$

The desired expression e is $u + y$. It is positive throughout the repetition process if $(x > 0) \wedge (y > 0)$ holds initially, and its value is reduced by 1 by every execution of the statements $z := z + y; \, u := u - 1$. So the repetition process is finite.

Consider now the division algorithm (8)

$$\begin{aligned}
&\textbf{begin } \{(x \geqslant 0) \wedge (y > 0)\} &\text{(8)}\\
&\quad q := \ 0; r := x;\\
&\quad \textbf{while } r \geqslant y \textbf{ do } \{r + y > 0\}\\
&\quad \textbf{begin } r := r - y;\\
&\qquad\qquad q := 1 + q\\
&\quad \textbf{end}\\
&\quad \{r + y > 0\}\\
&\textbf{end}
\end{aligned}$$

The desired expression is $r + y$, since $r \geqslant 0$ and $y > 0$ hold throughout the algorithm. The value of this expression is reduced by every execution of the statement **begin** $r := r - y; q := 1 + q$ **end**, and thus the termination is established.

Consider now a more complex example—the *gcd* algorithm (9) whose partial correctness was already established.

$$\begin{aligned}
&\textbf{begin } \{(x > 0) \wedge (y > 0)\} &\text{(9)}\\
&\quad a := x; b := y; \{(a > 0) \wedge (b > 0)\}\\
&\quad \textbf{repeat while } a > b \textbf{ do } a := a - b;\\
&\qquad\qquad\quad \{0 < a \leqslant b\}\\
&\qquad\quad \textbf{while } b > a \textbf{ do } b := b - a\\
&\qquad\quad \{0 < b \leqslant a\}\\
&\quad \textbf{until } a = b\\
&\textbf{end}
\end{aligned}$$

The expression we are looking for is $a + b$. From our previous analysis it follows that we can use the property $a + b > 0$ of this expression to verify that all the loops in (9) will terminate. First, we observe that $a + b > 0$ holds after the assignments $a := x; b := y$, and it remains true throughout execution of the rest of the algorithm. This last conclusion follows from our former analysis, some results of which are denoted as assertions in (9). The value of the expression $a + b$ is decreased by every execution of the statement $a := a - b$, as well as by every execution of the statement $b := b - a$, so both **while-do** loops in (9) are finite. Consequently, every execution of the composition of these loops will terminate and will decrease the value of $a + b$. Therefore the outer **repeat-until** loop must also terminate.

Proving Nontermination

When can we find a mistake in our program by showing that it does not terminate? Failing to come up with a suitable integer expression for proving termination does not, of course, permit us to conclude that our program does not terminate for some particular initial values of variables. We have to prove that it does not, and how we go about it will be illustrated by a slightly modified form of (9). The modification consists of changing the condition in the first inner loop from $a > b$ to $a \geqslant b$.

$$\begin{aligned}
&\textbf{begin } \{(x > 0) \wedge (y > 0)\} \quad\quad\quad\quad\quad\quad\quad\quad\quad\quad (10)\\
&\quad\quad a := x; b := y;\\
&\quad\quad \{(a > 0) \wedge (b > 0)\}\\
&\quad\quad \textbf{repeat while } a \geqslant b \textbf{ do } a := a - b;\\
&\quad\quad\quad\quad \{0 \leqslant a < b\}\\
&\quad\quad\quad\quad \textbf{while } b > a \textbf{ do } b := b - a\\
&\quad\quad\quad\quad \{0 < b \leqslant a\}\\
&\quad\quad \textbf{until}\quad a = b\\
&\textbf{end}
\end{aligned}$$

A careful inspection of the above program shows that the invariants changed as well—as was to be expected. The loop **while** $b > a$ **do** $b := b - a$ can now be reached with $a = 0$ and $b > 0$, and the loop will not terminate. For if $b > a = 0$, then $b > a$ will be an invariant of this loop, i.e., no matter how many times $b := b - a$ gets executed, $b > a$ will hold and so the process of execution of the loop will be infinite. Looking back at the loop **while** $a \geqslant b$ **do** $a := a - b$ we conclude that upon completion of execution of this loop $a = 0$ will hold if before entering this loop a was a multiple of b, i.e., $a = kb$ for some integer $k \geqslant 1$. An immediate conclusion is then that if x and y satisfy the condition:

$$(x > 0) \wedge (y > 0) \wedge \exists k((k \geqslant 1) \wedge (x = ky)) \quad\quad\quad\quad (11)$$

the algorithm (10) will not terminate.

It is interesting to find out what happens if we modify the algorithm (9) in such a way that we change the condition in the second inner loop from $b > a$ to $b \geqslant a$. (12) shows how this change will affect the invariants pertinent to termination.

$$\begin{aligned}
&\textbf{begin } \{(x > 0) \wedge (y > 0)\} \quad\quad\quad\quad\quad\quad\quad\quad\quad\quad (12)\\
&\quad\quad a := x; b := y;\\
&\quad\quad \{(a > 0) \wedge (b > 0)\}\\
&\quad\quad \textbf{repeat while } a > b \textbf{ do } a := a - b;\\
&\quad\quad\quad\quad \{0 < a \leqslant b\}\\
&\quad\quad\quad\quad \textbf{while } b \geqslant a \textbf{ do } b := b - a\\
&\quad\quad\quad\quad \{0 \leqslant b < a\}\\
&\quad\quad \textbf{until } a = b\\
&\textbf{end}
\end{aligned}$$

The problems caused by this change are now obvious. Upon completion of execution of the loop **while** $b \geqslant a$ **do** $b := b - a$ the condition $b < a$ will hold. This means that upon completion of every execution of the body of the **repeat-until** loop in (12) $a \neq b$ will hold, and thus this loop will never terminate.

Observe that in the above two examples of nonterminating programs we used the following reasoning. Suppose that we have a **while-do** loop:

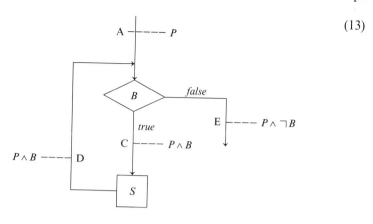

(13)

for which we want to establish that $\{P\}$ **while** B **do** S $\{P \wedge \neg B\}$. If we suspect that such a loop does not terminate, we have to prove that not only P, but $P \wedge B$ is an invariant of the loop. That is, we have to show that if $P \wedge B$ holds in A, the point D will be reached and $P \wedge B$ will hold whenever that point is reached. If we establish this, then obviously the loop does not terminate.

Similarly, suppose that we have a **repeat-until** loop:

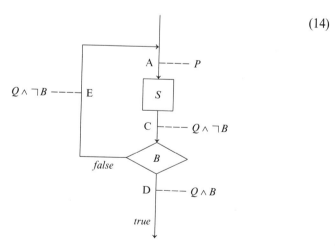

(14)

for which we want to establish $\{P\}$ **repeat** S **until** B $\{Q \wedge B\}$, but also that the loop terminates. If we are unable to prove termination, we can try to prove nontermination. In order to do that we have to show that if P holds when the point A is reached then when the point C is reached (if at all) not only Q, but $Q \wedge \neg B$ will hold. Because of $Q \wedge \neg B \supset P$ (which we need in order to prove $\{P\}$ **repeat** S **until** B $\{Q \wedge B\}$) we can conclude that $\neg B$ will hold whenever later on the point C is reached. But this then means that the process of execution of the loop (14) will not terminate.

The importance of the proof of nontermination is that it shows us why a particular program does not terminate. On the basis of the analysis which was necessary in order to establish nontermination we should be able to fix the given program to obtain a totally correct program.

Bibliographic Remarks

Our exposition of Pascal is based on Wirth (1972) and Jensen and Wirth (1974) and many of our programming examples are borrowed from these sources.

The technique presented for proving program correctness was originally suggested in Floyd (1967), where it was applied to flowcharts rather than pieces of program text. In the form in which it was described in this book it appeared first in Hoare (1969). The proof rules for the assignment and the conditional statement were first presented in Floyd (1967). The proof rule for the **while-do** statement was stated in Hoare (1969), and the proof rule for the **repeat-until** statement appeared in Hoare and Wirth (1973). The proof rule for the **for** statement is due to Hoare (1972c).

This axiomatic approach was extended to a semantic definition of almost complete Pascal in Hoare and Wirth (1973), where all of Pascal, except for real arithmetic and goto's was defined in terms of proof rules. A different line of research in establishing mathematical techniques for proving program properties and the relationship to the method presented in this book is given in Manna and Vuillemin (1972) and Manna, Ness and Vuillemin (1973).

The programming examples in this chapter, but not the proofs, are borrowed from Wirth (1972). Some simpler exercises are based on Conway and Gries (1975), but essentially all of the more involved examples are borrowed from Marmier (1975).

Exercises

1. Prove: $\qquad\qquad \{n < 0\}\ n := n * n\ \{n > 0\}$

2. Prove:
$$\{(a = a_0) \wedge (b = b_0)\}$$
begin $t := a$;
$\qquad a := b$;
$\qquad b := t$
end
$$\{(b = a_0) \wedge (a = b_0)\}$$

3. Prove:

$$\{(s = x * y) \wedge \neg odd(x)\}\ \textbf{begin}\ y := 2 * y;\ x := x\ \textbf{div}\ 2\ \textbf{end}\ \{s = x * y\}$$

where $odd(x)$ is *true* if x is an odd integer, and *false* if not.

4. Prove:

$$\{(z = a^b) \wedge \neg odd(b)\} \text{ begin } b := b \text{ div } 2; \ a := a * a \text{ end } \{z = a^b\}$$

5. Prove

$$\{(a \geqslant 0) \wedge (b \geqslant 0)\}$$
$$\text{if } a > b \text{ then } a := a - b$$
$$\text{else } b := b - a$$
$$\{(a \geqslant 0) \wedge (b \geqslant 0)\}$$

6. Prove:

$$\{(c = p * x^n) \wedge (x \neq 0) \wedge (n > 0)\}$$
$$\text{begin if } odd(n) \text{ then } p := p * x;$$
$$\qquad n := n \text{ div } 2; \ x := x * x$$
$$\text{end}$$
$$\{(c = p * x^n) \wedge (x \neq 0)\}$$

7. Write a conditional statement which interchanges the values of the variables x, y and z in such a way that after this interchange the variable x has the largest value and the variable z the smallest.

8. x, y and z are the lengths of the sides of a triangle if all of them are positive and the following relations hold: $x + y > z$, $x + z > y$, $y + z > x$. Write a statement S which tests whether x, y and z are the lengths of the sides of a triangle, and prove that it does indeed accomplish this test.

9. Prove:
$$\{true\} \text{ while } \neg odd(n) \text{ do } n := n \text{ div } 2 \ \{odd(n)\}$$

10. Prove

$$\{(s = c + t) \wedge (t \leqslant y)\}$$
$$\text{while } t \neq y \text{ do}$$
$$\text{begin } s := s + 1; \ t := t + 1 \text{ end}$$
$$\{s = c + y\}$$

11. Prove:

$$\{(s = c + t) \wedge (t < y)\}$$
$$\text{repeat } s := s + 1;$$
$$\qquad t := t + 1$$
$$\text{until } t = y$$
$$\{(s = c + y)\}$$

12. Verify that for the given precondition the loops in the previous two exercises terminate.

13. Prove that the more efficient version of the algorithm for computing the quotient and the remainder obtained on integer division presented in this chapter does actually terminate.

14. Prove that in the following compound statement:

$$\text{begin } x := x0; \ y := y0;$$
$$\qquad s := 0;$$
$$\qquad \text{repeat } \{s = (x0 - x) * y0\}$$
$$\qquad\qquad t := 0;$$
$$\qquad\qquad \text{repeat } \{s = (x0 - x) * y0 + t\}$$
$$\qquad\qquad\qquad s := s + 1; \ t := t + 1$$
$$\qquad\qquad \text{until } t = y$$
$$\qquad\qquad \{s = (x0 - x) * y0 + t\}$$
$$\qquad\qquad x := x - 1$$
$$\qquad \text{until } x = 0$$
$$\text{end} \quad \{s = x0 * y0\}$$

where $x0$, $y0$, x, y, s and t are integer variables, the annotated relations are indeed invariants.

15. Prove that in the following compound statement:

$$\begin{aligned}
&\textbf{begin } x := x0;\, y := y0; \\
&\qquad s := 0; \\
&\qquad \textbf{while } x \neq 0 \textbf{ do } \{s = (x0 - x) * y0\} \\
&\qquad \textbf{begin } t := 0; \\
&\qquad\qquad \textbf{while } t \neq y \textbf{ do } \{s = (x0 - x) * y0 + t\} \\
&\qquad\qquad \textbf{begin } s := s + 1;\, t := t + 1 \textbf{ end}; \\
&\qquad\qquad x := x - 1 \\
&\qquad \textbf{end} \\
&\qquad \{s = x0 * y0\} \\
&\textbf{end}
\end{aligned}$$

where $x0$, $y0$, x, y, s and t are non-negative integer variables, the annotated relations are indeed invariants.

16. The compound statement:

$$\begin{aligned}
&\textbf{begin } x := a;\, y := b; \\
&\qquad s := 0; \\
&\qquad \textbf{while } x \neq 0 \textbf{ do } \{s = a * b - x * y\} \\
&\qquad \textbf{begin while } \neg odd(x) \textbf{ do } \{s = a * b - x * y\} \\
&\qquad\qquad \textbf{begin } y := 2 * y; \\
&\qquad\qquad\qquad x := x \textbf{ div } 2 \\
&\qquad\qquad \textbf{end}; \\
&\qquad\qquad s := s + y;\, x := x - 1 \\
&\qquad \textbf{end}; \\
&\qquad \{s = a * b\} \\
&\textbf{end}
\end{aligned}$$

is intended to compute the product of non-negative integers a and b, leaving the result as the value of the integer variable s. x and y are auxiliary integer variables. Prove that the above compound statement does indeed accomplish the intended effect.

17. The compound statement:

$$\begin{aligned}
&\textbf{begin } x := x0;\, n := n0;\, \{n0 > 0\} \\
&\qquad p := 1; \\
&\qquad \textbf{if } x \neq 0 \textbf{ then} \\
&\qquad \textbf{while } n \neq 0 \textbf{ do } \{(p * x^n = x0^{n0}) \wedge (x \neq 0) \wedge (n > 0)\} \\
&\qquad \textbf{begin if } odd(n) \textbf{ then } p := p * x; \\
&\qquad\qquad n := n \textbf{ div } 2;\, x := x * x \\
&\qquad \textbf{end} \\
&\qquad \textbf{else } p := 0 \\
&\qquad \{p = x0^{n0}\} \\
&\textbf{end}
\end{aligned}$$

is intended to compute $x0^{n0}$, where $x0$ and $n0$ are integer variables, and $n0 > 0$. The result is represented as the value of the integer variable p. x and y are auxiliary integer variables. Prove that the above compound statement is correct.

18. Prove that the following compound statement performs multiplication of non-negative integers $x0$ and $y0$ and assigns this product to the integer variable x:

$$\textbf{begin } x := x0;\ y := y0;$$
$$z := 0;$$
$$\textbf{while } x \neq 0 \textbf{ do}$$
$$\textbf{begin if } odd(x) \textbf{ then } z := z + y;$$
$$y := y * 2;\ x := x \textbf{ div } 2$$
$$\textbf{end}$$
$$\{z = x0 * y0\}$$
$$\textbf{end}$$

x and y are auxiliary integer variables.

19. Prove that the following compound statement assigns the value of the expression $x0^{n0}$ to the integer variable z, where $x0$ and $n0$ are integer variables such that $n0 \geqslant 0$, and x and n are auxiliary integer variables:

$$\textbf{begin } x := x0;\ n := n0;\ \{n \geqslant 0\}$$
$$z := 1;$$
$$\textbf{while } n > 0 \textbf{ do}$$
$$\textbf{begin if } odd(n) \textbf{ then } z := z * x;$$
$$n := n \textbf{ div } 2;$$
$$x := x * x$$
$$\textbf{end}$$
$$\{x = x0^{n0}\}$$
$$\textbf{end}$$

20. The algorithm below is a generalization of the algorithm for computing the greatest common divisor gcd of $x0$ and $y0$, where $y0 \neq 0$. It computes the integers y, c and d such that the following holds

$$y = gcd(x0, y0) = c * x0 + d * y0$$

so $gcd(x0, y0)$ is computed also,

$$\textbf{begin } x := x0;\ y := y0;\ \{y \neq 0\}$$
$$c := 0;\ d := 1;\ u := 1;\ v := 0;$$
$$q := x \textbf{ div } y;\ r := x \textbf{ mod } y;$$
$$\{(gcd(y,r) = gcd(x0,y0)) \wedge (y = c * x0 + d * y0) \wedge (x = q * y + r) \wedge$$
$$(x = u * x0 + v * y0)\}$$
$$\textbf{while } r \neq 0 \textbf{ do}$$
$$\textbf{begin } \{y * q = (c * x0 + d * y0) * q\}$$
$$x := y;\ y := r;$$
$$t := u;\ u := c;\ c := t - q * c;$$
$$t := v;\ v := d;\ d := t - q * d;$$
$$q := x \textbf{ div } y;\ r := x \textbf{ mod } y$$
$$\textbf{end}$$
$$\{y = gcd(x0,y0) = c * x0 + d * y0\}$$
$$\textbf{end}$$

x, y, c, d, u, v, q, r, and t are integer variables. Prove correctness of the above algorithm.

21. Let $bin(n,k)$ be defined as follows:

$$bin(n,k) = 1 \qquad \text{if } k = n$$
$$bin(n,k) = bin(n,k+1) * (k+1) \textbf{ div } (n-k) \qquad \text{otherwise}$$

and consider the following algorithm

```
begin {n ⩾ k ⩾ 0}
    x := n; y := 1; b := 1;
    while x ≠ k do {b = bin(n,x) ∧ (x + y = n + 1) ∧ (y ⩾ 1)}
    begin b := b * x div y;
        x := x − 1; y := y + 1
    end
    {b = bin(n,k)}
end
```

Prove that if $n \geqslant k \geqslant 0$ holds before the above compound is executed, then $b = bin(n,k)$ will hold afterwards.

3
Data Types

3.1 Introduction

We have now built up a moderate amount of experience in the top-down design of algorithms, the translation of these algorithms into a programming language, and the verification of the correctness of the resultant programs. The rest of the book will develop each of these themes much further, providing the reader with a variety of useful tools and a rich experience in their use. For definiteness we have chosen the programming language Pascal, but it should be clear to the reader that most of the tools we introduce are valid far beyond Pascal, even though the fine details of their use will depend on the conventions used in setting up a particular programming language.

A program takes the given values of certain variables—these values provide the *input* data—manipulates them, using the values of other variables to store *intermediate* data, and puts out the answer to the problem as the *output* data. As we have already stressed in Section 1.2, although the value of a variable may change during the execution of a program, the set of values that the variable may possibly assume—and the operations permissible on those values—is fixed as part of the specification of the program. We thus speak of each variable as belonging to a particular *data type*. Each constant occurring in a program must also have an appropriate data type.

The need for data types is threefold:

a. It helps us gain logical clarity, by being quite clear about what each variable is, and what operations can thus be carried out upon it. This stops us from making silly mistakes like adding 'apples' to 'oranges' (unless they both occur in values of data type "fruit"). More realistically, it prevents a computer from adding the integer 1 to the real number 2.000 by lining up the rightmost digits to return the value 2.001—or some equally gross error, depending on the particular *internal form* in which the computer stores these data. Mixing these forms is almost always nonsensical.

b. When a real program is run on a real computer, the current value of each variable is stored in one or more storage units of computer memory. When we declare the data type of a variable, then, we give the compiler the information it needs to determine how many storage units must be set aside for the values of the variable, and on the necessary procedures for coding and decoding these values.

c. Each programming language comes with a repertoire of basic instructions, for testing the value of some variable to return a Boolean value, and for combining current values of certain variables to yield the new value of some variable. As our point in a. above should make clear, these operations must come with a clear specification of the data type of the variables the operation acts on (the *domain* of the action) as well as the data type of the result (the *codomain* of the action). This allows both the human designer and the computer compiler to check that operations are only used for data of the appropriate form.

Our job in this chapter is to see how basic data types are defined and how new (structured) data types are built up from old ones. New data types are built from the previously defined ones according to the rules of the chosen programming language. These rules are called rules of data structuring, and the types obtained by these rules are called *structured types*. We must also specify what operations are provided as "built-in equipment" for data types, both simple and structured. Of course, the whole point of programming is that, once we are given a basic repertoire of actions, we can build up programs which perform more and more intricate actions, by composing actions in the fashion described in Chapter 2. After a look at basic concepts of set theory, we focus on the basic data types in Section 3.3, turning to various ways of building *structured* data types in later sections. Throughout, we shall stress concepts valid in most modern programming languages, but will always provide the correct Pascal formalism for each concept.

3.2 A Primer on Set Theory

In this section, we summarize a number of basic concepts from set theory which are useful throughout modern mathematics and computer science. We use standard mathematical notation in this section, for it will help the reader to recognize these constructs when he meets them elsewhere. In later sections of this chapter, we shall see that most of these constructs are available in Pascal, and we shall set out the Pascal formalisms, and give examples of their use in programs.

Basically, a *set* is a collection of elements, and we usually think of the elements as defined by some rule. For example, the set of even numbers is defined by the rule 'leaves no remainder when divided by 2'. We write

$$a \in A \tag{1}$$

to denote that a is an element of the set A. We also read $a \in A$ as 'a belongs to A' and 'a is in A', and we use

$$a \notin A \text{ for } \neg(a \in A) \tag{2}$$

i.e., when a does not belong to A.

Often we write a set by listing its elements[1], so that

$$A = [2,3,7,9]$$

tells us that A has 4 elements, namely 2, 3, 7 and 9. The rule for testing membership is then just '$x \in A$ just in case x belongs to the list of elements of A'. This means that a set is *unordered*, so that we may also write

$$A = [2,9,7,3]$$
$$A = [9,7,3,2]$$

or even
$$A = [9,3,7,9,2,9]$$

since each list has the property of returning 2, 3, 7 and 9 as members of A when we apply the membership rule. We may sum up by saying that two sets are equal if and only if they contain exactly the same elements. As an exercise in the logical notation of Section 2.2, we can write this out as

$$A = B \text{ means } \forall x((x \in A) \equiv (x \in B)). \tag{3}$$

We say A is a *subset* of B, and write $A \leqslant B$, just in case every element of A is also an element of B.

We also read $A \leqslant B$ as B *contains* A, or A is contained in B. (We may also write $A \subset B$ instead of $A \leqslant B$). We thus have

$$A \leqslant B \text{ means } \forall x((x \in A) \supset (x \in B)). \tag{4}$$

For example, $[2,3,9] \leqslant [2,3,7,9]$. Note that any set is a subset of itself—$A \leqslant A$—and that each set contains

$$\text{the empty set, } [\ ] \tag{5}$$

which is defined as having zero elements. Be careful! The empty set with zero elements does *not* equal the set whose only element is zero: $[\ ] \neq [0]$.

Given any set A, we form a new set

$$PA, \text{ the } powerset \text{ of } A \tag{6}$$

whose elements are the subsets of A. For example:

$$P[2,3,7] = [[\ ], [2], [3], [7], [3,7], [2,7], [2,3], [2,3,7]]. \tag{6}$$

---

[1] Mathematicians usually employ { } to enclose the elements of a set, and write $\varnothing$ for the empty set. But we shall use the Pascal [ ] notation since the { } are already in heavy use for comments and relations.

Note that [2,3,7] has 3 elements and that $P[2,3,7]$ has $8 = 2^3$ elements. In general, if A has n elements, then PA has 2^n elements. Can you see why? For this reason—we shall see another later—PA is also denoted 2^A.

An important way of building subsets of a set A is to select those elements which satisfy some particular condition

$$[x \mid (x \in A) \wedge P(x)] \text{ means the set of those elements } x \text{ of } A \text{ for} \qquad (7)$$
$$\text{which the condition } P(x) \text{ holds.}$$

For example, we can define the set of *odd integers* by

$$odd\ integers = [x \mid x \text{ is an integer} \wedge (x \bmod 2 = 1)]. \qquad (8)$$

Given two sets A and B, we can build new sets as follows:

$A \cup B$ is the *union* of A and B, and contains all elements $\qquad$ (9)
which belong to A *or* B or both:

$$x \in A \cup B \text{ means } (x \in A) \vee (x \in B)$$

$A \cap B$ is the *intersection* of A and B, and contains all
elements which belong to A *and* B:

$$x \in A \cap B \text{ means } (x \in A) \wedge (x \in B)$$

$A - B$ is the *set difference* of A and B, and contains
just those elements of A which do not belong to B:

$$x \in A - B \text{ means } (x \in A) \wedge \neg(x \in B).$$

These three operations are indicated in Figure 3.1.

Another way of building sets is the *Cartesian product*:

$A \times B$ is the set of all *ordered pairs* of elements, $\qquad$ (10)
such that the first comes from A and the
second from B.

We use the notation (a,b) for an ordered pair. More generally, we use the notation $(x_1, \ldots ,x_n)$ for a *sequence* of n elements. A sequence is *ordered*, and two sequences are equal if and only if they are of the same length, and match at each position in order:

$$(x_1, \ldots ,x_m) = (y_1, \ldots ,y_n) \text{ means } (m = n) \wedge \forall j((1 \leqslant j \leqslant m) \supset (x_j = y_j)).$$
$$(11)$$

We can use this notion of a sequence to extend the definition of cartesian product to more than two sets:

$A_1 \times \cdots \times A_n$ is the set of all sequences of length n, where $\qquad$ (12)
the jth element belongs to A_j. Thus

$$x \in A_1 \times \cdots \times A_n \text{ means}$$

$$\exists a_1(\ldots (\exists a_n((x = (a_1, \ldots ,a_n)) \wedge \forall j((1 \leqslant j \leqslant n) \supset (a_j \in A_j)))) \ldots).$$

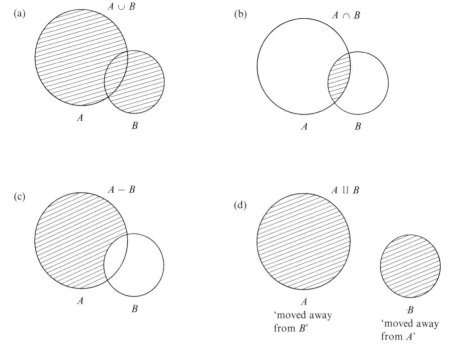

Figure 3.1   Basic set operations (a) union, (b) intersection, (c) difference, (d) disjoint union

For the two specific sets $A = [1,2,3]$ and $B = [3,4,5]$, their union $A \cup B = [1,2,3,4,5]$ has only 5 elements, because the occurrence of 3 in both A and B contributes only one element to $A \cup B$. In some applications, however, we want to keep a separate record of such multiple occurrences—we might, for example write $(3,A)$ and $(3,B)$ to distinguish the occurrences of 3 in A and B. Following the notation consistently, we have the disjoint union

$$A \amalg B = [(1,A), (2,A) (3,A), (3,B), (4,B), (5,B)]. \tag{13}$$

More generally, given any collection of sets $A_1, A_2, A_3, \ldots$ with distinct identifiers $t_1, t_2, t_3, \ldots$ we can define their *disjoint union* to be

$$A_1 \amalg A_2 \amalg A_3 \amalg \cdots = A_1 \times [t_1] \cup A_2 \times [t_2] \cup A_3 \times [t_3] \cup \cdots \tag{14}$$

whose typical element is (a_j, t_j) where a_j is in A_j.

Functions

Given two sets A and B, a *function* (also called a *map* or *mapping*) *from A to B* is any rule which assigns to each element of A a corresponding element of B. We use the notation

$$f : A \to B \tag{15}$$

to say that f takes elements from A (which is called the *domain* of f) to yield elements in B (which is called the *codomain* of f). We use a notation like $f(a)$ to indicate that, when applied to a in A, f yields the result $f(a)$ in B. We say that a function f is a *bijection* if each b in B is an $f(a)$ for one and only one a in A.

Now, consider the sets *Boolean* and *integer* (underlying the data types of the same name), and form the Cartesian product *integer* $\times$ *integer*. Then the following are familiar functions:

$\neg$: *Boolean* $\to$ *Boolean* is *negation*, which sends p to $\neg p$, where   (16)
$\neg$*false* $=$ *true*, and $\neg$*true* $=$ *false*.

$+$: *integer* $\times$ *integer* $\to$ *integer* is *addition*, which sends the pair
(a,b) of integers to their *sum*—which we
write $a + b$ instead of $+((a,b))$.

odd: *integer* $\to$ *Boolean* checks *parity*, with $odd(x) = true$ if x is
odd, while $odd(x) = false$ if x is even.

Given two sets A and B, we form a new set $[A \to B]$ whose elements are the functions from A to B. This set is called a *function space*. Suppose A and B are both finite sets, where A has m elements, and B has n elements. How many elements does $[A \to B]$ have? Let us write out the elements of A in some fixed order as $(a_1, \ldots, a_m)$. Then to define a function $f : A \to B$, we must specify the list

$$(f(a_1), \ldots, f(a_m)) \tag{17}$$

where each $f(a_j)$ belongs to B. Thus in defining f we have n choices for $f(a_1), \ldots$, down to n choices for $f(a_m)$—a total of n^m choices in all. Because of this, we often use the notation B^A for $[A \to B]$. If we use $|A|$ to denote the number of elements of A, etc., we then have the pleasing equality

$$|B^A| = |B|^{|A|}. \tag{18}$$

The notation B^A is a little confusing at first, since we read B^A as 'B *to the* A' while $[A \to B]$ is the set of maps *from* A *to* B. But the matching-up of the number of elements shown in (18) makes it worth learning to live with both notations.

The reader will notice that if A has n elements, then B^A may be identified with the cartesian product of n copies of B. We write $\simeq$ for 'may be identified with' (i.e., one set may be obtained from the other by suitably relabelling elements—in other words, there is a *bijection* between the two sets). We then have:

If $A = [a_1, \ldots, a_n]$ (where the n elements are distinct), then   (19)
$$B^A \simeq B_1 \times \cdots \times B_n$$

where each of the n sets B_j is a copy of B, under the correspondence

$f \in B^A$ corresponds to $(f(a_1), \ldots, f(a_n)) \in B_1 \times \cdots \times B_n$.

We can then consistently use the notation B^n for the cartesian product of n copies of B.

In computer science, we often consider a set B which is an *alphabet*, and we then think of B^n as the set of *words* of *length* n over the alphabet B. Thus a word in computer science is a more general notion than a word of English. For example

apple3   pear4

is a word of length 12 over an alphabet which includes letters, numbers *and the blank*. If we think of a word as the output of some device in a computer system, we must include the possibility of the *null word* of length 0, corresponding to no output at all. We use $\langle \ \rangle$ to denote the empty word, and $B^0 = [\langle \ \rangle]$. We often find it convenient to identify an element of B with a word of length 1, so that $B = B^1$. Distinguish carefully the following situations with respect to an alphabet B which contains the blank:

[ ]	the empty set; it contains 0 elements	(20)
[⟨ ⟩]	the 1 element set, B^0, whose only element is the null word	
[‘ ’]	the 1 element subset of B^1 whose only element is the blank character, which we show here in quotes to avoid confusion with [ ].	

Two sets of words are very important in computer science:

$$B^* = B^0 \cup B^1 \cup B^2 \cup \cdots \cup B^n \cup \cdots \tag{21}$$

$$B^+ = B^1 \cup B^2 \cup B^3 \cup \cdots \cup B^{n+1} \cup \cdots \tag{22}$$

B^* contains all words on the alphabet B including the null word, while B^+ contains all the nonnull words on the alphabet B.

Relations

Given a set A, a *relation* R on A is a set of pairs (a,b) such that both a and b are elements of A. In formal terms $R \subset A \times A$. It is customary to write aRb for a pair (a,b) which is a member of R.

We say a relation R is a *partial order* on A if for all a, b, c the following holds:

i.	*Transitivity*:	aRb and bRc implies aRc	(23)
ii.	*Reflexivity*:	aRa holds	
iii.	*Antisymmetry*:	aRb and bRa implies $a = b$.	

Note that if $A = PB$, the set of subsets of B, then the subset relation $\subset$ is a partial order on A. Again, the relation $\leqslant$ of numerical inequality is a partial order on the set of integers. Now, given any two integers a and b, it is either the case that $a \leqslant b$ or $b \leqslant a$—we say that the integers are *linearly ordered*. However, the subset relation is *not* linearly ordered: for example, if $a = [2,3]$ and $b = [3,9]$, as subsets of $[2,3,9]$, then neither $a \subset b$ nor $b \subset a$ holds.

Another important type of relation is an equivalence relation. We say R is an *equivalence relation* on A, if for all a, b, c the following holds:

> i. *Transitivity*: aRb and bRc implies aRc (24)
>
> ii. *Reflexivity*: aRa holds
>
> iii. *Symmetry*: If aRb holds, then so does bRa.

The classic example of an equivalence relation is, of course, equality, $=$. As another example of an equivalence relation on the integers, consider aRb to hold either if both a and b are odd or if both a and b are even. These are examples of the general property:

> Given an equivalence relation R on a set A, the set A can   (25)
> be *partitioned*—split into disjoint (that is, nonoverlapping)
> subsets—in such a way that a and b belong to the same
> subset in the partition, if and only if aRb holds.

Suppose that we start with $A = [1,2,3,4,5]$, and decree that R be an equivalence relation satisfying

$$2R5, \; 3R5 \text{ and } 1R4.$$

Then by symmetry, we also have $5R2$, $5R3$ and $4R1$. By transitivity we then have $2R3$ and $3R2$, while reflexivity yields aRa for each a in A. Thus if we partition A into the subsets

$$[1,4] \text{ and } [2,3,5]$$

we do indeed have that aRb if and only if a and b belong to the same subset in the partition.

A very important concept in computer science is that of *sorting*—rearranging the elements of a sequence so that they have some desirable property (e.g., arranging a sequence of numbers in increasing order, or a sequence of English words in alphabetical order). We say that one sequence is a *permutation* of another if it is obtained by rearranging the elements of the first sequence. More formally, we can define a relation *permute* on B^*, for any B, by the definition

> $(a_1, \ldots, a_n)$ *permute* $(b_1, \ldots, b_m)$ if and only if $m = n$ and there   (26)
> is a bijection
> $f : [1, \ldots, n] \to [1, \ldots, n]$ such
> that $b_j = a_{f(j)}$ for $1 \leqslant j \leqslant n$.

For example, $b = (4,6,5)$ is a permutation of $a = (5,4,6)$—and we can see this formally by defining $f:[1,2,3] \to [1,2,3]$ by $f(1) = 2$, $f(2) = 3$, $f(3) = 1$, so that $b_1 = a_{f(1)} = a_2 = 4$, etc.

3.3 Scalar Types and Simple Types

We have already met the basic data type

$$Boolean = (false, true)$$

in Section 2.2, where we learned that *Boolean* comes equipped with 3 basic actions:

$$\neg : Boolean \to Boolean \tag{1}$$

$$\wedge : Boolean \times Boolean \to Boolean \tag{2}$$

$$\vee : Boolean \times Boolean \to Boolean \tag{3}$$

and we saw that other actions, such as $\supset$ and $\equiv$, could be built up in terms of them. The notation *Boolean* $\to$ *Boolean* (1) says that $\neg$ takes a value p of type *Boolean* and returns a value $\neg p$ of type *Boolean*. The notation *Boolean* $\times$ *Boolean* $\to$ *Boolean* (2) says that $\wedge$ takes two values (p,q) of type *Boolean*, and returns a single value $p \wedge q$ of type *Boolean*. As a result, an expression like $3 \wedge true$ is meaningless, since 3 is not of type *Boolean* even though *true* is.

Scalar Types

We saw that Pascal views the values in *Boolean* as linearly ordered, with *false* < *true*. This is an example of what are called *scalar types* in Pascal—sets of values which are linearly ordered.[2] (Formally, a set is *linearly ordered* if, given any two values a and b of that set, just one of $a < b$, $a = b$ or $b < a$ must be true. In addition, we require that $a < b$ and $b < c$ implies $a < c$—so that we can imagine the values strung out along a *line* with '$a < b$' interpreted as 'a is to the left of b'.) We recall from 2.2 (5) that once we have a linear ordering $<$ on a data type, we can build up the relations $\leqslant$, $=$, $\geqslant$, $\neq$ and $>$ by using the Boolean operators:

New Relation	Definition	(4)
$a \leqslant b$	$\neg(b < a)$	
$a = b$	$(a \leqslant b) \wedge (b \leqslant a)$	
$a \neq b$	$\neg(a = b)$	
$a \geqslant b$	$b \leqslant a$	
$a > b$	$b < a$	

---

[2] Pascal differs from most other programming languages in requiring this linear order. In most languages, the basic data types are just sets of values, without any special ordering of those values.

When a new data type is defined, Pascal uses a type definition of the form

$$\textbf{type } t = T$$

where t is a hitherto unused string of symbols to be used as the identifier of the new type, and T is a description of the type which t denotes. A scalar type in Pascal may thus be introduced by an explicit definition of the form

$$\textbf{type } t = (c_1, c_2, \ldots, c_n) \tag{5}$$

which includes as a special case

$$\textbf{type } Boolean = (\textit{false, true}) \tag{6}$$

In (5) a type identifier t is introduced, as well as n constant identifiers $c_1, \ldots, c_n$. Enumeration of these n components corresponds to the linear order $<$ of the type t, i.e.,

$$c_i < c_j \text{ for } 1 \leqslant i < j \leqslant n. \tag{7}$$

Examples of scalar type definitions are:

$$\textbf{type } color = (\textit{red, blue, yellow})$$
$$\textbf{type } sex = (\textit{male, female})$$

It is possible in Pascal to use abbreviated notation when defining several types as in (8) where we do not repeat **type** beyond the first definition:

$$\textbf{type } workdays = (\textit{mon, tue, wed, thur, fri}); \tag{8}$$
$$freedays = (\textit{sat, sun})$$

We have already noted that a programming language associates certain basic operations with each of its data types. The fact that a scalar type is linearly ordered by (7) naturally leads to the introduction of the successor and the predecessor functions defined as follows:

$$succ(c_i) = c_{i+1} \text{ for } i = 1, \ldots, n-1 \tag{9}$$
$$pred(c_i) = c_{i-1} \text{ for } i = 2, \ldots, n.$$

Here $succ(c_n)$ and $pred(c_1)$ are undefined—any well-designed compiler should return an error message in response to any attempt to evaluate them. (This gives two examples of a *partial function*—a function which, in contrast to a *total function* need not be defined for all values of its domain. We shall have much more to say about these functions in later chapters).

The third standard function defined over scalar types is *ord*. *ord(x)* gives the ordinal number of x. For the type t defined in (5) this function is defined as $ord(c_j) = j$, which is equivalent to the following:

$$ord(c_1) = 1 \tag{10}$$
$$ord(succ(x)) = ord(x) + 1.$$

Given a scalar type it is often appropriate to define a new type which represents an interval of the original scalar type. In other words, we pick two elements *a* and *b* of the scalar type, and then form a new type whose elements run from *a* through *b*. A type defined in such a way is called a *subrange type* and the scalar type of which it represents an interval is called its *associated* scalar type.

The definition of a subrange type has the usual form **type** $t = T$, but in T the subrange is described by indicating the lower bound and the upper bound of the subrange, where the lower bound must be less than the upper bound:

$$\textbf{type } t = min \,.\,.\, max \tag{11}$$

and where *min* and *max* unambiguously identify elements of the original scalar type. An example of a definition of a subrange type is given by the second line of

$$\textbf{type } days = (mon, tue, wed, thur, fri, sat, sun); \tag{12}$$
$$workdays = mon \,.\,.\, fri$$

which defines workdays as a subrange of the type *days*.

Certain scalar types, such as *Boolean*, are used so frequently that they need not be introduced in a program by an explicit type definition. Furthermore, these types each come equipped with a predefined set of operators in addition to *succ*, *pred* and *ord* (9,10)—just as *Boolean* is supplied with $\neg$, $\wedge$ and $\vee$. Such types are called *standard types*. They include not only the logical truth values *Boolean*, but also suitable subsets of the integer and the real numbers, and a set of printable characters. We briefly examine this data type, *char*, of printable characters, and then turn to integer and real numbers.

The type *char* is a finite, ordered set of characters. The set of characters which are members of the type *char* depend upon the particular choice of computer system—it is the set available on the system's input and output equipment. We thus say that *char* is *implementation-dependent*.

Two standard functions are defined in conjunction with the type *char*, and are both implementation-dependent.

$$ord(c) \quad \text{the ordinal number of the character } c \tag{13}$$
$$chr(i) \quad \text{the character value with the ordinal } i.$$

These two functions are inverse to each other, that is, the following holds:

$$chr(ord(c)) = c \quad ord(chr(i)) = i. \tag{14}$$

To denote a constant of type *char*, it is customary to enclose the character in single quotes, as in the following examples:

$$\text{`*' `}B\text{' `}2\text{'.} \tag{15}$$

The following minimal properties are assumed to hold for the type *char* independent of the underlying implementation:

i. The character set contains the letters 'A'–'Z' and the digits '0'–'9', as well as the blank character.

ii. The subsets of letters and digits are ordered and coherent. This means that c is a (capital) letter only if 'A' $\leqslant c$ and $c \leqslant$ 'Z', and c is a digit if and only if '1' $\leqslant c$ and $c \leqslant$ '9'.

iii. 'A' $<$ 'B' 　 '1' $= succ($'0'$)$
　 'B' $<$ 'C' 　 '2' $= succ($'1'$)$
　 　 $\vdots$ 　 　 　 $\vdots$
　 'Y' $<$ 'Z' 　 '9' $= succ($'8'$)$

Types *integer* and *real*

The type *integer* is an *implementation-defined* subset of the set of integers, since the number of different integers which are storable will depend upon the (finite) number of bits set aside for each variable whose data type is *integer*. This subset is thus determined by an implementation dependent standard identifier *maxint*, so that the type *integer* is the set of integers x such that $|x| \leqslant maxint$. This set comes equipped with a set of familiar operations *integer* $\times$ *integer* $\rightarrow$ *integer* of integer arithmetic, defined informally as follows:

$+$　addition   (16)

$-$　subtraction

$*$　multiplication

div　integer division (i.e., with truncation of the possible fractional part)

mod　remainder of integer division.

We say 'informally' because $|a| \leqslant maxint$ and $|b| \leqslant maxint$ does not guarantee $|a * b| \leqslant maxint$ for example. However, the operators **div** and **mod** can be assumed to be implemented in such a way that the following relation holds for any pair a,b of integers:

$$a = ((a \textbf{ div } b) * b) + (a \textbf{ mod } b) \tag{17}$$

since $|a| \leqslant maxint$, $|b| \leqslant maxint$ does guarantee $|a \textbf{ div } b| \leqslant maxint$ and $|a \textbf{ mod } b| \leqslant maxint$.

In addition to the operators listed in (16) the type *integer* is also equipped with some standard functions which have as domain the data type of *integer*. These are:

odd: *integer* $\rightarrow$ *Boolean*　　*odd*(x) is *true* if x is   (18)
　　　　　　　　　　　　　　odd, and *false* otherwise

abs: *integer* $\rightarrow$ *integer*　　　*abs*(x) is the absolute value of x

sqr: *integer* $\rightarrow$ *integer*　　　*sqr*(x) is x squared.

We see from (18) that the codomain of the function *odd* is the type *Boolean*, whereas the codomain of the functions *abs* and *sqr* is the type *integer*. Note that only *sqr* runs into trouble because of the *maxint* limitation.

Of course, the type *integer*, just as any other scalar type, is equipped with the relational operators $<, \leqslant, =, \geqslant, >, \neq$, and the successor and predecessor functions. In this case, however, we have that:

$$succ(i) = i + 1 \tag{19}$$
$$pred(i) = i - 1.$$

Again because of space limitations which vary from computer to computer (and compiler to compiler) the type *real* is an *implementation-defined* subset of real numbers. It is equipped with the usual numerical inequality $<$ and with the familiar operations of addition ($+$), subtraction ($-$), multiplication ($*$) and division ($/$). Because of the limited precision of any computer these operations only *approximate* the ideal value of the operations on the full set of real numbers.

In modern digital computers, the so-called *floating-point* representation is used for real numbers, where two integers e and m of limited size can be used to represent the real number x satisfying

$$x = m * B^e \quad -E < e < E \quad -M < m < M \tag{20}$$

where B and the limits E and M are constants characteristic of a particular implementation. Then, for that implementation, *real* contains precisely those real numbers given by (20). m is called the *mantissa* and e the *exponent*. B is called the *base* of the floating-point representation and is usually not 10 but a small power of 2.

A given value x may be represented by many pairs (m,e). The *normalized* representation is defined by the additional relation

$$\frac{M}{B} \leqslant m < M \tag{21}$$

which is chosen since it gives the largest number of significant digits.

The type *real* is also equipped in Pascal with some standard functions, whose values approximate the specification on the right-hand side below:

abs(x)	the absolute value of x	(22)
sqr(x)	x squared	
sin(x)	sine of x	
cos(x)	cosine of x	
arctan(x)	arctangent of x	
ln(x)	natural logarithm of x	
exp(x)	e^x	
sqrt(x)	square root of x.	

Although in a mathematical sense the integers are a subset of real numbers, the computer representation of integers and reals is often different. It is thus appropriate to regard the types *integer* and *real* as disjoint. This is reflected in the specially chosen denotation of constants of these two types.

Examples of denotations of integers are:

$$1 \quad 100 \quad +30 \quad -403$$

and examples of denotations of real numbers are:

$$0.1 \quad 5e - 3 \quad 87.35e + 8.$$

Here e is called the scale factor and means: "times 10 to the power of." Thus, $5e - 3$ is a denotation for the number $5 * 10^{-3}$, in the usual floating-point notation. A number is of type integer if and only if its denotation contains neither a decimal point nor a scale factor. All numbers denoted with either a decimal point or a scale factor are assumed to be of type *real*. In order to make programming easier, two further conventions regarding the relationships between these two types are introduced:

i. Any real-valued operand may be replaced by an integer operand. No explicit transfer function from type *integer* to type *real* is necessary, but this transformation is, in fact, performed by a compiler, so that 2 and 2.0 may be treated as the same value of type *real*.

ii. If a *real* argument is used where an *integer* is expected, an explicit transfer function must be indicated. Two such functions defined over the type *real* are included in the standard repertoire of Pascal:

$$trunc(x) \qquad \text{the whole part of the real number } x, \qquad (23)$$
$$\text{i.e., the fractional part is discarded}$$

$$round(x) = \begin{cases} trunc(x + 0.5) & \text{for } x \geqslant 0 \\ -trunc(0.5 - x) & \text{for } x < 0 \end{cases}.$$

For example,

$$trunc(2.6) = 2, \, trunc(-2.6) = -2, \, round(3.8) = 4,$$

$$round(-3.8) = -4 \text{ etc.}$$

It is a logical consequence of what has been said so far about the type *real* that the functions *succ* and *pred* would not make much sense in the case of this type. The type *real* is the only simple type which is not equipped with these two functions. Because of this discrepancy, the type *real* is the one standard type which is not a scalar type.

The rest of this subsection briefly defines the impact of the implementation-based limitations of *integer* and *real* upon the usual, axiomatically defined properties of the "full sets" of integers and real numbers. A natural question to be asked is whether the operators defined in (16) satisfy the familiar axioms of integer arithmetic. This happens to be the case only if certain conditions regarding the operands are met.

We start with *integer*. If the result of some operation **op** from (16) is outside the range $|x| \leqslant maxint$ of the data type *integer*, the result of the operation will be undefined, or, to put it in the computer jargon, an *overflow* occurs. But, if the result is within this range, we demand of the implementation that $a \textbf{ op } b$ returns the usual value.

In order to illustrate what sort of a problem one can expect if overflow is not avoided, suppose that *maxint* = 1000 and consider the result of evaluation of

$$600 + (500 + (-400)) \tag{24}$$

Since all intermediate values are less than *maxint*, we obtain the correct result 700. However, the evaluation of

$$(600 + 500) + (-400) \tag{25}$$

gives an undefined value, since the result of evaluation of $600 + 500$ is undefined. Thus we see that the ordinary associative law of integer addition:

$$(a + b) + c = a + (b + c) \tag{26}$$

does not hold, unless all values x, including intermediate ones, satisfy $|x| \leqslant maxint$. Apart from this problem of overflow, in which case we assume that every reasonable implementation will terminate the computation and provide a warning signal, all operations defined over the type integer may be assumed to satisfy the familiar axioms of integer arithmetic.

The situation with the type *real* is much more complicated, since in this case the fact that types are always finite sets has particularly drastic consequences. The reason is that every arbitrarily small interval on the real axis contains infinitely many values. We say that the real axis forms a so-called continuum. Thus the type *real* is a finite set of representatives of intervals on the real continuum. The effects of performing computations with approximate instead of exact values are that at best the computed results represent approximations of the exact results. Estimation of inherent errors which occur in such inexact computations is a very hard task, as is the task of axiomatization of the properties of the values of type *real*. Presentation of such an axiomatization is beyond the scope of this book. Instead, we simply illustrate the sort of pitfalls one can expect. (This example does not use a proper normalized representation.) Consider, for example, the values

$$x = 9.900, \qquad y = 1.000, \qquad z = -0.999$$

stored in a hypothetical machine whose storage units can each hold the internal representation of a four-digit decimal number. Then

i. $(x + y) + z = 10.90 + -.9990 = 9.900$ \hspace{1em} (27)

ii. $x + (y + z) = 9.900 + 0.001 = 9.901.$

We see from (27) that the associativity axiom is violated. Suppose now that:

$$x = 1100. \qquad y = -5.000 \qquad z = 5.001.$$

Then we have

i. $(x * y) + (x * z) = -5500. + 5501. = 1.000$ \hspace{1em} (28)

ii. $x * (y + z) = 1100. * 0.001 = 1.100.$

We see from (28) that the distributive law of multiplication over addition is violated.

Variable Declarations and Constant Definitions

We now address the issue of representation of values in a program. We first look at constants. In a definition of a scalar type like (5), values of that type are represented by constant identifiers. Constants of standard types (excluding the type *Boolean*) occur so often in programs that they are represented not by identifiers, but by specific syntactic constructs which correspond to the familiar way of denoting integers, reals and characters. So we know how constants are represented in a program. It is often convenient to introduce an identifier as a synonym for a constant. This identifier may then be used in lieu of the constant. Thus if the identifier is appropriately chosen, its use makes a program more readable and acts as a convenient documentation aid. It also allows the programmer to group machine or example dependent quantities so that they can be easily changed without affecting the rest of the program.

In Pascal, an identifier is introduced as a synonym for a constant in a so-called *constant definition*, which has the form:

$$\textbf{const } i_1 = c_1; \dots; i_n = c_n; \tag{29}$$

where $c_j (j = 1, \dots, n)$ are constants and $i_j (j = 1, \dots, n)$ are identifiers. (29) introduces the identifier i_j as a synonym for the constant c_j, for $j = 1, \dots, n$. For example,

$$\textbf{const } pi = 3.14159; \tag{30}$$

makes pi a synonym for 3.14159, so that $2 + pi$ stands for $2 + 3.14159$.

As we saw in Section 1.2, the other way of representing values in a program is by variables. For each variable, there exists a memory area (of one or more storage units) which holds the current value of the variable. For each execution of the program a variable runs through a set of values of a given type *ordered in a time sequence*. At a given instant of time during the program execution a variable possesses a (possibly undefined) value which may be accessed or changed. The set of these values for all program variables comprises the computation state at that time. A variable is introduced in a program by a *variable declaration*, which introduces the identifier which denotes the variable and specifies its *data type*—that is, the range of values the variable may assume and the operations and tests which may be carried out upon it. A variable declaration in Pascal has the form:

$$\textbf{var } v : T \tag{31}$$

where v is the identifier of the new variable and T is its type (i.e., T denotes the set of values which the variable identified by v may assume). If several variables $v_1, \dots, v_m$ of the same type are declared, then the following short form can be used:

$$\textbf{var } v_1, v_2 \ldots v_m : T \qquad (32)$$

We close by reformulating the discussion which initiated this section, where we stressed that explicit specification of the type of a variable is essential in understanding a program. Without this explicit specification it is hard to determine the kind of objects that a variable represents, which certainly makes understanding a program much more difficult. But understanding a program is only one reason for explicit type definitions, and not the most important one. A further reason is that operators defined over a given type are applicable only to the elements of that type (with some exceptions—such as the conversion between *integer* and *real* which we have already discussed). Thus program correctness depends largely on whether variables which appear as arguments of operators (of course, operations are performed upon the current values of variables) are of the appropriate type. When the types of variables are explicitly specified, the compiler can be designed to detect programming errors of this kind.

Externally, i.e., within a program, a variable is represented by its identifier. Internally, i.e., within the computer, this identifier corresponds to a memory area which holds the current value of the variable. Internal representation of values of different types is usually different. In particular, the size of the memory area (the number of storage units) necessary to represent values of a type usually depends upon that type. Since internal representation of numbers of different types is usually different, implementation of arithmetic operators depends drastically upon the type of arguments. All this shows that explicit specification of the type of a variable is absolutely necessary.

In Pascal, every variable must be declared before it is used. This allows the compiler to do its job efficiently. A variable is declared in the heading of the appropriate part of the program. This is true for both type definitions and constant definitions.

Processing Reals

In this subsection we give an example in which values of type *real* are manipulated, but we do not attempt to prove correctness of the algorithms that we present.

We shall discuss a problem of water pollution described as follows:

i. The volume of a lake is 10^7 cubic feet and, on the day on which we start our study, it is 0.5 percent polluted, that is, the lake contains 0.5 percent $* 10^7 = 0.005 * 10^7 = 5 * 10^4 = 50{,}000$ cubic feet of polluting materials.

ii. A river flows into the lake, with an inflow of 45,000 cubic feet per day, which is 0.2 percent polluted.

iii. There is one town on the shore of the lake. It puts 5,000 cubic feet of sewage into the lake every day, out of which 10 percent are pollutants.

iv. The outflow of the river is 50,000 cubic feet per day (balancing the inflow of the river and sewage), and is at the lake's current pollution level.

Suppose that it is believed to be undesirable to live in the town if the lake ever becomes 1 percent polluted. This, of course, will eventually happen under the given conditions. Our task is to design a program segment which computes the quantity *days* which tells us in how many days the pollution in the lake will reach 1 percent.

In order to solve the posed problem we first set the variable *polut* to the initial quantity of pollutants in the lake, which is $0.005 * 10^7$ cubic feet. Then in every pass through a loop, which corresponds to a day, we add to *polut* the quantity of the pollutants from the sewage and the inflow from the river, and subtract the amount of pollutants which flows out by the river. This repetition process is continued until the percentage of pollutants $polut/10^7$ is greater than 1 percent. So we obtain the following simple program:

```
var polut: real;
    days: integer;
begin days := 0;
    polut := 0.005 * 1.e + 07;
    repeat days := days + 1;
        polut := polut + 0.002 * 45000. + 0.1 * 5000.;
        polut := polut - (polut/1.e + 07) * 50000.
    until polut/1.e + 07 > 0.01
end
```

As it turns out, the undesirable level of pollution will be reached in 271 days. So some corrective action is called for immediately. Suppose that it has been found out that if some plants in the town were closed and sewage treatment facilities built, the percentage of pollutants in the sewage going from the town into the lake would be reduced to 0.1 percent. In addition to that, if the septic tanks along the river were replaced by a sewer system, the percentage of pollutants in the river would drop to 0.03. The question is, if these measures were implemented, how long would it take to reduce the level of pollution in the lake to 0.1 percent.

The program segment given below, very similar to the preceding one, finds the answer to this question:

```
var polut: real;
    days: integer;
begin days := 0;
    polut := 0.005 * 1.e + 07;
    repeat days := days + 1;
        polut := polut + 0.0003 * 45000. + 0.001 * 5000.;
        polut := polut - (polut/1.e + 07) * 50000.
    until polut/1.e + 07 < 0.001
end
```

It is of some interest to note the flavor of a termination proof for this last program. The point to note is that *polut* starts at $5 * 10^4$, and the loop terminates only if *polut* falls below $1 * 10^4$. We analyze the effect on *polut* of a single loop traversal. If *polut* initially has the value a, then *polut* := $polut + 0.0003 * 45000. + 0.001 * 5000.$ changes it to $a + 13.5 + 5 = a + 18.5$. Then *polut* := $polut - (polut/1.e + 07) * 50000$ changes it to $(1 - 0.005)(a + 18.5) = 0.995a + 18.4$. In other words a decreases so long as $0.005a > 18.4$, i.e. so long as $a > 3682$. In fact, if $a \geqslant 10000$, then

$$a - (0.995a + 18.4) > 30$$

and so the *polut* drops by at least 30. This guarantees that the program will terminate. Running the programs shows that it takes 398 days for the level of pollution to drop down to 0.1 percent.

3.4 Arrays, Records, and Files

In this section, we give three constructions for building new data types from old ones. The old ones may be (*simple*) types, or may themselves be *structured types* which are built up from other types. We first look at three kinds of structured type—arrays, records and files—in the language of set theory introduced in Section 3.2, and then turn to the Pascal formats for each method of structuring. We shall defer discussion of *recursive* techniques for defining new data types—such as the use of pointers to define lists—until Chapter 6.

An Overview

Given any set A, we can form a new set A^N, whose typical element is a sequence

$$x = (a_1, \ldots, a_N) \tag{1}$$

of exactly N elements (possibly with repetitions) from A. We call each x as in (1) an *array* of N elements of A.

A^N comes equipped, then, with N operators which extract the ith component from each array,

$$[i]: A^N \to A \quad \text{for} \quad 1 \leqslant i \leqslant N \tag{2}$$
$$\text{satisfies } x[i] = a_i \quad \text{if} \quad x = (a_1, \ldots, a_N)$$
$$\text{so that } x = (x[1], \ldots, x[N]).$$

We call the value of the expression i which runs from 1 to N the *index* of the array. An important feature of the index is that it can be obtained by *evaluating an expression*. Given an index and a value in A we can change the corresponding entry in an array by a single assignment

$$x[i] := a. \tag{3}$$

For example, if the variable x of type $integer^3$ had the value (1,3,7) to start with, then after the assignment $x[2] := 5$ it would have the value (1,5,7). To change all the components of an array, Pascal uses a **for** statement which can systematically work through all the indices from 1 up to N, or some suitably selected subset.

Given several sets, $A_1, A_2, \ldots, A_N$, we can form their cartesian product $A_1 \times A_2 \times \cdots \times A_N$ with typical element

$$x = (a_1, a_2, \ldots, a_N) \text{ with } a_j \text{ in } A_j, 1 \leqslant j \leqslant N. \tag{4}$$

Each such sequence is called a *record*. Just as in (2), we have an operator

$$. s_j : A_1 \times A_2 \times \cdots \times A_N \to A_j \tag{5}$$

(where s_j is an *identifier* for A_j) which selects the A_j component $x . s_j = a_j$ from the record $x = (a_1, a_2, \ldots, a_N)$. The key difference between arrays and records is not so much that arrays are restricted to the same set for each component. Rather, the key point is that the indexes for an array are values of a scalar data type, and so can be processed in the given order (the **for** statement), or can be obtained by evaluating some expression. By contrast, the indexes for a record are just an unordered set of distinct fixed names. They do not form a data type. Thus components of a record must be individually named, rather than processed in sequence.

So far, we have considered records and arrays which are of fixed length. Recall, now, from Section 3.2, the set

$$B^* = B^0 \cup B^1 \cup B^2 \cdots \cup B^n \cup \cdots \tag{6}$$

of all "words on the alphabet B". More generally, we can think of B^* as the set of *variable length* arrays, where each component is from B. Now a number of programming languages offer a data structure like B^* but with *limited access*. Instead of being able to read arbitrary components from this structure f—which is called a *file*—we can only read from one position, as schematized by the read–write head in Figure 3.2(a). The reading is done via a buffer, which holds the value of the variable $f\uparrow$. The value of $f\uparrow$ can either be a value read from the file, or a value which is to be written in the file. The type of $f\uparrow$ is the same type as that of the file entries.

The position of the read–write head partitions the file into two portions f_L and f_R, so that if

$$f_R = \langle x_1, \ldots, x_n \rangle \tag{7}$$
$$f_L = \langle y_1, \ldots, y_m \rangle$$

then the content of the entire file is given by the *concatenation*

$$f = f_L f_R = \langle y_1, \ldots, y_m, x_1, \ldots, x_n \rangle \tag{8}$$

A read operation (Figure 3.2(a))—called *get* (f) in Pascal—moves the read head one square right, and transfers the contents of the newly scanned entry to $f\uparrow$. The program has no direct access to any entries on the file, only to the contents of $f\uparrow$. Thus, a program can read file entries *sequentially* by executing *get*(f) and then using the value of $f\uparrow$ in some appropriate way. The head cannot be moved to the left one square at a time, but can be *reset* to scan the first entry of the file (Figure 3.2(b)).

Writing can only occur at the rightmost end of the file. We thus require (Figure 3.2(c))

$$f_R = \langle \ \rangle \qquad\qquad (9)$$

before carrying out the write—called *put*(f) in Pascal—and after the operation we have

$$f_L = f_L \langle f\uparrow \rangle \qquad\qquad (10)$$
$$f_R = \langle \ \rangle$$

so that another write is then possible.

The *sequential file* (called, simply, *file* in Pascal) does not allow *rewriting* of individual components. The only way any component can be changed is by erasing the entire file, as shown in Figure 3.2(d).

Having now outlined the operators which let the programmer handle files, we can spell out the comparison of files and arrays. Both are sequences of elements of some component type, yet they differ greatly. Arrays are sequences of fixed length, whereas files can grow or be totally erased. Moreover, the implementation aspects require that files can be processed only sequentially, and that appending new elements can happen only at the end

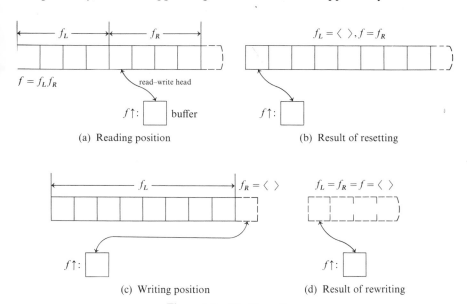

(a) Reading position   (b) Result of resetting

(c) Writing position   (d) Result of rewriting

Figure 3.2   File Operations

of the file. In fact, almost the whole file is kept in secondary storage, such as, for example, magnetic tape. The properties of the secondary storage dictate the kind of file operators one can have in order to achieve efficiency and economy of storage. Only a small portion of the file is kept in main store, and only one component $f\uparrow$ of that portion is accessible to the programmer at any time. Arrays are kept in main store, and that, in addition to sequential processing, also allows fast access to any array component. This last operation is impossible with files. In order to locate a random file element the file must be examined sequentially from the beginning. This is dictated by the storage medium, since, for example, it is not possible to quickly get to a particular place on a magnetic tape.

Arrays

Let $T0$ be a scalar or subrange type, where the *real* and *integer* types are excluded (but not subrange types of the type *integer*), and let T be any type. The type definition (11) introduces a new type A.

$$\textbf{type } A = \textbf{array } [T0] \textbf{ of } T \tag{11}$$

For example, **type** $A =$ **array** $[1 \, . \, . \, 20]$ **of** *integer* defines a type whose values are sequences of twenty integers. The type A is the set of all functions with domain $T0$ and codomain T (usually denoted as $[T0 \to T]$). In view of the fact that $T0$ is a linearly ordered set, each function can be viewed as a sequence of elements of type T. This sequence is *indexed* by the elements of $T0$, i.e., for each element of $T0$ we get an element of T. These sequences are called *arrays*. Their size is fixed by the declaration of their type and is equal to the number of elements of the type $T0$. $T0$ is called the *index type* and T the *component* or *base type* of A.

The above discussion introduces the so-called one-dimensional arrays. Multidimensional arrays are obtained if we choose T in (11) to be an array type itself. In that case we can write (11) explicitly as:

$$\textbf{type } A = \textbf{array } [T0] \textbf{ of array } [T1] \textbf{ of } T \tag{12}$$

The above type definition says that elements of the type A are arrays of arrays, or, to be more precise, A is a set of functions with domain $T0$ and codomain the set of functions from $T1$ into T. This set is usually denoted as $[T0 \to [T1 \to T]]$. It has a very interesting property. To each element in this set there corresponds an element of the set $[T0 \times T1 \to T]$, where $T0 \times T1$ is the cartesian product of sets $T0$ and $T1$, i.e., a set of pairs (x, y) such that $x \in T0$ and $y \in T1$. The other way around is also true, to each element g of the set $[T0 \times T1 \to T]$ there corresponds an element f of the set $[T0 \to [T1 \to T]]$. This correspondence is given by

$$f(a)(b) = g(a,b) \tag{13}$$

where $a \in T0$, $b \in T1$. Observe that $f(a) \in [T1 \to T]$, i.e., $f(a): T1 \to T$ is a function, which applied to b gives a value $f(a)(b)$ in T. The domain of the function g is the set $T0 \times T1$, and its codomain is the set T.

This equivalence justifies the following abbreviated notation for (12):

$$\textbf{type } A = \textbf{array } [T0, T1] \textbf{ of } T \tag{14}$$

In general, for a k-dimensional array we have that

$$\textbf{array } [T0, \ldots, Tk] \textbf{ of } T \quad \text{means} \quad \textbf{array } [T0] \textbf{ of array } [T1, \ldots, Tk] \textbf{ of } T \tag{15}$$

It is important to note that arrays in Pascal are static, i.e., the number of elements of each dimension is determined at the time the program is translated into the machine language. This simply follows from the general strategy adopted in Pascal that all types should be completely determined at compile time, which in particular means that the type $T0$ in (11) must also be completely determined at that time. It will be shown later that this decision leads to serious difficulties.

A variable of type A defined in (11) is more than just an array of elements of type T. It is, in fact, an array of component variables ot type T. For example, variable x declared as

$$\textbf{var } x: \textbf{array } [1 \ .. \ N] \textbf{ of } T \tag{16}$$

is in fact an array of N variables of type T. These N component variables are denoted as:

$$x[1], x[2], \ldots, x[N]. \tag{17}$$

For a multidimensional array such as **array** $[1 \ .. \ N, 1 \ .. \ M]$ **of** T rather than writing $x[i][j]$, the abbreviated notation $x[i, j]$ is used. In general, according to (15),

$$x[i_0, \ldots, i_k] \quad \text{means} \quad x[i_0][i_1, \ldots, i_k]. \tag{18}$$

Thus in order to denote a component of a k-dimensional array variable, the variable identifier is written followed by k expressions of k respective index types, enclosed in brackets [and]. These brackets in fact enclose arguments of a function, the same way the usual parentheses are used in (13). The expressions in the brackets are called *indexes*. What particular component variable $x[e1 \ldots, en]$ denotes is thus determined at run time, when the values of index expressions $e1, \ldots, en$ are computed. However, in normal implementations the time necessary to access an array component does not depend upon the values of these indexes. Because of this property, arrays are termed random access structures. We now give two examples which illustrate the above described conventions.

Given an array with components $A[1], \ldots, A[n]$ and a value x, the program given below sets the variable *found* to *false* if there is no k such that $A[k] = x$; otherwise it sets this variable to true and i to the first such k. The line "*found* := $A[i] = x$" says that found is assigned the value *true* just in case this is the Boolean value of the assertion "$A[i] = x$."

$$\begin{aligned}
&\textbf{var}\quad i: 0 \; .. \; n; \; found: Boolean; \hfill (19)\\
&\qquad A: \textbf{array} \; [1 \; .. \; n] \; \textbf{of} \; T;\\
&\textbf{begin} \; \{\text{assignment of values to } A\}\\
&\qquad \ldots\\
&\qquad i := 0;\\
&\qquad \textbf{repeat} \; i := i + 1;\\
&\qquad\qquad found := A[i] = x\\
&\qquad \textbf{until} \;\; found \vee (i = n)\\
&\textbf{end}
\end{aligned}$$

The line of dots indicates omitted details which are irrelevant to the present discussion.

The above solution can be made much more efficient if the array is sorted, i.e., if $A[i] < A[j]$ for all $i < j$. We apply the following strategy: We first select the middle array element, i.e., the one with the index $k = (1 + n) \; \textbf{div} \; 2$ and compare it with x. There exist three possibilities: the first one is that $A[k] = x$. This means that the desired element is found. The second case is $A[k] < x$. This means that no element with index less than k can be equal to x, and so further search, which applies the same strategy, should be restricted to the elements with indexes greater than k. The third case is $A[k] > x$. For analogous reasons further search should be restricted to the elements with indexes less than k. We use i and j as variables for the low and high ends of the range to which search is restricted.

$$\begin{aligned}
&\textbf{var} \; i,j,k: integer; \; found: Boolean; \hfill (20)\\
&\qquad A: \textbf{array} \; [1 \; .. \; n] \; \textbf{of} \; T;\\
&\textbf{begin} \; \{\text{assignment of values to } A\}\\
&\qquad \ldots\\
&\qquad i := 1; j := n; \; found := false;\\
&\qquad \textbf{repeat} \; k := (i + j) \; \textbf{div} \; 2;\\
&\qquad\qquad \textbf{if} \; A[k] = x \; \textbf{then} \; found := true\\
&\qquad\qquad \textbf{else if} \; A[k] < x \; \textbf{then} \; i := k + 1\\
&\qquad\qquad\qquad \textbf{else} \; j := k - 1\\
&\qquad \textbf{until} \; found \vee (i > j)\\
&\textbf{end}
\end{aligned}$$

While the number of necessary comparisons in the algorithm (19) is on the average $n/2$, that number in the case of the search (20) is $log_2 \, n$ on the average. Thus if the array A is large (i.e., if n is large), the algorithm (20) becomes considerably more efficient than the algorithm (19). This example reminds us that it is not enough for a program to be correct—it must also be *efficient* in its use of time and resources. The algorithm (20) is both called *binary search* because of its successive splitting of the array in two, and *logarithmic search* because of the average number of comparisons.

for Statement

Situations in which arrays are scanned strictly sequentially are so frequent that a special notation is introduced to denote such actions. This notation is similar to the notation introduced for the **repeat-until** and **while-do** statements. In order to explain it, assume that S is a statement, and v a scalar variable (so not of type *real*), and that a and b are expressions of the same type as v. Then the statement (21)

$$\textbf{for } v := a \textbf{ to } b \textbf{ do } S \tag{21}$$

specifies the action which consists of execution of the statements which assign v the value x and then execute S,

$$v := x;\ S \tag{22}$$

once for each value x in the interval from a to b. If we decide that these repetition steps are executed sequentially, and that the values x are selected in ascending order from a to b, then the effect of (21) is equivalent to the effect of the following statement:

$$\textbf{if } a \leqslant b \textbf{ then} \tag{23}$$
$$\textbf{begin } v := v_1;\ S;\ v := v_2;\ S; \ldots ;\ v := v_n;\ S \textbf{ end}$$

where $v_1 = a$, $v_n = b$ and $v_i = succ(v_{i-1})$ for $i = 2, \ldots, n$. It follows then that the successor function must be defined on the type of v, and that is why the type *real* was excluded. (23) may be expressed in a closed form (24) in terms of the statement composition rules introduced in Chapter 2.

$$\textbf{if } a \leqslant b \textbf{ then} \tag{24}$$
$$\textbf{begin } v := a;\ S;$$
$$\textbf{while } v < b \textbf{ do}$$
$$\textbf{begin } v := succ(v);$$
$$S$$
$$\textbf{end}$$
$$\textbf{end}$$

An alternative form of the **for** statement is:

$$\textbf{for } v := a \textbf{ downto } b \textbf{ do } S \tag{25}$$

which is equivalent to:

$$\textbf{if } a \geqslant b \textbf{ then} \tag{26}$$
$$\textbf{begin } v := v_1;\ S;\ v := v_2;\ S; \ldots ;\ v := v_n;\ S \textbf{ end}$$

where $v_1 = a$, $v_n = b$, and $v_i = pred(v_{i-1})$ for $i = 2, \ldots, n$. (26) can be expressed in closed form as follows:

$$
\begin{aligned}
&\textbf{if } a \geqslant b \textbf{ then} \hspace{5.5cm} (27)\\
&\textbf{begin } v := a;\ S;\\
&\hspace{1.2cm} \textbf{while } v > b \textbf{ do}\\
&\hspace{1.2cm} \textbf{begin } v := pred(v);\\
&\hspace{2.4cm} S\\
&\hspace{1.2cm} \textbf{end}\\
&\textbf{end}
\end{aligned}
$$

The definitions (24) and (27) of the **for** statements (21) and (25) are admittedly elegant, but they do not reflect some additional and fundamental requirements imposed on the **for** statement. These requirements are: S in (21) and (25) may change neither the value of the controlled variable v, nor the values a and b.

Since the values of a and b thus remain unchanged during the repetition process, they are evaluated only once, at the beginning of execution of the **for** statement. With these requirements fulfilled, the **for** statement has a property which distinguishes it in a very important way from both the **while-do** and **repeat-until** statements: if S in (21) and (25) terminates for each value of x in the range bounded by a and b, then both (21) and (25) terminate.

In order to define the proof rule for the **for** statement we introduce the following notation for open and closed intervals:

$$
\begin{aligned}
[a \ldots b] &= \text{the set of } i \text{ such that } a \leqslant i \leqslant b \hspace{2cm} (28)\\
[a \ldots x) &= \text{the set of } i \text{ such that } a \leqslant i < x\\
(x \ldots b] &= \text{the set of } i \text{ such that } x < i \leqslant b\\
[\ ] &= \text{the empty set.}
\end{aligned}
$$

Observe that the above definitions imply $[a \ldots a) = (b \ldots b] = [\ ]$.

Denote now with $P(w)$ an assertion about the interval w, and suppose that S in **for** $x := a$ **to** b **do** S satisfies the *induction* property:

$$
\{P([a \ldots x))\}\ S\ \{P([a \ldots x])\} \text{ for all } x \text{ such that } a \leqslant x \leqslant b \hspace{1cm} (29)
$$

which tells us that each application of S extends the interval over which P is valid. Furthermore, suppose that $P([a \ldots a))$, i.e., $P([\ ])$ holds. Then according to (29) at the end of the first iteration $P(w_1)$ will hold, where

$$
w_1 = [a \ldots a] = [a \ldots succ(a)). \hspace{3cm} (30)
$$

On completion of the second iteration (if any) $P(w_2)$ will hold, where:

$$
w_2 = [a \ldots succ(succ(a))). \hspace{3cm} (31)
$$

Finally, at the end of the last iteration we have that

$$
P([a \ldots b]) \hspace{4cm} (32)
$$

holds. The analysis leads to the following proof rule:

$$\frac{\{(a \leqslant x \leqslant b) \land P([a \mathinner{\ldotp\ldotp} x))\} \ S \ \{P([a \mathinner{\ldotp\ldotp} x])\}}{\{P([\ ])\} \ \textbf{for} \ x := a \ \textbf{to} \ b \ \textbf{do} \ S \ \{P([a \mathinner{\ldotp\ldotp} b])\}} \ . \tag{33}$$

Similar reasoning leads to the following proof rule

$$\frac{\{(a \leqslant x \leqslant b) \land P((x \mathinner{\ldotp\ldotp} b])\} \ S \ \{P([x \mathinner{\ldotp\ldotp} b])\}}{\{P([\ ])\} \ \textbf{for} \ x := b \ \textbf{downto} \ a \ \textbf{do} \ S \ \{P([a \mathinner{\ldotp\ldotp} b])\}} \ . \tag{34}$$

As an example of the application of the proof rule (33) we show that the program

$$\textbf{var} \ i,m : a \mathinner{\ldotp\ldotp} b; \tag{35}$$
$$A : \textbf{array} \ [a \mathinner{\ldotp\ldotp} b] \ \textbf{of} \ T;$$
$$\textbf{begin} \ m := a; \ max := A[a];$$
$$\textbf{for} \ i := a \ \textbf{to} \ b \ \textbf{do}$$
$$\textbf{if} \ A[i] > max \ \textbf{then}$$
$$\textbf{begin} \ max := A[i]; \ m := i \ \textbf{end}$$
$$\textbf{end}$$

finds the maximal value *max* of the elements of the array A and assigns the index of a maximal element (in fact, the first—but we shall not prove this) to m. Let

$$P([a \mathinner{\ldotp\ldotp} i)) \ \text{be} \ (a \leqslant m \leqslant b) \land (max = A[m])$$
$$\land \ \forall k((a \leqslant k < i) \supset (A[k] \leqslant max)). \tag{36}$$

Observe that $P([a \mathinner{\ldotp\ldotp} b])$ is the relation that we wish to hold after (35). Proof of (35) now proceeds in the following steps: The first pair of assignments "sets up" $P([a \mathinner{\ldotp\ldotp} a))$:

$$\{true\} \ m := a; \ max := A[a] \ \{P([a \mathinner{\ldotp\ldotp} a))\} \tag{37}$$

for we have $(a \leqslant a \leqslant b) \land (max = A[a])$ while $a \leqslant k < a$ is always false in $\forall k((a \leqslant k < a) \supset (A[k] \leqslant max))$, and thus the implication part is true for all k. According to the proof rule for the **for** statement, it remains to establish:

$$\{(a \leqslant i \leqslant b) \land P([a \mathinner{\ldotp\ldotp} i))\} \ \textbf{if} \ A[i] > max \ \textbf{then} \tag{38}$$
$$\textbf{begin} \ max := A[i]; \ m := i \ \textbf{end}$$
$$\{P([a \mathinner{\ldotp\ldotp} i])\}.$$

In order to prove (38) we apply the proof rule for the **if-then** statement. We proceed as follows:

$$(a \leqslant i \leqslant b) \land P([a \mathinner{\ldotp\ldotp} i)) \land (A[i] > max) \tag{39}$$
$$\text{implies}$$
$$(a \leqslant i \leqslant b) \land \forall k((a \leqslant k \leqslant i) \supset (A[k] \leqslant A[i]))$$
$$\{(a \leqslant i \leqslant b) \land \forall k((a \leqslant k \leqslant i) \supset (A[k] \leqslant A[i]))\} \tag{40}$$
$$max := A[i]$$
$$\{(a \leqslant i \leqslant b) \land \forall k((a \leqslant k \leqslant i) \supset (A[k] \leqslant max)) \land (max = A[i])\}$$

$$\{(a \leqslant i \leqslant b) \wedge \forall k((a \leqslant k \leqslant i) \supset (A[k] \leqslant max)) \wedge (max = A[i])\} \quad (41)$$
$$m := i$$
$$\{(a \leqslant m \leqslant b) \wedge (max = A[m]) \wedge \forall k((a \leqslant k \leqslant i) \supset (A[k] \leqslant max))\}.$$

So we have proved that

$$\{(a \leqslant i \leqslant b) \wedge P([a \mathrel{..} i)) \wedge (A[i] > max)\} \qquad (42)$$
$$\textbf{begin } max := A[i]; \ m := i \textbf{ end}$$
$$\{P([a \mathrel{..} i])\}.$$

In addition, we have:

$$(a \leqslant i \leqslant b) \wedge P([a \mathrel{..} i)) \wedge \neg(A[i] > max) \qquad (43)$$
$$\text{implies}$$
$$P([a \mathrel{..} i]).$$

According to the proof rule of the **if-then** statement (39), (42) and (43) imply (38). (38) implies (44) by the proof rule of the **for** statement.

$$\{P([\ ])\} \textbf{ for } i := a \textbf{ to } b \textbf{ do} \qquad (44)$$
$$\textbf{if } A[i] > max \textbf{ then}$$
$$\textbf{begin } max := A[i]; \ m := i \textbf{ end}$$
$$\{P([a \mathrel{..} b])\}$$

Applying now the proof rule for the compound statement to (37) and (44) we obtain the desired result:

$$\{true\} \textbf{ begin } m := a; \ max := A[a]; \qquad (45)$$
$$\textbf{for } i := a \textbf{ to } b \textbf{ do}$$
$$\textbf{if } A[i] > max \textbf{ then}$$
$$\textbf{begin } max := A[i]; \ m := i \textbf{ end}$$
$$\textbf{end } \{P([a \mathrel{..} b])\}$$

Records

Let $s_1, \ldots, s_m$ be distinct identifiers, and $T_1, \ldots, T_m$ type identifiers. Then

$$\textbf{type } T = \textbf{record } s_1 : T_1; \ s_2 : T_2; \ \ldots \ ; \ s_m : T_m \textbf{ end} \qquad (46)$$

defines a new type T. The type T is a set of m-tuples $(x_1, \ldots, x_m)$ where x_i is of type T_i, for $i = 1, \ldots, m$. Employing the usual terminology of mathematics, we say that T is the cartesian product of the sets $T_1, \ldots, T_m$. Components of the *record-type* T are called *fields* and the s_i ($i = 1, \ldots, m$) are called *field identifiers*.

A variable x of type T is an m-tuple of variables, where the ith component variable is of the type T_i and is denoted as $x \cdot s_i$. Thus we can manipulate the whole structured value of x, or select a particular component of it, and manipulate the component. But even if $T_1 = T_2 = \cdots = T_m$ in (46) the difference between such a record and an array of the type **array** $(1 \mathrel{..} m]$ **of** T_1 is fundamental. Array components are accessed via computable indexes, so that if x is of the type **array** $[1 .. m]$ **of** T_1, and e is an expression of the type $1 .. m$, it is only at run time that it is determined which component $x[e]$ denotes. On the other hand, record components are denoted by field identifiers, so that if x is a variable of type T, the compiler determines which component $x . s_i$ denotes.

Consider now some examples:

$$\textbf{type } \textit{time} = \textbf{record } \textit{hour}: 1 .. 24; \qquad\qquad (47)$$
$$\textit{min}: 1 .. 60;$$
$$\textit{sec}: 1 .. 60$$
$$\textbf{end}$$

And now let x be a variable of type $\textit{time}$. Then the following assignments may be written:

$$x . \textit{hour} := 11; \qquad\qquad (48)$$
$$x . \textit{min} := 20;$$
$$x . \textit{sec} := 35$$

In the above example the components (fields) were all of simple types. But in (46) no restriction of that sort is imposed, which means that any T_i $(i = 1, \dots, m)$ can be a structured type. So far we have introduced just two rules for structuring types (array and record), and in the example that follows we see how more complex types can be expressed using these rules.

$$\textbf{type } \textit{authortype} = \textbf{record } \textit{firstname}: \textbf{array } [1 .. 10] \textbf{ of } \textit{char}; \qquad (49)$$
$$\textit{middlinit}: \textbf{array } [1 .. 2] \textbf{ of } \textit{char};$$
$$\textit{lastname}: \textbf{array } [1 .. 15] \textbf{ of } \textit{char}$$
$$\textbf{end};$$
$$\textit{bookcard} = \textbf{record } \textit{callnumber}: \textit{integer};$$
$$\textit{author}: \qquad \textit{authortype};$$
$$\textit{title}: \qquad \textbf{array } [1 .. 20] \textbf{ of } \textit{char}$$
$$\textbf{end}$$

The type $\textit{bookcard}$ defined in (49) is a record type. Two of its fields are structured types. The field $\textit{author}$ is a record itself, whose fields are arrays of characters. The field $\textit{title}$ is also an array of characters. If we now let $\textit{title}$ be a variable of type $\textit{bookcard}$ and $\textit{writer}$ be a variable of type $\textit{authortype}$, then the following assignments may be made:

$$\textit{writer} . \textit{firstname} := \text{`robert'}; \qquad\qquad (50)$$
$$\textit{writer} . \textit{middlinit} := \text{`l.'};$$
$$\textit{writer} . \textit{lastname} := \text{`stevenson'};$$
$$\textit{title} . \textit{callnumber} := 631;$$
$$\textit{title} . \textit{author} := \textit{writer};$$
$$\textit{title} . \textit{title} := \text{`kidnapped'}$$

Note the use of quotes to distinguish a string of characters from its use as an identifier. Observe that in (50) no confusion arises since the variable $\textit{title}$ of

type *bookcard* is easily distinguishable from the variable *title* . *title* of type
array [1 . . 20] **of** *char*. However, it is good programming practice to avoid
such clashes.

In order to simplify the above definition, a notational abbreviation is
used in Pascal, called the **with** statement. Its simplest form is:

$$\textbf{with } x \textbf{ do } S \tag{51}$$

where x is a variable of record type and S is a statement. S is called the *scope*
of the **with** statement (51). Within S, components of x can be referenced by
field identifiers only, without preceding them with x. Thus, within S, field
identifiers of x act as variable identifiers. For example,

$$\textbf{with } writer \textbf{ do} \tag{52}$$
$$\textbf{begin } firstname := \text{`}robert\text{'};$$
$$middlinit := \text{`}l.\text{'};$$
$$lastname := \text{`}stevenson\text{'}$$
$$\textbf{end}$$

It is important to observe that in (51), following the general philosophy
of record types, all references to components are determined at compile
time. But this would not be possible in a case like this:

$$\textbf{with } a[i] \textbf{ do} \tag{53}$$
$$\textbf{begin } . . . .$$
$$i := i + 3$$
$$. . . .$$
$$\textbf{end}$$

and so (53) is not allowed.

A more general form of the **with** statement is

$$\textbf{with } x_1, x_2, \ldots, x_m \textbf{ do } S \tag{54}$$

where the x_i ($i = 1, \ldots, m$) are variables. (54) is equivalent to

$$\textbf{with } x_1 \textbf{ do} \tag{55}$$
$$\textbf{with } x_2 \textbf{ do}$$
$$. . .$$
$$\textbf{with } x_n \textbf{ do } S$$

Use of (54) requires that the field identifiers for $x_1, \ldots, x_m$ are all distinct.
For example, we could write:

$$\textbf{with } title \textbf{ do} \tag{56}$$
$$\textbf{begin } callnumber := 631;$$
$$\textbf{with } writer \textbf{ do}$$
$$\textbf{begin } firstname := \text{`}robert\text{'};$$
$$middlinit := \text{`}l.\text{'};$$
$$lastname := \text{`}stevenson\text{'}$$
$$\textbf{end};$$
$$title := \text{`}kidnapped\text{'}$$
$$\textbf{end}$$

or, equivalently:

$$\begin{aligned}
&\textbf{with } \textit{title, writer } \textbf{do} \hspace{4cm} (57)\\
&\textbf{begin } \textit{callnumber} := 631;\\
&\qquad \textit{firstname} := \text{`robert'};\\
&\qquad \textit{middlinit} := \text{`l.'};\\
&\qquad \textit{lastname} := \text{`stevenson'};\\
&\qquad \textit{title} := \text{`kidnapped'}\\
&\textbf{end}
\end{aligned}$$

Instead, if we take account of the equivalence expressed in (54) and (55) we see that (56) and (57) accomplish the same effect.

The proof rule for the **with** statement is quite straightforward. Let x be a variable of type **record** $s_1 : T_1; \ldots s_m : T_m$ **end**. Then we have

$$\frac{\{P^{x \cdot s_1, \ldots, x \cdot s_m}_{s_1 \quad , \ldots, s_m}\} \ S \ \{Q^{x \cdot s_1, \ldots, x \cdot s_m}_{s_1 \quad , \ldots, s_m}\}}{\{P\} \textbf{ with } x \textbf{ do } S \ \{Q\}}.$$

Disjoint Unions

If $T_1, \ldots, T_n$ are types, then we can define a new type T in such a way that T, viewed as a set, represents a *disjoint union* of sets $T_1, \ldots, T_n$. This means that a distinct copy of each T_i (for $i = 1, \ldots, n$) is present in T, even if $T_i \cap T_j \neq [\ ]$ (empty set) for some $i, j \in [1, \ldots, n]$. Furthermore, it is possible to define T in such a way that given an element a of T, we can determine to which T_i $(i = 1, \ldots, n)$ this element belongs. A variable x of type T assumes during its lifetime values which belong to only one of the types T_i $(i = 1, \ldots, n)$ at each time. This type is the *current type* of the variable x.

Type unions are expressed in Pascal in terms of *records with variants*. If we want to be able to determine what the current type of a variable x of type T (defined above) is, then this variable must have a record structure. The first (fixed) component of that record is a *tag* which tells us what the current type of the variable is, and the second (*variant*) part is the current value of the variable (which is of one of the types T_i $(i = 1, \ldots, n)$). The format for expressing this is:

$$\begin{aligned}
&\textbf{type } T = \textbf{record} \hspace{4cm} (58)\\
&\qquad \textbf{case } \textit{tag}: (c_1, \ldots, c_n) \textbf{ of}\\
&\qquad\quad c_1: (s_{1,1}: T_{1,1}; \ldots; s_{1,m_1}: T_{1,m_1});\\
&\qquad\quad c_2: (s_{2,1}: T_{2,1}; \ldots; s_{2,m_2}: T_{2,m_2});\\
&\qquad\qquad \cdots\\
&\qquad\quad c_n: (s_{n,1}: T_{n,1}; \ldots; s_{n,m_n}: T_{n,m_n})\\
&\textbf{end}
\end{aligned}$$

where *tag* is the identifier of the tag field which is declared to be of the scalar type $(c_1, \ldots, c_n)$ where $c_1, \ldots, c_n$ are constant identifiers, $s_{i,j}$ are field identifiers and $T_{i,j}$ are their corresponding types $(i = 1, \ldots, n, j = 1, \ldots, m)$.

The full syntax for expressing records with variant structure may be found in the appendix. See exercise 17 and Sections 6.3 and 6.4 for examples of the use of type *union*.

Files

If T is a type identifier then the type declaration for introducing a *file type F* whose values are files with entries of type T is

$$\textbf{type } F = \textbf{file of } T \tag{59}$$

When we declare a variable f to be of the type **file of** T

$$\textbf{var } f : \textbf{file of } T \tag{60}$$

we automatically introduce an additional variable, denoted $f\uparrow$, which is of type T, and is called a *buffer variable*.

The underlying set of $F = \textbf{file of } T$ is $T^* \times T^*$. In other words, a variable f of type F is given by a pair of variables (f_L, f_R), each taking as value a sequence (possibly empty) of values of type T.

It will be useful to associate two partial functions (why are they partial?) with T^*—they are not part of Pascal, but will help us understand the operators that Pascal associates with the data type **file of** T.

$$first: T^* \to T \quad \text{ sends } \quad \langle x \rangle f \text{ to } x \tag{61}$$
$$rest: T^* \to T^* \quad \text{ sends } \quad \langle x \rangle f \text{ to } f$$

where x is in T and f is in T^*.

We are to imagine, as in Figure 3.2 on page 77 that the buffer is connected via a read–write head to the leftmost symbol of f_R. The read–write head can only scan the file sequentially. Applying the operator $get(f)$ is permitted only if the read–write head is not at the end of the file, i.e., if $\neg eof(f)$ holds, where

$$eof(f) \text{ means } f \text{ is at the end of the file, i.e., } f_R = \langle \ \rangle. \tag{62}$$

Then $get(f)$ reads the value in the scanned square into the buffer, and advances the read–write head one step to the right:

$$f\uparrow := first(rest(f_R)) \tag{63}$$
$$f_L := f_L \, first(f_R)$$
$$f_R := rest(f_R)$$

Note that after $get(f)$ has been applied, we have:

$$f\uparrow = first(f_R) \tag{64}$$

Reading normally moves sequentially, one entry at a time, from left to right. To read an entry k squares to the right of the current position, k consecutive *gets* are required. In the Pascal file it is *not* possible to move entry-by-entry left—and it is certainly not possible to access random components as is possible with arrays and records. In fact, the only way to move left is to move all the way left, using the operation $reset(f)$ which has the combined effect of the following assignments:

$$f_R := f_L f_R \qquad\qquad (65)$$
$$f_L := \langle\ \rangle$$
$$f\uparrow := first(f_R)$$

Once again, (64) holds. However, this need not hold after other operations are executed. For example, $f\uparrow$ can be assigned a value:

$$f\uparrow := e$$

by a program, prior to writing that value into the file. This writing is carried out by the operator put, which may only be applied when the read–write head is at the end of the file, i.e., just in case $eof(f)$ is true. Then the effect is to write the contents of $f\uparrow$ at the end of the file, and move the read–write head on to the end of the file once more.

$$f_L := f_L \langle f\uparrow \rangle. \qquad\qquad (66)$$

The value of f_R does not change since it is empty at all times during a write; and $f\uparrow$ is undefined after $put(f)$.

Finally, note that writing only occurs at the end of a file. We cannot change a component that is already written, except by erasing the *entire* file, by applying the operation $rewrite(f)$, which has the effect of the assignments

$$f_L := \langle\ \rangle \qquad\qquad (67)$$
$$f_R := \langle\ \rangle$$

We may summarize the effect of the Pascal file operations in the following proof rules:

$$\{\neg eof(f) \wedge P_{f_L\ first(f_R),\ first(rest(f_R)),\ rest(f_R)}^{f_L\quad f\quad f_R}\}\ get(f)\ \{P\} \qquad (68)$$

$$\{P_{\langle\rangle,\ first(f),\ f_L f_R}^{f_L\ f\uparrow\ f_R}\}\ reset(f)\ \{P\} \qquad (69)$$

$$\{eof(f) \wedge P_{f_L\langle f\uparrow\rangle}^{f_L}\}\ put(f)\ \{P \wedge eof(f)\} \qquad (70)$$

$$\{P_{\langle\rangle,\ \langle\rangle}^{f_L\ f_R}\}\ rewrite(f)\ \{P \wedge eof(f)\} \qquad (71)$$

We close with a simple program which reads a file f of real numbers and computes their sum S:

$$\begin{aligned}
&\textbf{begin}\ S := 0;\ reset(f); \qquad\qquad\qquad\ (72)\\
&\qquad \textbf{while}\ \neg eof(f)\ \textbf{do}\\
&\qquad\qquad \textbf{begin}\ S := S + f\uparrow;\\
&\qquad\qquad\qquad get(f)\\
&\qquad\qquad \textbf{end}\\
&\textbf{end}
\end{aligned}$$

3.5 Processing Arrays

We have now learnt how to build those structured data types which have the form of arrays, records and files; and we have seen the different operators that Pascal gives us for handling each of these structures. In this and the subsequent section, we build on this material by studying a number of useful programs for handling arrays, files and records.

A Two-Dimensional Array

Suppose that a department in a university has a number of courses, to be represented by the value of the variable *numcor*, and a number of students, *numstud*. Grades of the students can be stored in a two-dimensional array *grade* of the type **array** [1 . . *numcor*, 1 . . *numstud*] **of** *integer* (assuming integer grades), where $grade[i,j]$ represents the grade of the *j*th student in the *i*th course.

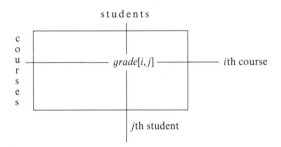

We shall accept the convention that zero means no grade. Suppose now that we want to compute the average grade *avgrade*, of type *real*, in the *i*th course. This can be accomplished by the following program segment:

```
begin totgrade := 0;
      numgrades := numstud;
      for j := 1 to numstud do
      begin gr := grade[i,j];
            if gr ≠ 0 then totgrade := totgrade + gr
            else numgrades := numgrades − 1
      end;
      if numgrades ≠ 0 then avgrade := totgrade/numgrades
      else avgrade := 0
end
```

A similar task is computing the average grade *studavg* of the *j*th student for all of his courses. This can be accomplished by the following program segment:

```
begin sumgrade := 0;
      numgrades := numcor;
      for i := 1 to numcor do
      begin gr := grade[i,j];
            if gr ≠ 0 then sumgrade := sumgrade + gr
            else numgrades := numgrades − 1
      end;
      if numgrades ≠ 0 then studavg := sumgrade/numgrades
      else studavg := 0
end
```

Finally, the task of computing the overall average grade *ovavg* of all students in all courses could be obtained by the following program segment:

```
begin gsum := 0;
      for j := 1 to numstud do
      begin sumgrade := 0;
            numgrades := numcor;
            for i := 1 to numcor do
            begin if grade[i,j] ≠ 0 then
                  sumgrade := sumgrade + grade[i,j]
                  else numgrades := numgrades − 1
            end;
            if numgrades ≠ 0 then studavg := sumgrade/numgrades
            else studavg := 0;
            gsum := gsum + studavg
      end;
      ovavg := gsum/numstud
end
```

Manipulating Numbers in Positional Notation

In order to further illustrate the use of the **for** statement, we now discuss algorithms which provide the reader with a feel for multiple precision arithmetic, and which show the natural use of **downto** in a **for** statement:

i. addition and subtraction of n-place integers, giving an n-place answer and a carry.
ii. multiplication of an n-place integer by an m-place integer, giving an $(m + n)$-place answer.
iii. division of an $(m + n)$-place integer by an n-place integer, giving an $(m + 1)$-place quotient and an n-place remainder.

By the term n-place integer, we mean an integer less than b^n, where b is the base (radix) of the conventional positional notation in which the numbers are written. Such numbers can be written using at most n places in the positional notation. Assume, for simplicity, that such numbers are represented as arrays of integers, rather than as arrays of characters, since in the latter case we would often have to use the transformation functions which map characters into integers and vice-versa. A further simplification is the assumption that the numbers we deal with are nonnegative. The additional work for computing the signs is straightforward, although sometimes tedious.

Consider first the algorithm (1) for addition of n-place integers $u_1 u_2 \ldots u_n$ and $v_1 v_2 \ldots v_n$ to obtain their sum $w_0 w_1 \ldots w_n$ where w_0 is the carry, and is always equal to 0 or 1. In the algorithm, we use j to index the components currently being added, and k for the carry digit from the previous addition.

$$
\begin{aligned}
&\textbf{var } u,v \colon \textbf{array } [1 \mathinner{\ldotp\ldotp} n] \textbf{ of } integer; \qquad\qquad\qquad (1)\\
&\phantom{\textbf{var }} w \colon \textbf{array } [0 \mathinner{\ldotp\ldotp} n] \textbf{ of } integer;\\
&\phantom{\textbf{var }} j,k,t \colon integer;\\
&\textbf{begin } \ldots\\
&\qquad k := 0;\\
&\qquad \textbf{for } j := n \textbf{ downto } 1 \textbf{ do}\\
&\qquad \textbf{begin } t := u[j] + v[j] + k;\\
&\qquad\qquad w[j] := t \textbf{ mod } b;\\
&\qquad\qquad k := t \textbf{ div } b\\
&\qquad \textbf{end};\\
&\qquad w[0] := k\\
&\textbf{end}
\end{aligned}
$$

Observe that in (1) k is set to 1 or 0 depending upon whether a carry occurred or not, i.e., whether $u[j] + v[j] + k \geqslant b$ or not. We always have $u[j] + v[j] + k \leqslant (b-1) + (b-1) + 1 < 2b$ so that at most one carry is possible during the two additions in $u[j] + v[j] + k$.

Since we have only used **mod** and **div** for nonnegative integers to date, we state here that if t is negative, but b positive, we set

$$
\begin{aligned}
&t \textbf{ div } b = -1 - abs(t) \textbf{ div } b \qquad\qquad\qquad\qquad (2)\\
&t \textbf{ mod } b = b - abs(t) \textbf{ mod } b\\
&\text{so that}\\
&t = -abs(t)\\
& = -(b * abs(t) \textbf{ div } b\\
& + abs(t) \textbf{ mod } b)\\
& = -(b * (-1 - t \textbf{ div } b)\\
& + b - t \textbf{ mod } b)\\
& = b * t \textbf{ div } b + t \textbf{ mod } b
\end{aligned}
$$

as desired. For example $-3 \textbf{ mod } 10 = 7$ and $-3 \textbf{ div } 10 = -1$.

Consider now the algorithm (3) for subtraction of nonnegative n-place integers $u_1 u_2 \ldots u_n$ and $v_1 v_2 \ldots v_n$ where $u_1 u_2 \ldots u_n > v_1 v_2 \ldots v_n$. The nonnegative difference is $w_1 w_2 \ldots w_n$. Again, j marks the position, while this time k is the borrow digit.

$$\textbf{var } u,v,w: \textbf{ array } [1 \mathinner{\ldotp\ldotp} n] \textbf{ of } integer; \qquad (3)$$
$$j.k,t: integer;$$
$$\textbf{begin } \ldots$$
$$k := 0;$$
$$\textbf{for } j := n \textbf{ downto } 1 \textbf{ do}$$
$$\textbf{begin } t := u[j] - v[j] + k;$$
$$w[j] := t \textbf{ mod } b;$$
$$k := t \textbf{ div } b$$
$$\textbf{end}$$
$$\textbf{end}$$

Observe that in (3) k is set to -1 or 0 depending upon whether a borrow occurred or not, i.e., whether $u[j] - v[j] + k < 0$ or not. Observe also that in the calculation of $w[j]$ we have $-b = 0 - (b-1) + (-1) \leqslant u[j] - v[j] + k \leqslant (b-1) - 0 + 0 < b$, i.e., $-b \leqslant u[j] - v[j] + k \leqslant b$, i.e., $0 \leqslant u[j] - v[j] + k + b < 2b$ so that $0 \leqslant w[j] \leqslant b - 1$. When the algorithm terminates we should have $k = 0$. The condition $k = -1$ occurs if and only if $v_1 v_2 \ldots v_n > u_1 u_2 \ldots u_n$, contrary to the assumption.

We now present an algorithm (4) for multiplication of an n-place non-negative integer $u_1 u_2 \ldots u_n$ by an m-place integer $v_1 v_2 \ldots v_m$ to form their product $w_1 w_2 \ldots w_{m+n}$. A more conventional algorithm would be based on forming the partial products $u_1 u_2 \ldots u_n$ times v_j first, for $1 \leqslant j \leqslant m$, and then adding these products together with an appropriate scale factor. In algorithm (4), however, the addition is done concurrently with the multiplication which results in a more efficient procedure.

$$\textbf{var } u: \textbf{ array } [1 \mathinner{\ldotp\ldotp} n] \textbf{ of } integer; \qquad (4)$$
$$v: \textbf{ array } [1 \mathinner{\ldotp\ldotp} m] \textbf{ of } integer;$$
$$w: \textbf{ array } [1 \mathinner{\ldotp\ldotp} m + n] \textbf{ of } integer;$$
$$i,j,k,t: integer;$$
$$\textbf{begin } \ldots$$
$$\textbf{for } i := 1 \textbf{ to } n \textbf{ do } w[m + i] := 0;$$
$$\textbf{for } j := m \textbf{ downto } 1 \textbf{ do}$$
$$\textbf{if } v[j] = 0 \textbf{ then } w[j] := 0$$
$$\textbf{else begin } k := 0;$$
$$\textbf{for } i := n \textbf{ downto } 1 \textbf{ do}$$
$$\textbf{begin } t := u[i] * v[j] + w[i + j] + k; \{0 \leqslant t < b^2\}$$
$$w[i + j] := t \textbf{ mod } b;$$
$$k := t \textbf{ div } b; \{0 \leqslant k < b\}$$
$$\textbf{end};$$
$$w[j] := k$$
$$\textbf{end}$$
$$\textbf{end}$$

The final algorithm in this subsection is division of an $(n + m)$-place integer by an n-place integer to obtain an $(m + 1)$-place quotient and an n-place remainder. If we follow the logic of the ordinary division algorithm we conclude that the general problem breaks down into m simpler steps, each of which consists of the division of an $(n + 1)$-place number u by an n-place divisor v, where $0 \leqslant u/v < b$. The remainder after each step is less than v, so it may be used in the succeeding step. So our problem reduces to the following problem: Find an algorithm to determine $q = u$ **div** v and $r = u$ **mod** v where $u = u_0 u_1 \ldots u_n$ and $v = v_1 \ldots v_n$ are nonnegative integers such that $u/v < b$.

The usual strategy in solving this problem is to make a guess about q based on the most significant digits of u and v. This trial quotient qt is obtained by dividing the two leading digits of u by the leading digit of v; and if the result is b or more it is replaced by $(b - 1)$:

$$qt = min((u_0 b + u_1) \textbf{ div } v_1, b - 1). \tag{5}$$

This value qt is always a very good approximation to the desired answer q, since the following result holds:

$$\text{If } v_1 \geqslant b \textbf{ div } 2 \quad \text{then} \quad qt - 2 \leqslant q \leqslant qt. \tag{6}$$

One simple way to satisfy $v_1 \geqslant b$ **div** 2 is to divide both u and v by b **div** $(v_1 + 1)$. This does not change the value of u/v, and it always makes the new value of v_1 large enough. The latter follows from the following result: If v and b are integers such that $1 \leqslant v < b$, then the following holds:

$$b \textbf{ div } 2 \leqslant v * b \textbf{ div } (v + 1) < (v + 1) * b \textbf{ div } (v + 1) \leqslant b. \tag{7}$$

The division algorithm (10) uses a slightly improved choice of qt which guarantees that $q = qt$ or $q = qt - 1$. This improved choice is made on the basis of the following observations:

$$\text{If } (u_0 * b + u_1 - qt * v_1) * b + u_2 - v_2 * qt < 0 \text{ then } q < qt \tag{8}$$

$$\text{If } (u_0 * b + u_1 - qt * v_1) * b + u_2 - v_2 * qt \geqslant 0 \text{ then } qt = q \text{ or } q = qt - 1. \tag{9}$$

The algorithm (10) contains particular types of multiplication and division algorithms: the algorithm for multiplication of an n-place integer by a one-place integer and the algorithm for division of an n-place integer by a one-place integer.

```
var u: array [0 .. m + n] of integer {dividend};                        (10)
    v: array [0 .. n] of integer {divisor};
    r: array [1 .. n] of integer {remainder};
    q: array [0 .. m] of integer {quotient};
    d,k,k1,t,t1,r1,i,j: integer;
begin d := b div (v[1] + 1);
      {u[0] ... u[m + n] := u[1] ... u[m + n] times d}
      k := 0;
      for j := m + n downto 1 do
```

```
begin t := u[j] * d + k;
      u[j] := t mod b;
      k := t div b
end; u[0] := k;
{v[1] . . . v[n] := v[1] . . . v[n] times d};
k := 0;
for j := n downto 1 do
begin t := v[j] * d + k;
      v[j] := t mod b;
      k := t div b
end;
for j := 0 to m do
begin {divide u[j] . . . u[j + n] by v[1] . . . v[n] to get q[j]}
      {calculate trial quotient}
      if u[j] = v[1] then qt := b − 1
      else qt := (u[j] * b + u[j + 1]) div v[1];
      while (u[j] * b + u[j + 1] − qt * v[1]) * b + u[j + 2] − qt * v[2] < 0
      do qt := qt − 1;
      {replace u[j] . . . u[j + n] by u[j]u[j + 1] . . . u[j + n] −
                                  (qt times v[1] . . . v[n])}
      k := 0; k1 := 0;
      for i := n downto 1 do
      begin t := v[i] * q1 + k1;
            t1 := t mod b; k1 := t div b;
            t := u[j] − t1 + k;
            u[j] := t mod b; k := t div b
      end;
      q[j] := qt;
      if k < 0 then begin q[j] := q[j] − 1;
                          {add v₀v₁ . . . vₙ to uⱼuⱼ₊₁ . . . uⱼ₊ₙ}
                          k := 0;
                          for i := n downto 1 do
                          begin t := u[j + i] + v[i] + k;
                                u[j + i] := t mod b;
                                k := t div b
                          end
                    end; u[j] := u[j] + k
end;
{q[0] . . . q[m] is the quotient and the remainder is obtained by
dividing u[m + 1] . . . u[m + n] by d}
r1 := 0;
for j := m + 1 to m + n do
begin t := r1 * b + u[j];
      r[j − m] := t div d;
      r1 := t mod d
end {r[1] . . . r[n] is the remainder}
end
```

The reader who has struggled through (10)—which is typical of the way in which programs are presented and documented—may come to understand the advantages of a top-down approach to presenting a program.

3.6 Processing Files and Records

In this section we consider algorithms which illustrate how the standard file operators are used.

File Merging

Suppose that we have two *sorted* files of integers:

$$f_1 f_2 \ldots f_m \quad \text{and} \quad g_1 g_2 \ldots g_n \tag{1}$$

which means that the following relations hold:

$$\forall i,j((1 \leqslant i < j \leqslant m) \supset (f_i \leqslant f_j)) \tag{2}$$
$$\forall i,j((1 \leqslant i < j \leqslant n) \supset (g_i \leqslant g_j)).$$

Our task is to merge the files f and g into a sorted file h, i.e., in such a way that the following relation holds:

$$(\forall i,j)((1 \leqslant i < j \leqslant (m+n)) \supset (h_i \leqslant h_j))$$
$$\wedge ((f_1 \ldots f_m g_1 \ldots g_n) \; permute \; (h_1 \ldots h_{m+n})) \tag{3}$$

where the relation *permute* was defined in (26) of Section 3.2. The strategy used to perform merging simply consists of comparing the next incoming elements of f and g. The smaller of them is then transported to h, and the file position of the file from which this element is taken is advanced, as well as the file position of h. This whole process is continued until either the end of f or of g is reached. The remaining part of f or g (whichever—if either—is nonempty) is then copied to h. So we obtain the following algorithm:

```
begin reset(f); reset(g);                                            (4)
      rewrite(h);
      while ¬(eof(f) ∨ eof(g)) do
      begin if f↑ < g↑ then
                begin h↑ := f↑;
                      get(f)
                end
            else begin h↑ := g↑;
                        get(g)
                  end;
            put(h)
      end;
      copy tail of f;
      copy tail of g;
end
```

In refining the abstract statements *copy tail of f* and *copy tail of g* we do it in such a way that these statements have no effect if the tail (i.e., the file) is empty. That is why in (5) we use the **while-do** statement.

$$
\begin{array}{lll}
\textbf{while } \neg eof(g) \textbf{ do} & \textbf{while } \neg eof(f) \textbf{ do} & (5)\\
\textbf{begin } h\!\uparrow := g\!\uparrow; & \textbf{begin } h\!\uparrow := f\!\uparrow; & \\
\quad put(h); get(g) & \quad put(h); get(f) & \\
\textbf{end} & \textbf{end} &
\end{array}
$$

Looking back at (4) we observe that it is somewhat inefficient to have a rather complicated Boolean expression $\neg(eof(f) \vee eof(g))$ as the continuation condition of the main loop of the algorithm. In the final algorithm which is presented in (6), this main loop is made more efficient by introducing an auxiliary Boolean variable *endfg* which is set to *true* if either $eof(f)$ or $eof(g)$ is *true*. In (6) only one of $eof(f)$ and $eof(g)$ gets evaluated each time around the loop, and in addition one assignment is made to *endfg*. In the previous version (4), both $eof(f)$ and $eof(g)$ get evaluated every time around the loop, as well as one disjunction operation $\vee$.

$$
\begin{array}{ll}
\textbf{begin } reset(f); reset(g); & (6)\\
\quad rewrite(h); \\
\quad endfg := eof(f) \vee eof(g); \\
\quad \textbf{while } \neg endfg \textbf{ do} \\
\quad \textbf{begin if } f\!\uparrow < g\!\uparrow \textbf{ then} \\
\qquad\quad \textbf{begin } h\!\uparrow := f\!\uparrow; \\
\qquad\qquad\quad get(f); \\
\qquad\qquad\quad endfg := eof(f) \\
\qquad\quad \textbf{end} \\
\qquad\quad \textbf{else} \\
\qquad\quad \textbf{begin } h\!\uparrow := g\!\uparrow; \\
\qquad\qquad\quad get(g); \\
\qquad\qquad\quad endfg := eof(g) \\
\qquad\quad \textbf{end}; \\
\qquad\quad put(h) \\
\quad \textbf{end}; \\
\quad \textbf{while } \neg eof(g) \textbf{ do} \\
\quad \textbf{begin } h\!\uparrow := g\!\uparrow; \\
\qquad\quad put(h); get(g) \\
\quad \textbf{end}; \\
\quad \textbf{while } \neg eof(f) \textbf{ do} \\
\quad \textbf{begin } h\!\uparrow := f\!\uparrow; \\
\qquad\quad put(h); get(f) \\
\quad \textbf{end} \\
\textbf{end}
\end{array}
$$

Registration Files

We consider the problem of updating two files maintained by a university: the file *students* contains information on students who are currently registered; the file *dropouts* contains information on students who have left the university without completing their studies. The file *students* is consulted very often, and so is kept sorted according to increasing order of the student's registration numbers. The file *dropouts*, however, is consulted very seldom. We shall assume that because of that it is sorted only from time to time. So, when adding new records of drop-out students to this file, we shall simply append them at the end of the file. The update operation we are to perform is based on the file *in* (short for 'input number') which contains registration numbers of those students who are dropping out of the university. We assume that this file is sorted. The program is to update *dropouts* (without sorting) as well as to produce a new, sorted, file of students (*newstudents*) which contains only those students who are still enrolled, and a file of errors which contains those numbers in the file *in* for which a corresponding student record was not found in the file of students.

The types of records in the files *students*, *newstudents* and *dropouts* are defined below:

type *date* = **record** *year*: *integer*;   (7)
                 month: (*jan, feb, mar, apr, may, jun, jul, aug,*
                        sep, oct, nov, dec);
                 day: 1 . . 31
       end;
    studentrec : = **record** *num*: *integer*;
                 name: **array** [1 . . 35] **of** *char*;
                 major: (*math, phys, comsci, art, phil,*
                        eeng, ceng, exci, chem);
                 year: (*freshman, sophmore, junior, senior*);
          end;
    dropout = **record** *record*: *studentrec*;
                 dropdate: *date*
      end

The file variables necessary for this program are declared as follows:

        var *students, newstudents*: **file of** *studentrec*;   (8)
           dropouts: **file of** *dropout*;
           in, error: **file of** *integer*

In addition to these, a global variable *today*, which holds the current date, must be appropriately initialized. With the above conventions, our algorithm takes the following form:

        begin *reset*(*students*); *reset*(*dropouts*);   (9)
          reset(*in*);
          rewrite(*error*); *rewrite*(*newstudents*);
          {advance to end of file prior to adding new entries}
          while ¬*eof*(*dropouts*) **do** *get*(*dropouts*);
          while ¬*eof*(*in*) **do**

begin while *in*↑ > *students*↑ . *num* **do**
    {copy a student record to the file *newstudents*}
    begin *newstudents*↑ := *students*↑;
        put(*newstudents*); *get*(*students*)
    end;
    if *in*↑ < *students*↑ . *num* **then**
    begin {error}
        error↑ := *in*↑;
        put(*error*)
    end
    else begin {append a new drop-out}
            dropouts↑ . *record* := *students*↑;
            dropouts↑ . *dropdate* := *today*;
            put(*dropouts*); *get*(*students*)
        end
    get(*in*)
  end
end

Bank Files

The example that follows is from business data processing. The task is to write a program which updates the file of bank loans on the basis of the file of repayments. In addition to that, the program is to generate a file of statements (a statement is generated in case there was a repayment so that the balance must be calculated) and a file of refund records (a refund record is put out in case the repayment exceeds the amount due.) We assume that records of these files have the following types:

type *loan* = **record** *number*: *integer*;   (10)
                    name: **array** [1 . . 30] **of** *char*;
                    principal: *integer*;
                    interestrate: *real*
            end;
repayment = **record** *number*: *integer*;
                        amount: *integer*
               end;
refund = **record** *number*: *integer*;
                  name: **array** [1 . . 30] **of** *char*;
                  amount: *integer*
            end;
statement = **record** *number*: *integer*;
                    name: **array** [1 . . 30] **of** *char*;
                    principal: *integer*;
                    interestrate: *real*;
                    payment: *integer*;
                    balance: *integer*
            end;

We assume that the file of loans and the file of repayments are sorted in ascending order of the values of the field number, and that no two loans have the same number. The abstract algorithm in (11) is then designed to work properly so long as each repayment is for an existing loan.

At any time, a loan involves a certain principal—the amount owed to the bank. The program is used once a month, and starts by computing the month's interest. If there is no repayment on the loan, then the interest is simply added to the principal. If there is a repayment, then the balance is obtained by subtracting the amount of this repayment from the sum of principal and interest—forming a refund record if the balance is negative. Finally, the program generates a statement for each repayment.

In a sequential file, we can only add entries at the end—we cannot modify entries in the middle. We thus introduce a new file called *loans2* and copy into it each processed loan with its updated balance, using *update loans2*. Then at the end of the program we must copy the entire *loans2* to provide the new correct data in the *loans* file, using *restore loans*.

being *rest(loans)*; *reset(repayments)*; *rewrite (loans2)*; (11)
    rewrite(refunds); *rewrite(statements)*;
    while ¬(*eof(repayments)*) **do**
    begin *compute interest*;
        if *loans↑ . number ≠ repayments↑ . number* **then**
        add interest to principal
        else
        begin *compute balance*;
            if *balance* < 0 **then begin** *output refund record*;
                        balance := 0 **end**;
            set principal to balance;
            output statement;
            get(repayments)
        end;
        update loans2
    end;
    while ¬*eof(loans)* **do**
    begin *compute interest*;
        add interest to principal;
        update loans2
    end
    restore loans
end

We now refine the abstract statements in (11).

{*compute interest*} (12)
interest := *round(loans↑ . principal ∗ loans↑ . interestrate* **div** 12).

Here *round* is used to convert a real value to an integer—to give the interest in the smallest unit of currency. *interestrate* holds the annual rate.

$$\{add\ interest\ to\ principal\} \qquad\qquad (13)$$
$$loans\uparrow . principal := loans\uparrow . principal + interest$$

$$\{compute\ balance\}$$
$$balance := loans\uparrow . principal + interest - repayments\uparrow . amount \quad (14)$$

$$\{output\ refund\ record\} \qquad\qquad (15)$$
begin *refunds*↑ . *number* := *loans*↑ . *number*;
    refunds↑ . *name* := *loans*↑ . *name*;
    refunds↑ . amount := −*balance*;
    put(*refunds*)
end

$$\{set\ principal\ to\ balance\} \qquad\qquad (16)$$
$$loans\uparrow . principal := balance$$

$$\{output\ statement\} \qquad\qquad (17)$$
begin *statements*↑ . *number* := *loans*↑ . *number*;
    statements↑ . *name* := *loans*↑ . *name*;
    statements↑ . *principal* := *loans*↑ . *principal*;
    statements↑ . *interestrate* := *loans*↑ . *interestrate*;
    statements↑ . *payment* := *repayments*↑ . *amount*;
    statements↑ . *balance* := *balance*;
    put(*statements*)
end

Note that each time we get to the instruction *update loans2* in (11), the value of *loans*↑ is just the current loan with the principal updated either by (13) or by (16). Thus *loans*↑ contains precisely the information to be appended to *loans2*.

$$\{update\ loans2\} \qquad\qquad (18a)$$
begin *loans2*↑ := *loans*↑;
    put (*loans2*); *get* (*loans*)
end

Finally, when all the loans are processed we must copy the updated loans as filed in *loans2* back into *loans* so that the correct data will be available for processing next month's payments.

{*restore loans*}   (18b)
begin *rewrite* (*loans*); *reset* (*loans2*);
   while ¬(*eof* (*loans2*)) **do**
    begin *loans*↑ := *loans2*↑;
      put (*loans*); *get* (*loans2*)
   end
end

Textfiles

Files whose components are printable characters are called *textfiles*. Their role is fundamental since the input and output of most programs are textfiles. A computational process in such cases may be viewed as a transformation converting one textfile called *input* into another textfile called *output*. Because of that, two standard variables *input* and *output*, and the standard type *text* are introduced. They are assumed to be predefined in the environment of every program as follows:

$$\textbf{type } text = \textbf{file of } char \qquad (19)$$
$$\textbf{var } input, output: text$$

The two standard variables denote the two standard input and output media of a computer system (for example the card reader and the line printer). Because of this, the following conventions apply to these two standard files: The file *input* can only be inspected, i.e., only the file operator *get* is applicable. The file *output* can only be generated, i.e., only the file operator *put* is applicable. Since these two standard files occur in practically every complete computer program, an abbreviated notation is introduced as in (20).

Explicit notation	*Abbreviated notation*	(20)
c := *input*↑; *get*(*input*)	*read*(*c*)	
output↑ := *e*; *put*(*output*)	*write*(*e*)	
eof(*input*)	*eof*	

At this point we give an example which demonstrates operations on textfiles. The program in (21) copies the nonempty file *input* onto the file *output* so that every subsequence of blanks is reduced to a single blank (denoted ' '). In this case, the same *c* serves as both input buffer and output buffer. The last character of the input file is not a blank.

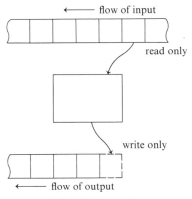

Figure 3.3   Input and output

```
var c: char;                                                    (21)
begin while ¬eof do
        begin read(c); write(c);
              if c = ' ' then
              begin repeat read(c)
                    until c ≠ ' ';
                    write(c)
        end
    end
end
```

Texts are logically subdivided into *lines*, and the line-by-line arrangement of *input* and *output* can be controlled using the following special textfile operators.

writeln	Terminate the current line of the textfile *output*	(22)
readln	Skip to the beginning of the next line of the textfile *input*. *input↑* becomes the first character of the next line.	
eoln	If the end of the current line of the textfile *input* has been reached *eoln* yields *true*. In that case *input↑* corresponds to the position of a line separator, but *input↑* is blank.	

At the level of computer implementation, the separation of two consecutive lines is obtained by using a special *control character*, which is in addition to the printed characters. Thus *writeln* corresponds to writing a control character, *readln* corresponds to searching ahead for the next control character in the input file, and then getting the next character.

In order to illustrate the operations on textfiles, assume that the standard file *input* contains persons' first and last names. Each name (first and last) represents a single line in the file *input*. The first name is separated from the last name by a blank character. Given this file, we want to print those last names which begin with the letter '*t*'. A program that accomplishes this task is given in (23).

We assume that there are no blanks at the start of the line, exactly one blank between the first and last name, and at least one blank after the last name. We print each last name beginning with a *t*, followed by a blank, on a separate line.

```
begin while ⌐eof do                                              (23)
      begin readln;
            repeat read(ch) until ch = ' ';
            read(ch);
            if (ch = 't') then
            begin repeat write(ch); read(ch) until (ch = ' ');
                  write(' '); writeln
            end
      end
end
```

The file operators *read* and *write* as defined so far operate on single characters. In some situations this can get rather cumbersome. For example, the external representation of Boolean values is by constant identifiers *true* and *false*. These identifiers, although sequences of characters, represent values of the simple type *Boolean*. An extension of the procedures *read* and *write* which simplifies programming a great deal consists of allowing that in *read(v)* and *write(v)*, *v* may be of a type which is not only *char*. Thus if *v* is of type *Boolean*, then the whole sequence of characters representing externally the current Boolean value of *v* will be written by *write(v)*. Similarly, *read(v)*, where *v* is of type Boolean, will read the whole sequence of characters representing externally a Boolean value and assign the internal representation of that value to *v*.

The other two types of *v* in *read(v)* and *write(v)* which are permitted are *integer* and *real*. Externally, these values are represented as sequences of characters. According to the syntax of numbers discussed before, their internal representation is quite different from that. If *v* in *read(v)* is of type *integer* or *real* then a sequence of characters will be read according to the syntax of numbers, consecutive numbers must be separated by blanks. The internal representation which corresponds to the external representation of the number read in will be assigned to *v*. Likewise, if in *write(v)*, *v* is of type *integer* or *real*, then a transformation from the internal number representation into the external number representation will be performed and the external representation (a sequence of characters) will be printed according to some implementation-dependent conventions. These conventions have to do with the field width (number of output characters) which a number occupies. Reals are output in the decimal floating-point form.

The operators *read* and *write* are in fact generalized even further, but for the purposes of our exposition the restricted facilities defined so far will be quite enough.

In order to illustrate the application of the extended file operators discussed above, suppose that we are to read a sequence of numbers from the file input and process them in the order in which they appear.

Let x be a variable of type *integer*, and $P(x)$ denote some processing of x. If we do not know how many numbers are to be read and the sequence of numbers is not terminated by a special symbol, then the following program schemat should be used:

$$read(x);   \qquad (24)$$
$$\textbf{while} \ \neg eof \ \textbf{do}$$
$$\textbf{begin} \ P(x);$$
$$read(x)$$
$$\textbf{end}$$

3.7 Set Manipulation in Pascal

We now study how many of the set manipulations of Section 3.2 can be applied to data types in Pascal.

We use Pascal notation for set expressions. In that notation a set is denoted by enumerating the set elements (i.e., expressions of the base type) and enclosing them in set brackets [and]. [ ] denotes the empty set. The expression [m .. n] denotes the set of all elements i of the base type such that $m \leqslant i \leqslant n$. Thus if $m > n$, [m .. n] denotes the empty set. Examples of use of this notation are:

$$[1 .. 9] \qquad (1)$$
$$['A' .. 'Z']$$
$$['0' .. '9'].$$

It is important to observe that the above notation in fact stands for the operation of constructing a set out of the given elements. For example, if s is a variable which takes subsets of [1,2,3] as its values, then the following assignments are equally valid:

$$s := [1,2] \qquad (2)$$
$$s := [1 .. 2]$$

Observe that on the right-hand side of both assigments (2) we have a set expression—the value of this expression is the set which consists of two elements: 1 and 2.

If $T1$ is a scalar type or subrange type, then:

$$\textbf{type } T2 = \textbf{set of } T1 \tag{3}$$

introduces a new type $T2$ which is the set of all subsets of the set $T1$. $T2$ is thus the *powerset* of the set $T1$ (denoted $PT1$ in set theory), and contains two characteristic elements: the empty set and the set $T1$ itself. $T1$ is called the *base type* of $T2$.

For example, if $T1$ is the subrange $1 . . 3$ of *integer* then $T2$ defined by (3) consists of the following elements (sets):

$$[\ ]\ [1]\ [2]\ [3]\ [1,2]\ [1,3]\ [2,3]\ [1,2,3] \tag{4}$$

Several standard operations which construct new sets out of the given ones are defined as follows, where A and B are of the type **set of** for some basic type T:

$A + B$ — The union of the sets A and B, i.e., the set which consists of elements which are either in A or in B or in both. (Set theory notation: $A \cup B$).

$A * B$ — The intersection of the sets A and B, i.e., the set of those elements of A which are also elements of B. (Set theory notation: $A \cap B$).

$A - B$ — The difference of the sets A and B, i.e., the set of all elements of A which are not elements of B.

In addition to the above construction operators which yield new sets of type **set of** T; every powerset type is equipped with the following relational operators:

$A = B$ — The value of this expression is *true* if A and B are equal sets and *false* otherwise.

$A \neq B$ — The value of this expression is the same as the value of expression $\neg(A = B)$.

$A \leqslant B$ — The value of this expression is *true* if A is a subset of B; i.e., if every element of A is also an element of B, otherwise the value of the expression is *false*.

$A \geqslant B$ — The value of this expression is the same as the value of expression $B \leqslant A$.

a **in** B — The value of this expression is *true* if a is an element of the set B, otherwise it is *false*. Thus a must be of some scalar or subrange type T, and B must be of the type **set of** T. (Set theory notation: $a \in B$).

We illustrate the above operations and relations by some examples. Suppose that we want to pick the smallest element of a *nonempty* set A of type **set of** $1 . . N$. Let x be declared as a variable of type $1 . . N$. Then the following piece of program accomplishes the desired goal:

$$\textbf{begin } x := 1; \tag{5}$$
$$\textbf{while } \neg(x \textbf{ in } A) \textbf{ do } x := succ(x)$$
$$\textbf{end}$$

Upon execution of the above compound statement, the value of the variable x will be the element of the set A which is smallest with respect to the ordering of the base type $1 .. N$.

With the conventions defined above, and with n being a variable of type $0 .. N$ and $A1$ of type **set of** $1 .. N$, the piece of program (6) is designed to compute the number of elements n in the set A.

$$\textbf{begin } n := 0; \tag{6}$$
$$\textbf{if } A \neq [\ ] \textbf{ then}$$
$$\textbf{begin } x := 1; A1 := A;$$
$$\textbf{repeat while } \neg(x \textbf{ in } A1) \textbf{ do } x := succ(x);$$
$$n := n + 1; A1 := A1 - [x]$$
$$\textbf{until } A1 = [\ ]$$
$$\textbf{end}$$
$$\textbf{end}$$

Now let f be a function with domain $1 .. N$ and codomain $1 .. N$, and let A and B be sets of type **set of** $1 .. N$. Suppose that our task is to compute the set I whose elements x satisfy the relation $(x \textbf{ in } A) \wedge (f(x) \textbf{ in } B)$. The piece of program (7) accomplishes this task. As before, $A1$ is of type **set of** $1 .. N$.

$$\textbf{begin } I := [\ ]; \tag{7}$$
$$\textbf{if } (A \neq [\ ]) \wedge (B \neq [\ ]) \textbf{ then}$$
$$\textbf{begin } A1 := A; x := 1;$$
$$\textbf{repeat while } \neg(x \textbf{ in } A1) \textbf{ do } x := succ(x);$$
$$\textbf{if } f(x) \textbf{ in } B \textbf{ then } I := I + [x];$$
$$A1 := A1 - [x]$$
$$\textbf{until } A1 = [\ ]$$
$$\textbf{end}$$

Our next example is somewhat more involved. It deals with equivalence relations. To get a feel for the task, suppose that $A = 1 .. 9$, and that an equivalence relation R on A is defined to include the following set of pairs:

$$(2,5)\ (3,7)\ (5,6)\ (7,9)\ (6,4) \tag{8}$$

But then on the basis of the properties of transitivity, symmetry and reflexivity, we can conclude that $(2,6)$, $(3,9)$, $(5,4)$, $(4,6)$, etc are also elements of R. In general, as we stated in Section 3.2, given an equivalence relation R on a set A, the set A can be split into disjoint subsets (forming a partition) such that a and b in A belong to one such subset if and only if aRb holds. These partitions are called *equivalence classes*. We now look into an algorithm which constructs equivalence classes of a set $1 .. N$ from an equivalence relation which is given as a sequence of some of the related pairs as in (8). This sequence will be represented by an array of records thus:

$$\textbf{var } eq: \textbf{array } [1 \mathinner{.\,.} K] \textbf{ of} \qquad\qquad (9)$$
$$\textbf{record } a,b: integer \textbf{ end}$$

The essence of the algorithm is very simple. We start with each element of A alone in one class. Then we repeatedly read equivalent pairs (elements of eq) and test which classes they belong to. We call this abstract statement *find classes to which eq[i] . a and eq[i] . b belong*. If they belong to different classes, we merge these two classes into a single class. The collection of equivalence classes will be represented by an array of sets as follows:

$$\textbf{var } class: \textbf{array } [1 \mathinner{.\,.} N] \textbf{ of} \qquad\qquad (10)$$
$$\textbf{set of } 1 \mathinner{.\,.} N$$

In order to keep track of indexes of class which correspond to the collecttion of classes built so far, we introduce a set variable, *active*, of the type **set of** $1 \mathinner{.\,.} N$. Upon completion of this algorithm the variable *active* will contain indexes to the array *class* of equivalence classes of the equivalence relation defined by (9).

So we have the following abstract algorithm:

```
begin active := [1 .. N];                                         (11)
    for i := 1 to N do class[i] := [i];
    for i := 1 to K do
    begin find classes to which eq[i] . a and eq[i] . b belong;
        if eq[i] . a and eq[i] . b in different classes then
        merge classes
    end
end
```

Refinement of the abstract statement *find classes to which eq[i] . a and eq[i] . b belong* consists of testing the membership of $eq[i] . a$ and $eq[i] . b$ in the equivalence classes $class[j]$ for successive active indexes j. This is performed by first locating j such that either $eq[i] . a \in class[j]$ or $eq[i] . b \in class[j]$. When such j is found, then if $eq[i] . a \in class[j]$ (in which case a Boolean variable p is set to *true*) what we have to do is to find the next active j such that $eq[j] . b \in class[j]$. Similarly, if j is found such that $eq[i] . b \in class[j]$ (in which case a Boolean variable q is set to *true*) then we have to find the next active j such that $eq[i] . a \in class[j]$. Apart from the Boolean variables p and q, two more variables of type $1 \mathinner{.\,.} N$ are needed: np which denotes the index j such that $eq[i] . a \in class[j]$ and nq which denotes the index j such that $eq[i] . b \in class[j]$. The idea is that if we find p and q true with $np \neq nq$, we may merge $class[np]$ and $class[nq]$ to form a new $class[np]$, and then delete nq from the *active* list. With this discussion in mind we obtain the following refinement of *find classes to which eq[i] . a and eq[i] . b belong*. The point is that on each iteration, $eq[i]$. a is in exactly one $class[j]$, and similarly for $eq[i]$. b.

> {*find classes to which $eq[i]$. a and $eq[i]$. b belong*}
> **repeat** *pick next j in active*;
> $p := eq[i]$. a **in** $class[j]$;
> $q := eq[i]$. b **in** $class[j]$
> **until** $p \lor q$;
> **if** p **then**
> **begin** $np := j$;
> $nq :=$ *index of class to which $eq[i]$. b belongs*
> **end**
> **else begin** $nq := j$;
> $np :=$ *index of class to which $eq[i]$. a belongs*
>   **end**

In refining the statements $np :=$ *index of class to which $eq[i]$. a belongs* and $nq :=$ *index of class to which $eq[i]$. b belongs* we have to bear in mind that $eq[i]$. a and $eq[i]$. b may be in the same class $class[j]$. That is the reason why in the refinements of these two statements given below we have to use the **while-do** rather than the **repeat-until** statement.

> {$nq :=$ *index of class to which $eq[i]$. b belongs*}
> **while** $\neg(eq[i]$. b **in** $class[j])$ **do**
> *pick next j in active*;
> $nq := j$

> {$np :=$ *index of class to which $eq[i]$. a belongs*}
> **while** $\neg(eq[i]$. a **in** $class[j])$ **do**
> *pick next j in active*;
> $np := j$

The abstract statement *pick next j in active* occurs in three refinements developed so far. Recalling that the type of *active* is **set of** $1 .. N$, and that j is of type $1 .. N$ we may refine this statement and complete refinement of the statement *find classes to which $eq[i]$. a and $eq[i]$. b belong*.

> {*pick next j in active*}
> **while** $\neg(j$ **in** $active)$ **do** $j := succ(j)$

Since np and nq have been set in *find classes to which $eq[i]$. a and $eq[i]$. b belong* to indexes of those classes to which $eq[i]$. a and $eq[i]$. b respectively belong, the abstract test $eq[i]$. a *and* $eq[i]$. b *in different classes* reduces to $np \neq nq$. Finally, merging classes is performed as follows:

> {*merge classes*}
> **begin** $class[np] := class[np] + class[nq]$;
> $active := active - [nq]$
> **end**

This completes the development of the desired algorithm which is, in its final form, given in (12).

begin *active* := [1 .. *N*];   (12)
      for *i* := 1 **to** *N* **do** *class*[*i*] := [*i*];
      for *i* := 1 **to** *K* **do**
      begin { *find classes to which eq*[*i*] . *a and eq*[*i*] . *b belong*}
            j := 1;
            repeat {*pick next j in active*}
                    while $\neg$(*j* **in** *active*) **do** *j* := *succ*(*j*);
                    {*test membership*}
                    p := *eq*[*i*] . *a* **in** *class*[*j*];
                    q := *eq*[*i*] . *b* **in** *class*[*j*]
            until   *p* $\vee$ *q*;
            if *p* **then**
            begin *np* := *j*;
                  {*nq* := *index of class to which eq*[*i*] . *b belongs*}
                  while $\neg$(*eq*[*i*] . *b* **in** *class*[*j*]) **do**
                  {*pick next j in active*}
                  while $\neg$(*j* **in** *active*) **do** *j* := *succ*(*j*);
                  nq := *j*
            end
            else begin *nq* := *j*;
                  {*np* := *index of class to which eq*[*i*] . *a belongs*}
                  while $\neg$(*eq*[*i*] . *a* **in** *class*[*j*]) **do**
                  {*pick next j in active*}
                  while $\neg$(*j* **in** *active*) **do** *j* := *succ*(*j*);
                  np := *j*
               end;
            if *np* $\neq$ *nq* **then** {*merge classes*}
            begin *class*[*np*] := *class*[*np*] + *class*[*nq*];
                active := *active* − [*nq*]
            end
      end
end

Bibliographic Remarks

The basic references for the material presented in this chapter are Wirth (1972), Jensen and Wirth (1974), Wirth (1974), Hoare and Wirth (1973) and Wirth (1976). Although we relied on these references and borrowed a number of examples from them, our approach in presenting the material on data types is very different. The proof rule for the **for** statement is due to Hoare (1972c), and the example of its use is adapted from the same source. The proof rules for the standard file operators appeared in Hoare and Wirth (1973). The proof rule for the **with** statement appeared in the same paper. The algorithms for addition, subtraction and multiplication of integers in positional notation are structured versions of the algorithms given in Knuth (1969). The file merge example is from Jensen and Wirth (1974), and the file processing business example is adapted from Hoare (1968). The students' grades example is adapted from Conway, Gries and Zimmerman (1976) while the pollution example is based on J. L. Gross and W. S. Brainerd: *Fundamental Programming Concepts*, Harper and Row (1972). Useful texts for discrete mathematics are L. S. Bobrow and M. A. Arbib: *Discrete Mathematics: Applied Algebra for Computer and Information Science*, Hemisphere Books (1974) and D. F. Stanat and D. F. McAllister: *Discrete Mathematics in Computer Science*, Prentice-Hall (1977).

Exercises

The purpose of the following two exercises is to illustrate operations with real numbers.

1. Consider the following sum:

$$s_i = 1 + x + \frac{x^2}{2!} + \cdots + \frac{x^i}{i!}$$

s_i can be written as $\sum_{j=0}^{i} t_j$, where the terms t_j are defined as follows:

$$t_0 = 1$$
$$t_j = t_{j-1} * x/j \quad \text{for} \quad j > 0.$$

As j grows, t_j decreases, and the sum of t_j's converges to a fixed limit which is the exponential function $exp(x)$.

Write an algorithm which approximates $exp(x)$ by stopping when the last term is less than some degree of accuracy eps.

2. Consider the following sum:

$$s_i = x - \frac{x^3}{3!} + \frac{x^5}{5!} + \cdots + (-1)^{2i-1} * \frac{x^{2i-1}}{(2i-1)!}$$

s_i can be written shortly $\sum_{j=0}^{i} t_j$ where the terms t_j are defined as follows:

$$t_0 = x \qquad k_0 = 1$$
$$\left. \begin{array}{l} t_j = -t_{j-1} * \dfrac{x^2}{k_j * (k_{j-1})} \\[2mm] k_j = k_{j-1} + 2 \end{array} \right\} \text{for } j > 0.$$

The sum converges to the limit $sin(x)$. Write an algorithm which approximates $sin(x)$ by stopping when the last term is less than some degree of accuracy eps.

3. Given an $n \times n$ matrix A, we construct another $n \times n$ matrix B in such a way that $b_{ij} = a_{ji}$, where a denotes an element of A and b an element of B. This operation is called *transposition*. Write an algorithm which performs this operation.

4. Prove that after completion of execution of the **for** statement in the following block

> **const** $n = 100$;
> **type** *index* $= 1 \ .. \ n$;
> **var** a: **array** [*index*] **of** *integer*;
> i: *index*;
> **begin for** $i := 1$ **to** n **do** $\{\forall j((1 \leqslant j < i) \supset (a[j] = 0))\}$
> $a[i] := 0$
> **end**

the logical formula

$$\forall j((1 \leqslant j \leqslant n) \supset (a[j] = 0))$$

has the value *true*.

5. Assuming that $\{true\}$ $read(x,y)$ $\{(x \geqslant 0) \wedge (y \geqslant 0)\}$ holds for the *read* statement in the block:

> **var** x,y,s,i,j: *integer*;
> **begin** $read(x,y)$;
> $\{\text{assume } (x \geqslant 0) \wedge (y \geqslant 0)\}$;
> $s := 0$;
>   **for** $i := 1$ **to** x **do** $\{(s = (i-1) * y) \wedge (y \geqslant 0)\}$
>   **for** $j := 1$ **to** y **do** $\{(s = (i-1) * y + j\}$
> $s := s + 1$;
> $\{s = x * y\}$
> **end**

prove that the annotated relations in the above block are indeed invariants. $read(x, y)$ stands for $read(x)$; $read(y)$.

6. Consider the following block:

> **var** s: *real*; i: *integer*;
> x,y: **array** [$1 \ .. \ n$] **of** *real*;
>   **begin** $\{\text{assignment of initial values to } x \text{ and } y\} \ldots$
> $s := 0$; $i := 0$;
>   **repeat** $i := i + 1$;
> $s := s + x[i] * y[i]$
>   **until** $i = n$
> $\left\{ s = \sum_{j=1}^{n} x[j] * y[j] \right\}$
>   **end**

Prove that upon execution of the **repeat-until** statement in the above block the relation

$$s = \sum_{j=1}^{n} x[j] * y[j]$$

holds.

7. The following block is intended to store all x with the property *sol* into an array a.

```
const max = 100;
type candidate = 1 . . max; candidate0 = 0 . . max;
     index = 1 . . max; index0 = 0 . . max;
var x: candidate0;
    a: array [index] of candidate;
    n: index0; b: Boolean;
begin x := 0; n := 0;
      while x < max do
      begin x := x + 1;
            b := sol(x);
            if b then
            begin n := n + 1; a[n] := x end
      end
end
```

In the above block *sol* is a known function with the domain *candidate* and codomain *Boolean*. In order to prove correctness, we have to show three things:

i. All x with the property *sol* are stored. This is formulated in the predicate:

$$\forall y((1 \leqslant y \leqslant max) \supset (sol(y) \supset \exists j((1 \leqslant j \leqslant n) \wedge (a[j] = y))))$$

ii. Nothing else but those x with the property *sol* are stored. This is formulated in the following predicate:

$$\forall i((1 \leqslant i \leqslant n) \supset (sol(a[i]) \wedge (1 \leqslant a[i] \leqslant max)))$$

iii. No two stored x are the same. This is formulated in the following predicate:

$$\forall j,k((1 \leqslant j < k \leqslant n) \supset (a[j] < a[k]))$$

Prove correctness.

8. Give an example of an update operation of a record of the type *student* defined below:

```
type alfa = array [1 . . 30] of char;
     campusresidence = record address: array [1 . . 30] of char;
                              telephone: array [1 . . 7] of char;
                              dininghallcode: array [1 . . 3] of char
                       end;
     homedata = record parentguardian: alfa;
                       address: array [1 . . 30] of char;
                       telephone: array [1 . . 10] of char
                end;
     registratdata = record college: array [1 . . 12] of char;
                            class: array [1 . . 2] of char;
                            gradeaverage: real;
                            adviser: alfa;
                     end;
     student = record name: alfa;
                      campus: campusresidence;
                      home: homedata;
                      registration: registratdata
               end
```

9. Define a record type which represents the following personal data: name (first, last), sex, date of birth. Give an example of assignment of sample personal data to a record variable of this type.

10. Using the **with** statement write the assignments from the previous two exercises in a notationally simpler manner.

11. Write a program which reads a sequence of integers from the standard file *input*, and outputs (writes into the standard file *output*) the maximum of the numbers read in.

12. Given positive integers n and m, write a program which prints all powers of n which are less than m.

13. Elements of a file f are records with three *integer* fields. Write a program which reads the file f, and writes into the file q those read in records whose fields represent the lengths of the sides of a triangle. Prove correctness of the constructed program.

14. The Fibonacci numbers of order 1 are defined by the following rules:
$$f_0 = 0; \qquad f_1 = 1;$$
$$f_n = f_{n-1} + f_{n-2} \qquad \text{for} \qquad n > 1.$$

Write a program which outputs the first n Fibonacci numbers. Prove correctness of this program using the previously established correctness of the algorithm for generation of the Fibonacci numbers.

15. Define the type *color* whose elements are colors represented as sets of basic colors. For example, the color *orange* is represented as the set [*red, yellow*].

16. Define the type *hand* whose elements are hands of playing cards.

17. Define a type whose elements contain personal data as follows:

> name (first, last)
>
> social security number
>
> date of birth
>
> number of dependents
>
> marital status (*married, widowed, divorced, single*).

If the marital status is *married* or *widowed*, the date of marriage or husband's death should be included. If the marital status is *divorced*, then the date of the divorce should be included as well as an indication of whether the divorce was the first one or not. Finally, if the marital status is *single* an indication of whether the person has an independent residency or not should be given.

18. Give a sample assignment to a variable of the type defined in the previous exercise, setting its fields to some appropriate values.

4

Developing Programs
with Proofs of Correctness

4.1 Introduction

As we stressed in Chapter 1, a complex programming problem should not be analyzed immediately in terms of the detailed facilities of a particular programming language, for then the number of details that the programmer has to deal with at once is beyond the bounds of his intellectual capabilities, and may lead to inappropriate global decisions. At the early stages of solving a complex problem, attention should be directed mainly toward the global problems, and one should pay little attention to specific details. This first draft of the solution should be expressed in terms natural to the problem itself and formulated in a higher-level, quite possibly natural, language. Because of this, such a formulation is called an *abstract algorithm* and its constituents are called *abstract statements* and *abstract data*. An abstract algorithm expresses only the general strategy for solving the problem together with the general structure of the solution yet to be developed.

From an abstract algorithm, program development proceeds in refinement steps. In each refinement step, abstract statements and abstract data are decomposed in such a way that the representation obtained is expressed more directly in terms of the program and data structuring facilities of the chosen programming language. Thus we can say that each refinement step leads to a program on a lower level of abstraction. This process is continued until the point is reached where the whole program is represented in the given programming language, i.e., when we have developed a specific program. If one views the stepwise decomposition of the problem and the simultaneous development and refinement of the program as a gradual progression to greater and greater depth, then it can be characterized as the top-down approach to problem solving. This development process leads to a program with an inherently clear structure and it is important that the target programming language allows us to express clearly this emerging program structure.

Even though the development process must be guided by the available facilities of the programming language, the notation natural to the problem should be used as long as possible and decisions regarding details of particular computer and programming language representation should be postponed until they are really necessary. This approach results in programs which are easier to adapt to changes in languages or computers, where different specific details of representation may be necessary.

Each refinement step implies a number of design decisions based upon a set of design criteria. Among these criteria are efficiency, storage economy, clarity and regularity of structure. The programmer should be conscious of the decisions involved and should critically examine and reject solutions, even if they are correct as far as the final result of executing the algorithm is concerned. Various aspects of design alternatives should be weighed in the light of these design criteria. In particular, at some stage it may become clear that earlier decisions were inappropriate and so must be reconsidered, possibly anulling a number of decisions made in the later stages of program development. This process of *back-up* may even send us back to the very first draft of the solution. The process of back-up will be illustrated in the development of an algorithm for sorting arrays by merging in Section 4.3.

The examples that follow are chosen with the aim of demonstrating the above described method of stepwise program development. Other examples of program development will show up throughout the rest of the book.

One of the advantages of program development by stepwise refinement is that it leads to programs with a high degree of modularity. This means that the whole program is expressed in terms of a relatively small number of abstract primitives (modulues), which appear in the program in different contexts. Such a program can be easily adapted to changes in its objectives. It is usually possible to perform this modification by changing the global program structure, and retaining most of the modules in terms of which the original solution was built. Even if some modules have to be changed, the elegant structure typical of programs developed in the top-down manner helps to isolate these modules and determine what changes are necessary. We shall see an example of this at the end of Section 4.3.

Another important feature of stepwise program refinement is that it can go hand in hand with the proof of correctness. Observe that the program proofs exhibited so far are fairly laborious in spite of the simplicity of the chosen examples. Thus direct line-by-line application of proof techniques is out of the question when we deal with large programs. Yet it is precisely for large programs that proofs of correctness are most needed. The solution lies in developing a proof of correctness level-by-level together with the program. At each level of abstraction, a proof of correctness of that level is given on the assumption that further refinements to the next lower level of abstraction preserve the desired correctness criteria. We start with the first, most abstract version of the program, and prove its correctness, on the assumption that the abstract statements and operations in terms of which this program is written are refined correctly. Since abstract programs are much shorter than the real ones, proofs of their correctness are consequently easier and less tedious. In the next step we apply the same approach to the abstract statements, and so on, until we reach the level where each operation is expressed in the chosen programming language. Each section in this chapter will give at least one example of the co-ordinated development of proof and program.

4.2 Squares and Palindromes

To illustrate the technique of developing a top-down proof of correctness along with the top-down construction of an algorithm we first consider a relatively simple example: finding numbers whose squares are palindromes. A palindrome is a sequence of characters which reads the same from both ends. English palindromes include 'radar', while '1', '232' and '121' are number palindromes. Both '1' and '121' are also squares. More precisely, suppose we are to list all integers between 1 and N whose squares have a decimal representation which is a palindrome. We base our algorithm on the fact that it is easier to test palindromes than squares. Thus the algorithm generates each square and checks whether the decimal representation is a palindrome. The first, most abstract, program draft has the following form:

$$n := 0; \tag{1}$$
$$\textbf{repeat } n := n + 1;$$
$$\quad \textit{generate square};$$
$$\quad \textbf{if } \textit{decimal representation of square}$$
$$\quad\quad \textit{is a palindrome } \textbf{then } \textit{write}(n)$$
$$\textbf{until } n = N$$

Before we embark on the correctness proof of (1), we perform one more step in program development, refining the abstract statements in (1) into a form closer to the chosen programming language. In order to do that, we have to introduce auxiliary variables which represent the result of one step of computation and the argument of the successive step. Inspection of (1) clearly indicates that we need the following variables:

i. A variable s which holds the value of the computed square

ii. An array variable d to hold the decimal representation of s. Thus the decimal representation of s will have the form:

$d[L]$ ... $d[1]$ where L is the number of computed digits, also a variable.

iii. A Boolean variable p which holds the result of the test for the palindrome property.

With the above conventions (1) may be refined to the following form:

$$
\begin{aligned}
&n := 0; \hspace{5cm} (2)\\
&\textbf{repeat } n := n + 1;\\
&\qquad s := n * n;\\
&\qquad d := \textit{decimal representation of } s;\\
&\qquad p := \textit{d is a palindrome};\\
&\qquad \textbf{if } p \textbf{ then } \textit{write}(n)\\
&\textbf{until } n = N
\end{aligned}
$$

The two abstract statements in (2) which are still to be refined are $d :=$ *decimal representation of s* and $p := d$ *is a palindrome*. But (2) is sufficiently precise to allow us to formulate criteria under which these two abstract statements should be refined.

Consider first the statement $d :=$ *decimal representation of s*. Before execution of this statement the relation $s = n^2$ certainly holds (see (2)). After execution of this abstract statement we must have $n^2 = \sum_{k=1}^{L} d[k] *$ 10^{k-1}, which says that the decimal representation of n^2 is $d[L]$ ... $d[1]$. In addition to that, we require that $d :=$ *decimal representation of s* does not affect the value of n, for obvious reasons.

Consider now the abstract statement $p := d$ *is a palindrome*. This statement should be refined in such a way that it does not affect values of the variables n, d and L. Without this requirement the algorithm (2) would not make any sense. This requirement, in particular, means that $p := d$ *is a palindrome* should be refined in such a way that it leaves the relation $n^2 = \sum_{k=1}^{L} d[k] * 10^{k-1}$ invariant. Furthermore, if p is *true* after execution of $p := d$ *is a palindrome*, then $d[L]$ ... $d[1]$ must indeed be a palindrome.

Formally, we require that after execution of $p := d$ *is a palindrome*, the relation $p \equiv \forall k((1 \leqslant k < (L + 1)/2) \supset (d[k] = d[L - (k - 1)]))$ holds. Observe that k and $L - (k - 1)$ are symmetric subscripts of d. Also, $(L + 1)/2$ is the subscript of the middle element of the array d, if it has one, i.e., if L is odd. Note that if the length L of d is odd (and this includes the case $L = 1$), the middle digit $d[i]$ for $i = (L + 1)/2$, is—so to speak—automatically symmetric, and so need not be checked in the predicate p.

Suppose now that the statements $d :=$ *decimal representation of s* and $p :=$ *d is a palindrome* are refined in such a way that the above criteria are satisfied.

Then we can prove that the algorithm (2) is correct, i.e., that whenever n is printed, the following relations hold:

$$1 \leqslant n \leqslant N \tag{3}$$

$$n^2 = \sum_{k=1}^{L} d[k] * 10^{k-1}$$

$$\forall k \left(\left(1 \leqslant k < \frac{L+1}{2} \right) \supset (d[k] = d[L - (k - 1)]) \right).$$

This simply says that every printed number is less than or equal to N and that the decimal representation of its square is a palindrome.

We also have to show that if a number is not printed, the decimal representation of the square is not a palindrome. In order to prove this, it suffices to prove that $p \equiv \forall k((1 \leqslant k < (L + 1)/2) \supset (d[k] = d[L - (k - 1)]))$ holds whenever, in the process of program execution, the conditional **if** p **then** $write(n)$ is reached—and to see that it must be reached for every n with $1 \leqslant n \leqslant N$. Thus if $\neg p$ at that point, (the number will not be printed), we conclude that $\neg \forall k((1 \leqslant k < (L + 1)/2) \supset (d[k] = d[L - (k - 1)]))$, i.e., d is not a palindrome.

In order to prove the above, consider (2) annotated with appropriate relations (these will, in fact, be proved to be invariants).

$$n := 0; \tag{4}$$

repeat $\{0 \leqslant n < N\}$

$\quad n := n + 1;$

$\quad \{1 \leqslant n \leqslant N\}$

$\quad s := n * n;$

$\quad \{(1 \leqslant n \leqslant N) \wedge (s = n^2)\}$

$\quad d := decimal\ representation\ of\ s;$

$\quad \left\{ (1 \leqslant n \leqslant N) \wedge \left(n^2 = \sum_{k=1}^{L} d[k] * 10^{k-1} \right) \right\}$

$\quad p := d\ is\ a\ palindrome;$

$\quad \left\{ (1 \leqslant n \leqslant N) \wedge \left(n^2 = \sum_{k=1}^{L} d[k] * 10^{k-1} \right) \wedge \right.$

$\quad\quad \left. (p \equiv \forall k((1 \leqslant k < (L + 1)/2) \supset (d[k] = d[L - (k - 1)]))) \right\}$

$\quad$**if** p **then** $\left\{ (1 \leqslant n \leqslant N) \wedge \left(n^2 = \sum_{k=1}^{L} d[k] * 10^{k-1} \right) \wedge \right.$

$\quad\quad\quad \left. \forall k((1 \leqslant k < (L + 1)/2) \supset (d[k] = d[L - (k - 1)])) \right\}$

$\quad\quad write(n)$

$\quad\quad \{1 \leqslant n \leqslant N\}$

until $n = N$

$\{n = N\}$

The previously stated requirements for correct refinement of $d := decimal$ $representation$ of s and $p := d$ is a $palindrome$ are now formulated as:

$$\{(1 \leqslant n \leqslant N) \wedge (s = n^2)\} \tag{5}$$

$$d := decimal\ representation\ of\ s$$

$$\left\{(1 \leqslant n \leqslant N) \wedge \left(n^2 = \sum_{k=1}^{L} d[k] * 10^{k-1}\right)\right\}$$

$$\left\{(1 \leqslant n \leqslant N) \wedge \left(n^2 = \sum_{k=1}^{L} d[k] * 10^{k-1}\right)\right\} \tag{6}$$

$$p := d\ is\ a\ palindrome$$

$$\left\{(1 \leqslant n \leqslant N) \wedge \left(n^2 = \sum_{k=1}^{L} d[k] * 10^{k-1}\right) \wedge (p \equiv \forall k((1 \leqslant k < (L+1)/2)\right.$$

$$\left. \supset (d[k] = d[L - (k-1)])))\right\}.$$

If we assume that (5) and (6) are true, then the proof of correctness of (4) is straightforward. In fact, careful inspection of (4) should be convincing enough.

So the next step is to refine $d := decimal\ representation\ of\ s$ and $p := d\ is\ a$ $palindrome$ in such a way that (5) and (6) hold.

$d := decimal\ representation\ of\ s$ is refined as follows:

$$L := 0; \tag{7}$$
$$\textbf{repeat } L := L + 1;$$
$$d[L] := s \textbf{ mod } 10;$$
$$s := s \textbf{ div } 10$$
$$\textbf{until } s = 0$$

Suppose that S_1, S_2, S_3 are such that

$$\{P_1\}\ S_1\ \{P_2\} \tag{8}$$

$$\{P_2\}\ S_2\ \{P_3\} \tag{9}$$

and

$$\{P_4\}\ S_3\ \{P_5\} \tag{10}$$

while

$$P_3 \supset P_4 \tag{11}$$

Then we may deduce that

$$\{P_3\}\ S_3\ \{P_5\} \tag{12}$$

and it then follows that

$$\{P_1\}\ S_1; S_2; S_3\ \{P_5\} \tag{13}$$

It will often be convenient to summarize the argument in the following form:

$$\{P_1\} \tag{14}$$
$$S_1$$
$$\{P_2\}$$
$$S_2$$
$$\{P_3\}$$
$$\text{implies}$$
$$\{P_4\}$$
$$S_3$$
$$\{P_5\}.$$

Therefore

$$\{P_1\}\ S_1\ ;S_2\ ;S_3\ \{P_5\} \tag{15}$$

Let us apply this in the proof that (7) is correct. It is obvious that (7) leaves the relation $1 \leqslant n \leqslant N$ invariant. In order to complete the proof of (5) recall that $x = (x\ \textbf{div}\ y) * y + \textbf{mod}\ y$ holds for every pair (x,y) of natural numbers. Proof of (7) now relies on the following steps:

$$\left\{ n^2 = s * 10^L + \sum_{k=1}^{L} d[k] * 10^{k-1} \right\} \tag{16}$$

$$L := L + 1$$

$$\left\{ n^2 = s * 10^{L-1} + \sum_{k=1}^{L-1} d[k] * 10^{k-1} \right\}$$

$$\text{implies}$$

$$\left\{ n^2 = (s\ \textbf{div}\ 10) * 10^L + (s\ \textbf{mod}\ 10) * 10^{L-1} + \sum_{k=1}^{L-1} d[k] * 10^{k-1} \right\}$$

$$d[L] := s\ \textbf{mod}\ 10$$

$$\left\{ n^2 = (s\ \textbf{div}\ 10) * 10^L + \sum_{k=1}^{L} d[k] * 10^{k-1} \right\}$$

$$s := s\ \textbf{div}\ 10$$

$$\left\{ n^2 = s * 10^L + \sum_{k=1}^{L} d[k] * 10^{k-1} \right\}.$$

Thus we have the loop-invariant

$$\left\{ n^2 = s * 10^L + \sum_{k=1}^{L} d[k] * 10^{k-1} \right\}$$

for

$$\textbf{begin}\ L := L + 1;\ d[L] := s\ \textbf{mod}\ 10;\ s := s\ \textbf{div}\ 10\ \textbf{end}$$

Now certainly

$$\{s = n^2\} \tag{17}$$

$$L := 0$$

$$\left\{ n^2 = s * 10^L + \sum_{k=1}^{L} d[k] * 10^{k-1} \right\}$$

while

$$\left(n^2 = s * 10^L + \sum_{k=1}^{L} d[k] * 10^{k-1} \right) \wedge (s \neq 0) \tag{18}$$

implies

$$n^2 = s * 10^L + \sum_{k=1}^{L} d[k] * 10^{k-1}$$

and

$$\left(n^2 = s * 10^L + \sum_{k=1}^{L} d[k] * 10^{k-1} \right) \wedge (s = 0) \tag{19}$$

implies

$$n^2 = \sum_{k=1}^{L} d[k] * 10^{k-1}.$$

(16)–(19) imply

$$\{s = n^2\} \; L := 0; \tag{20}$$
$$\textbf{repeat } L := L + 1;$$
$$d[L] := s \textbf{ mod } 10;$$
$$s := s \textbf{ div } 10$$
$$\textbf{until } s = 0 \left\{ n^2 = \sum_{k=1}^{L} d[k] * 10^{k-1} \right\}$$

Since we have already observed that (7) does not affect the relation $1 \leqslant n \leqslant N$, the proof that the refinement (7) of $d := decimal\ representation\ of\ s$ satisfies (5) is completed.

Let us now refine $p := d\ is\ a\ palindrome$ as follows:

$$i := 1; j := L; \tag{21}$$
$$\textbf{repeat } p := d[i] = d[j];$$
$$i := i + 1; j := j - 1$$
$$\textbf{until } (i \geqslant j) \vee \neg p$$

That the relation $(1 \leqslant n \leqslant N) \wedge \left(n^2 = \sum_{k=1}^{L} d[k] * 10^{k-1} \right)$ is not affected by (21) is obvious. It remains to be proved that

$$\{true\}\ p := d\ is\ a\ palindrome\ \{p \equiv \forall k((1 \leqslant k < (L+1)/2) \supset$$
$$(d[k] = d[L - (k-1)]))\} \tag{22}$$

The proof of (22) proceeds as follows so long as $L > 1$:

$$\{true\} \tag{23}$$
$$i := 1; j := L$$
$$\{(i < j) \wedge (j = L - (i - 1)) \wedge \forall k((1 \leqslant k < i) \supset (d[k] = d[L - (k - 1)]))\}$$
$$p := d[i] = d[j]$$
$$\{(i < j) \wedge (j = L - (i - 1)) \wedge (p \equiv \forall k((1 \leqslant k \leqslant i) \supset (d[k]$$
$$= d[L - (k - 1)])))\}$$
$$i := i + 1; j := j - 1$$
$$\{(j = L - (i - 1)) \wedge (p \equiv \forall k((1 \leqslant k < i) \supset (d[k] = d[L - (k - 1)])))\}$$

But we also have

$$(j = L - (i - 1)) \wedge (p \equiv \forall k((1 \leqslant k < i) \supset (d[k]$$
$$= d[L - (k - 1)]))) \wedge \neg(i \geqslant j) \wedge p \tag{24}$$
$$\text{implies}$$
$$(i < j) \wedge (j = L - (i - 1)) \wedge \forall k((1 \leqslant k < i) \supset (d[k] = d[L - (k - 1)]))$$

while

$$(j = L - (i - 1)) \wedge (p \equiv \forall k((1 \leqslant k < i) \supset (d[k]$$
$$= d[L - (k - 1)]))) \wedge ((i \geqslant j) \wedge \neg p) \tag{25}$$
$$\text{implies}$$
$$(p \equiv \forall k((1 \leqslant k < (L + 1)/2) \supset (d[k] = d[L - (k - 1)])))$$

(22) follows from (23)–(25) applying appropriate proof rules. The reader should supply the missing treatment for $L = 1$.

4.3 Sorting Arrays and Files

In this section we develop a number of algorithms for sorting the components of an array or file in ascending order. We first develop an algorithm for sorting an array by selection, and develop the corresponding proof of correctness. The remaining algorithms are developed without proof of correctness. We first show how to sort an array by merging those subarrays that are already correctly ordered. We then show how to sort files by merging. We first develop an algorithm that uses 3 files and then—to illustrate the adaptability afforded by the modularity of a program obtained by top-down design—we modify the algorithm to increase efficiency by using a fourth file.

Sorting Arrays by Selection

Let us be given an array A with index bounds 1 to N, and scalar components. Our sorting task is to *permute* the elements of the array so that at the end of the algorithm, we have $A[1] \leqslant A[2] \leqslant \cdots \leqslant A[N]$. We say that the array is *sorted* when the ordering holds. The algorithm we now develop rests on viewing A as partitioned into two sections $A[1 \, . . \, i-1]$ and $A[i \, . . \, N]$, where $A[1 \, . . \, i-1]$ denotes the elements $A[1], \ldots, A[i-1]$ and $A[i \, . . \, N]$, the elements $A[i], \ldots, A[N]$. At the start of the algorithm the section $A[1 \, . . \, 0]$ is empty—and thus sorted!—while $A[1 \, . . \, N]$ is possibly unsorted. Thus, for $i = 1$, the partition $A[1 \, . . \, i-1]$ is sorted, and in each step of the algorithm we extend this sorted partition by one element (increase i), and shorten the partition $A[i \, . . \, N]$ by one element. At the end of the algorithm, the partition $A[i \, . . \, N]$ is empty. This means that the whole array is sorted.

The immediate question is thus how to accomplish the basic step of the algorithm: extending the partition $A[1 \ldots i-1]$ by one array element and shortening the partition $A[i \ldots N]$ by one array element. Of course, the only operation we are allowed to perform upon the array is permutation of its elements, i.e., the resulting array must be the same as the original one, up to the permutation of its elements. So in each step of the algorithm we permute the elements of the partition $A[i \ldots N]$ in such a way that the smallest element of this partition is put in $A[i]$, and then move $A[i]$ to the other block. We thus start from the following first draft of the algorithm:

for $i := 1$ **to** $N - 1$ **do**

permute values of $A[i \, . . \, N]$ to put smallest in $A[i]$.   (1)

Upon completion of the above **for** loop the array $A[1 \, . . \, N]$ will be sorted, i.e., the following must hold:

$$\forall p,q((1 \leqslant p < q \leqslant N) \supset (A[p] \leqslant A[q])). \qquad (2)$$

Let us describe the desired state of computation of (1) before the ith step in (1) is executed. The section $A[1 \, . . \, i-1]$ would be sorted, i.e., the assertion $P([1 \, . . \, i))$ holds, where

$$P([1 \, . . \, i)) \quad \text{is} \quad \forall p,q((1 \leqslant p < q < i) \supset (A[p] \leqslant A[q]). \qquad (3)$$

The array A is partitioned in two parts: $A[1 \, . . \, i-1]$ and $A[i \, . . \, N]$ in such a way that each element in the partition $A[i \, . . \, N]$ is greater than or equal to any element of the partition $A[1 \, . . \, i-1]$, i.e., the assertion $Q([1 \, . . \, i))$ holds where:

$$Q([1 \, . . \, i)) \quad \text{is} \quad \forall p,q((1 \leqslant p < i \leqslant q \leqslant N) \supset (A[p] \leqslant A[q])). \qquad (4)$$

This desired state of computation may be expressed by the following diagram:

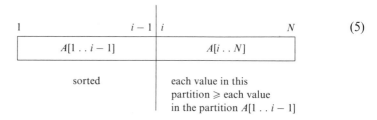

(5)

Since $[1 \mathinner{\ldotp\ldotp} i + 1) = [1 \mathinner{\ldotp\ldotp} i]$, we see that (3) and (4) yield the definitions

$$P([1 \mathinner{\ldotp\ldotp} i]) \quad \text{is} \quad \forall p,q((1 \leqslant p < q \leqslant i) \supset (A[p] \leqslant A[q])) \qquad (6)$$

$$Q([1 \mathinner{\ldotp\ldotp} i]) \quad \text{is} \quad \forall p,q((1 \leqslant p \leqslant i < q \leqslant N) \supset (A[p] \leqslant A[q])) \qquad (7)$$

Now if we refine the instruction to *permute values of A[i .. N] to put smallest in A[i]*, by just permuting values of the array section $A[i \mathinner{\ldotp\ldotp} N]$, this will not affect $P([1 \mathinner{\ldotp\ldotp} i))$ and $Q([1 \mathinner{\ldotp\ldotp} i))$. Furthermore, the assertion:

$$M([i \mathinner{\ldotp\ldotp} N]) \text{ is } \forall q((i \leqslant q \leqslant N) \supset (A[i] \leqslant A[q])) \qquad (8)$$

should hold upon execution of this abstract statement ($A[i]$ is the smallest element of the array section $A[i \mathinner{\ldotp\ldotp} N]$). In other words, we will obtain the situation shown in (9).

Now observe that:

$$P([1 \mathinner{\ldotp\ldotp} i)) \wedge Q([1 \mathinner{\ldotp\ldotp} i)) \supset P([1 \mathinner{\ldotp\ldotp} i]). \qquad (10)$$

$$Q([1 \mathinner{\ldotp\ldotp} i)) \wedge M([i \mathinner{\ldotp\ldotp} N]) \supset Q([1 \mathinner{\ldotp\ldotp} i]). \qquad (11)$$

So we conclude that upon execution of the ith step the state of computation may be described by the diagram (12) below:

Just before *permute values of A[i .. N] to put smallest in A[i]* is executed again (if at all), the state of computation will be again described by (5) since i is increased by 1 in the meantime. Thus if we define:

$$I([1 \mathinner{\ldotp\ldotp} i)) \quad \text{as} \quad P([1 \mathinner{\ldotp\ldotp} i)) \wedge Q([1 \mathinner{\ldotp\ldotp} i)) \qquad (13)$$

and if the abstract statement to *permute the values of A[i . . N] to put the smallest in A[i]* is refined in such a way that

$$\{(1 \leqslant i \leqslant N) \wedge I([1 \ . \ . \ i))\} \ \textit{permute values of } A[i \ . \ . \ N] \qquad (14)$$
$$\textit{to put smallest in } A[i] \ \{I([1 \ . \ . \ i])\}$$

then according to the proof rule for the **for** statement we conclude that:

$$\{I([\ ])\} \ \textbf{for} \ i := 1 \ \textbf{to} \ N - 1 \ \textbf{do} \qquad (15)$$
$$\textit{permute values of } A[i \ . \ . \ N]$$
$$\textit{to put smallest in } A[i] \ \{I([1 \ . \ . \ N])\}$$

Observe that $I([\ ]) = I([1 \ . \ . \ 1))$ is true since in $P([1 \ . \ . \ i))$, $(1 \leqslant p < q < 1)$ is always *false* and in $Q([1 \ . \ . \ i))$, $(1 \leqslant p < 1)$ is always *false*. In fact $I([\ ]) = I([1 \ . \ . \ 1))$ describes the initial state of the array A which is obtained from (5) setting $i = 1$:

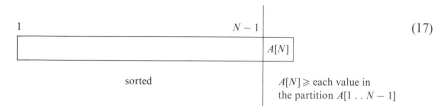

1 N (16)

possibly unsorted array

The section $A[1 \ . \ . \ i - 1]$ is empty, and thus trivially sorted, and the section $A[i \ . \ . \ N]$ is the whole array so that trivially each value in this section $\geqslant$ each value in the partition $A[1 \ . \ . \ i - 1]$. Furthermore, $I([1 \ . \ . \ N - 1])$ means that the array section $A[1 \ . \ . \ N - 1]$ is sorted and that $A[N]$ is greater than any element of the array section $A[1 \ . \ . \ N - 1]$. This follows from (6) and (7). So $I([1 \ . \ . \ N - 1])$ implies (2), and we conclude that (1) is correct if the abstract statement *permute values of A[i . . N] to put the smallest in A[i]* is refined in such a way that (14) holds. In fact $I([1 \ . \ . \ N - 1])$ means that the array A looks like this:

1 $N - 1$ (17)

$A[N]$

sorted $A[N] \geqslant$ each value in
                                  the partition $A[1 \ . \ . \ N - 1]$

which simply means that the whole array is sorted. Thus our task now is to refine the abstract statement *permute values of A[i . . N] to put smallest in A[i]* in such a way that (10) holds. Consider the following:

$$m := i; \qquad\qquad\qquad\qquad\qquad (18)$$
$$\textbf{for} \ j := i + 1 \ \textbf{to} \ N \ \textbf{do}$$
$$\textbf{if} \ A[j] < A[m] \ \textbf{then} \ m := j;$$
$$\textit{exchange } A[i] \textit{ and } A[m]$$

Now clearly (18) does not affect the array section $A[1 .. i - 1]$, so that $P([1 .. i))$ remains invariant over the program part (18). Since (18) only permutes elements of the array section $A[i .. N]$, we conclude that $Q([1 .. i))$ is also unaffected by (18). Of course, we assume that *exchange $A[i]$ and $A[m]$* is refined in such a way that it does not cause any undesired side effects. If it does just what it is supposed to, i.e., if it exchanges the values of $A[i]$ and $A[m]$, then this won't affect $P([1 .. i))$ and $Q([1 .. i))$. So upon completion of (18) $P([1 .. i))$ and $Q([1 .. i))$ hold, and what remains to be proved is that at that point $M([i .. N])$ holds, since then

$$P([1 .. i)) \wedge Q([1 .. i)) \wedge M([i .. N]) \supset I([1 .. i]) \tag{19}$$

and thus (14) is established.

Consider the **for** statement in (18) and let

$$R([i + 1 .. j)) \text{ be } \forall q((i \leqslant q < j) \supset (A[m] \leqslant A[q])). \tag{20}$$

Observe that $R([i + 1 .. i + 1))$ reduces to $A[m] \leqslant A[i]$ which certainly holds after the assignment $m := i$, i.e., just before the **for** loop in (18) is executed.

$$\{true\} \; m := i \; \{R([i + 1 .. i + 1))\}. \tag{21}$$

Since $R([i + 1 .. i + 1)) = R([\;))$, we prove

$$\{R([\;))\} \; \textbf{for } j := i + 1 \textbf{ to } N \textbf{ do} \tag{22}$$
$$\textbf{if } A[j] < A[m] \textbf{ then } m := j \; \{R([i + 1 .. N])\}.$$

But if $R([i + 1 .. N])$ holds before the exchange operation, then $M([i .. N])$ should hold after it, i.e., the abstract statement *exchange $A[i]$ and $A[m]$* should be refined in such a way that

$$\{R([i + 1 .. N])\} \; exchange \; A[i] \; and \; A[m] \; \{M([i .. N])\}. \tag{23}$$

The obvious refinement

$$t := A[i]; \; A[i] := A[m]; \; A[m] := t \tag{24}$$

clearly satisfies (23).

So let us prove (22). According to the proof rule of the **for** statement we have to prove

$$\{R([i + 1 .. j))\} \; \textbf{if } A[j] < A[m] \textbf{ then } m := j \; \{R([i + 1 .. j])\}. \tag{25}$$

(25) is established using the proof rule of the **if-then** statement and observing that

$$\{R([i + 1 .. j)) \wedge (A[j] < A[m])\} \; m := j \; \{R([i + 1 .. j])\} \tag{26}$$
$$R([i + 1 .. j)) \wedge \neg(A[j] < A[m]) \supset R([i + 1 ... j]).$$

Sorting Arrays by Merging

In this section, we give an example of designing a program and then backing up when we find that the program draft is not correct.

Suppose now that we have a sequence of records

$$r_1, r_2, \ldots, r_n \tag{27}$$

of the type

$$\textbf{type } rec = \textbf{record } key: keytype; \qquad\qquad (28)$$
$$\{\text{other components}\}$$
$$\textbf{end}$$

and suppose that *keytype* is linearly ordered—any scalar or subrange type would do. For such keyed records, the task of *sorting* consists of permuting the elements of the sequence (1) in such a way that the resulting sequence $r_{p1}, r_{p2}, \ldots, r_{pn}$ satisfies the property:

$$r_{p1} \cdot key \leqslant r_{p2} \cdot key \leqslant \cdots \leqslant r_{pn} \cdot key \qquad\qquad (29)$$

where $a \leqslant b$ means $(a < b) \vee (a = b)$, as usual.

There are, of course, many ways of approaching this problem, but a particularly natural one starts with the observation that any sequence like (27) is, in fact, partially sorted, to a lesser or higher degree. Indeed, (27) is a sequence of ordered subsequences $r_i, \ldots, r_j$, where

$$r_k \cdot key \leqslant r_{k+1} \cdot key \quad \text{for} \quad k = i, \ldots, j-1 \qquad\qquad (30)$$
$$r_{i-1} \cdot key > r_i \cdot key \quad \text{or} \quad i = 1$$
$$r_j \cdot key > r_{j+1} \cdot key \quad \text{or} \quad j = n$$

A sequence $r_i, \ldots r_j$ which satisfies (30) is called a *run*. So a run is a maximal ordered subsequence. For example, suppose that *keytype* is *integer*. If we disregard the information associated with a key, since it affects the sorting algorithm only to the extent that it is moved together with the key, then in (31) runs are underlined by a single arrow.

$$\underset{\rightarrow}{43} \quad \underset{\longrightarrow}{18 \quad 21 \quad 30} \quad \underset{\longrightarrow}{13 \quad 52} \quad \underset{\longrightarrow}{51 \quad 75 \quad 80} \quad \underset{\rightarrow}{62} \qquad\qquad (31)$$

A special case of (30) occurs when $i = 1$ and $j = n$, which means that the whole sequence (27) is a run, i.e., it is sorted. And this is precisely what we have to achieve. If the given sequence has only two runs, then we can merge these two runs into a single run by repeated comparison and selection of the smaller element of the two runs. For example, given runs

$$18 \quad 21 \quad 30 \qquad\qquad (32)$$
$$13 \quad 52$$

we may merge them into a single run as follows

$$13 \quad \begin{cases} 18 \\ 52 \end{cases} \quad 21 \quad 30 \qquad\qquad (33)$$

$$13 \quad 18 \quad \begin{cases} 21 \\ 52 \end{cases} \quad 30$$

$$13 \quad 18 \quad 21 \quad \begin{cases} 30 \\ 52 \end{cases}$$

$$13 \quad 18 \quad 21 \quad 30 \quad \begin{cases} \\ 52 \end{cases}$$

$$13 \quad 18 \quad 21 \quad 30 \quad 52$$

Suppose now that two runs are given as arrays x and y of respective type **array** $[1 \ .. \ m]$ **of** *rec* and **array** $[1 \ .. \ n]$ **of** *rec*. Then the result of merging these two runs will be an array z of type **array** $[1 \ .. \ m + n]$ **of** *rec*, and the algorithm that performs this operation is given in (34).

$$i := 1; j := 1; k := 1; \tag{34}$$

while $(i \leqslant m) \wedge (j \leqslant n)$ **do**
begin if $x[i] \ . \ key \leqslant y[j] \ . \ key$ **then**
  begin $z[k] := x[i]$;
    $k := k + 1; i := i + 1$
  end
  else
  begin $z[k] := y[j]$;
    $k := k + 1; j := j + 1$
  end
end;
append tail of x-run;
append tail of y-run.

Observe that the repeated selection of the smaller element of the runs x and y exhausts one of them, and the remaining part of the nonempty run must be copied at the end of the created run z. The refinements of the abstract statements *append tail of x-run* and *append tail of y-run* are given in (35) and (36) respectively.

$$\{append \ tail \ of \ x\text{-}run\} \tag{35}$$

while $i \leqslant m$ **do**
begin $z[k] := x[i]$;
  $k := k + 1; i := i + 1$
end

$$\{append \ tail \ of \ y\text{-}run\} \tag{36}$$

while $j \leqslant n$ **do**
begin $z[k] := y[k]$;
  $k := k + 1; j := j + 1$
end

Analysis of the special case presented above hopefully gives the reader a better feel for the general problem we want to solve. The general strategy now emerges from the analysis of the above two special cases (one run and two runs). The essence of it is that we have to merge longer and longer runs until we finally have two runs which, when merged, give a sorted sequence. But in order to apply this strategy, we need two sources (input sequences) of runs which are merged into longer runs forming the output sequence. Now from this output sequence we have to form two sequences of runs, and repeat the merging process, and so on. Since we are initially given a single sequence, we can subdivide this sequence into two sequences of runs, merge them into a single sequence, and repeat the step. We observe that the algorithm then consists of repeating a basic step which consists of two actions: distribution and merging. Thus the abstract algorithm we are talking about has the following form:

$$\textbf{repeat } distribute\ runs; \qquad\qquad (37)$$
$$merge\ runs$$
$$\textbf{until }\quad one\ run$$

and it can be graphically represented as follows:

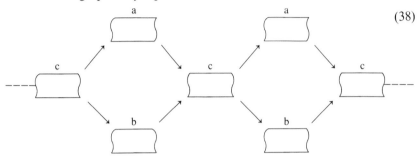

Sequences can be represented in several ways: as arrays, as lists, or as files. Further development of the ideas behind the abstract algorithm (37) crucially depends upon the data representation for sequences. In this subsection, we assume that sequences are represented as arrays, as above. In the next subsection, we discuss the problem of sorting files using this approach, while the problem of sorting lists will be left to the reader as an exercise in Chapter 6, after the Pascal list structures have been introduced.

So if we have an array a of type **array** $[1 . . n]$ **of** rec, where rec is defined in (28), and we want to sort it using the strategy (37), then the fact that we can easily access *any* array element becomes very important. Rather than distributing the sequence a into two sequences, we realize that we can actually pick runs from both sides of the array a. Both ends are easily accessible, and then reading the array from both ends inwards, we obtain two input sequences of runs. So the distribution of initial runs comes for free. The question is where we deposit the merged runs. Remembering from (38) that the merge and distribution operations alternate, we deposit the merged runs into another array a' of the same type as the array a, and we do it in such a way that the actions of depositing a new run at the left-hand side of the array a' and at the right-hand side alternate. This process is illustrated by the sequence (39) of integer keys, in which we see that a and a' alternate roles as the process continues:

$$
\begin{array}{lcccccccccc}
a & 43 & 18 & 21 & 30 & 13 & 52 & 51 & 75 & 80 & 62 & \qquad(39)\\
a' & 43 & 62 & 80 & 13 & 51 & 52 & 75 & 30 & 21 & 18 \\
a & 18 & 21 & 30 & 43 & 62 & 75 & 80 & 52 & 51 & 13 \\
a' & 13 & 18 & 21 & 30 & 43 & 51 & 52 & 62 & 75 & 80 \\
a & 13 & 18 & 21 & 30 & 43 & 51 & 52 & 62 & 75 & 80
\end{array}
$$

In the diagram (39), runs are denoted by arrows indicating the direction in which the array is scanned. During the sorting process runs are transported from a to a', and then from a' to a as illustrated by (40).

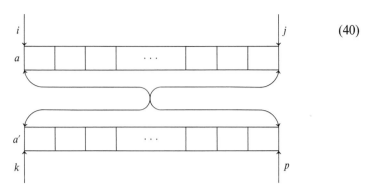

In order to indicate two access points of these arrays, we need two pairs (i, j) and (k, p) of integer variables. We also need an integer variable m which denotes the number of runs merged. In addition to that, a Boolean variable *up* will denote the direction in which the array elements are transported, i.e., *up* will be *false* if we are transporting elements from a to a' and *true* if the direction is reversed. With these conventions we obtain the abstract algorithm (41).

$$up := false;\qquad\qquad\qquad\qquad\qquad\qquad\qquad\qquad (41)$$

> **repeat** *initialize* i, j, k *and* p;
> $\quad m := 0$; {number of runs merged}
> $\quad$ *merge runs from* i *and* j *to* k
> $\quad$ *and* p;
> $\quad up := \neg up$ {reverse direction}
> **until** $m = 1$;
> **if** *up* **then** *copy* a' *to* a

If it is acceptable that the result of the sorting process may be left in either a or a', then the last statement in (12) is not necessary.

By now we realize that we have departed considerably from the initial strategy outlined in (37) and represented in (38). The essential difference is that the operation of merging and distribution are now combined, and so figure (42) is the graphical representation of the sorting process defined by the algorithm we are developing. This is an example of *recasting the top-down design* as we proceed towards the details of implementation.

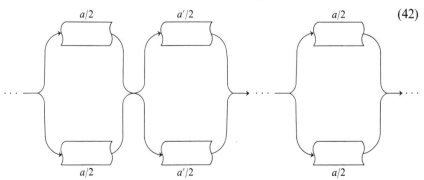

(42)

Since the distribution operation is in effect avoided as a separate step, the number of copying operations required in each step of the algorithm is reduced by half, and thus the efficiency of the algorithm is considerably improved.

It follows from the above that we in fact do not need two arrays. An array A of type **array** $[1 .. 2 * n]$ **of** *rec* will suffice, if we represent the array a by the first half of A (indexes $1 .. n$) and the array a' by the second half of A (indexes $n + 1 .. 2 * n$). With this convention the abstract statement *initialize i, j, k and p* is refined to:

$$\{initialize\ i, j,\ k\ and\ p\} \tag{43}$$
if *up* **then**
begin $i := 1; j := n;$
          $k := n + 1; p := 2 * n$
end
else
begin $k := 1; p := n;$
          $i := n + 1; j := 2 * n$
end

Consider now the abstract statement *merge runs from i and j to k and p*. This statement will be expressed as a repetitive statement in which the basic action of each repetition step is merging a run. In doing this, elements are taken from the access points determined by i and j. The destination alternates between the points determined by k and p. Thus if in one repetition step the destination is determined by k, in the next repetition it will be determined by p. But it is possible that k denotes the destination at all times, if we exchange the values of k and p after the operation of merging a run is performed (i.e., before the next repetition step). But then the increment must alternate between $+1$ and -1. We introduce an additional variable h whose value will represent the current increment, and this leads to the refinement (44) of the abstract statement *merge runs from i and j to k and p*.

$$\{merge\ runs\ from\ i\ and\ j\ to\ k\ and\ p\} \tag{44}$$
$h := 1;$
repeat *merge one run from i and*
          j to k;
          $h := -h;$
          $m := m + 1;$
          exchange k and p
until $i = j$

Refinement of the abstract statement *exchange k and p* requires an auxiliary variable t, and is given in (45).

$$\{exchange\ k\ and\ p\} \tag{45}$$
$$t := k; k := p; p := t$$

Refinement of the abstract statement *merge one run from i and j to k* is very similar to (34). We repeatedly compare the keys of the incoming records (the records at the access points i and j), select the lesser one and transport it to $A[k]$, stepping up appropriate indexes. Every time we perform this, we test whether the end of the run is reached. The value of the Boolean variable *eor* will hold the result of this test. This process is continued until the end of one of the runs is reached. After that, the tail of the remaining nonempty run is copied to the destination. We thus obtain the following refinement. Recall that $h = +1$ or $h = -1$ as we alternate the direction of merging in consecutive runs.

$$\{merge\ one\ run\ from\ i\ and\ j\ to\ k\} \qquad (46)$$
repeat if $A[i]\ .\ key < A[j]\ .\ key$ **then**
    begin $A[k] := A[i];$
        $i := i + 1;$
        $eor := A[i - 1]\ .\ key > A[i]\ .\ key$
    end
    else
    begin $A[k] := A[j];$
        $j := j - 1;$
        $eor := A[j + 1]\ .\ key > A[j]\ .\ key$
    end;
    $k := k + h$
until *eor*;
append tail of i-run;
append tail of j-run

The reader should inspect it carefully to see if it is correct. (46) is designed in such a way that the appending operation has no effect if the tail is empty. Because of that, the use of the **while-do** statement rather than the **repeat-until** statement is cruical in the refinements (47) and (48) of the abstract statements *append tail of i-run* and *append tail of j-run* respectively.

$$\{append\ tail\ of\ i\text{-}run\} \qquad (47)$$
while $A[i]\ .\ key \leqslant A[i + 1]\ .\ key$ **do**
begin $A[k] := A[i];$
    $k := k + h; i := i + 1$
end

$$\{append\ tail\ of\ j\text{-}run\} \qquad (48)$$
while $A[j]\ .\ key \leqslant A[j - 1]\ .\ key$ **do**
begin $A[k] := A[j];$
    $k := k + h; j := j - 1$
end

However, the developed form of (46)–(48), although simple and natural, is *not quite correct*. One reason for that is that when a run in (46) is exhausted, the corresponding pointer (i or j) is moved to the first element of the next run. Thus (47) or (48) will copy that run to the current destination, and the corresponding pointer will be moved to the next run etc. So the algorithm certainly does not do what it is supposed to, as an attempted proof would show. We have to *back up* and consider (46) again.

The modification of (46) which is called for consists of replacing the unconditional increase of the pointer to the source (i or j) by a conditional increase of that pointer, i.e., by increase of that pointer only if the end of run is not yet reached. If it is, the Boolean variable *eor* (end of run) is set to *true*. So we obtain the following new refinement of the abstract statement *merge one run from i and j to k*.

repeat if $A[i]$. $key < A[j]$. key **then**   (46a)
$\qquad$ **begin** $A[k] := A[i]$;
$\qquad\qquad$ **if** $A[i]$. $key > A[i + 1]$. key **then** $eor := true$
$\qquad\qquad$ **else** $i := i + 1$
$\qquad$ **end**
$\qquad$ **else** $A[k] := A[j]$;
$\qquad\qquad$ **if** $A[j]$. $key > A[j - 1]$. key **then** $eor := true$
$\qquad\qquad$ **else** $j := j - 1$;
$\qquad$ $k := k + h$
until *eor*
append tail of i-run
append tail of j-run

Now the problem which made us change (46) to (46a) is solved, but the algorithm is still not correct. It still does not handle properly the fairly frequent situation, illustrated by the first line in (39), in which the runs 13 52 and 52 51 overlap. With *merge one run from i and j to k* as refined in (46a), the refinements (47) and (48) of *append tail of i-run* and *append tail of j-run* respectively have to be modified in order to prevent double copying of the elements of the overlapping run in the middle of the array. What we have to prevent is crossing of the pointers i and j. This observation leads to the following modifications of (47) and (48):

$\qquad$ {*append tail of i-run*}   (47a)
$\qquad$ **while** $(A[i]$. $key \leqslant A[i + 1]$. $key) \wedge (i < j)$ **do**
$\qquad$ **begin** $A[k] := A[i]$;
$\qquad\qquad$ $k := k + h; i := i + 1$
$\qquad$ **end**

$\qquad$ {*append tail of j-run*}   (48a)
$\qquad$ **while** $(A[j]$. $key \leqslant A[j - 1]$. $key) \wedge (i < j)$ **do**
$\qquad$ **begin** $A[k] := A[j]$;
$\qquad\qquad$ $k := k + h; j := j - 1$
$\qquad$ **end**

The only statement in the abstract algorithm (41) still to be refined is *copy a to a′*. Its refinement (49) is very straightforward indeed.

$\qquad$ **for** $i := n + 1$ **to** $2 * n$ **do** $a[i - n] := a[i]$ (49)

Sorting Files by Merging

Suppose now that the sequence which we have to sort is represented as a file. Let it be given as the value of the variable c declared as:

$$\textbf{var } c \colon \textbf{file of } rec \qquad\qquad (50)$$

where rec was defined in (28). The properties of this data representation differ greatly from the properties of the array representation. These differences will affect the development of the sort merge algorithm to be presented in this subsection. Another difference comes from the following: If we have four files (which often means four tapes), then we can merge runs from two of them (input tapes) and distribute them to the other two (output tapes). In the next step we switch the input and the output tapes. This approach would then be very similar to the approach chosen in the development of the algorithm presented in the previous subsection. But we assume here that we do not want to pay the price of the fourth tape. With only three tapes a, b, and c, the sorting process will be less efficient. It will correspond to diagram (38). In the next subsection we study how to modify our algorithm to make use of a fourth tape.

If we assume that a, b, and c are variables of type **file of** rec, and that the initial sequence is given as the value of the variable c, the abstract algorithm which we are looking for takes the form (51)

$$
\begin{aligned}
&\textbf{repeat } rewrite(a);\ rewrite(b);\ reset(c); \qquad (51)\\
&\qquad distribute\ runs;\\
&\qquad reset(a);\ reset(b);\ rewrite(c);\\
&\qquad n := 0;\ \{\text{number of runs merged}\}\\
&\qquad merge\ runs\\
&\textbf{until } n = 1
\end{aligned}
$$

In (51) n is an integer variable. The idea is that the *merge runs* algorithm is to increment n by one each time it merges a run from the a file with a run from the b file to get a run on the c file, or when a run is copied onto the c file from the a file or the b file. Thus, on completion of *merge runs*, n will be the number of runs on the c file. Hence, sorting is complete if and only if $n = 1$ at this stage.

Consider now the abstract statement *distribute runs*. Its task is to distribute evenly the runs from c to a and b. Its refinement is given in (52).

$$
\begin{aligned}
&\{distribute\ runs\} \qquad\qquad (52)\\
&\textbf{repeat } copy\ run\ from\ c\ to\ a;\\
&\qquad \textbf{if } \neg eof(c)\ \textbf{then}\\
&\qquad\quad copy\ run\ from\ c\ to\ b\\
&\textbf{until } eof(c)
\end{aligned}
$$

The abstract statement *copy run from c to a* will simply consist of a loop in which the next record of *c* is copied to *a* until the end of the current run on *c* is reached. So we get the following:

$$\{copy\ run\ from\ c\ to\ a\} \tag{53}$$
repeat *copy record from c to a;*
   test end of c-run
until *end of c-run*

The abstract statement *copy run from c to b* is refined likewise.

The abstract components of the algorithm (53) are very simple to refine. We postpone that for later, and attack the problem of the refinement of the crucial operation of the whole algorithm: *merge runs*. This statement is refined as a loop in which a run is merged from *a* and *b* and deposited into *c*. This merge run operation is repeated until the end of *a* or *b* is reached. At that point the loop is terminated, and the remaining runs of the input file whose end has not been reached yet are copied to *c*. So we get (54)

$$\{merge\ runs\} \tag{54}$$
repeat *merge one run from*
   a and b to c;
   $n := n + 1$
until $eof(a) \vee eof(b);$
copy rest of a-runs;
copy rest of b-runs

And now remembering (46), we refine the abstract statement *merge one run from a and b to c* as

$$\{merge\ one\ run\ from\ a\ and\ b\ to\ c\} \tag{55}$$
repeat if $a\uparrow\ .\ key < b\uparrow\ .\ key$ **then**
   begin *copy record from a to c;*
     test end of a-run
   end
   else
   begin *copy record from b to c;*
     test end of b-run
   end
until *end of a-run* $\vee$ *end of b-run;*
copy tail of a-run;
copy tail of b-run

Refinement of the abstract statements *copy tail of a-run* and *copy tail of b-run* is parallel to (47) and (48):

$$\{copy\ tail\ of\ a-run\} \tag{56}$$
while $\neg$ *end of a-run* **do**
begin *copy record from a to c;*
   test end of a-run
end

$$\{copy\ tail\ of\ b\text{-}run\} \qquad\qquad (57)$$
while $\neg end\ of\ b\text{-}run$ **do**
begin *copy record from b to c*;
        test end of b-run
end

Now we go back to (54) and refine the abstract statements *copy rest of a-runs* and *copy rest of b-runs*. These refinements are given in (58) and (59) respectively.

$$\{copy\ rest\ of\ a\text{-}runs\} \qquad\qquad (58)$$
while $\neg eof(a)$ **do**
begin repeat *copy record from a to c*;
         test end of a-run
    until *end of a-run*;
    $n := n + 1$
end

$$\{copy\ rest\ of\ b\text{-}runs\} \qquad\qquad (59)$$
while $\neg eof(b)$ **do**
begin repeat *copy record from b to c*;
         test end of b-run
    until *end of b-run*;
    $n := n + 1$
end

Note that (54), (58) and (59) do indeed update n in the fashion specified by our discussion immediately following (51). At this point the whole algorithm is expressed in terms of the abstract primitives of the form:

$$copy\ record\ from\ x\ to\ y \qquad\qquad (60)$$

$$test\ end\ of\ x\text{-}run \qquad\qquad (61)$$

$$end\ of\ x\text{-}run \qquad\qquad (62)$$

where x and y are file variables. Refinement of these abstract primitives is straightforward. If we introduce an auxiliary variable *buf* of type *rec*, then (60) is refined in (63)

$$\{copy\ record\ from\ x\ to\ y\} \qquad\qquad (63)$$
read(x, buf);
write(y, buf)

In order to refine (61) we introduce a Boolean variable *eorx* (end of x-run), so that for the whole program we need three Boolean variables: *eora*, *eorb*, *eorc*. Then the refinement of (61) is given in (64), and the refinement of the abstract expression (62) is given in (65).

$$\{test\ end\ of\ x\text{-}run\} \qquad\qquad (64)$$
if $eof(x)$ **then** $eorx := true$
else $eorx :\Rightarrow buf\ .\ key > x{\uparrow}\ .\ key$
    $\{end\ of\ x\text{-}run\} \qquad\qquad (65)$
    eorx

Observe that (64) is designed on the basis of the observation that the end of a run can be reached if either the end of the file is reached $(eof(x))$, or the key of the incoming file record is smaller than the key of the last record read in $(buf . key > x\uparrow . key)$. Rather than writing the conditional statement in (64) one would perhaps, *hope* to do it more simply as:

$$eorx := eof(x) \vee (buf . key > x\uparrow . key) \qquad (66)$$

but that would be wrong. If $eof(x)$ is true, then evaluation of the expression $eof(x) \vee (buf . key > x\uparrow . key)$ leads to access to a nonexisting variable $x\uparrow . key$, and so (64) is really the only way of doing the test.

Bringing in an Extra File

Note the high degree of modularity achieved in the design of the above algorithm for sorting file entries by merging. The whole algorithm is essentially expressed in terms of the abstract primitives (60), (61) and (62). In order to illustrate the adaptability of a program designed with a high degree of modularity we modify the file sort algorithm to take advantage of a fourth tape. We try to modify the previous algorithm in such a way that it makes use of the fourth tape so that merging and distribution of runs are performed at the same time. When runs are merged from a and b, the resulting runs are distributed to c and d. In the next pass, runs are merged from c and d and distributed to a and b, and so on. So we have two input tapes and two output tapes, and if a and b are input tapes in one pass, then they become the output tapes in the next pass. This way a separate distribution step before every merge operation is avoided. If we do not take into account the first distribution which is still necessary, then we can say that this approach reduces the number of copying operations by 50%. Thus the program becomes considerably more efficient.

If we assume that the initial file given is c, then the abstract algorithm (51) of the previous section gets modified in the following way:

$$\begin{aligned}
&rewrite(a); rewrite(b); reset(c); &&(67)\\
&\textit{distribute runs};\\
&\textbf{repeat } n := 0;\\
&\qquad reset(a); reset(b); rewrite(c); rewrite(d);\\
&\qquad \textit{merge runs from a and b to c and d};\\
&\qquad \textbf{if } n \neq 1 \textbf{ then}\\
&\qquad \textbf{begin } rewrite(a); rewrite(b); reset(c); reset(d);\\
&\qquad\qquad \textit{merge runs from c and d to a and b}\\
&\qquad \textbf{end}\\
&\textbf{until } n = 1
\end{aligned}$$

The module *distribute runs* remains unchanged, but the previous module *merge runs from a and b to c* now clearly has to be modified to obtain the

module *merge runs from a and b to c and d*. The same strategy of changing
the global program structure and retaining the previous modules if possible
will be applied in this case as well, and so we get the following:

$$\{\textit{merge runs from a and b to c and d}\} \tag{68}$$
repeat *merge one run from a and b to c*;
    $n := n + 1$;
    if $\lnot(\textit{eof}(a) \lor \textit{eof}(b))$ **then**
    begin *merge one run from a and b to d*;
        $n := n + 1$
   end
until $\textit{eof}(a) \lor \textit{eof}(b)$;
copy rest of a-runs;
copy rest of b-runs

    The module (55), *merge one run from a and b to c* (and consequently the
module *merge one run from a and b to d*), does not require any changes.
However, the modules *copy tail of a-runs* (56) and *copy tail of b-runs* (57)
clearly have to be modified, since the destination to which the remaining runs
are sent should alternate between c and d, if we want to achieve even distribution of runs. In modifying these modules we again attempt to retain the original modules and change the global structure. This leads to the following:

$$\{\textit{copy rest of a runs}\} \tag{69}$$
while $\lnot \textit{eof}(a)$ **do**
begin repeat *copy record from a to c*;
         test end of a-run
    until *end of a-run*;
    $n := n + 1$;
    if $\lnot \textit{eof}(a)$ **then**
    begin repeat *copy record from a to d*;
          test end of a-run
      until *end of a-run*;
        $n := n + 1$
   end
end

This completes the modification process.

4.4 Manipulating Sets

The Sieve of Eratosthenes

A *prime* number is an integer p greater than 1 with the property that the only
divisors of p are 1 and p itself. For example, 2, 3, 5, 7 and 11 are primes, but
4, 6, 9 and 10 are not. Any number greater than 1 can be written as a product

of the primes that divide it. For example $7 = 7$ while $420 = 2 \cdot 2 \cdot 3 \cdot 5 \cdot 7$. The *sieve of Eratosthenes* is an efficient algorithm for generating all primes less than or equal to the given natural number N. The basic idea of this algorithm is quite simple. We start with the set of numbers which are greater than 1 and less than or equal to N. Let this set be represented by a set variable *sieve*. Then numbers which are multiples of other numbers are gradually removed ("sifted out") from the sieve until at the end the sieve contains precisely the primes $\leqslant N$. (We use *multiple* for $k * p$ with $k \neq 1$.)

The following notation will be convenient in stating the formal requirements which the algorithm must satisfy:

$[2 \mathinner{\ldotp\ldotp} k]$—the set of integers between 2 and k inclusive, as before;

primes $([2 \mathinner{\ldotp\ldotp} k])$—the set of all primes up to and including k.

With the above notation the desired *end result* of the algorithm may be formulated as:

$$sieve = primes([2 \mathinner{\ldotp\ldotp} N]) \tag{1}$$

The algorithm is designed in such a way that two essential properties remain invariant throughout the process of removal of nonprimes from the sieve. The first property is that a prime is never removed from the sieve, i.e.,

$$primes([2 \mathinner{\ldotp\ldotp} N]) \leqslant sieve \tag{2}$$

The second property is that the sieve contains only numbers from the range 2 to N, i.e.,

$$sieve \leqslant [2 \mathinner{\ldotp\ldotp} N] \tag{3}$$

Since we do not want the sieve to contain any even numbers greater than 2, it is initialized to $[2] + [n \,|\, (n \textbf{ in } [2 \mathinner{\ldotp\ldotp} N]) \wedge odd(n)]$, with all multiples of 2 already gone from the sieve. So the first prime whose multiples should be removed from the sieve is 3. Having done that, we remove all multiples of 5, the next prime after 3, and so on. Let p be the prime whose multiples are to be removed next from the sieve. At that point multiples of primes less than p have already been removed from the sieve. We show that the sifting process may stop as soon as $p^2 > N$, by showing that any $s \in sieve$ must then be a prime.

Suppose, by way of contradiction, that s is not a prime. Then s may be factored into prime factors. Let q be its smallest prime factor. Then $q^2 \leqslant s$ must hold (s must be representable as a product of at least two primes, q being less than or equal to each one of them). By assumption, $s \in [2 \mathinner{\ldotp\ldotp} N]$, i.e., $s \leqslant N$. Thus if $p^2 > N$, we have:

$$q^2 \leqslant s \leqslant N < p^2 \tag{4}$$

which implies $q \leqslant p - 1$. Since q is a prime less than p, its multiples, s in particular, have—by assumption—already been removed from the sieve. So $p^2 > N$ and $s \in sieve$ but $s \notin primes([2 \mathinner{\ldotp\ldotp} N])$ leads to a contradiction and we conclude that $s \in sieve$ implies $s \in primes([2 \mathinner{\ldotp\ldotp} N])$. In other words, $p^2 > N$ implies

$$sieve \leqslant primes([2 \mathinner{\ldotp\ldotp} N]) \tag{5}$$

which, together with the invariant property (2) of the algorithm, gives the desired result (1).

The abstract version of the desired algorithm given in (6) is constructed on the basis of the above considerations. In (6) $sift(p)$ denotes the operation of removing all multiples of p from the sieve, where p is an integer variable.

$$sieve := [2] + [n \,|\, (n \text{ in } [2 .. N]) \wedge odd(n)]; \tag{6}$$

$$p := 3;$$

while $p^2 \leqslant N$ **do**

begin $sift(p);$

$\qquad p := next \ prime \ after \ (p)$

end

Before we prove correctness of the above program, let us introduce the following notation:

$sifted(q)$—all multiples of q have been removed from the sieve
$sifted([2 .. p))$—all multiples of any prime less than p have been removed from the sieve.

After initialization of the variables $sieve$ and p, (2) and (3) hold, and in addition:

$$sifted([2 .. p)) \tag{7}$$

holds in view of the fact that the sieve contains 2 and all odd numbers up to N. 2 is the only prime less than the current value of p (which is 3), and no odd number is a multiple of 2, hence (7).

Assume now that the operation $sift(p)$ is refined in such a way that the relations:

$$primes([2 .. N]) \leqslant sieve \tag{8}$$

$$sieve \leqslant [2 .. N]$$

$$sifted([2 .. p))$$

are preserved. By this we mean that if (8) holds before $sift(p)$ is executed, it will also hold after it is executed. In addition to this, let us also assume that after $sift(p)$ is executed:

$$sifted(p) \tag{9}$$

holds. (8) and (9) now define precisely how the operation $sift(p)$ should be refined and together represent the correctness criterion of $sift(p)$. If we assume that $sift(p)$ is refined in such a way that the above criteria are satisfied, and that $p := next \ prime \ after \ (p)$ is refined in such a way that it does not affect the value of the variable $sieve$, we can prove that the algorithm in (6) is correct.

Note that we have already proved:

$$(primes([2 .. N]) \leqslant sieve \leqslant [2 .. N]) \wedge sifted([2 .. p)) \wedge (p^2 > N) \tag{10}$$

$$\text{implies}$$

$$sieve = primes([2 .. N]).$$

With this in mind all we have to prove is that (8) is invariant over the loop in (6), or more precisely, that if (8) and $p^2 \leqslant N$ hold before the body of the loop is executed, (8) will hold after its execution.

By the previously made assumption, (8) and (9) will hold after $sift(p)$ if (8) holds before it. Now

$$sifted([2 \ldots p)) \wedge sifted(p) \tag{11}$$

implies

$$sifted([2 \ldots next\ prime\ after\ (p))).$$

Indeed, let q be a prime less than $next\ prime\ after\ (p)$. If $q \leqslant p - 1$, then $sifted(q)$ holds because of $sifted([2 \ldots p))$. If $q = p$, then $sifted(q)$ follows from $sifted(p)$. The situation

$$p < q \leqslant next\ prime\ after\ (p) - 1$$

is impossible since q is a prime. So (11) is indeed a valid inference. But if $sifted([2 \ldots next\ prime\ after\ (p)))$ holds before $p := next\ prime\ after\ (p)$ is executed, then $sifted([2 \ldots p))$ must hold upon execution of this assignment.

If this assignment does not affect the value of the variable $sieve$ (this is one of the assumptions that we made), then clearly it does not affect (8) and (9). So we conclude that if (8) and $p^2 \leqslant N$ hold before the body of the loop in (6) is executed, (8) will hold upon completion of its execution. But then appealing to the verification rule of the **while-do** statement, we conclude that (8) and $p^2 > N$ will hold upon termination of the loop. By (10) we conclude that at that point the correctness criterion $sieve = primes([2 \ldots N])$ is satisfied.

The condition $p^2 \leqslant N$ comes essentially into the picture if we want to show how to compute the next prime after p in the context of the body of the loop.

Recall that before $p := next\ prime\ after\ (p)$ is executed

$$primes([2 \ldots N]) \leqslant sieve \leqslant [2 \ldots N] \tag{12}$$
$$sifted([2 \ldots next\ prime\ after\ (p)))$$
$$p^2 \leqslant N$$

holds. Denote by p' the smallest element of the sieve which is greater than p. Then we can prove that (12) implies

$$next\ prime\ after\ (p) = p' \tag{13}$$

Indeed first of all we have $p < p'$ and $p' \in sieve$. Since $primes([2 \ldots N]) \leqslant sieve$

$$p < p' \leqslant next\ prime\ after\ (p) \tag{14}$$

must hold. To establish that in fact $p' = next\ prime\ after\ (p)$ in (14), it is sufficient to prove that p' is prime. Suppose that it was not. Then it can be factored into primes—let r be the smallest prime factor of p', so that $r \leqslant p'$ holds. Suppose that $r < p'$ holds. If so, then from (14) and $sifted([2 \ldots (next\ prime\ after\ (p)))$ follows that $sifted(r)$ holds, which contradicts the assumption that p' is in the sieve and is not a prime. Thus we conclude that p' must be

equal to its smallest prime factor, i.e., that it is a prime. This by (14) implies
(13). To show that $p' \in sieve$ is in fact *true*, we have to appeal to a result in
number theory which says that there is always a prime between p and p^2.
The desired conclusion then follows from $p^2 \leqslant N$. So we get the following
refinement of the abstract statement $p := next\ prime\ after\ (p)$:

$$\textbf{repeat } p := succ(p) \textbf{ until } \neg p \textbf{ in } sieve \qquad (15)$$

The next step is to refine the operation $sift(p)$. At that, (8), which holds
before $sift(p)$ is executed, must hold upon completion of execution of $sift(p)$.
At that point (9) must also hold.

The operation $sift(p)$ consists of generation of multiples of p and their
removal from the sieve. This process may be efficiently designed on the basis
of the following reasoning. $(p > 2) \wedge odd(p)$ holds before $sift(p)$. Also,
$sifted([2 .. p))$ holds at that point. $(p > 2) \wedge sifted([2 .. p))$ implies $sifted(2)$.
This means that all even multiples of p are already gone from the sieve, and so
it remains to remove only odd multiples of p. At that, the first number to be
removed is $p * p$, since all multiples of all primes less than $p - 1$ have been
removed. The latter follows from $sifted([2 .. p))$. So the sequence of
numbers to be generated and removed from the sieve is

$$p * p, p * (p + 2), \ldots$$

or

$$p^2, p^2 + 2p, \ldots$$

The termination condition for this process is the same as in (6). So we
have the following proposal for refinement of the operation $sift(p)$:

$$\begin{aligned}
&step := p + p; \qquad\qquad\qquad\qquad\qquad\qquad\qquad\qquad\qquad (16)\\
&s := p * p;\\
&\{(s \textbf{ mod } 2p = p) \wedge\\
&\forall s' \textbf{ in } sieve * [2 .. (s - 1)]((p\ divides\ s') \supset (p = s'))\}\\
&\textbf{while } s \leqslant N \textbf{ do}\\
&\textbf{begin } sieve := sieve - [s];\\
&\qquad s := s + step\\
&\textbf{end}
\end{aligned}$$

The program (16) has not been annotated by all invariants, but just with those
which will require some proving. Other obvious loop invariants are:

$$s \geqslant 2 \qquad\qquad\qquad (17)$$
$$odd(p)$$
$$p > 2.$$

In fact, $p > 2$ and $odd(p)$ are invariants of the whole program (16).

Let us now prove that $s \textbf{ mod } 2p = p$ and $\forall s' \in sieve * [2 .. (s - 1)]((p$
$divides\ s') \supset (p = s'))$ hold after execution of $s := p * p$. First observe that
since p is odd, $(p * p) \textbf{ mod } 2p = p$ must hold. Indeed, $p = (2k + 1)$ (for
some k) implies $p * p = (2k + 1)(2k + 1) = 2k(2k + 1) + 2k + 1 = 2kp + p$

and hence $(p * p) \bmod 2p = p$ is immediate. This implies that after the assignment $s := p * p$, the relation $s \bmod 2p = p$ will hold.

To prove that:

$$\forall s' \in sieve * [2 \ldots (s - 1)]((p \text{ divides } s') \supset (p = s')) \tag{18}$$

holds after the assignment $s := p * p$, we prove

$$sifted([2 \ldots p)) \wedge (p > 2) \tag{19}$$

implies

$$\forall s' \in sieve * [2 \ldots (p * p - 1)]((p \text{ divides } s') \supset (p = s')).$$

Let $s' \in sieve * [2 \ldots (p^2 - 1)]$ and p divide s', but suppose that s' is not a prime. If so, then s' may be factored into primes—let r be its smallest prime factor. Then $r^2 \leqslant s'$, which together with $s' < p^2$ give $r^2 < p^2$ by transitivity. This implies $r \leqslant p - 1$. Now $sifted(r)$ follows from $sifted([2 \ldots p))$ contradicting the assumption that r is a prime factor of s' different from s. Hence $r = s'$, i.e., s' is a prime. But if s' is a prime, then p divides s' implies $p = s'$, which completes the proof of (19). The relation $s \bmod 2p = p$ is invariant over the loop in (16) since $s \bmod 2p = p$ implies $(s + 2p) \bmod 2p = p$. Thus if $s \bmod 2p = p$ holds before the assignment $s := s + step$ the same relation will hold after it.

It remains to be proved that (19) holds after execution of the loop in (16). To put it simply, the new values of $sieve$ and s, which are $sieve - [s]$ and $s + step$ respectively, must satisfy the relation (19). Since before the assignments $sieve := sieve - [s]$; $s := s + step$ (19) holds, we prove that it implies $s' \in (sieve - [s]) * [2 \ldots (s + 2p - 1)]((p \text{ divides } s') \supset (p = s'))$. But if the last relation holds before $sieve := sieve - [s]$; $s := s + step$, then (19) will hold after these assignments. So let us prove that in the context of (19) the following holds:

$$\forall s \in sieve * [2 \ldots (s - 1)]((p \text{ divides } s') \supset (p = s')) \tag{20}$$

implies

$$\forall s \in (sieve - [s]) * [2 \ldots (s + 2p - 1)]((p \text{ divides } s') \supset (p = s')).$$

Let $(s' \in (sieve - [s])) \wedge (s' \leqslant s + 2p - 1) \wedge (p \text{ divides } s')$. Since $s = s'$ is impossible because $s' \in (sieve - [s])$, either $s' < s$ or $s' > s$. If $s' < s$ then $p = s'$ follows from the antecedent in (20), i.e., from (19). If $s' > s$ then we have $s < s' \leqslant s + 2p - 1$, i.e., $s < s' < s + 2p$. Since p divides both s and s', it must be that $s' = s + p$. Now recall that $s \bmod 2p = p$ holds in the context in which we want (20) to hold. $s' = s + p$ and $s \bmod 2p = p$ imply $s' \bmod 2p = 0$, i.e., 2 divides s'. $sifted([2 \ldots p)) \wedge (2 \text{ divides } s') \wedge (p > 2)$ implies $(2 = s')$, which contradicts $s' > s \geqslant 2$ (see (17)). So the case $s' > s$ is impossible. This completes the proof of (20).

It now becomes clear that $sift(p)$ as refined in (16) does not affect the relations (8). Indeed, in $sieve := sieve - [s]$, s satisfies $s \bmod 2p = p$, which means that for some $k \geqslant 0$, $s = (2k + 1)p$ holds. So s is not a prime. This means that $sift(p)$ affects the value of the variable *sieve* only to the extent that it removes nonprimes from it. Removal of a nonprime from the sieve clearly does not affect the relation (8).

It still remains to be proved that upon completion of execution of $sift(p)$, $sifted(p)$ holds. This follows from

$$(s > N) \land (sieve \geqslant [2 .. N]) \land$$

$$\forall s' \in sieve * [2 .. (s - 1)]((p \; divides \; s') \supset (p = s')). \quad (21)$$

It is sufficient to prove that (21) implies $sieve * [2 .. (s - 1)] = sieve$. $sifted(p)$ then follows from $\forall s' \in sieve * [2 .. (s - 1)]((p \; divides \; s') \supset (p = s'))$. But if $s > N$ then $[2 .. N] \leqslant [2 .. (s - 1)]$. Now $sieve \leqslant [2 .. N] \leqslant [2 .. (s - 1)]$ implies $sieve * [2 .. (s - 1)] = sieve$.

Refinement of the abstract statement $sieve := [2] + [n | (n \; \textbf{in} \; [2 .. N]) \land odd(n)]$ still remains to be made. One way of doing it is:

$$sieve := [2]; n := 3; \quad\quad\quad\quad\quad (22)$$
$$\textbf{while } n \leqslant N \textbf{ do}$$
$$\textbf{begin } sieve := sieve + [n];$$
$$n := n + 2$$
$$\textbf{end}$$

We have to prove that upon completion of (22), $sieve = [2] + [n | (n \; \textbf{in} \; [2 .. N]) \land odd(n)]$ but that proof is left to the reader.

Finding the Coarsest Partition of a Set

We now present the systematic development of an algorithm for set manipulation, but this time we omit the proof of correctness. The problem starts with the following as given: a set S, a function $f : S \rightarrow S$, and a collection $B_1, \ldots, B_p$ of subsets of S which are pairwise disjoint, i.e., $B_i \cap B_j = [\;]$ for $i \neq j$. The task is to find a collection of pairwise disjoint subsets $E_1, E_2, \ldots, E_q$ of S which satisfies the following requirements:

   i. Each E_i is a subset of some B_j (23)

   ii. If $a \in E_k$ and $b \in E_k$ for some k then $f(a) \in E_j$ and $f(b) \in E_j$ for some j

   iii. Any collection of pairwise disjoint subsets of S which satisfies the requirements (i) and (ii) has at least as many sets as the collection $E_1, \ldots, E_q$.

Collections like $B_1, \ldots, B_p$ and $E_1, E_2, \ldots, E_q$ are called *partitions* of the set S. Each set in such a collection is called a *block*. The partition $E_1, E_2, \ldots, E_q$ is said to be compatible with $B_1, \ldots, B_p$ and f.

One obvious way of solving the above problem consists of examining the values $f(a)$ for a in some block B_i. Then two elements a and b of B_i are placed into the same block (or subblock of B_i) if and only if $f(a)$ and $f(b)$ belong to the same block B_j. This process is repeated for each B_i until no further division of blocks into subblocks is possible. For example, let $S = [1,2, \ldots ,n]$, $f : S \rightarrow S$ be defined as $f(i) = i + 1$ for $1 \leqslant i < n$ and $f(n) = n$, and let the initial partition consist of two blocks $B_1 = [1,2, \ldots , n - 1]$ and $B_2 = [n]$. In the first pass we partition $[1,2, \ldots , n - 1]$ into $[1,2, \ldots , n - 2]$ and $[n - 1]$. This requires $n - 1$ evaluations of f, since each element of B_1 must be tested. Progressing further this way we end up with the partition $[1]$, $[2]$, $[3]$, $\ldots$, $[n - 1]$, $[n]$.

Although the above method is certainly acceptable, it is not particularly satisfactory. Indeed, in dividing a block into two subblocks the effort of performing this partition is proportional to the larger subblock. This is particularly unfortunate when the smaller subblock is much smaller. In the above example we had to perform p tests in order to remove just one element from a partition with p elements. So it pays to try to devise a more efficient partitioning algorithm.

An algorithm in which the effort to divide a block into two subblocks is proportional to the smaller subblock is based on the reasoning which is, in a way, opposite to the one described above. Given a block B_i, we partition each other block B_j in such a way that $B_j = B_j' + B_j''$ where

$$B_j' = \{b \,|\, b \in B_j \text{ and } f(b) \in B_i\} \tag{24}$$

$$B_j'' = \{b \,|\, b \in B_j \text{ and } f(b) \notin B_i\}.$$

If we denote with $f^{-1}(B_i)$ the set $\{b \,|\, f(b) \in B_i\}$, then clearly if $B_j \cap f^{-1}(B_i) = [\ ]$, B_j' is empty. Also, if $B_j \leqslant f^{-1}(B_i)$, then B_j'' is empty. So the partitioning (24) should be applied to those blocks B_j which contain at least one element in $f^{-1}(B_i)$ and one element not in $f^{-1}(B_i)$.

The above analysis suggests several first steps of the development of the desired algorithm. We assume that $S = 1 \ldots n$, although the development that follows applies to any other scalar or subrange type. The partitioning of S will be represented by the variable B of type **array** $[1 \ldots n]$ **of set of** $1 \ldots n$, i.e., B is an array of subsets of S. We assume that the initial partition $B_1, \ldots , B_p$ is given by initializing appropriately the components $B[1], \ldots ,B[p]$ of B. The final partitioning will be $B[1], \ldots ,B[q]$, where q is a variable of type $1 \ldots n$. An additional variable *waitlist* of type **set of** $1 \ldots n$ is also needed. Its value will be the set of indexes of those blocks with respect to which partitioning still remains to be done. Finally, a variable i of type $1 \ldots n$ is also needed, as indicated in the first draft (25) of the algorithm.

$$\begin{aligned}
&\textbf{begin } waitlist := [1 \ldots p]; \hspace{4cm} (25)\\
&\qquad q := p;\\
&\qquad \textbf{while } waitlist \neq [\ ] \textbf{ do}\\
&\qquad \textbf{begin } i := any\ member\ of\ waitlist;\\
&\qquad\qquad waitlist := waitlist - [i];\\
&\qquad\qquad partition\ with\ respect\ to\ B[i]\\
&\qquad \textbf{end}\\
&\textbf{end}
\end{aligned}$$

Of course, the above abstract algorithm tells us nothing about how the actual partitioning is performed. This will be specified in the refinement of the abstract statement: *partition with respect to B[i]*. The analysis given above suggests the following ideas for the refinement of this statement. We first compute the set $f^{-1}(B_i)$, call it *inverse*. Then for any B_j such that $B_j \cap$ *inverse* $\neq [\;]$ and $B_j \not\supseteq$ *inverse* we divide B_j into two blocks: $B_q = B_j \cap$ *inverse* and $B_j = B_j - B_q$. This way every suitable B_j (i.e. such that $B_j \cap$ *inverse* $\neq$ $[\;]$ and $B_j \not\supseteq$ *inverse*) is divided into two blocks, and having performed this division, we have to update *waitlist*. So we get the refinement (26) of the abstract statement *partition with respect to B[i]*, where we must use Pascal notation $*$ instead of $\cap$ for the intersection and $\leqslant$ instead of $\subseteq$ for the subset notation.

$$inverse := f^{-1}(B[i]);$$

$$j := 1; \qquad\qquad\qquad\qquad\qquad\qquad\qquad\qquad (26)$$

repeat if $(B[j] * inverse \neq [\;]) \wedge \neg (B[j] \leqslant inverse)$ **then**
$\qquad$ **begin** $q := q + 1;$
$\qquad\qquad B[q] := B[j] * inverse;$
$\qquad\qquad B[j] := B[j] - B[q];$
$\qquad\qquad$ *update waitlist*
$\qquad$ **end**;
$\qquad j := j + 1$
until $j > q$

An obvious improvement in the efficiency of (26) consists of introducing an additional variable and computing $B[j] * inverse$ only once.

Let us now concentrate on the problem of updating *waitlist* after subdivision of $B[j]$ into two blocks. This is the most delicate operation among the ones still to be refined.

If j was in *waitlist* before we split $B[j]$ according to (26), then clearly q must be added to *waitlist*. It may look as if both q and j should be added to *waitlist* if j was not in *waitlist* before $B[j]$ was split, but in fact that is not the case, as the following argument shows: Suppose that for some k we have, $\forall b \in B_k \; f(b) \in B_j$, and suppose that B_j was split into B'_j and B''_j. So B_k now has to be partitioned with respect to B'_j and B''_j, and we get the following four sets:

$$[b \,|\, b \in B_k \text{ and } f(b) \in B'_j] \qquad\qquad (27)$$
$$[b \,|\, b \in B_k \text{ and } f(b) \notin B'_j]$$
$$[b \,|\, b \in B_k \text{ and } f(b) \in B''_j]$$
$$[b \,|\, b \in B_k \text{ and } f(b) \notin B''_j].$$

Since B_j is a disjoint union of B_j' and B_j'', we conclude that the second and the third sets in (27) are equal, as well as the first and the fourth set in (27). This means that we have to partition B_k with respect to only one of the sets B_j' and B_j'', and we naturally choose the smaller one. So we get the following refinement of the abstract statement *update waitlist*, where we note that (26) has the effect that $j' = q$ while $j'' = j$.

$$\textbf{if } j \textbf{ in } \textit{waitlist} \textbf{ then } \textit{waitlist} := \textit{waitlist} + [q] \qquad (28)$$
$$\textbf{else begin } p := \textit{card}(B[j]) \leqslant \textit{card}(B[q]);$$
$$\textbf{if } p \textbf{ then } \textit{waitlist} := \textit{waitlist} + [j]$$
$$\textbf{else } \textit{waitlist} := \textit{waitlist} + [q]$$
$$\textbf{end}$$

In (28) p is a Boolean variable, and $\textit{card}(B)$ denotes the cardinality of the set B, i.e., the number of elements in B.[1]

In the algorithm (6) of Section 3.7, we showed how the cardinality of a set can be computed, and so refinement of the abstract statement $p := \textit{card}(B[j]) \leqslant \textit{card}(B[q])$ is no problem. But here we show an alternative, faster, way of refining this abstract statement:

$$Bj := B[j]; \; Bq := B[q]; \; x := 1; \qquad (29)$$
$$\textbf{while } (Bj \neq [\;]) \wedge (Bq \neq [\;]) \textbf{ do}$$
$$\textbf{begin while } \neg(x \textbf{ in } Bj) \wedge \neg(x \textbf{ in } Bq) \textbf{ do } x := \textit{succ}(x);$$
$$\textbf{if } x \textbf{ in } Bj \textbf{ then } Bj := Bj - [x]$$
$$\textbf{else } Bq := Bq - [x]$$
$$\textbf{end};$$
$$\textbf{if } Bj = [\;] \textbf{ then } p := \textit{true}$$
$$\textbf{else } p := \textit{false}$$

In (29) Bj and Bq are variables of type **set of** $1 \; .. \; n$, and x is a variable of type $1 \; .. \; n$.

Two abstract statements: $i := \textit{any number of waitlist}$ and $\textit{inverse} := f^{-1}(B[i])$ remain to be refined, but in both cases we know how to do it by Section 3.7 on set types. Pascal does not provide a primitive for picking a random element from a set. So we refine the statement $i := \textit{any number of waitlist}$ in such a way that the first element of waitlist is assigned to i:

$$i := 1; \qquad (30)$$
$$\textbf{while } \neg(i \textbf{ in } \textit{waitlist}) \textbf{ do } i := \textit{succ}(i)$$

[1] In the Zurich implementation of Pascal (CDC 6000 series) *card* is included in the repertoire of standard functions.

And finally, computing the set *inverse* may be accomplished in the following way:

$$inverse := [\ ];$$ (31)
$$\textbf{for } x := 1 \textbf{ to } n \textbf{ do}$$
$$\textbf{if } f(x) \textbf{ in } B[i] \textbf{ then } inverse := inverse + [x]$$

Observe that if Pascal had had a standard (and efficient) primitive for picking the first element of a set (represented as a sequence), that feature would have made the set manipulation algorithms much more satisfactory.

Bibliographic Remarks

The classical reference on structured programming is Dahl, Dijkstra and Hoare (1972). The method of program development by stepwise refinement was originally suggested by Dijkstra. Excellent references on this topic are Wirth (1971), Dijkstra (1972), Wirth (1972) and Wirth (1974b). Useful introductory texts are Conway and Gries (1975) and Conway, Gries and Zimmerman (1976). Our exposition of top-down program design is based on the following sources: The algorithm for sorting arrays by natural merging is adapted from Knuth (1973). The algorithm for sorting files by natural merging is adapted from Wirth (1976). The algorithm for finding the coarsest partition of a set is adapted from Aho, Hopcroft and Ullman (1974).

The idea of developing a program and its proof of correctness together (a constructive approach to the problem of program correctness) appeared in Dijkstra (1968b). The formal approach presented in this book is due to Hoare (1971b). Other related papers are Hoare (1972a) and Hoare (1972b). A proof of correctness of the algorithm 'The Sieve of Eratosthenes' appeared in Hoare (1972b). Two other top-down structured proofs (sort by successive minima and squares and palindromes) are ours. (The program for the problem of squares and palindromes is due to Wirth (1974b), the sorting algorithm is a standard algorithm).

Sources for exercises include Conway, Gries and Zimmerman (1976), Dijkstra (1976), Knuth (1973) and Wirth (1972, 1976).

Exercises

1. The algorithm for sorting arrays by straight insertion is based on the following reasoning: In each step of the algorithm, starting with $i = 2$, the sequence $a_1 a_2 \ldots a_n$ to be sorted is divided into two subsequences: $a_1 \ldots a_{i-1}$ and $a_i \ldots a_n$, where

$a_1 \ldots a_{i-1}$ is already sorted. Every step extends the subsequence $a_1 \ldots a_{i-1}$ and shortens the subsequence $a_i \ldots a_n$ by one element, inserting a_i at the appropriate place in $a_1 \ldots a_{i-1}$. Following this reasoning, develop this algorithm and its proof of correctness in the top-down fashion.

2. In the section on file types an algorithm for merging two sorted files into a single sorted file was given as a finished product. Exhibit the top-down structure of this algorithm and using this structure provide a proof of correctness.

3. The comments in the algorithm for division of nonnegative integers in the positional notation (Section 3.5 (Processing Arrays)) are in fact abstract statements on the higher level of abstraction. Using the top-down structure of this algorithm, as well as the analysis which preceded the presentation of the algorithm, provide its proof of correctness.

4. The algorithm for sorting arrays by merging presented in this chapter is efficient if the array to be sorted tends to be partially sorted. If that's not the case, then the efficiency of the algorithm can be improved by merging runs of fixed, precomputed size. This way frequent tests for end of run are avoided. The basic idea is this: we regard the original array as a sequence of runs of length 1. Merging these runs we obtain runs of length 2. Merging runs of length 2, we obtain runs of length 4, etc. This approach is called straight two-way merge sort. The approach presented earlier is called natural two-way merge sort. Modify the natural two-way merge sort algorithm to obtain a straight two-way merge sort algorithm.

5. Develop a program which updates the file of bank accounts on the basis of the file of transactions, and produces a file of statements. Elements of each of the above three files are records defined as follows:
   i. A bank account record contains the account number and the account balance.
   ii. A transaction record contains the account number, an indication whether the transaction is a deposit or withdrawal, and the transaction amount.
   iii. A statement record contains the account number, the initial balance, the number of deposits and withdrawals, and the final balance.

6. Construct a proof of correctness of the algorithm for finding the coarsest partition of a set, developing this proof through the levels of abstraction.

7. Develop an algorithm for computing the smallest prime factor of a large integer $N > 1$. The algorithm should be developed together with its proof of correctness. Assume that the additive operations and comparisons are very fast compared with arbitrary multiplications and divisions. Here is one proposal for the first draft of the algorithm: Successive primes are investigated in the increasing order of magnitude as possible factors. Since a divisible number has at least one prime factor not exceeding its square root, this search continues in the worst case, until the square of the currently considered prime is greater than N. If this prime is still not a factor of N, then N must be prime.

8. As pointed out before, most implementations of Pascal restrict the size of the base type of a set type. So the algorithms which manipulate sets, presented so far, are all right if the sets are small. The question is then how to represent large sets. One

way of doing it consists of representing a large set as an array of small sets. Using this data representation for sets, modify the algorithm for finding the coarsest partition of a set so that it works for large sets as well.

9. Adapt the algorithm for the sieve of Eratosthenes developed in this chapter so that it works for large sets as well. Provide a proof of correctness of this adapted algorithm.

5
Procedures and Functions

5.1 Procedures and Block Structure

We have seen how to design an algorithm to solve a problem by decomposing the overall problem into precisely specified subproblems and then verifying that if each subproblem is solved correctly, and the solutions are fitted together in a specified way, then the original problem will be solved correctly. In other words, in order to understand an abstract algorithm and prove it correct, we have to know and specify precisely what the abstract statements do, but not how they do it. However, on the lower levels of abstraction, abstract statements are refined into sequences of actual statements of the chosen programming language, at which point we specify how each abstract statement accomplishes its task. Since an abstract statement is denoted by a sequence of symbols which names the action it performs, we can say that, in the process of program development, we associate a sequence of statements with each such name. These named sequences of statements are called *procedures* in Pascal, and the association between a name and a sequence of statements is specified in a procedure declaration. For example, given a procedure *exchange* which, applied to two variables, exchanges their values, we would call it (after it has been declared, of course) simply by listing

$$exchange(a,b)$$

as a line of our program, where a and b are the names of the variables whose values we want exchanged.

The point is that the top-down approach, by its very nature, structures a Pascal program into a set of procedures. In addition to using procedures to define abstract statements, Pascal uses *functions* to define abstract expressions. For example, once we have declared a function *multiply* which applies to two integer variables to return their product, we can use it in building up complex instructions. It could then appear in a statement like

$$c := multiply(a + b, a + b) + a + b$$

where it is used just like the basic operators with which Pascal is equipped.

In short, any step of an algorithm that requires further refinement can be implemented as a subprogram (procedure or function) reference. The internal mechanics of the subprogram can then be deferred until the design of the algorithm at the abstract level is completed and verified. We devote this section to procedures and block structure, turning to Pascal functions in Section 5.3. An example of the simplest form of *procedure declaration* is:

$$
\begin{aligned}
&\textbf{procedure } exchange; \qquad\qquad\qquad\qquad (1)\\
&\textbf{begin } t := x;\\
&\qquad x := y;\\
&\qquad y := t\\
&\textbf{end}
\end{aligned}
$$

A procedure declaration consists of two parts: the procedure heading, which is followed by the procedure body. An example of the simplest (parameter-free) form of a procedure heading is the first line in (1). It consists of the basic symbol **procedure** which is followed by the identifier *exchange*. This identifier names the procedure, and because of that it is called the *procedure identifier*. The *procedure body* in (1) consists of the statements enclosed between **begin** and **end** which determine the action the procedure *exchange* accomplishes.

In order to indicate that the action *exchange* should be performed when a point in a program is reached during its execution, it is sufficient to write the procedure identifier at that point. Such an occurrence of a procedure identifier is called a *procedure statement* or a *procedure call*. We stress again that the concept of procedure allows us to formulate explicitly the top-down program structure, and express it in terms of logically closed components. It can also save memory space and effort in writing a program. Indeed, if the same procedure body is to be executed at various places in a program, then only one copy of it will be present together with procedure calls at those places in the program where this body is needed. The criterion for using a procedure is that it embodies a single action on the upper level of abstraction in program development.

Local and Global Objects

The procedure *exchange* exchanges values of the variables x and y. These two variables, as well as the auxiliary variable t necessary for performing the *exchange* operation, are defined in the environment of the procedure *exchange*, i.e., in the program in which the procedure is declared. Because of that these variables are called *global variables* of the procedure *exchange*. Since the effect of execution of a procedure call is the same as the effect of execution of the corresponding procedure body, we conclude that execution of the call *exchange* changes the environment of the procedure (and the call), in the sense that it changes the values of variables declared in the environment.

A little reflection about the procedure *exchange* leads to the conclusion that this effect upon the values of the variables x and y is exactly what we want. On the other hand, the variable t, as well as its value, are absolutely insignificant *for the environment* of the procedure *exchange*. This variable becomes of interest only when we look into the problem of how to exchange the values of the variables x and y. This clearly indicates that the significance of the variable t should be restricted to the inside of the procedure *exchange*. In other words, the variable t should be declared as a *local variable* of the procedure *exchange*. This declaration, according to the rules of Pascal, is expressed as follows:

$$\text{\textbf{procedure} } exchange; \qquad\qquad\qquad\qquad (2)$$
$$\text{\textbf{var} } t: integer;$$
$$\text{\textbf{begin} } t := x; x := y; y := t \text{ \textbf{end}}$$

The body of procedure *exchange* (lines 2 and 3 of (2)) is an example of a block. As we shall see later, blocks also occur as the body of programs and functions. A *block* consists of a *declaration part* and a *statement part*. The declaration part defines those objects referenced in the statement part which are not defined outside the block. These are called *local* objects—the ones defined in the environment are called *global* objects. The objects can be constants, types, variables, procedures, functions (and, see Chapter 7, labels). The statement part of a block has the structure of a compound statement. It describes the actions performed by the block.

It is sound programming practice to declare every identifier which is not referenced outside the procedure as local to that procedure. It is also convenient and conceptually a logical consequence of the notion of locality that these identifiers should have the 'most local scope'—that is, that they may be freely chosen, without regard to the choice of identifiers that occur in the procedure environment. It then may happen that the same identifier was both chosen as local to a procedure and also declared in its environment. The following example illustrates such a situation:

$$\text{\textbf{var} } x,y: integer; \qquad\qquad\qquad\qquad (3)$$
$$t := integer;$$
$$\text{\textbf{procedure} } exchange;$$
$$\text{\textbf{var} } t: integer;$$
$$\text{\textbf{begin} } t := x; x := y; y := t \text{ \textbf{end}};$$
$$\text{\textbf{begin} } x := 5; y := 3; t := 1;$$
$$exchange;$$
$$\{x = 3, y = 5, t = 1\}$$
$$\text{\textbf{end}}$$

Program (3) has t for two variables—one is declared in the environment of the procedure *exchange*, and the other one is declared as local to this procedure. In spite of the fact that it is the same identifier, it names two different variables, one of which is local to the procedure *exchange* and the other one which is global to it. An occurrence of t within the procedure *exchange* is a reference to the local variable denoted by t. In fact, we cannot refer to the global variable t within the procedure *exchange* for that variable is effectively inaccessible within the body of *exchange*. On the other hand, any occurrence of t outside the procedure *exchange* is a reference to the global variable t. Here, the variable t which is local to the procedure *exchange* is not accessible. The local t exists only within the scope of *exchange*, and is allocated a memory area to hold its value each time *exchange* is called. Once the computation leaves the scope of *exchange*, this memory cell is effectively deallocated, i.e. it is not associated with the identifier t any more. Thus, assignments to t within the procedure *exchange* do not affect the value of the global variable t, and vice versa. This is illustrated by the comment in (3).

Existence of a variable means existence of a memory area of appropriate size which holds the current value of the variable. Upon each call of a procedure (we also say activation of a procedure) this memory area is allocated for the local variables of that procedure. Upon completion of execution of its procedure body, this memory is freed, and used subsequently for other purposes. In other words, local variables are created when the procedure is entered, and anihilated when its execution is completed. Each activation of a procedure has its private instances of local variables declared within that procedure.

The attributes local and global apply not only to variables, but also to types, constants and procedures themselves. This means that a type, a constant and a procedure can be declared as local to some procedure. The fact that procedures may be declared within other procedures is particularly interesting, and it requires more careful analysis of the rules which determine the scope of validity of an identifier. An example of nested procedure declarations (and thus nested blocks) is given in Figure 5.1. In principle, the scope of an identifier is the whole block in which this identifier is declared, including all the blocks nested inside this block, apart from those in which that identifier is redeclared. Alternatively, given an identifier in a program, its meaning (i.e., the corresponding declaration) is found by first looking into the declarations of the smallest block in which that identifier occurs, and if its declaration is not found there, proceeding to the next textually enclosing block, and so on. It follows then that if we assume that all the identifiers declared in the procedures given in Fig. 5.1 are distinct, (i.e., no identifier is redeclared within an inner block), the following can be stated about their scopes:

Identifiers defined in blocks:	The scope of the identifiers are blocks:
A	A,B,C,D,E,F
B	B,D
C	C,E,F
D	D
E	E
F	F

We shall further discuss Pascal block structure in Section 5.4.

It should be observed that this is a different sort of block structure from the one offered by Algol 60 and some other languages. In Pascal, all declarations are given at the procedure level, and the whole program should be regarded, conceptually, as a procedure. In Algol 60, it is possible to open one block inside another just by introducing new variable declarations (in Algol 60 this is done after the **begin** symbol, and not before it as in Pascal). This means that using Algol 60 it is possible to achieve localization of variables without explicit use of procedures. In order to illustrate how this affects the program development process, consider the following abstract algorithm for sorting by selection:

$$\textbf{var } A: \textbf{array } [1 \,.\,.\, N] \textbf{ of } integer; \tag{4}$$
$$i: 1 \,.\,.\, N;$$
$$\textbf{begin for } i := 1 \textbf{ to } N - 1 \textbf{ do}$$
$$\quad permute\ the\ elements\ A[i], \ldots ,A[N]$$
$$\quad to\ put\ smallest\ in\ A[i]$$
$$\textbf{end}$$

In the next refinement step we discover that, in order to refine the abstract statement *permute the elements $A[i], \ldots ,A[N]$ to put smallest in $A[i]$*, we need two integer variables m and j. However, it is clear that these variables are local to the abstract statement, and certainly do not belong to the environment of this statement, for which only its effect upon the array A matters. (This effect is the external specification which the refinement must satisfy). So we get the following refinement of the abstract statement:

$$\textbf{var } m,j: 1 \,.\,.\, N; \tag{5}$$
$$\textbf{begin } m := i;$$
$$\quad \textbf{for } j := i + 1 \textbf{ to } N \textbf{ do}$$
$$\quad \textbf{if } A[j] < A[m] \textbf{ then } m := j;$$
$$\quad exchange\ A[i]\ and\ A[j]$$
$$\textbf{end}$$

The same thing happens when we attempt to refine the abstract statement *exchange $A[i]$ and $A[j]$*. In order to do that, we need an auxiliary integer variable t, which clearly belongs to the internal structure of the module

procedure *A*

    – – – – – – – – – –

    procedure *B*

       – – – – – – – – – –

       procedure *D*

         – – – – – – – – –

         begin

         – – – – – – – – – –

         end; {*D*}
       begin

         – – – – – – – – –

       end; {*B*}
       procedure *C*

         – – – – – – – – –

         procedure *E*

            – – – – – – – – – –

         begin

            – – – – – – – – –

         end; {*E*}
         procedure *F*

            – – – – – – – – – –

         begin

            – – – – – – – – –

         end; {*F*}
       begin

         – – – – – – – – – –

       end; {*C*}
begin

    – – – – – – – – – –

end {*A*}

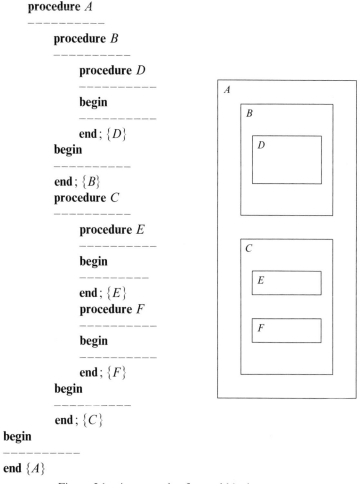

Figure 5.1   An example of nested block structure.

Note that the figure shows, for example, *B* as nested inside *A*. This is true of the scope of the variables. However, the main body of *A* corresponding to the last **begin** . . . **end** does not contain the text of *B*, but only statements which call *B* (and this, of course, is a feature of top-down design).

exchange A[i] and A[j], and in fact should not be accessible for the environment of that module. So we get the following refinement:

$$
\begin{aligned}
&\textbf{var } t\colon integer;\\
&\textbf{begin } t := A[i];\\
&\qquad A[i] := A[j];\\
&\qquad A[j] := t\\
&\textbf{end}
\end{aligned}
\tag{6}
$$

Now in Algol 60 one can (using a somewhat different notation) put the block (6) inside the block (5) in place of the abstract statement *exchange A[i] and A[j]*, and then put the block obtained this way inside the block (4) in place of the abstract statement *permute the elements A[i], . . . ,A[N] to put smallest in A[i]*. In order to achieve this in Pascal, however, one has to explicitly use the procedure declaration and the procedure call mechanisms.

Parameters

The procedure *exchange* as declared in (2) exchanges values of two fixed variables x and y. Its restrictions in that sense would be a serious drawback for a program in which the exchange operation would have to be performed several times, and each time on different variables. Because of this, modern programming languages offer the generality (and flexibility) of letting us make procedure declarations which do not fix the specific variables to which the action described in the procedure declaration should be applied. Rather, specific variables are supplied in a procedure call, as illustrated in (7).

$$\text{var } a,b,c,d,i: integer; \qquad\qquad\qquad\qquad (7)$$

        $A:$ **array** $[1 \; . . \; 10]$ **of** *integer*;
        procedure *exchange*(**var** $x,y:$ *integer*);
        var $t:$ *integer*;
        begin $t := x; x := y; y := t$ **end**;
    begin {main program body}

       ----

       exchange(a,b);

       ----

       exchange(c,d);

       ----

       exchange(A[i], A[i + 5]);

       ---

    end

In the heading of the procedure *exchange* as declared in (7), we observe a new part (on the third line in (7)) which is called the *formal parameter section*. In this section two identifiers x and y are introduced, and they stand for the variables whose values should be exchanged in a specific call of the procedure exchange. x and y are called *formal parameters*, and the actual variables supplied in each procedure call (such as a and b, c and d, $A[i]$ and $A[i + 5]$ in (7)) are called *actual parameters*. The formal parameter section, apart from quoting formal parameters in the chosen order, also specifies that both x and y stand for variables (which is what the symbol **var** indicates) of type *integer*. Inside the procedure body, x and y are used to identify the formal parameters, and as such they have no significance outside the procedure body. If x and y are declared in the environment of the procedure or its call, then there they denote completely different objects, and these declarations are superceded within the procedure body. In that respect, formal parameters behave just like variables, but they should *by no means* be identified with local variables.

The distinction becomes clear if we discuss the dynamic aspects of procedure parameters, i.e., the effects of a procedure call. A procedure call now, apart from the procedure identifier, also contains the actual parameters. The effect of a call is the same as the effect of execution of the procedure body in which the formal parameters are replaced by the corresponding actual parameters in the left-to-right order. For example, the effect of the call *exchange*(*a,b*) is the same as the effect of executing **begin** $t := a$; $a := b$; $b := t$ **end**, where t is a temporarily introduced integer variable. So the requirement is that the actual parameters must be of the same type as the corresponding formal parameters, and they must be supplied in a procedure call in the order in which they should be substituted for the formal parameters. If the actual parameter is indexed (such as the parameters in the call *exchange*(*A*[*i*], *A*[*i* + 5])), the operation of indexing is performed, and the component variable obtained that way is substituted for the corresponding formal parameter.

Possible conflicts between the identifiers of the local variables of a procedure and the variables which are substituted for the formal parameters are easy to resolve by systematic substitution of identifiers, just as was done with the predicate formulas in our discussion of quantification in Section 2.2. This is performed by the compiler, and so the programmer does not have to be concerned with that.

With the above conventions, one would write the usual multiplication algorithm for positive integers as a procedure in the following way:

$$\begin{aligned}
&\textbf{procedure } \mathit{multiply}(\textbf{var } x,y,z: \mathit{integer}); \qquad\qquad (8)\\
&\textbf{var } u: \mathit{integer};\\
&\textbf{begin } u := y; z := 0;\\
&\qquad \textbf{repeat } z := z + x;\\
&\qquad\qquad u := u - 1\\
&\qquad \textbf{until } u = 0\\
&\textbf{end}
\end{aligned}$$

The arguments are given here as the first and second parameters, and the result of the multiplication operation is assigned to the third parameter. But then it would be convenient to be able to write a call in the form of a complex statement such as

$$\mathit{multiply}(a + b, a - b, d) \qquad\qquad (9)$$

where the first two actual parameters are integer expressions. Indeed, looking into (8) we realize that it is sufficient that in the process of substitution of actual parameters for the formal ones the procedure *multiply* gets only the *values* of the first two parameters. That does not hold for the third parameter. It must be a *variable*, since we want to assign the result of the procedure to it.

There are two types of substitution mechanisms in Pascal. The first one (which we would apply to the first two parameters of the procedure *multiply*) is called *value substitution* and the second one (which should be applied to the third parameter of *multiply*) is called *variable substitution*. Variable substitution is indicated by the symbol **var** which, in the first parameter section, precedes the formal parameter (or parameters) to which this substitution mechanism applies.[1] If the desired substitution mechanism is value substitution, the symbol **var** is simply omitted. With these conventions the declaration (8) looks like this:

$$\begin{aligned}
&\textbf{procedure } multiply(x, y: integer; \textbf{var } z: integer); \qquad\qquad (10)\\
&\textbf{var } u: integer;\\
&\textbf{begin } u := y; z := 0;\\
&\qquad \textbf{repeat } z := z + x;\\
&\qquad\qquad\quad u := u - 1\\
&\qquad \textbf{until } u = 0\\
&\textbf{end}
\end{aligned}$$

Now consider $multiply(x, y: integer; \textbf{var } z: integer)$. It tells the compiler that it should so compile $multiply(a + b, a - b, d)$ that a call starts with the following two steps:

i. Carry out *value substitution* for x and y: it sets aside memory areas for the formal parameters x and y, then places the current value of the actual parameter $a + b$ in the memory location for x and the current value of $a - b$ in the memory location for y.

ii. Carry out *variable substitution* for z: for the duration of the call, the formal parameter z of the procedure *multiply* refers to the variable d.

Thus, in variable substitution, the actual parameter must be a variable, whereas in value substitution the actual parameter can be an expression (of which variables form a special case).

Note, then, that there are in principle two ways by which a procedure call can affect its environment. The first way consists of changing the values of global variables which occur in the procedure body, and the second is by assignments to the parameters for which variable substitution is specified.

The point to note here is that execution of $multiply(a + b, a - b, c)$ changes the value of c, but does *not* change the values of $a + b$ or $a - b$. It is the values of the local variables which correspond to the formal parameters x and y and which are initialized to the values of $a + b$ and $a - b$, respectively, that may change during execution. (If one were sloppy enough to use a and b as global variables which actually occur in the body of *multiply*, then the values of a and b might in fact change. At completion of *multiply* there would then be no guarantee that the value of c would equal the product

---

[1] Perhaps unfortunately, the standard terms for value and variable substitution are *call by value* and *call by reference* respectively.

of the *current* values of $a + b$ and $a - b$. This would clearly be an example of bad programming practice.)

To repeat, any assignment to a parameter called by value is an assignment to the corresponding local variable, and it cannot affect the actual parameter. This is an important and often very desirable property. If the actual value parameter is an expression, its evaluation must yield a value whose type is the same as the type of the corresponding formal parameter. With this in mind we observe that (10) can be written in the following way:

> **procedure** *multiply*(x, y: *integer*; **var** z: *integer*);   (11)
> **begin** $z := 0$;
>   **repeat** $z := z + x$;
> $y := y - 1$;
>   **until** $y = 0$
> **end**

Given the above, one would tend to conclude that if a parameter is an argument of a procedure (such as x and y in the procedure *multiply*), then value substitution is appropriate. On the other hand, if a parameter is a result of a procedure, then variable substitution should be specified. Although this is true in general, there are cases where the exceptions to this rule are required for reasons of economy of storage and efficiency of execution. For example, if a parameter of a procedure is an array, then we would often want variable substitution, even if no assignment is performed to the components of the array in the procedure body. For example, see (12) below. The reason for this is the value substitution mechanism explained above. Indeed, if the substitution mechanism is value substitution, then every procedure call would create an instance of a local array variable, and the array which is supplied as the actual parameter will be copied into this memory area. This, of course, can be a costly operation.

Specifying the Size of Arrays

Pascal requires that the type of each parameter be completely determined at compile time, so that all necessary checks of correspondence between actual and formal parameters can be performed when the program is being translated into machine language. This means that these checks are not included in the translated (machine) version of the program. Inclusion of these checks into the translated program would of course affect its efficiency, and so it becomes clear why this approach is adopted in Pascal. But if every attribute of a type is to be determined at compile time (this means that types are static), then the size of arrays (the number of elements of each dimension) must also be determined at compile time. So changing the size of an array in a Pascal program requires its recompilation. Worse than that, specification of the type of an array parameter includes its size, and this seriously restricts the use of procedures with array parameters. For example, suppose that we have a program with the following declarations:

$$\begin{aligned}
&\textbf{var } a\colon \textbf{array } [1 \, . \, . \, 100] \textbf{ of } \textit{real}; &(12)\\
&\quad b\colon \textbf{array } [0 \, . \, . \, 63] \textbf{ of } \textit{real};\\
&\textbf{procedure } \textit{sqnorm}(\textbf{var } A\colon \textbf{array } [1 \, . \, . \, 100] \textbf{ of } \textit{real};\\
&\qquad\qquad\qquad\quad \textbf{var } r\colon \textit{real});\\
&\textbf{var } i\colon \textit{integer};\\
&\textbf{begin } r := 0;\\
&\quad \textbf{for } i := 1 \textbf{ to } 100 \textbf{ do } r := r + A[i] * A[i]\\
&\textbf{end}
\end{aligned}$$

Note that we specify variable substitution for A to save storage space, and to save the time required to copy an array into new work space. This economy has no side-effects, since the body of the procedure has no assignments to any $A[i]$. However, in Section 5.4 we shall see a procedure *Partition* which has an array A as formal parameter which permutes elements of the array. This is reminiscent of assignments like $x := x + 1$, where x appears on both sides of the assignment.

The procedure *sqnorm* can be now used only to compute the *squared norm* (sum of squares of components) of the vector a, and of any vector of the type **array** $[1 \, . \, . \, 100]$ **of** *real*. It is not possible to use the same procedure to compute the squared norm of the vector b, where the origin is 0 and the number of elements is 64 rather than 100, not even if we introduce two additional integer value parameters u and v so that the **for** loop in (12) looks like this:

$$\textbf{for } i := u \textbf{ to } v \textbf{ do } r := r + A[i] * A[i] \qquad (13)$$

We still have to specify the index type of the array A when declaring the procedure *sqnorm*, and this must include such specification of the lower and upper bounds of the subrange that these can be determined at compile time. This is very unfortunate and certainly presents a serious problem if we want to apply consistently the programming methodology advocated so far.

Although Algol 60 is inferior to Pascal in many respects, it allows arrays with dynamic bounds, which means that the size of each array dimension is determined at run time, upon entrance to the block in which the array is declared. But introducing such a feature in Pascal is not easy at all. One has to have in mind all the complexity of behavior of structures which are obtained if dynamic arrays are included and other type structuring rules of Pascal are applied. So a more restrictive feature was proposed by Wirth: parametric array definitions. For the example (12), such a parametric type definition would have the form:

$$\textbf{type } \textit{vector}(m,n) = \textbf{array } [m \, . \, . \, n] \textbf{ of } \textit{real} \qquad (14)$$

So the parameter A in (12) would be declared of the type $\textit{vector}(m,n)$, and the variables a and b in (12) would be declared as:

$$\begin{aligned}
&\textbf{var } a\colon \textit{vector}(1,100); &(15)\\
&\quad b\colon \textit{vector}(0,63)
\end{aligned}$$

Now (12) takes the following form:

type *vector(m,n)* = **array** [*m . . n*] **of** *real*;   (16)
var *a*: *vector*(1,100);
      b: *vector*(0,63);
procedure *sqnorm*(**var** *A*: *vector*; *u,v*: *integer*;
                        var *r*: *real*);
var *i*: *integer*;
begin *r* := 0;
      for *i* := *u* **to** *v* **do** *r* := *r* + *A*[*i*] * *A*[*i*]
end

and specific calls would now look like this:

sqnorm(*a*,1,100,*r*1);   (17)
sqnorm(*b*,0,63,*r*2);

where *r*1 and *r*2 are real variables.

Wirth also suggested that parameterization should be restricted to index bounds of array types, and that only constants should be allowed as actual parameters in variable declarations (like (15)). Any further generalization, he suggests, would destroy many advantages of the Pascal approach to the concept of type.

5.2 Functions and Their Proof of Correctness

We now discuss the Pascal function mechanism, which allows us to introduce new function symbols with which to build up expressions.

Given types T_1 and T_2, a function F from domain T_1 into codomain T_2 determines, for a given element x of T_1, a unique corresponding element of T_2 which is customarily denoted by $F(x)$. Following this mathematical definition, we would say that in order to specify a function, it is necessary to specify its domain type, its codomain type and a rule, which for a given value of the domain type, determines uniquely the corresponding value of the codomain type. In Pascal, this rule is given as an algorithm, which is specified in a form which is very similar to a procedure declaration. For example, the function which multiplies two positive integers may be declared as follows:

function *multiply*(*x,y*: *integer*): *integer*;   (1)
var *z*: *integer*;
begin *z* := 0;
      repeat *z* := *z* + *x*;
            y := *y* − 1
      until *y* = 0
      multiply := *z*
end

The differences between a procedure declaration and a function declaration may be summarized briefly as follows: A function declaration is indicated by the basic symbol **function**. The function heading includes the formal parameter section defining the local names of the domain arguments and their types, followed by a colon after which follows the identifier of the codomain type (the type of the computed value). We may specify variable substitution for some of the arguments of a function—for the same reasons of storage economy that we discussed for procedures in the previous section. Thus a function can certainly affect the value of a global variable if it is used as an actual parameter via variable substitution—as well as if the variable occurs explicitly as a global variable in the function body.

Unlike a procedure, we do *not* name the result variable in the heading of a function. Instead, within the procedure body there is an indication of what the computed value is, this is given in the form on an assignment of the computed value to the function identifier. Such an assignment must get executed during execution of the function body. Pascal rules require that the resulting type of a function—indicated in the function heading—must be a scalar, a subrange or (see Chapter 6) a pointer type.

A function call is an expression—unlike a procedure call, which is a statement. Thus a function call can appear in any expression where a value of the same type as the function result type is expected. This is illustrated in the program (2).

$$\begin{aligned}
&\textbf{var } a,b,c\colon integer; \hspace{4em} (2)\\
&\textbf{function } multiply(x,y\colon integer)\colon integer;\\
&\textbf{var } z\colon integer;\\
&\textbf{begin } z := 0;\\
&\quad\quad \textbf{repeat } z := z + x;\\
&\quad\quad\quad\quad\quad\; y := y - 1\\
&\quad\quad \textbf{until } y = 0;\\
&\quad\quad multiply := z\\
&\textbf{end};\\
&\textbf{begin } \{\text{main program}\}\\
&\quad\quad a := 7; b := 5;\\
&\quad\quad c := multiply(a + b, a + b) + a + b\\
&\textbf{end}
\end{aligned}$$

A careful reader might have observed that the above differences do not exclude possible effects of a function call upon its environment. So a function, apart from computing and delivering the desired value, can—as discussed on p. 160—also change the values of its global variables, in the same way as procedures can. But in the case of functions, such assignments to global variables of a function should be strongly discouraged. They make programs hard to understand, since the effect of a function call cannot then be explained as simply computation of the desired value; this may also lead to situations where even in the case of integer type the familiar axioms of integer arithmetic do not hold. This is illustrated by the following example:

$$\textbf{function } f(x: \textit{integer}): \textit{integer}; \qquad (3)$$
$$\textbf{begin } a := x + 1; f := a \textbf{ end};$$
$$\textbf{function } g(\textbf{var } x: \textit{integer}): \textit{integer};$$
$$\textbf{begin } x := a + 2; g := a \textbf{ end}$$

In the above two function declarations, a is a global integer variable for both functions. Suppose that a is initialized to 0 and consider the expressions $f(a) + g(a)$ and $g(a) + f(a)$. One would expect their values to be equal, but this turns out not to be the case. Indeed, suppose that the implementation of integer addition is such that evaluation of an expression of the form $x + y$ is performed in such a way that x is evaluated first, then y is evaluated, and then their values are added. If the order is reversed (and on a conventional computer it must be one way or the other) we could again come up with an example which illustrates the problem described below. Then if the calls occur in the order listed below on the left, the situation after them is described on the right.

$$f(a) \qquad\qquad a = 1, f(a) = 1 \qquad (4)$$
$$g(a) \qquad\qquad a = 3, g(a) = 3$$
$$f(a) + g(a) = 1 + 3 = 4.$$

However, if the order of the calls is reversed, we get the following situation:

$$g(a) \qquad\qquad a = 2, g(a) = 2 \qquad (5)$$
$$f(a) \qquad\qquad a = 3, f(a) = 3$$
$$g(a) + f(a) = 2 + 3 = 5.$$

Some of the proof rules stated so far hold only in the absence of these side effects of functions. In general, in the presence of the side effects the concept of a function in programming languages is more general than the usual mathematical definition from which we started our discussion of functions. Such excessive generality can lead to serious problems.

A Proof Rule for Functions

Let

$$\textbf{function } f(L): T; S \qquad (6)$$

be a function declaration, where L is the parameter specification part, T the type of the result, and S the function body. Let x be the list of parameters declared in L. We assume that no assignments are made within S to either parameters with variable substitution specified or to global variables. This means that f causes no side effects.

The effect of execution of such a function call is the execution of the function body with the actual parameters replacing the formal ones. The function name is used as a variable to store the result of the function. It follows then that in order to establish some property which is to hold for every function call, we have to establish that property for the function body. So suppose that $\{P\}\ S\ \{Q\}$ has been proved for the body S of the function f declared in (6). At that, Q will include the function name f denoting the result of the function, and both P and Q will include the formal parameters of the function. If global variables occur within S, then these will in general appear in P and/or Q. From this assumption, we may conclude that P implies the truth of Q in which each occurrence of the function name f is replaced by $f(x)$. Furthermore, this is true for all values of variables involved in this assertion. To put it briefly, we have:

$$\frac{\{P\}\ S\ \{Q\}}{\forall x(P \supset Q^f_{f(x)})}. \tag{7}$$

The property $\forall x(P \supset Q^f_{f(x)})$ is then used when proving properties of expressions in which calls of the function f occur.

The function *root* in (10) is intended to compute the greatest natural number x smaller than or equal to $\sqrt{a}$, i.e., the following property is intended to hold:

$$\forall a((a \geqslant 0) \supset (root(a)^2 \leqslant a < (root(a) + 1)^2)). \tag{8}$$

The algorithm in (10) is designed on the basis of the fact that:

$$1 + 3 + 5 + \cdots + (2n - 1) = n^2 \text{ for every } n > 0. \tag{9}$$

So we start with $x := 0$ (for $n - 1$ with $n = 1$), $z := 1$ (for $2n - 1$ with $n = 1$) and $y := 1$ (for n^2 with $n = 1$).

```
function root(a: integer): integer;                    (10)
var x,y,z: integer;
begin x := 0; y := 1; z := 1;
    while y ≤ a do
    begin x := x + 1;
          z := z + 2;
          y := y + z
    end;
    root := x
end
```

With the function *root* in (10) the efficiency of the Sieve of Eratosthenes algorithm discussed in Section 4.4 may be improved as follows:

```
rootN := root(N);                                      (11)
sieve := [2] + [n|(n in [2 .. N]) ∧ odd(n)];
p := 3;
while p ≤ rootN do
begin sift(p);
      p := next prime after (p)
end
```

We now turn to a proof of correctness for (10). To use the proof rule (7) we must prove

$$\{a \geqslant 0\}\ S\ \{root^2 \leqslant a < (root + 1)^2\} \tag{12}$$

where S is the body of the function $root$ in (10).

Consider now the body of $root$ annotated with some invariants which indicate the major guidelines of the proof:

$$\{a \geqslant 0\} \tag{13}$$
$$\textbf{begin}\ x := 0;\ y := 1;\ z := 1;$$
$$\{(x^2 \leqslant a) \wedge (y = (x + 1)^2) \wedge (z = 2x + 1)\}$$
$$\textbf{while}\ y \leqslant a\ \textbf{do}$$
$$\textbf{begin}\ x := x + 1;$$
$$z := z + 2;$$
$$y := y + z$$
$$\textbf{end};$$
$$\{(x^2 \leqslant a) \wedge (a < y) \wedge (y = (x + 1)^2)\}$$
$$root := x$$
$$\{root^2 \leqslant a < (root + 1)^2\}$$
$$\textbf{end}$$

Proof of (13) proceeds in the following steps:

$$\{a \geqslant 0\}\ x := 0;\ y := 1;\ z := 1\ \{(x^2 \leqslant a) \wedge (y = (x + 1)^2) \wedge (z = 2x + 1)\} \tag{14}$$

$$\{(y \leqslant a) \wedge (x^2 \leqslant a) \wedge (y = (x + 1)^2) \wedge (z = 2x + 1)\} \tag{15}$$
$$x := x + 1$$
$$\{(y \leqslant a) \wedge (y = x^2) \wedge (z = 2(x - 1) + 1)\}$$
$$\text{implies}$$

$$\{(x^2 \leqslant a) \wedge (y = x^2) \wedge (z = 2x - 1)\} \tag{16}$$

$$z := z + 2 \tag{17}$$
$$\{(x^2 \leqslant a) \wedge (y = x^2) \wedge (z = 2x + 1)\}$$

$$y := y + z \tag{18}$$
$$\{(x^2 \leqslant a) \wedge (y = (x + 1)^2) \wedge (z = 2x + 1)\}$$

(15) to (18) imply:

$$\{(y \leqslant a) \wedge (x^2 \leqslant a) \wedge (y = (x + 1)^2) \wedge (z = 2x + 1)\} \tag{19}$$
$$x := x + 1;\ z := z + 2;\ y := y + z$$
$$\{(x^2 \leqslant a) \wedge (y = (x + 1)^2) \wedge (z = 2x + 1)\}$$

From (19) we now conclude

$$\{(x^2 \leqslant a) \wedge (y = (x + 1)^2) \wedge (z = 2x + 1)\} \qquad (20)$$
$$\textbf{while } y \leqslant a \textbf{ do}$$
$$\textbf{begin } x := x + 1;$$
$$z := z + 2;$$
$$y := y + z$$
$$\textbf{end}$$
$$\{(x^2 \leqslant a) \wedge (y = (x + 1)^2) \wedge (z = 2x + 1) \wedge (y > a)\}$$

The desired conclusion (12) now follows from (14) and (20) observing that

$$(x^2 \leqslant a) \wedge (y = (x + 1)^2) \wedge (z = 2x + 1) \wedge (y > a) \supset (x^2 \leqslant a < (x + 1)^2)$$
$$(21)$$

and

$$\{x^2 \leqslant a < (x + 1)^2\} \; root := x \; \{root^2 \leqslant a < (root + 1)^2\} \qquad (22)$$

Extreme care must be exercised in treating properly the issue of termination when designing a function. Indeed, if for some x execution of the function call $f(x)$ does not terminate, then an assignment such as $y := f(x)$ does not make sense, since $f(x)$ is not defined. In fact, if the termination is not ensured, then the proof rule (7) can lead to contradictions. This will be illustrated by the following example:

$$\textbf{function } f(x: integer): integer; \qquad (23)$$
$$\textbf{begin while } true \textbf{ do } f := x$$
$$\textbf{end}$$

We can easily prove:

$$\{true\} \textbf{ while } true \textbf{ do } f := x \; \{false \wedge f = x\} \qquad (24)$$

and then applying the proof rule (7) we conclude that the following holds

$$\forall x(true \supset (false \wedge f(x) = x)) \qquad (25)$$

which is obviously a contradiction. The lesson to be learned from this is that when proving $\{P\} S \{Q\}$ for (7) we must make sure that if P holds before S is executed, S will in fact terminate.

Procedures and Functions as Parameters

So far we have discussed only variable and value parameters. Procedures and functions may also be parameters of a procedure or function. In the formal parameter section such a parameter is preceded by the symbol **procedure** or **function**. If a parameter is a function, then the type of the *result value* is also indicated. An example of this sort is the general summation function defined below, where *term* is a function whose codomain is the data type *real*.

While in all other cases, Pascal requires complete specification of the type of the formal parameters, in the case of a parameter which is a procedure or a function that is not the case. In the specification of such a parameter specification of the number of its parameters and their type is not given. This is why, in (26), we write **function** *term*: *real* instead of **function** *term* (*j*: *integer*): *real*.

$$\begin{aligned}
&\textbf{function } sum(\textbf{function } term\colon real;\ k\colon integer)\colon real; \qquad (26)\\
&\textbf{var } s\colon real;\ j\colon integer;\\
&\textbf{begin } s := 0;\\
&\qquad \textbf{for } j := 1 \textbf{ to } k \textbf{ do } s := s + term(j);\\
&\qquad sum := s\\
&\textbf{end}
\end{aligned}$$

The above function sums the terms of some series from 1 to k. During a call of the function *sum*, the function which is the first actual parameter (i.e., the one which corresponds to the formal parameter *term*) is called once each time around the **for** loop in (26). This function specifies the rule for computing the jth term (j is its parameter). So the function *sum* can be used to compute different sums, and it would be appropriate in a program where different summations are needed.

A somewhat similar example is the procedure *update* declared in (27). It can be used to perform various operations f on all elements of an array. The first parameter of the procedure *update* is a function which defines the operation to be performed upon each element of the array.

$$\begin{aligned}
&\textbf{procedure } update(\textbf{function } f\colon real;\ \textbf{var } A\colon \textbf{array } [1\ ..\ 100]\ \textbf{of } real); \quad (27)\\
&\textbf{var } i\colon integer;\\
&\textbf{begin for } i := 1 \textbf{ to } 100 \textbf{ do}\\
&\qquad A[i] := f(A[i])\\
&\textbf{end}
\end{aligned}$$

Because of Pascal's incomplete type specification for procedures and functions which occur as formal parameters, it would be very difficult for a compiler to discover the kind of error illustrated by the example (28).

$$\begin{aligned}
&\textbf{procedure } P(\textbf{procedure } Q); \qquad\qquad\qquad ,(28)\\
&\textbf{begin } Q(1,\text{'}A\text{'}) \textbf{ end};\\
&\textbf{procedure } R(x\colon Boolean);\\
&\textbf{begin } write(x) \textbf{ end};\\
&\textbf{begin } \{\text{main program}\}\\
&\qquad P(R)\\
&\textbf{end}
\end{aligned}$$

With the requirement of full specification of the formal parameters the heading of the procedure P would have one of the following two forms:[2]

$$\textbf{procedure } P(\textbf{procedure } Q(integer, char)) \qquad (29)$$

$$\textbf{procedure } P(\textbf{procedure } Q(Boolean)). \qquad (30)$$

[2] This change has been suggested in Lecarme and Desjardins (1975).

In the first case the compiler would detect an error in the call $P(R)$ in (28), since the number and types of the actual parameters (there is only one) in this call do not correspond to the number and types of the formal parameters of the procedure P. In the second case the compiler would detect an error in the call $Q(1,`A')$ since now the first parameter of P is specified as a procedure which has only one parameter of type *Boolean*.

As it is, the compiler can hardly perform all necessary checks of the correspondence of actual and formal parameters and so can either fail to do all of them properly or insert into the compiled program machine instructions which perform these tests when the translated program is executed. The first possibility hardly needs a comment, the second means decreasing program efficiency.

5.3 Proofs of Correctness of Procedures

In our exposition of proofs of correctness of procedures, we first concentrate on two special kinds of procedures. The first kind consists of procedures without parameters. Procedures of this type communicate with their environment i.e., the collection of blocks which enclose the procedure, through their global variables. The second kind consists of procedures which communicate with their environment entirely through their parameters. Procedures of this second type are independent of the context of their use. In general, a procedure may be a mixture of the above two extreme cases: it has global variables occurring in its body, as well as parameters. If we show how to prove correctness of the first two types of procedures, then proofs of correctness of procedures of the third type do not involve any new conceptual difficulties.

Procedures without Parameters

Let

$$\textbf{procedure } p:S \tag{1}$$

be a declaration of a parameterless procedure p with procedure body S. The effect of a call of this procedure is execution of its body S. Thus if we want to prove that

$$\{P\}\, p\, \{Q\} \tag{2}$$

holds for a procedure call p, we have to prove

$$\{P\}\, S\, \{Q\}. \tag{3}$$

P and Q above will naturally include global variables of the procedure p.

The proof rule that we have just formulated thus has the form:

$$\frac{\{P\} \, S \, \{Q\}}{\{P\} \, p \, \{Q\}} \tag{4}$$

where p is a procedure declared without parameters as in (1).

Procedures without Global Variables

Consider now the kind of procedure with formal parameters and with no global variables occurring in its body. Let

$$\textbf{procedure } p(L);S \tag{5}$$

be a declaration of such a procedure, where p is its name, L is the formal parameter specification part and S is the procedure body. Let x be the list of formal parameters of p.

Suppose that we had proved

$$\{P\} \, S \, \{Q\} \tag{6}$$

where P and Q involve the formal parameters of the procedure p. Then what we would like to establish is that any procedure call of p satisfies the property (6), i.e.,

$$\forall x(\{P\} \, p(x) \, \{Q\}). \tag{7}$$

In other words, for a call $p(a)$, where a is a list of actual parameters, we want

$$\{P_a^x\} \, p(a) \, \{Q_a^x\} \tag{8}$$

to hold. A tentative form of the proof rules for procedures is

$$\frac{\{P\} \, S \, \{Q\}}{\forall x(\{P\} \, p(x) \, \{Q\})} \tag{9}$$

$$\frac{\forall x(\{P\} \, p(x) \, \{Q\})}{\{P_a^x\} \, p(a) \, \{Q_a^x\}} \tag{10}$$

where p is a procedure with the body S and list of formal parameters x. We shall provide a more rigorous version below.

For example, suppose that we have a procedure declared as:

$$\textbf{procedure } random(\textbf{var } k: integer; m,n: integer); e$$

where e is the body of the above procedure. Suppose now that

$$\{m \leqslant n\} \, e \, \{m \leqslant k \leqslant n\} \tag{11}$$

has been established for the procedure body e. From (12) we want to conclude that

$$\{m \leqslant n\} \, random(k,m,n) \, \{m \leqslant k \leqslant n\} \tag{12}$$

holds for every m, n and k, and then, applying (12) to a particular call we get

$$\{1 \leqslant q + 1\} \; random(r, 1, q + 1) \; \{1 \leqslant r \leqslant q + 1\}.$$

However, the logic formulated in (5)–(8) is correct only if the actual parameters in the list x obey the following discipline: Let x_1 be a list of formal parameters of p subject to change in S and x_2 a list of all other parameters of p. Let a_1 be the actual parameters corresponding to the formal parameters x_1 and a_2 the actual parameters which correspond to the formal parameters x_2. Then all variables in a_1 must be distinct, and none of them may be contained in a_2. Denote this condition by $dis(a)$—where dis is short for *distinctness condition*. If the actual parameters do not meet this requirement, then the proof of the body of the procedure is no longer valid as a proof of correctness of the call.

Consider the following example of a procedure:

$$\textbf{procedure } p(\textbf{var } x\colon integer; \; v\colon integer); \tag{13}$$
$$\textbf{begin } x := v + 1 \textbf{ end}$$

Since

$$\{true\} \; x := v + 1 \; \{x = v + 1\} \tag{14}$$

we conclude

$$\forall x, v (\{true\} \; p(x, v) \; \{x = v + 1\}). \tag{15}$$

The call $p(a, a)$ does not satisfy the above formulated requirements for the actual parameters, and from (15) we conclude

$$\{true\} \; p(a, a) \; \{a = a + 1\} \tag{16}$$

which is an obvious contradiction.

We now state the rigorous proof rule

$$\frac{\{P\} \; S \; \{Q\}}{\forall x(dis(x) \supset \{P\} \; p(x) \; \{Q\})} \tag{17}$$

where S is the body of the procedure p, and

$$\frac{dis(a), \; \forall x(dis(x) \supset \{P\} \; p(x) \; \{Q\})}{\{P_a^x\} \; p(a) \; \{Q_a^x\}}. \tag{18}$$

Another problem in applying the proof strategy outlined in (5)–(18) is collision of variables. For example, P and/or Q may contain some variables k which do not occur in x, but which do occur in a. In such a case, it is necessary to make a systematic change of the variables k in P and Q, replacing them by some variables which do not occur in a, and then to apply the proof rule given in (9) and (10). Observe that the sequel to (12) represents a correct application of this proof rule.

The Procedure Partition

We now give a proof of correctness of a procedure of the second type. All the proofs given in Chapter 4, on top-down program and proof construction, are proofs of correctness of procedures of the first special type, and we shall give another such example in the next subsection.

The procedure *Partition* is designed to arrange the elements of an array A between $A[m]$ and $A[n]$ in two overlapping sequences. All the elements in the lower partition $A[m], \ldots, A[i-1]$ are less than or equal to the elements in the upper partition $A[j+1], \ldots, A[n]$, where $j < i$. The situation is shown below where a_j is the value of $A[j]$, for $1 \leqslant j \leqslant N$, before *Partition*$(A,i,j,m,n)$ is applied, and the second line shows the situation after the call. Note that this A is an example of variable substitution in a procedure where the actual parameter supplies an argument for the procedure that can be modified by the procedure.

Given A, m and n with $m \leqslant n$ (19)

Partition(A,i,j,m,n) rearranges $A[m], \ldots, A[n]$ and determines $j < i$ in such a way that

$$(j < i) \wedge \forall p,q((m \leqslant p < i) \wedge (j < q \leqslant n) \supset (A[p] \leqslant A[q])) \qquad (20)$$

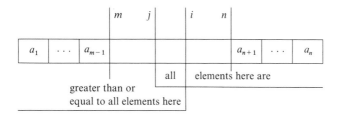

(It is rather disturbing that the procedure is called *Partition*, for i and j divide A into two *overlapping* sequences, not into two disjoint pieces. However, it is worth noting that there are *three* disjoint sequences in (21): $p \leqslant j$, $j < p < i$ (which will be empty if $j + 1 = i$, so that we do then have a genuine two-fold partition), and $i \leqslant p$. Note that (20) implies that if p and q satisfy $j < p < i$ and $j < q < i$, then $A[p] = A[q]$.) If we assume that the index bounds of the array A are 1 to N, then clearly before every call of the procedure *Partition* we must have that m and n are within these bounds. We assume that $1 \leqslant m \leqslant n \leqslant N$. In addition to (20) we require that after a call of *Partition* the array A is equal to the original one up to permutation of its elements between $A[m]$ and $A[n]$. This part of the correctness criterion will not be formalized, since it will be clear from the proposed solution that it is satisfied. But since we won't be doing anything apart from permuting the array elements between m and n, this will hold throughout the procedure *Partition*. $1 \leqslant m \leqslant n \leqslant N$ will also be dropped from further discussion, but this discussion makes sense only if it is satisfied.

The procedure *Partition* and its proof of correctness will be developed in the top-down fashion described previously. The first, abstract, version of the algorithm is formulated on the basis of the following reasoning. The array is scanned from left and from right starting at $A[m]$ and $A[n]$ respectively. Two pointers (integer variables) i and j, indicate the current points reached in these two scans. The scan from the left is performed in such a way that all the elements with subscripts which are strictly less than i are less than or equal to r, where r is $A[(m + n) \textbf{ div } 2]$. The scan from the right is designed in such a way that all the elements with subscripts greater than j are greater than or equal to r. These two conditions may be expressed formally as

$$(m \leqslant i) \wedge \forall p((m \leqslant p < i) \supset (A[p] \leqslant r)) \qquad (21)$$
$$(j \leqslant n) \wedge \forall q((j < q \leqslant n) \supset (r \leqslant A[q]))$$

and are diagrammed in (22)

$A[p] \leqslant r$		$r \leqslant A[q]$	(22)
$\longleftarrow \quad \mid i$		$j \mid \longrightarrow$	
$A[m]$	$r = A[k]$	$A[n]$	
$m \leqslant p < i$	$k = (m + n)\textbf{ div } 2$	$j < q \leqslant n$	

So the process of increasing i and decreasing j is designed in such a way that (21) always holds. This process is continued until $j < i$. At that point (21) yields (20) by transitivity. Observe also that the initial values of i and j which are m and n respectively, satisfy the invariants (21). This follows from the fact that $m \leqslant p < m$ and $n < q \leqslant n$ are always *false*.

The procedure *Partition* is declared in (23)

```
procedure Partition(var A: array [1 .. N] of integer;          (23)
       var i,j: integer; m,n: integer);
   var r: integer;
   begin r := A[(m + n) div 2];
       i := m; j := n;
       while i ≤ j do increase i and
                           decrease j
   end
```

We now give the body of *Partition* annotated with invariants as comments:

$\{m \leqslant n\}$ (24)

begin

    $r := A[(m + n) \textbf{ div } 2];$

    $i := m; j := n;$

    $\{(m \leqslant (m + n)/2 \leqslant n) \land$

    $(m \leqslant i) \land \forall p((m \leqslant p < i) \supset (A[p] \leqslant r)) \land$

    $(j \leqslant n) \land \forall q((j < q \leqslant n) \supset (r \leqslant A[q]))\}$

    while $i \leqslant j$ **do** *increase i and*

                    decrease j

end $\{(j < i) \land \forall p, q((m \leqslant p < i) \land (j < q \leqslant n) \supset (A[p] \leqslant A[q]))\}$

Suppose now that *increase i and decrease j* in (24) is refined correctly, i.e., in such a way that (21) is preserved. Then (24) is correct, as was already shown in the discussion which preceded (23) and (24). Note that the precondition $m \leqslant n$ guarantees that the element $A[(m + n) \textbf{ div } 2]$ is one of the elements between $A[m]$ and $A[n]$ inclusive.

Let us now refine the operation *increase i and decrease j*. The first action to be specified is repeated increase of the value of i as long as $A[i] < r$ is satisfied. This is accomplished by the loop:

$$\textbf{while } A[i] < r \textbf{ do } i := i + 1. \tag{25}$$

The next action is to repeatedly decrease the value of j as long as the condition $r < A[j]$ is satisfied. This action is specified by the loop:

$$\textbf{while } r < A[j] \textbf{ do } j := j - 1. \tag{26}$$

Upon termination of both loops we have that $A[j] \leqslant r \leqslant A[i]$ holds. If $i \leqslant j$ at this point, we are not yet done, and increasing i and decreasing j should be continued. In order to preserve the invariants (21), which state that i passes only over those values which satisfy $A[i] \leqslant r$ and j over those which satisfy $r \leqslant A[j]$, we exchange $A[i]$ and $A[j]$ to put them in their proper places. After this exchange $A[i] \leqslant r \leqslant A[j]$ will hold and this justifies further increase of i and decrease of j. The proposed refinement of *increase i and decrease j* is given in (27):

                    $\textbf{while } A[i] < r \textbf{ do } i := i + 1;$ (27)

                    $\textbf{while } r < A[j] \textbf{ do } j := j - 1;$

                    $\textbf{if } i \leqslant j \textbf{ then}$

                    $\textbf{begin } exchange\ A[i]\ and\ A[j];$

                            $i := i + 1; j := j - 1$

                  $\textbf{end}$

Assume now that the operation *exchange A[i] and A[j]* in (27) is refined in such a way that the invariants (21) are preserved. Furthermore, suppose that after *exchange A[i] and A[j]* the relation $A[i] \leqslant r \leqslant A[j]$ holds. Then we can prove that the refinement (27) of *increase i and decrease j* is correct, i.e., that it preserves (21).

Let us first show that the loops (25) and (26) preserve the required invariants. So suppose that

$$(A[i] < r) \wedge (m \leqslant i) \wedge \forall p((m \leqslant p < i) \supset (A[p] \leqslant r)) \tag{28}$$

holds before $i := i + 1$ is executed. (28) implies:

$$(m \leqslant i + 1) \wedge \forall p((m \leqslant p < i + 1) \supset (A[p] \leqslant r)). \tag{29}$$

But if (29) holds before $i := i + 1$ is executed, then (21) must hold upon completion of this assignment. Applying now the proof rule for the **while-do** statement, we conclude that $r \leqslant A[i]$ and (21) will hold upon termination of the loop (25) in (27). The second loop in (27) does not affect these relations in any way. In order to prove the desired property of the second loop in (27), suppose that:

$$(r < A[j]) \wedge (j \leqslant n) \wedge \forall q((j < q \leqslant n) \supset (r \leqslant A[q])) \tag{30}$$

holds before $j := j - 1$ is executed. (30) implies

$$(j - 1 \leqslant n) \wedge \forall q((j - 1 < q \leqslant n) \supset (r \leqslant A[q])). \tag{31}$$

But if (31) holds before the assignment $j := j - 1$, then (21) will hold after it. Applying the inference rule for the **while-do** statement, we conclude that $A[j] \leqslant r$ and (21) will hold upon termination of the second loop in (27).

The body of the conditional in (27) is not executed if $j > i$, in which case (21) certainly holds. If $i \leqslant j$, then (21) was assumed to hold after *exchange A[i] and A[j]*, as well as $A[i] \leqslant r \leqslant A[j]$. Following the same argument as before, we conclude that

$$(A[i] \leqslant r) \wedge (m \leqslant i) \wedge \forall p((m \leqslant p < i) \supset (A[p] \leqslant r)) \tag{32}$$

implies (29), which implies that (21) will hold after the assignment $i := i + 1$. Similarly, from

$$(r \leqslant A[j]) \wedge (m \leqslant j) \wedge \forall q((j < q \leqslant n) \supset (r \leqslant A[q])) \tag{33}$$

we conclude that (31) holds which implies that (21) will hold after the assignment $j := j - 1$. This completes the proof that the refinement (27) of *increase i and decrease j* is correct if *exchange A[i] and A[j]* is refined correctly.

The operation of exchanging the values of $A[i]$ and $A[j]$ is programmed simply as:

$$\begin{aligned} &w := A[i]; \\ &A[i] := A[j]; \\ &A[j] := w \end{aligned} \tag{34}$$

If $A[j] \leqslant r \leqslant A[i]$ holds before (34) is executed, then clearly $A[i] \leqslant r \leqslant A[j]$ will hold after execution of (34). Before execution of (34) we have that

$$(m \leqslant i \leqslant j) \wedge \forall p((m \leqslant p < i) \supset (A[p] \leqslant r)) \tag{35}$$

holds. That $m \leqslant i$ holds after the exchange operation is clear. Furthermore, if $m \leqslant p < i \leqslant j$, then $p \neq i$ and $p \neq j$. Since the exchange operation affects only the values of the array elements with subscripts i and j, we conclude that $\forall p((m \leqslant p < i) \supset (A[p] \leqslant r))$ holds after execution of the exchange operation. Similarly, if

$$(i \leqslant j \leqslant n) \wedge \forall q((j < q \leqslant n) \supset (r \leqslant A[q])) \tag{36}$$

holds before the exchange operation is executed, then certainly $j \leqslant n$ is not affected by this execution. If $i \leqslant j < q \leqslant N$ holds before execution of (34), then $q \neq i$ and $q \neq j$. Since the exchange operation affects only the array elements with subscripts i and j, we conclude that $\forall q((j < q \leqslant N) \supset (r \leqslant A[q]))$ will hold after the exchange operation.

This completes the proof that (34) is a correct refinement of *exchange* $A[i]$ *and* $A[j]$.

At this point all abstract statements have been expressed in terms of the chosen programming language. Thus we have gradually developed the whole procedure, as well as its proof of correctness. The complete procedure declaration is:

```
procedure Partition(var A: array [1 .. N] of integer;        (37)
                    var i,j: integer; m,n: integer);
var r,w: integer;
begin
        r := A[(m + n) div 2];
        i := m; j := n;
        while i ≤ j do
        begin while A[i] < r do i := i + 1;
              while r < A[j] do j := j − 1;
              if i ≤ j then
              begin w := A[i];
                    A[i] := A[j];
                    A[j] := w;
                    i := i + 1; j := j − 1
              end
end
end
```

Observe that the solution (37) satisfies not only (20), but also the informally stated part of the correctness criterion. Indeed, the only manipulation of the array A performed in (37) is an exchange of two elements between $A[m]$ and $A[n]$.

Correctness Proofs of Blocks and Programs

A program is much like a procedure, save that the head of its declaration starts with **program** rather than **procedure** and a '.' appears after the final **end**. Consider, for example, the program (38) which performs a frequency count on letters in the *input* file while copying the *input* file onto the *output* file. When copying is complete, the program outputs the *count* information. In what follows, recall that *eof* is the end-of-file test for the input file.

```
program fcount(input, output);                                    (38)
var ch: char;
    count: array ['a' .. 'z'] of integer;
    letter: set of 'a' .. 'z';
begin letter := ['a' .. 'z'];
    for ch := 'a' to 'z' do count[ch] := 0;
    while ¬eof do
    begin read(ch); write(ch);
        if ch in letter then count[ch] := count[ch] + 1
    end;
    write(' ')
    for ch := 'a' to 'z' do
    begin write(ch);
        write(' ');
        write(count[ch]);
        write(' ')
    end
end.
```

This has the structure of a complete program. It includes the program heading which specifies the program name (the identifier which follows the symbol **program**) and program parameters (*input* and *output* in the above example). Program parameters denote entities (usually files) through which the program communicates with its environment. These entities are called external, and must be declared in the program, save for the two standard files *input* and *output*, which only have to be listed as parameters.

A program heading is followed by a block. A block contains a declaration part and a statement part. The *declaration part* defines all objects referenced in the statement part, and in particular it contains constant definitions, type definitions (type definitions are implicit in (38)) and variable declarations. The *statement part* of a block has the structure of a compound statement. It describes the actions performed by the program.

An example of a program which contains two external files, f and g is given below:

$$\begin{aligned}
&\textbf{program } copy(f,g); \hspace{4cm} (39)\\
&\textbf{var } f,g\colon \textbf{file of } real;\\
&\textbf{begin } reset(f); \; rewrite(g);\\
&\quad \textbf{while } \neg eof(f) \textbf{ do}\\
&\qquad \textbf{begin } g\!\uparrow := f\!\uparrow;\\
&\qquad\qquad put(g); \; get(f)\\
&\qquad \textbf{end}\\
&\textbf{end}.
\end{aligned}$$

The above program simply copies the file f of real numbers into the file g.

The program in (40) carries out line-by-line copying from the input file to the output file, preserving the line structure. Apart from two external variables *input* and *output*, it also contains a variable *ch*. This variable has no significance outside the program and is thus a local variable of the program in (40).

$$\begin{aligned}
&\textbf{program } copytext(input, output); \hspace{3cm} (40)\\
&\textbf{var } ch\colon char;\\
&\textbf{begin while } \neg eof \textbf{ do}\\
&\quad \textbf{begin while } \neg eoln \textbf{ do}\\
&\qquad \textbf{begin } read(ch); \; write(ch) \textbf{ end};\\
&\qquad writeln; \; readln\\
&\quad \textbf{end}\\
&\textbf{end}.
\end{aligned}$$

The block in the above program is the scope of the declaration **var** *ch*: *char* The variable *ch* exists only within its scope, which means that a memory cell is allocated to hold the value of the variable within its scope. Upon leaving this scope this memory cell is effectively deallocated. In particular, it is not associated with the identifier *ch*.

Let us now look explicitly at how declarations enter in our program proving methodology. In other words, we study how to prove correctness of a block like the one in (40). Let

$$D;S \hspace{6cm} (41)$$

be such a block, where D is a sequence of declarations (constant and type definitions, and variable declarations) and S is a compound statement. Declarations in D introduce named objects (constants, types, variables) and prescribe their properties. Let the set of assertions which specify these properties be denoted by H. In the case of the constant definitions the assertions in H are nothing but the list of equations themselves. In the case of type definitions, H contains axioms which describe the properties of the newly introduced types. In the case of a variable declaration **var** $x\colon T$, the corresponding assertion in H is that the set of values which x may assume is T, and thus T determines the axioms which govern operations on these values.

Suppose that P and Q are assertions which do not contain local identifiers declared in D. If this is not the case, then we have to perform an alphabetic change of identifiers first. The properties H may be assumed to hold in any proof which establishes that some properties hold within the scope of D. Thus if we prove that from H one can conclude that $\{P\}\ S\ \{Q\}$ holds, then this implies that $\{P\}\ D;S\ \{Q\}$ also holds. So the proof rule which allows us to establish the desired properties of an entire block is:

> If the set H of assertions captures the properties introduced $\qquad$ (42)
> by the declaration D, then
> $$\frac{H \vdash \{P\}\ S\ \{Q\}}{\{P\}\ D;S\ \{Q\}}\ .$$

Here the top line is to be read using the general interpretation of '$H_1, \ldots,$ $H_n \vdash H_{n+1}$' as 'H_{n+1} can be deduced from the collection $H_1, \ldots, H_n$ of assertions'. In order to illustrate the above procedure, consider again the program (39). The formal criterion of correctness of (39) may be expressed as follows:

$$\{f = f_1 f_2 \ldots f_n\}\ copy$$
$$\{(f_L = f_1 \ldots f_n) \wedge (f_R = \langle\ \rangle) \wedge (g_L = f_L) \wedge (g_R = \langle\ \rangle)\}\quad (43)$$

In order to prove (43), we have to show:

$$\{f = f_1 f_2 \ldots f_n\}\ \textbf{begin}\ reset(f);\ rewrite(g);\qquad\qquad (44)$$
$$\textbf{while}\ \neg eof(f)\ \textbf{do}$$
$$\textbf{begin}\ g\!\uparrow := f\!\uparrow;$$
$$put(g);\ get(f)$$
$$\textbf{end}$$
$$\textbf{end}\ \{(f_L = f_1 \ldots f_n) \wedge (f_R = \langle\ \rangle) \wedge (g_L = f_L) \wedge (g_R = \langle\ \rangle)\}$$

When proving (44) we use the properties of the file variables f and g, in particular those that define the effect of the standard file operators eof, $reset$, $rewrite$, put and get. These properties were given in the form of the proof rules in Chapter 4. Since the proof of (44) is elementary but tedious, we leave it to the reader. Having proved (44), we can conclude (43) by the proof rule (42).

Bibliographic Remarks

The formal basis for proofs of correctness of functions was first given by Clint and Hoare (1972). It was later extended in Hoare and Wirth (1973).

Proof rules for procedures without formal parameters and procedures with formal parameters but without global variables are due to Hoare (1971a). These rules were later extended for procedures that include both parameters and global variables (Hoare and Wirth (1973)).

Proof of the algorithm used for the function *root* is borrowed from Manna and Vuillemin (1972). Proof of correctness of the procedure *Partition* is from Hoare (1971b) and Foley and Hoare (1971). The problems in applying the proof rule for functions were pointed out in Ashcroft, Clint and Hoare (1976).

The exercises in this chapter are either borrowed or adapted from Wirth (1972), Gries (1971), Marmier (1975), Manna (1974) and Wirth (1976).

Exercises

1. Consider the following block:

> **var** i: *integer*;
> a: **array** $[1 .. 2]$ **of** *integer*;
> **procedure** $P(x$: *integer*);
> **begin** $i := i + 1$;
> $x := x + 2$
> **end**;
> **begin** {main program}
> $a[1] := 10; a[2] := 20$;
> $i := 1$;
> $P(a[i])$
> **end**

What will be the value of the array a after the call $P(a[i])$ if the type of substitution for the parameter x is

> a. value substitution
> b. variable substitution.

2. Consider the following procedure declaration

> **procedure** p(**var** x,i: *integer*);
> **begin** $i := 1; x := 5; i := 2; x := 7$ **end**

and suppose that b is an integer array variable whose value is (5,7,13,15). Let j be an integer variable initialized to 2, and consider the following procedure call:

$$p(b[j * 2], j)$$

What does the array b look like after the above call if

(a) Subscripting in $b[j * 2]$ is performed first, and then the obtained variable is substituted for the formal parameter x (this is what the rules of Pascal prescribe)

(b) $b[j * 2]$ is substituted for the variable parameter x, and subscripting is performed every time this parameter is encountered during execution of the procedure body (this happens if call by name substitution mechanism from Algol 60 is used).

3. Consider the following block:

> **var** i: *integer*;
> $\quad$ b: **array** $[1 .. 2]$ **of** *integer*;
> **procedure** $q(x$: *integer*$)$;
> **begin** $i := 1; x := x + 2;$
> $\quad$ $b[i] := 10;$
> $\quad$ $i := 2; x := x + 2$
> **end**;
> **begin** $b[1] := 1; b[2] := 1;$
> $\quad$ $i := 1;$
> $\quad$ $q(b[i])$
> **end**

What would be the effect of the call $q(b[i])$ upon the array b if the substitution mechanism for the formal parameter x of the procedure q is defined to be
i. variable substitution
ii. value substitution.

4. Certain problems are inherent in the variable substitution mechanism. They come from the fact that the same variable may be denoted by more than one identifier. Because of that the programmer should, as explained in Section 5.3, follow strictly the following discipline: No two actual variable parameters should be the same. Also, no actual variable parameter should occur in the expression for some actual value parameter of the same call. If this discipline is not followed, wrong results are possible. This will be illustrated by an example which deals with arrays, where departures from the above discipline may be particularly dangerous. Consider the following procedure which performs matrix multiplication:

> **procedure** *mult*(**var** A: **array** $[1 .. m, 1 .. p]$ **of** *real*;
> $\qquad\qquad$ **var** B: **array** $[1 .. p, 1 .. n]$ **of** *real*;
> $\qquad\qquad$ **var** C: **array** $[1 .. m, 1 .. n]$ **of** *real*;
> **var** $i:1 .. m; j:1 .. n; k:1 .. p; s:real$;
> **begin for** $i := 1$ **to** m **do**
> $\quad$ **for** $j := 1$ **to** n **do**
> $\quad\quad$ **begin** $s := 0;$
> $\quad\quad\quad$ **for** $k := 1$ **to** p **do** $s := s + A[i,k] * B[k,j];$
> $\quad\quad\quad$ $C[i,j] := s$
> $\quad\quad$ **end**
> **end**

Suppose, for example, that $m = p = n = 2$, and that the matrices A and B are given as:

$$A = \begin{pmatrix} 2 & 1 \\ -1 & 3 \end{pmatrix} \qquad B = \begin{pmatrix} 3 & -1 \\ 1 & 2 \end{pmatrix}.$$

Investigate the correctness of the effects of the following procedure calls:
i. $mult(A,B,C)$
ii. $mult(A,B,A)$
iii. $mult(A,B,B)$.

5. Rewrite the algorithm for sorting files by natural merging developed in the chapter on program development using explicitly the procedure declaration and the procedure call facilities.

6. Rewrite the algorithm for sorting files by merging using four tapes (balanced sort-merge) using explicitly the procedure declaration and the procedure call facilities.

7. Declare a function which finds a zero of a function by bisection. The function should have three parameters: a real valued function parameter f, which specifies the function whose zero is sought, and two real valued parameters a and b which determine the interval on the real axis in which a zero of the function f is to be found. The method works as follows: Suppose that initially $f(a) < 0$ and $f(b) > 0$. $f((a + b)/2.0)$ is computed. If $f((a + b)/2.0) > 0$, then further search is confined to the interval $(a, (a + b)/2.0)$ otherwise there must be a zero of the function f in the interval $((a + b)/2.0, b)$. This way a zero is computed with some degree of accuracy eps. We assume that f is continuous.

8. The Fibonacci members of order 1 are defined by the following rules:

$$f_0 = 0; f_1 = 1;$$
$$f_n = f_{n-1} + f_{n-2} \quad \text{for} \quad n > 1.$$

The above rules define the following sequence of numbers:

$$0, 1, 1, 2, 3, 5, 8, 13, 21, 34, 55, \ldots$$

Consider now the following function declaration:

```
function fib(n: integer): integer;
var i,a,b: integer;
begin a := 1; b := 0;
    for i := 1 to n do
    begin b := a + b; a := a - b end;
    fib := b
end
```

Prove that the following holds:

$$\forall n((n \geqslant 0) \supset (fib(n) = f_n)).$$

9. Consider the following block:

```
var a,b,c,d,e,f: integer;
procedure m(x,y: integer; var z: integer);
begin z := 0;
    while x ≠ 0 do
    begin if odd(x) then z := z + y;
        y := y * 2; x := x div 2
    end
end;
begin a := 5; b := 7; d := 11; e := 13;
    m(a,b,c);
    {c = 35}
    m(d − b, e − a, f)
    {f = 32}
end
```

Prove that after the call $m(a,b,c)$ the relation $c = 35$ holds, and that after the call $m(d - b, e - a, f)$ the relation $f = 32$ holds.

10. Express explicitly the top-down structure of the algorithm for sorting arrays by natural merging, using the procedure declaration and the procedure call facilities. Then supply proof of correctness of the algorithm obtained that way using the proof rules for procedures.

11. Rewrite the algorithm for sorting arrays by selection as well as its proof of correctness in such a way that procedures are used explicitly.

12. Consider the following block:

```
const m = 1; n = 100;
type index = m .. n;
var a: array [index] of integer;
    x: integer; i,j,k: index;
function f(i,j: index): index;
begin f := (i + j) div 2
end;
begin {array a initialization and sorting}
    ———
    read(x);
    i := m; j := n;
    while i ≠ j do
    begin k := f(i,j);
             if a[k] < x then i := k + 1
             else j := k
    end
end
```

Prove that if we apply this block to a sorted array, then upon exit from the **while-do** loop in the above program the following holds:

$$(a[k] \neq x) \supset \forall i((m \leqslant i \leqslant n) \supset (a[i] \neq x)).$$

13. Consider the following procedure declaration:

```
const m = 1; n = 100;
type domain = m .. n;
procedure q(function f: domain; x: integer; var i: domain);
var j,k: domain;
begin if (f(m) ≤ x) ∧ (x < f(n)) then
      begin i := m; j := n;
            while i < j − 1 do {(i < j) ∧ (f(i) ≤ x < f(j))}
            begin k := (i + j) div 2;
                     if f(k) ≤ x then i := k
                     else j := k
            end
            {f(i) ≤ x < f(i + 1)}
      end
end
```

It is intended to find an argument i of a monotone function f such that the input x lies between $f(i)$ and $f(i + 1)$. Prove that if the function f satisfies the property

$$\forall y1, y2((m \leqslant y1 < y2 \leqslant n) \supset (f(y1) < f(y2)))$$

then a call of $q(f, x, i)$ accomplishes the desired effect.

6
Recursion

6.1 Introduction

We say a function or procedure or data type is *recursive*, or is defined by *recursion*, if the use of the definition recurs within that definition itself.

To see this for functions, consider the familiar function $n! = fact(n)$, which is defined for all integers $n \geqslant 1$ to be the product of all integers from 1 up to n, with $0! = 1$. One way to compute $fact(n)$ is to use the following program:

$$\{n \geqslant 0\} \tag{1}$$
$$\textbf{begin } m := n; r := 1;$$
$$\quad \textbf{while } m > 0 \textbf{ do}$$
$$\quad\quad \textbf{begin } r := m * r; m := m - 1 \textbf{ end}$$
$$\textbf{end } \{fact(n) = r\}.$$

This is *not* a recursive definition. No reference is made to *fact* within the definition itself. However (3) *is* recursive, and uses the familiar equality

$$n * (n - 1) * \ldots * 2 * 1 = n * ((n - 1) * \ldots * 2 * 1). \tag{2}$$

We simply take

$$fact(n) = \begin{cases} 1 \text{ if } n = 0 \\ n * fact(n - 1) \text{ if } n > 0. \end{cases} \tag{3}$$

This unpacks as follows for $n = 3$.

$$\text{Since } 3 \neq 0, fact(3) = 3 * fact(2) \tag{4}$$
Since $2 \neq 0, fact(2) = 2 * fact(1)$ and so $fact(3) = 6 * fact(1)$
Since $1 \neq 0, fact(1) = 1 * fact(0)$ and so $fact(3) = 6 * fact(0)$
Since $0 = 0, fact(0) = 1$ and so $fact(3) = 6$.

To see an example of a recursive definition of a data type, consider the set B^+ of all sequences of one or more elements of a fixed alphabet B. We can define B^+ recursively as follows:

i. If $b \in B$, then $\langle b \rangle \in B^+$ (5)

ii. If $w \in B^+$ and $b \in B$, then $w\langle b \rangle \in B^+$.

Note that the definition is recursive because of the phrase "If $w \in B^+$" in (5) ii. Note that on this definition, the sequence (1,3,4,7) would be represented in B^+ in the form $\langle 1 \rangle \langle 3 \rangle \langle 4 \rangle \langle 7 \rangle$.

We now return to the introductory chapter of this book for an example of a recursive function, and we shall then give an example of a recursive procedure definition in Pascal. We defer further discussion of recursive data structures to our discussion of pointers in Section 6.3.

In Chapter 1, we designed an algorithm for computing the greatest common divisor (gcd) of two nonnegative integers. Recall that the fundamental property which we used was:

$$gcd(m,n) = gcd(n, m \bmod n).\qquad(6)$$

Bearing in mind the relation

$$gcd(m,0) = m\qquad(7)$$

one natural way of defining the desired algorithm would be:

GCD : **if** $n = 0$ **then** answer is m (8)
           else the answer is obtained
           by applying the algorithm GCD
           to n and m **mod** n.

Following a very similar argument to that in Chapter 1, we can show that this algorithm makes sense, since it reduces the problem of computing $gcd(m,n)$ to the problem of $gcd(n, m \bmod n)$, where certainly $0 \leqslant m \bmod n < n$. Thus this process must lead in a finite number of steps to the computation of $gcd(a,b)$ where $b = 0$. But not only does the algorithm terminate, it computes precisely $gcd(m,n)$ since, by (6) the value of this expression remains invariant under the change of parameters.

The major characteristic of the way this version of the GCD algorithm was developed in (8) is that the algorithm is defined in terms of itself or *recursively*. In order to express it in Pascal we have to use recursive procedures and functions. In (9) the algorithm (8) is defined as a recursive function:

function $gcd(m,n: integer): integer$;   (9)
begin if $n = 0$ **then** $gcd := m$
      else $gcd := gcd(n, m \bmod n)$
end

In the declaration of a recursive function, then, calls to that very function occur in the body of the function. Such a recursive call is recognized by an occurrence of the function identifier on the righthand side of an assignment statement such as $gcd(n,m \bmod n)$ in (9). If we have a recursive procedure, then calls of that procedure occur among the statements which constitute the body of the procedure.

Recursive procedures and functions allow us to express explicitly a special type of composition of actions—recursive composition. As we shall now spell out, we have already met this type of composition in the semantics of **while-do** and **repeat-until** statements. With the knowledge that we have at this point, we can say that the semantics of **while** B **do** S can be defined to be the same as that of the call $whiledo(B,S)$ of the recursive procedure $whiledo$ defined in (10).

$$
\begin{aligned}
&\textbf{procedure } whiledo(B\colon Boolean;\ \textbf{procedure } S);\qquad\quad(10)\\
&\textbf{begin if } B \textbf{ then}\\
&\qquad \textbf{begin } S;\\
&\qquad\qquad whiledo(B,S)\\
&\qquad \textbf{end}\\
&\textbf{end}
\end{aligned}
$$

Similarly, the meaning of the statement **repeat** S **until** B can be defined as equivalent to the meaning of the call $repeatuntil(S,B)$ of the recursive procedure $repeatuntil$ declared in (11).

$$
\begin{aligned}
&\textbf{procedure } repeatuntil(\textbf{procedure } S;B\colon Boolean);\qquad(11)\\
&\textbf{begin } S;\\
&\qquad \textbf{if } \neg B \textbf{ then}\\
&\qquad repeatuntil(S,B)\\
&\textbf{end}
\end{aligned}
$$

Because of this simple way of expressing repetition in terms of recursion, many people would say that recursion is the basic composition rule, at least from the conceptual viewpoint. They would then argue that repetition be derived from it. One further justification for this view is that going the other way is in general not at all easy. However, we shall see below that the indiscriminate use of recursion causes severe storage problems in any actual implementation. First however, note that the fundamental problem of possible infinite execution processes is, of course, present in the case of recursive procedures and functions, just as it is present in the case of repetitive composition. This problem can be illustrated by (12), which reexpresses as a Pascal procedure the recursive definition of (3).

$$
\begin{aligned}
&\textbf{procedure } Fact(n\colon integer;\ \textbf{var } r\colon integer);\qquad\quad(12)\\
&\textbf{var } w\colon integer;\\
&\textbf{begin if } n = 0 \textbf{ then } r := 1\\
&\qquad \textbf{else begin } Fact(n-1,\,w);\\
&\qquad\qquad\qquad r := n * w\\
&\qquad\qquad \textbf{end}\\
&\textbf{end}
\end{aligned}
$$

The procedure *Fact* computes the factorial of *n* and assigns the result to *r*. Any call *Fact(m,k)* where $m \geqslant 0$ will cause a finite number of recursive calls, and eventually the execution process will terminate. But if $m < 0$, then the execution of the call *Fact(m,k)* will give rise to an infinite number of recursive calls, since the condition $n = 0$ will never be satisfied. This teaches us that extreme care should be exercised when designing and calling recursive procedures and functions—an issue to be discussed more carefully later in this chapter.

A further very important dynamic aspect of recursive procedures and functions has to do with local variables. The reader is reminded that a local variable of a procedure (or a function) is brought into existence by every activation of that procedure (function) via a procedure (function) call. That instance of the local variable ceases to exist upon completion of that activation of the procedure (function). This in particular holds for recursive procedure (function) calls. It follows that the call *Fact(3,k)* gives rise to 4 instances of the local variable *w*.

Every procedure call requires some overhead, which has to do with parameter substitution, creation and annihilation of local variables, keeping track of the changes in the environment etc. Recursive procedures and functions although very often offering elegant ways of solving certain types of problems, are not always very efficient, and sometimes can be very inefficient when compared with some repetitive algorithms. In order to illustrate this, consider the following problem:

Compute the number of ways in which a natural number *N* can be represented as a sum of natural numbers (we only count once those sums—such as $4 + 1$ and $1 + 4$—which differ only in the order in which the numbers are added):

$$\text{Example—If } N = 5, \text{ there are 7 ways} \qquad (13)$$
$$5, 4 + 1, 3 + 2, 3 + 1 + 1, 2 + 2 + 1,$$
$$2 + 1 + 1 + 1, 1 + 1 + 1 + 1 + 1.$$

The solution to this problem can be expressed in terms of the function *f* such that $f(m,n)$ is the number of ways in which *m* can be expressed as a sum so that each summand is not greater than *n*. If we manage to define the function *f*, then the desired answer is computed as $f(N,N)$.

The function *f* can be defined as follows:

$$
\begin{aligned}
f(1,n) &= 1 && \text{for all } n && (14)\\
f(m,1) &= 1 && \text{for all } m \\
f(m,n) &= f(m,m) && \text{if } m < n \\
f(m,m) &= 1 + f(m, m-1) \\
f(m,n) &= f(m, n-1) + f(m-n, n) && \text{if } m > n.
\end{aligned}
$$

A recursive function declaration follows immediately from the above definitions:

$$\begin{aligned}
&\textbf{function } f(m,n: integer): integer; \qquad\qquad (15)\\
&\textbf{begin if } (m = 1) \vee (n = 1) \textbf{ then } f := 1\\
&\qquad \textbf{else if } m \leqslant n \textbf{ then } f := 1 + f(m, m - 1)\\
&\qquad\qquad \textbf{else } f := f(m, n - 1) + f(m - n, n)\\
&\textbf{end}
\end{aligned}$$

And now let us look into the sequence of calls which the call $f(6,4)$ gives rise to. These are represented by the diagram (16).

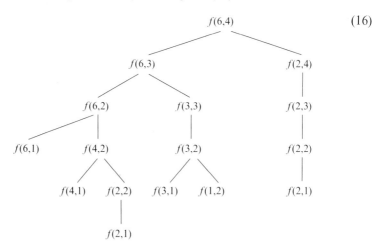

(16)

Not only is the number of calls large, but some of them get repeated ($f(2,1)$ and $f(2,2)$). For larger m and n (and for some particular m and n) the number of repeated calls becomes much larger. Altogether, the performance of the algorithm can be very poor. This type of problem has turned a number of programmers against recursive procedures and functions. It is certainly true that recursion, in spite of its elegance, can lead to considerable inefficiency. Because of that recursion should not be used in those cases where there exists a simple and efficient repetitive solution. But there are many solutions where use of recursion is quite appropriate and justified, and two such complex examples will be presented in the next section.

Proof Rules for Recursive Procedures

A very interesting problem arises when we want to prove correctness of a recursive procedure. Consider, for example, the following procedure for computing the factorial of a given nonnegative integer:

> **procedure** *fact*(**var** *r*: *integer*; *n*: *integer*);   (17)
> **var** *w*: *integer*;
> **begin if** *n* = 0 *then* *r* := 1
>   **else**
>   **begin** *fact*(*w*, *n* − 1);
>   *r* := *n* * *w*
>   **end**
> **end**

In order to prove that a call of the procedure *fact* satisfies the desired property, we have to prove that the procedure body satisfies that property, just as we did in Section 5.4. Thus, more formally, in order to prove

$$\{n \geqslant 0\}\; fact(r,n)\; \{r = n!\} \tag{18}$$

for every *n* and *r*, we have to prove

$$\{n \geqslant 0\}\; body_{fact}\; \{r = n!\} \tag{19}$$

This simple strategy does not take us very far, however, since the procedure body contains a call *fact*(*w*, *n* − 1). The correct methodology is to assume that the inner call satisfies the property (18) and then prove the property (19) for the procedure body. This proof rule is easy to justify appealing to *mathematical* induction.

Let us now prove (19) by induction. If $n \geqslant 0$ before the body is executed, then either $n = 0$ or $n > 0$.

Basis Step. If $n = 0$ then $1 = 0!$ implies $1 = n!$. Thus $\{n = 0\}\; r := 1$ $\{r = n!\}$, and so $\{n = 0\}\; fact(r,n)\; \{r = n!\}$.

Induction Step. If $n > 0$, then $n - 1 \geqslant 0$. We can thus use the assumption $\{n - 1 \geqslant 0\}\; fact(w, n - 1)\; \{w = (n - 1)!\}$ about the inner call of the procedure body to conclude that $w = (n - 1)!$ will hold after the call *fact*(*w*, $n - 1$). But then after the assignment $r := n * w$, $r = n * (n - 1)!$ holds, that is, $r = n!$ holds.

So we have proved that if $n \geqslant 0$ holds before the procedure body is executed, $r = n!$ will hold after its execution. Thus formally, we have used the following proof rules:

$$\frac{\forall x(\{P\}\; p(x)\; \{Q\}) \vdash \{P\}\; S\; \{Q\}}{\forall x(\{P\}\; p(x)\; \{Q\})} \tag{20}$$

where *S* is the body of the recursive procedure *p*.

$$\frac{\forall x(\{P\}\; p(x)\; \{Q\})}{\{P_a^x\}\; p(a)\; \{Q_a^x\}} . \tag{21}$$

Application of these proof rules requires a careful discipline on the use of variables—recall the $dis(x)$ condition of (17) and (18) in Section 5.3.

Proof of (20) proceeds as follows:

> The assumption of the theorem is
> i. $\forall x(\{P\}\ p(x)\ \{Q\}) \vdash \{P\}\ S\ \{Q\}$
> and we have to prove
> ii. $\forall x(\{P\}\ p(x)\ \{Q\})$.

We do this by induction on the number of levels of recursion caused by the procedure call $p(x)$:

Basis Step. Suppose that $p(x)$ gives rise to no inner recursive calls, i.e., no recursive call $p(x)$ in the body S of p gets executed when p is called and thus only one activation of S occurs. Then it follows from the assumption i. of the theorem that $\{P\}\ S\ \{Q\}$. According to the proof rule for procedures, if $\{P\}\ S\ \{Q\}$ holds, then a call of the procedure p satisfies $\forall x(\{P\}\ p(x)\ \{Q\})$, so ii. holds in this case.

Induction Step. Assume now that ii. holds if a call of p gives rise to (at most) n levels of recursion, i.e., each inner recursive call in S gives rise to (at most) n recursive calls of p (inductive hypothesis). Then i. permits us to conclude that $\{P\}\ S\ \{Q\}$ holds, and according to the proof rule for procedures, we conclude that ii. holds where now $p(x)$ causes $n + 1$ levels of recursion (including the top-most activation of S). Thus the inductive step is established, and proof of (18) is completed.

6.2 Design and Correctness of Recursive Procedures

In Chapter 5, the concept of a procedure allowed us to make an explicit distinction between two levels of abstraction in program development. On the level of the main program, a procedure call represents a simple action. On that level we were concerned only with what the procedure does. How it does it was irrelevant on this level of abstraction. However, on the level of the procedure itself, we were concerned with how it accomplishes its task regardless of how it is used. Unfortunately, this clear distinction of two semantic levels does not apply to recursive procedures. A recursive procedure has to be understood and conceived on a single semantic level and as such it represents a composition of actions like the other composition schemes we have discussed. Because of this, design of a recursive procedure requires a mental skill different from the skill required for design of the sort of programs discussed so far. Design methodology for recursive procedures will be illustrated on the problem of 8 queens. We will then turn to a proof of correctness for the recursive *Quicksort* algorithm.

The Eight Queens Problem

The 8-queens problem is: Find all configurations of 8 queens on a chess-board of 8×8 squares such that—as in the example of Figure 6.1—no queen may be taken by any other queen. In other words, no two queens may be on the same row, on the same column or the same diagonal.

The algorithm that we provide is an example of the stepwise construction of a solution by repeated trial and error. The essential characteristic of this method is that candidates for a solution are generated in a systematic manner and tested according to the criteria characterizing the solution. Roughly speaking, we hope to find a representation of trial solutions x of the form $[x_1, \ldots, x_n]$, such that x can be generated in steps which produce $[x_1]$, $[x_1, x_2], \ldots, [x_1, \ldots, x_n]$. The decomposition $[x_1, \ldots, x_n]$ of x must be such that:

i. Every step (a passage from $[x_1, \ldots, x_j]$ to $[x_1, \ldots, x_j, x_{j+1}]$)   (1)
   must be considerably simpler than the computation of the
   entire candidate x.

ii. If q is the predicate characterizing a solution to the problem,
   then we must have

$$\forall j ((1 \leqslant j \leqslant n) \supset (q(x) \supset q([x_1, \ldots, x_j]))).$$

Clause ii. means that in order to obtain a full and correct solution, we have to extend a partial solution in such a way that it satisfies the desired correctness criterion. But it may happen that a partial solution may not be extensible in such a way. If this happens for a trial solution at step j, we have to annul some of the previous extensions of the trial solution, i.e., we have to shorten it to $[x_1, \ldots, x_i]$ where $i < j$, and then try a different extension of $[x_1, \ldots, x_i]$. This process is called *backtracking*.

We now apply this methodology to the 8-queens problem. If we number the rows and columns of our chessboard, as in Figure 6.1, with integers 0 through 7, then systematic construction of trial solutions to the 8-queens

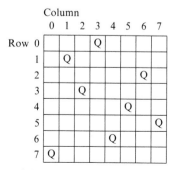

Figure 6.1   One of the 92 solutions to the eight-queens problem.

problem consists of positioning queens in successive rows starting with the row 0 and adding a safe queen (i.e., one which cannot be taken by any other already positioned queen) in the next row in each step. Obviously, a partial configuration not satisfying the mutual safety condition can never be extended by this method into a full solution. Also, since during the *j*th step only pairs of queens including the *j*th queen have to be tested for mutual safety, finding a partial solution at step *j* requires less effort than finding a complete solution. Recall that these were the criteria ii. and i. which we placed above on the representation of trial solutions. Now, more precisely, the algorithm puts the queen of row 0 in column 0. This queen remains there until all safe configurations with queen 0 in that position are generated. Only then is this queen moved one square to the right to the next column. For each position of queen 0, queen 1 will walk from left to right in row 1—skipping the squares that are covered by queen 0. For each combined position of the first two queens, queen 2 walks along row 2 from left to right, skipping all squares covered by the preceding queens etc. Figure 6.2 shows the first placement of queens 0 through 4, and makes clear the need for backtracking.

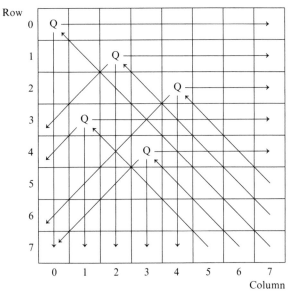

Figure 6.2   Placement of first 5 queens at start of algorithm developed in the text. Note that each queen is placed in the leftmost square of its row not covered by the "lines of attack" of queens in earlier rows. At this stage, there are *no* 'safe' squares in row 5 (or rows 6 or 7) and so *backtracking* is required—searching by trial and error for positions for the queens in earlier rows which will yield a 'safe' square in row 5.

Note that squares with equal sum of their coordinates lie on the same *downward* diagonal, and squares with equal differences of their coordinates lie on the same *upward* diagonal.

Generating partial configurations (for the moment we forget about the printing of those configurations that form full solutions) may be accomplished by the following loop.

$$\textit{initialize empty board}; \qquad\qquad (2)$$
$$h := 0;$$
$$\textbf{repeat } \textit{set queen on square } (0,h);$$
$$\qquad\qquad \textit{generate all configurations with}$$
$$\qquad\qquad \textit{queen 0 fixed};$$
$$\qquad\qquad \textit{remove queen from square } (0,h);$$
$$\qquad\qquad h := h + 1$$
$$\textbf{until } h = 8$$

In order to generate all configurations with queen 0 fixed we proceed using the same strategy, given in the program below:

$$h1 := 0; \qquad\qquad (3)$$
$$\textbf{repeat if } \textit{square}(1,h1) \textit{ safe } \textbf{then}$$
$$\qquad \textbf{begin } \textit{set queen on square}(1,h1);$$
$$\qquad\qquad \textit{generate all configurations with}$$
$$\qquad\qquad \textit{first 2 queens fixed};$$
$$\qquad\qquad \textit{remove queen from square } (1,h1)$$
$$\qquad \textbf{end}$$
$$\qquad h1 := h1 + 1$$
$$\textbf{until } h1 = 8$$

For *generate all configurations with first 2 queens fixed* we could write a similar piece of program and so on. Inserting these programs into each other would result in a correct program with 8 nested loops. These loops would be very similar. Such a program, although correct, would be clumsy, repetitious and unadaptable to changes in board size. What we want to achieve is that all these loops be executed under control of the same program text. Thus we have to make the texts of the 8 loops identical.

The exceptional loops are the outermost and the innermost ones. The outermost loop is exceptional in that it does not test whether the square $(0,h)$ is safe since we know that it is. But then there is no harm in inserting the conditional clause

$$\textbf{if } \textit{square}(0,h) \textit{ safe } \textbf{then} \qquad\qquad (4)$$

which is superfluous in the case of the first loop, but makes it identical with the next six loops.

In the design of the innermost loop we have to take into account what we neglected at first: printing a configuration as soon as 8 queens have been safely placed on the board. In order to make this loop identical with the preceding seven, we replace the statement *generate* in each loop by the statement:

$$\textbf{if } board\ full \textbf{ then } print\ configuration \qquad (5)$$
$$\textbf{else } generate\ all\ configurations$$
$$extending\ the\ current\ one$$

If we introduce a global variable n which represents the number of queens currently on the board, then *board full* may be refined into $n = 8$, and the operations on squares may have n as their first subscript. But then the only remaining difference between the eight loops is that each has its private h. At this point it becomes clear that sequencing through the eight nested loops can be evoked with the aid of a recursive procedure with local variable h. The procedure (with global variable n) is defined as:

```
procedure generate;                                    (6)
var h: integer;
begin h := 0;
      repeat if square(n,h) safe then
             begin set queen on square(n,h);
                   n := n + 1;
                   if n = 8 then print configuration
                   else generate;
                   n := n - 1;
                   remove queen from square(n,h)
             end;
             h := h + 1
      until h = 8
end
```

The desired program then reduces to:

```
initialize empty board;                                (7)
n := 0;
generate
```

Each activation of *generate* will introduce its private local variable h and thus we effectively obtain variables $h, h1, \ldots, h7$ which we would need when writing eight nested loops. The fact that each recursive call of *generate* creates its private instance of the local variable h makes *backtracking* work in the developed algorithm. Rather than analyzing what happens in general on some level of recursion n, $0 \leqslant n < 8$, let us consider a particular case. The algorithm given by (6) and (7) positions the first five queens as shown in Figure 6.2. Now the test *square(5,h) safe* fails for all h, $0 \leqslant h < 8$. Observe that h here stands for $h5$. That means that the **repeat-until** loop in (6) is terminated as well as the sixth activation of the procedure *generate*. We end up at the point after the call *generate*, where we are now on the level of the fifth activation of the procedure *generate*, and h thus stands for $h4$. $(4,h4)$ is the position of the queen placed in the fourth row. $h4$ is now increased by one $(h := h + 1$ in (6)$)$, and the square $(4,4)$ is tested for safety. Since it is not safe, the squares $(4,5)$, $(4,6)$ and $(4,7)$ will be tested for safety to discover that

(4,7) is the first safe one. So queen number 5 is placed on the square (4,7), and we proceed to row number 5, calling *generate* at the sixth level of its activation.

In order to complete the refinement process, we have to decide how to represent the configuration on the board. For that purpose we introduce an array variable x declared as:

$$\textbf{var } x \colon \textbf{array } [0 \ . \ . \ 7] \textbf{ of } integer \qquad (8)$$

adopting the convention that $x[i]$ $(0 \leqslant i \leqslant 7)$ denotes the number of the column occupied by the queen in the ith row.

There is no logical need to introduce additional variables, since the abstract test *square(n,h) safe* can be refined in such a way that safety of the square (n,h) is determined solely on the grounds of x, i.e., on the basis of the positions of the queens placed thus far on the board. This requires testing whether there is a queen on the column, the "upward" diagonal and the "downward" diagonal passing through the square (n,h). However, this is a time-consuming operation which occurs very often in (6). Thus in order to obtain a more efficient solution, we represent the information required by *square(n,h) safe* by the three Boolean variables *col*, *up* and *down* as follows:

$$col[k] = true \colon \text{no queen is positioned in the } k\text{th column} \qquad (9)$$

$$up[k] = true \colon \text{no queen is positioned in the } k\text{th upward}$$
$$\text{diagonal}$$

$$down[k] = true \colon \text{no queen is positioned in the } k\text{th downward}$$
$$\text{diagonal.}$$

Squares with equal sum of their coordinates lie on the same downward diagonal and the squares with equal differences of their coordinates lie on the same upward diagonal. Because of this, the arrays are declared as:

$$\begin{aligned}
\textbf{var } col \colon \quad & \textbf{array } [0 \ . \ . \ 7] \textbf{ of } Boolean; \qquad (10)\\
up \colon \quad & \textbf{array } [-7 \ . \ . \ +7] \textbf{ of } Boolean;\\
down \colon \ & \textbf{array } [0 \ . \ . \ 14] \textbf{ of } Boolean
\end{aligned}$$

Now the test *square[n,h] safe* simply reduces to

$$col[h] \wedge up[n - h] \wedge down[n + h]. \qquad (11)$$

The statement *set queen on square(n,h)* is now refined as:

$$\begin{aligned}
& x[n] := h; \qquad\qquad\qquad\qquad (12)\\
& col[h] := false;\\
& up[n - h] := false;\\
& down[n + h] := false
\end{aligned}$$

and the statement *remove queen from square(n,h)* as:

$$down[n + h] := true; \ up[n - h] := true; \ col[h] := true \qquad (13)$$

Note that (13) works because a queen is not placed on a square unless (11) holds beforehand.

The gain in speed comes from the fact that the test *square(n,h) safe* is executed far more often than the statements *set queen on square(n,h)* and *remove queen from square(n,h)*.

The complete program is presented in (14). It is interesting that the developed algorithm is asymmetric; it tests rows and columns differently in spite of the fact that the original problem was symmetric in that respect. Instead of introducing an array variable x to represent configurations on the board, we could have introduced a Boolean square matrix (two-dimensional array) B with $B[i,j] = true$ meaning that square (i,j) is occupied. This data representation of relevant facts of the algorithm would certainly closely reflect a chessboard, but it is fairly evident that the representaton that we chose is more suitable than a Boolean matrix in terms of simplicity of instructions and of storage economy. Thus this example teaches us also to consider asymmetric algorithms in the design process.

```
program queens(output);                                              (14)
var n,k: integer; x: array [0 . . 7] of integer;
    col: array [0 . . 7] of Boolean; up: array [−7 . . 7] of Boolean;
    down: array [0 . . 14] of Boolean;
procedure generate;
var h: integer;
begin h := 0;
      repeat if {square(n,h) safe} col[h] ∧ up[n − h] ∧ down[n + h] then
             begin {set queen on square(n,h)}
                   x[n] := h; col[h] := false; up[n − h] := false;
                   down[n + h] := false; n := n + 1;
                   if {board full} n = 8 then
                   begin {print configuration}
                         k := 0; repeat write(x[k]);
                                        k := k + 1
                                 until k = 8; writeln;
                   end
                   else generate;
                   n := n − 1; {remove queen from square(n,h)}
                   down[n + h] := true; up[n − h] := true;
                   col[h] := true
             end;
             h := h + 1
      until h = 8
end;
begin {main program}
{initialize empty board}
n := 0;
k := 0; repeat col[k] := true; k := k + 1 until k = 8;
k := 0; repeat up[k − 7] := true; down[k] := true; k := k + 1 until k = 15;
generate
end.
```

The Quicksort Algorithm

The next example to be discussed is the *Quicksort* algorithm. The purpose of the example is to illustrate how correctness of a modular program is proved on the basis of the already established correctness of any procedures which it uses.

   The procedure *Quicksort* is designed for sorting the elements from $A[m]$ to $A[n]$ of an array A—elements with subscripts below m and above n are left untouched. Thus the desired result of the program is expressed formally as:

$$\forall p,q((m \leqslant p \leqslant q \leqslant n) \supset (A[p] \leqslant A[q])) \tag{14}$$

with an additional requirement that the array A after execution of *Quicksort* is the same as before, except for the fact that its elements from $A[m]$ to $A[n]$ are permuted. This second requirement will not be specified formally, since it will be clear from the proposed solution that it is satisfied. As in the case of the procedure *Partition*, if we assume that the index bounds of the array A are 1 and N, then the condition which must hold before every call of the procedure is

$$1 \leqslant m \leqslant n \leqslant N \tag{15}$$

and every call of the procedure should leave this relation unaffected.

   Partition(A,i,j,m,n) is given the array A and the integers m and n. It returns integers i and j, as well as permuting the elements of A. It does this by rearranging only the array elements between $A[m]$ and $A[n]$ in such a way that (16) below holds (Fig. 6.3). Note that this is just (20) of Section 5.3.

$$(j < i) \wedge \forall p,q((m \leqslant p < i) \wedge (j < q \leqslant n) \supset (A[p] \leqslant A[q])). \tag{16}$$

   Note that (16) implies that the elements between $A[j]$ and $A[i]$ are not only already sorted—they are equal. Indeed, if $j < p \leqslant q < i$ then both $m \leqslant p < i$ and $j < q \leqslant n$, which according to (16) implies $A[p] \leqslant A[q]$. Similarly, $m \leqslant q < i$ and $j < p \leqslant n$ implies $A[q] \leqslant A[p]$. In other words, (16) implies

$$\forall p,q((j < p \leqslant q < i) \supset (A[p] = A[q])). \tag{17}$$

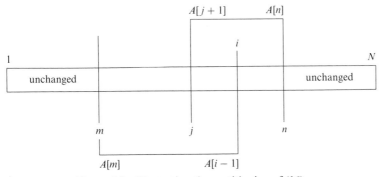

Figure 6.3   Illustrating the partitioning of (16).

More importantly (16) tells us that

$$\forall p,q((m \leqslant p \leqslant j) \wedge (j < q \leqslant n) \supset (A[p] \leqslant A[q])) \tag{18}$$
$$\forall p,q((m \leqslant p < i) \wedge (i \leqslant q \leqslant n) \supset (A[p] \leqslant A[q])).$$

But if (17) and (18) hold after a call to the procedure *Partition* which, in particular, returns i and j, then all that remains to be done is to sort the array elements with subscripts between (and including) m and j, and i and n. This is achieved by two recursive calls of *Quicksort*, so that the proposed program is:

```
procedure Quicksort(var A: array [1 . . N] of integer; m,n: integer);   (19)
var i,j: integer;
begin if m < n then
       begin Partition(A,i,j,m,n);
             Quicksort(A,m,j);
             Quicksort(A,i,n)
       end
end
```

It is obvious now that *Quicksort* satisfies the second, informally stated criterion of correctness. This follows from the fact that the only manipulation that the procedure *Partition* performs with the array elements between $A[m]$ and $A[n]$ is exchanging two at a time. This operation is a permutation, and since the composition of permutations is a permutation, we are assured that the required result holds.

To prove that *Quicksort* satisfies (14), consider the body of *Quicksort* annotated with invariants as comments:

```
if  m < n then                                                          (20)
begin {m < n}
      Partition(A,i,j,m,n);
      {(j < i) ∧ ∀p,q((m ≤ p < i) ∧ (j < q ≤ n) ⊃ (A[p] ≤ A[q])}
      Quicksort(A,m,j);
      {∀p,q((m ≤ p ≤ q ≤ j) ⊃ (A[p] ≤ A[q]))}
      Quicksort(A,i,n);
      {∀p,q((i ≤ p ≤ q ≤ n) ⊃ (A[p] ≤ A[q]))}
end
{∀p,q((m ≤ p ≤ q ≤ n) ⊃ (A[p] ≤ A[q]))}
```

The first thing to be proved is that the correctness criterion is satisfied if the body of the conditional is not executed at all, i.e., when $n \leqslant m$. Formally, $n \leqslant m$ implies the correctness criterion (14) since in that case $m \leqslant p \leqslant q \leqslant n$ implies $n = m$, i.e., there is only one element to be sorted. If $m < n$ then after the call of the procedure *Partition*, (18) holds, since it follows from (16). (18) remains unaffected by the two recursive calls to the procedure *Quicksort*, since i and j are—at the level we are discussing—external to these calls of *Quicksort*. After the call, $Quicksort(A,m,j)$ $\forall p,q((m \leqslant p \leqslant q \leqslant j) \supset (A[p] \leqslant$

$A[q])$) holds and remains unaffected by the call $Quicksort(A,i,n)$, after which $\forall p,q((i \leqslant p \leqslant q \leqslant n) \supset (A[p] \leqslant A[q]))$ holds. (Recall that it is our inductive hypothesis that the inner recursive calls work correctly). Thus in the end we have that the following conditions hold:

$$\forall p,q((m \leqslant p \leqslant j) \wedge (j \leqslant q \leqslant n) \supset (A[p] \leqslant A[q])) \tag{21}$$
$$\forall p,q((m \leqslant p \leqslant i) \wedge (i \leqslant q \leqslant n) \supset (A[p] \leqslant A[q]))$$
$$\forall p,q((m \leqslant p \leqslant q \leqslant j) \supset (A[p] \leqslant A[q]))$$
$$\forall p,q((i \leqslant p \leqslant q \leqslant n) \supset (A[p] \leqslant A[q]))$$

the above conditions clearly imply

$$\forall p,q((m \leqslant p \leqslant q \leqslant n) \supset (A[p] \leqslant A[q])) \tag{22}$$

which completes the proof of $Quicksort$.

6.3 Recursive Data Types

In this section, we study the use of *pointers* to build up recursive data types and exemplify their use in recursively defining lists and the s-expressions of the list-manipulating language Lisp. We then study the use of recursive procedures and functions in processing recursive data structures.

Pointers, Dynamic Variables, and Lists

If T is a type, then the Pascal declaration

$$\textbf{type } P = \uparrow T \tag{1}$$

defines a new type P which is a set of values *pointing* to elements of the type T. Because of that P is called a *pointer type* and is said to be *bound* to T. Every pointer type includes **nil** amongst its possible values. **nil** points to no element at all. A variable of the type P is called a *pointer variable bound to the type T*. If p is such a variable, then p is a *reference* to a variable of type T. This variable of type T to which p points is denoted by $p\uparrow$. This is illustrated in (2)

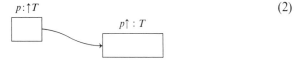

$$\tag{2}$$

Pointer variables are used to reference variables which do not occur in explicit variable declarations and thus cannot be referenced directly by identifiers. Variables of this sort are called *dynamic variables*. These variables are generated dynamically, but independently of the static program structure, as opposed to the static variables whose generation is reflected by the static program structure. A *static variable* is explicitly declared and subsequently denoted by its identifier. It exists during the entire execution of the block to which it is local. A dynamic variable is brought into existence via a call of the standard procedure *new*. If p is of type $\uparrow T$ then

$$new(p) \tag{3}$$

allocates a new variable x of type T and assigns a reference to that variable to the variable p. x is subsequently accessed via p and is denoted as $p\uparrow$.

Allocation of a new variable means allocation of a memory region of the appropriate size. If that variable later becomes unnecessary, again independently of the static program structure, some means should be provided to indicate that the memory region allocated for that variable is once again available. This is done by a call of the standard procedure *dispose*, which has the form

$$dispose(p) \tag{4}$$

The actual effect of (4) depends upon the implementation, which may use the information provided by (4) to retrieve storage, or just ignore it.

Pointers are used to construct and manipulate *directed finite graphs* such as that shown in Figure 6.4(a). Here we see a set of *nodes* and *edges*, with each edge directed *from* one node to another. If the graph takes the linear form shown in Figure 6.4(b), and if a word of information is stored at each node, then our directed graph takes the form of a list.

If all the nodes bear data of the same type, we may view the set of *lists* (including the empty list) as forming a recursive data type. We let a node

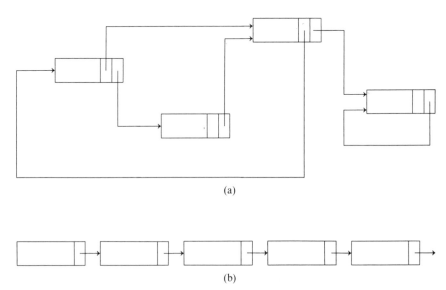

(a)

(b)

Figure 6.4   (a) A directed graph. Note that different nodes may have different numbers of successors, and that a node may be its own successor; (b) A list viewed as a linear directed graph.

be an element of a given type T. Then:

   i. The empty set of nodes is a list.   (5)

  ii. If h is a node and t is a list, then an ordered pair (h,t) is a list. h is called the *head*, and t the *tail* of the list (h,t).

In a graphical representation such as Figure 6.4(b) of a list (h,t), we draw a directed edge from the node h to the head of the list t on condition, of course, that t is nonempty. In terms of the data structuring facilities introduced so far, this directed edge is represented by a pointer. In (6), then, we represent each node as a pair comprising a character (the data stored at the node) and a *link* (a pointer to the next node). If the link component takes the value **nil**, then the node is the last in the list.

$$\textbf{type } \textit{link} = \uparrow\textit{node};\qquad\qquad\qquad(6)$$
$$\textit{node} = \textbf{record } \textit{info}: \textit{char};$$
$$\textit{next}: \textit{link}$$
$$\textbf{end}$$

Observe that in (6) the name of the type *node* is used indirectly within its own type definition. That is, we defined the new type *node* in such a way that one of its component types is defined in terms of the same type *node*. This circularity which comes from the recursive nature of the type *node* is permitted only in situations like (6) where the field *next* is of a pointer type bound to the type *node*. In other words, a type name may not be used directly or indirectly within its own definition in Pascal unless a pointer "intervenes" between any two uses of the type name. If p is a variable of type *link*, then the effect of *new*(p) consists of creating a new variable p of type *link*, and the variable $p\uparrow$ of type *node*, and setting p to point to $p\uparrow$. As we see from

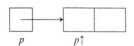

$$p\qquad\qquad p\uparrow$$

the variable $p\uparrow$ contains a field of type *info* and a field of type *link*. The latter should be set to the head of a list whose elements are of type *node*. The simplest way of doing this is for the list to be empty, so that $p\uparrow$. *link* is set to **nil**. In this case, p points to a one-element list. Going back to definition (5), we see how it is implemented using pointers.

In (7) we see *head* as the link which points to the actual list:

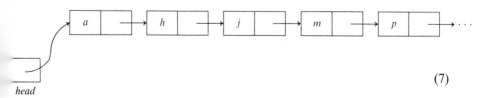

$$(7)$$

head

In order to create a list of this sort which has *n* elements we read *n* characters
from the standard file *input* and create successive list elements, assigning the
characters to the *info* fields in turn:

```
var head, pt: link; i: integer; ch: char;
begin head : = nil;
      for i := 1 to n do
      begin read(ch); new(pt);
            pt↑ . next := head;
            pt↑ . info := ch;
            head := pt
      end
```

Observe that in the above program the list pointed at by the variable *head*
is created appending new list elements at the beginning of the list created so
far, where we start with the empty list.

To see what happens when we need to add elements at the end of a list,
we consider the problem of reading a sequence of values (characters) from
the standard file *input* and using them to create a list, in the order of occurrence in the file. If we do not know how many elements that file has but we
know that it has at least one, then the following program will do the job:

```
var head, pt, newp: link; ch: char;                          (8)
begin new(head); read(ch);
      head↑ . info := ch;
      head↑ . next := nil; pt := head;
      while ¬eof do
      begin read(ch);
            new(newp); newp↑ . info := ch;
            newp↑ . next := pt↑ . next;
            pt↑ . next := newp;
            pt := newp
      end
end
```

If we wish to add elements at the end of the list, without having to search
the list every time in order to discover its end, a separate pointer *pt* is maintained which, as shown in (9), points to the end of the list.

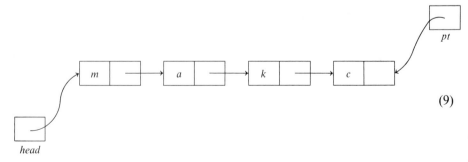

(9)

Consider the pair of assignments

$$newp\uparrow . next := pt\uparrow . next; \qquad (10)$$
$$pt\uparrow . next := newp$$

which occurs in (8). Note that $pt\uparrow . next$ is the *link* field of the node, $pt\uparrow$, which is pointed to by pt. (10) inserts a new record pointed at by $newp$ after the record of the list pointed at by pt. In other words, if the situation before (10) is executed is:

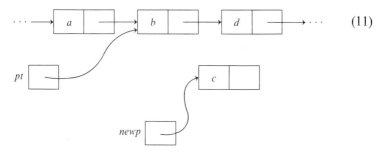

$$(11)$$

so that $pt\uparrow . next$ points to the node containing the character d, then after execution of (10) the situation is:

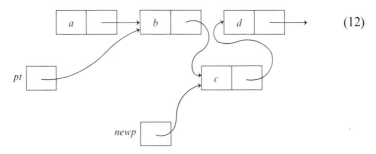

$$(12)$$

Of course, in (8) we know that $pt\uparrow . next$ is always **nil**, and so we should really use $newp\uparrow . next := $ **nil** rather than $newp\uparrow . next := pt\uparrow . next$. So insertion of an element after the element pointed at by pt is no problem, but the question is whether we can insert an element before the element pointed at by pt. In fact, this operation arises very often when one performs list manipulation. Suppose, for example, that we have an *ordered* list (elements are linked according to the ascending order of the value of the field *info*), and that we want to insert a new list element into the list at the appropriate place. Then we would first search the list (the operation to be explained shortly) to find the element whose field *info* has the value which is just greater (greater or equal if we allow duplicate values of this field) than the value of this field of the element to be inserted. Having found such an element (it is also possible that we reach the end of the list this way, and in that case we simply add the new element at the end of the list), we want to insert this element before the located element. It seems that one-way links would not allow this operation to be performed, unless we have a pointer to the element which precedes the located element. And, in fact, this is one way of accomplishing this insertion: maintaining two pointers which point to two adjacent list elements. But this approach requires special care if the boundary cases are to be handled properly (a one element list, for example, or empty list). It comes perhaps as a surprise that it is in fact easy to insert an element into a list before some element. This trick is explained in (13), which inserts an element with the field *info* equal to this character before the element pointed at by *pt*. Figure 6.5 explains this manipulation graphically.

$$new(newp);   \tag{13}$$
$$newp\uparrow := pt\uparrow;$$
$$pt\uparrow . info := ch;$$
$$pt\uparrow . next := newp$$

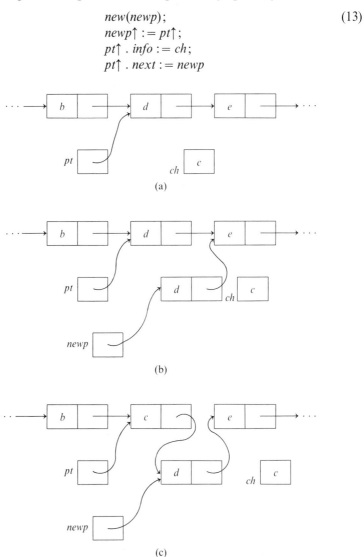

(a)

(b)

(c)

Figure 6.5   A graphical demonstration of inserting a character in a list using (13).

The key point to note is that in creating the new pointer *newp*, we also create a new node to which it points—so that $newp\uparrow := pt\uparrow$ gets *newp* to point to a *replica* of the node to which *pt* points, not to that target node itself.

Although (13) does insert an element in a list in front of the element pointed to by *pt*, the instruction $newp\uparrow := pt\uparrow$ copies the *info* field as well as the pointer field of $pt\uparrow$. But one reason for using lists is to avoid such copying of information fields of list elements, and to perform insertions (or deletions) of list elements by manipulating only the pointer fields, rather than entire elements. We shall see this illustrated in examples and exercises below.

Deletion from a list of the node which follows the list element pointed out by *pt* is performed by a single statement:

$$pt\uparrow . next := pt\uparrow . next\uparrow . next \qquad (14)$$

Thus if the situation before execution of (14) is

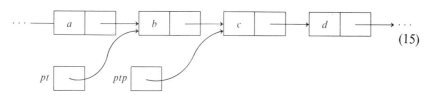

$$(15)$$

then after execution of (14) the situation is

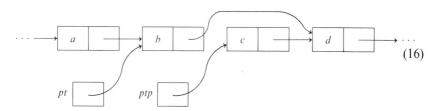

$$(16)$$

In order not to lose free storage which results after execution of the assignments (14), we write:

$$dispose(ptp) \qquad (17)$$

A trick similar to inserting an element before the designated element can be used here if we know that the designated element has a successor. If so, then we can move the successor fields to the fields of the designated element, and then delete the successor. So we obtain the following piece of program:

> **if** $pt\uparrow . next \neq$ **nil then**   (18)
> **begin** $q := pt\uparrow . next$;
> $pt\uparrow := q\uparrow$;
> $pt\uparrow . next := pt\uparrow . next\uparrow . next$;
> $dispose(q)$
> **end**

Deleting the element pointed at by *ptp* itself is more complicated. One way of doing it consists of maintaining two pointers, one that points to that element of the list which is to be deleted, call it *ptp*, and the other, call it *pt*, which points to the element which precedes the element pointed at by *ptp*. Deletion is then performed by the following assignments:

$$ptp := ptp\uparrow . next; \tag{19}$$
$$pt\uparrow . next := ptp$$

But here, just as in the case of insertion, special cases have to be taken into account, such as the case of a one-element list or empty list.

Consider now two typical search operations. The first search operation, already mentioned, consists of locating the node of the list pointed at by *head* such that the *info* field of that node has value $>$ '*c*'. If we do not know whether such a list element does indeed exist, then we also have to take into account the possibility that we may reach the end of the list without having discovered the desired element. One way of performing the desired search is by the following program part:

$$pt := head; b := true; \tag{20}$$
while ($pt \neq$ **nil**) **and** b **do**
if $pt\uparrow . info >$ '*c*' **then** $b := false$
else $pt := pt\uparrow . next.$

The other basic search operation is traversing the entire list to perform some operation on each element of the list. An example of this kind is printing a list, which may be accomplished as follows:

$$pt := head; \tag{21}$$
while $pt \neq$ **nil do**
begin $write(pt\uparrow . info);$
        $pt := pt\uparrow . next$
end

On the basis of the operations on lists previously discussed, one can draw some simple and important conclusions. If we have a sequence of elements of the same type, then representing it as a list would be particularly suitable in those situations where operations of deleting and/or inserting arbitrary elements of the sequence are to be performed frequently, and where search operations would be of the second type described above. Arrays and files are certainly inferior to lists as far as the operations of deletions and/or insertions of arbitrary elements are concerned. Arrays require shifting of elements, and files require complete rewriting. Sequential processing of arrays is somewhat faster than sequential processing of lists, and sequential processing of files slower. Arrays have definite advantages over lists in accessing a random element, and searching an ordered array for a desired element is particularly efficient. This type of search is very slow for lists, on the average it requires $n/2$ accesses of list elements and comparisons.

If we expect to access elements in the middle or at the end of a list, then rather than searching it sequentially, several pointers to these parts of the list should be kept. We conclude this section by an example which includes sequential processing of list elements, insertions and deletions. Suppose that we want to perform operations on polynomials in one variable. For example, adding the polynomials

$$3x^4 + 5x^3 + 2x - 2 \qquad -2x^3 + 5x^2 + 5 \tag{22}$$

we get the polynomial

$$3x^4 + 3x^3 + 5x^2 + 2x + 3. \tag{23}$$

It is clear that as a result of operations like the addition above, polynomials can grow and shrink, so a suitable representation of a polynomial is a list of elements of the following type:

$$\textbf{type } element = \textbf{record } coef : integer; \tag{24}$$
$$exp : integer;$$
$$link : \uparrow element$$
$$\textbf{end}$$

where a polynomial term ax^b is represented by a list element whose field $coef$ is equal to a and whose field exp is equal to b. Elements of such a list are arranged in decreasing order of exp field. In order to avoid the problem of the empty list, which corresponds to the polynomial 0, and in order to make tests in loops simple (and thus loops more efficient), we introduce an extra node in each such list. This node will appear as the last element, its field exp will always be set to -1 (all other elements have this field non-negative) with field $coef$ 0. This node acts as a 'sentinel' for the search operation. With these conventions the polynomial $3x^4 + 5x^3 + 2x - 2$ will be represented in the following way:

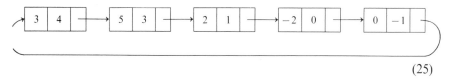

$$\tag{25}$$

where we observe that the field $next$ of the sentinel is linked to the first element of the list. This way we obtain a $circular\ list$ or a $ring$, just one of the structures more intricate than simple lists that can be built using pointers. A reference to such a structure is given by a pointer to its sentinel element. Suppose that p and q are two such pointer variables, and suppose that we want to add the polynomial p to the polynomial q, so that the result of addition will be the polynomial q. The algorithm which follows accomplishes this task. The list p is unchanged, and when the algorithm terminates p and q return to their starting points. Additional pointer variables $q1$ and $q2$ are needed in the algorithm. The pointer variable $q1$ follows the pointer variable

q around the list, for the reasons which we explained when we discussed insertions and deletions of elements.

```
{initialize}                                                    (26)
p := p↑ . link; q1 := q; q := q↑ . link;
while p↑ . exp > 0 do
begin while p↑ . exp < q↑ . exp do
        begin {move to the next element of q}
        q1 := q; q := q↑ . link
        end
if p↑ . exp = q↑ . exp then
begin {add coefficients of equal terms}
        q↑ . coef := p↑ . coef + q↑ . coef;
        if q↑ . coef ≠ 0 then
        begin {proceed to the next elements in p and q}
                q1 := q;
                p := p↑ . link; q := q↑ . link
        end
                else begin {delete term with zero coefficient}
                        q2 := q; q := q↑ . link;
                        q1↑ . link := q;
                        dispose(q2);
                        p := p↑ . link
                end
end
else    {insert new term in q}
begin new(q2);
        q2↑ . coef := p↑ . coef;
        q2↑ . exp := p↑ . exp;
        q2↑ . link := q; q1↑ . link := q2;
        q1 := q2; p := p↑ . link
end
end
```

s-Expressions

In order to illustrate the above definitions consider the *s-expressions*—the data structures which form the basis of pure Lisp. Suppose that *element* is a scalar-type, whose members will be called *atoms*. Then the set of s-expressions is defined recursively as the smallest set such that:

    i. *Atoms* are s-expressions   (27)

    ii. If s_1 and s_2 are s-expressions, then so is the pair (s_1, s_2).

Apart from the fact that the above type definition is a disjoint union of types, it is also recursive, so we have to use pointers to express it in Pascal. Hence the following type definition:

$$\textbf{type } \textit{sexpr} = \textbf{record} \tag{28}$$

$$\textbf{case } \textit{tag} \colon (\textit{single}, \textit{pair}) \textbf{ of}$$
$$\textit{single} \colon (a \colon \textit{element});$$
$$\textit{pair} \colon (\textit{first} \colon {\uparrow}\textit{sexpr};$$
$$\textit{second} \colon {\uparrow}\textit{sexpr})$$

$$\textbf{end}$$

$$\textbf{end}$$

The reader should review the discussion of disjoint unions in Section 3.4. Here the *tag* indicates that an expression is either single—an *atom* as in (27)i—or a pair—as in (27)ii.

In order to manipulate s-expressions we need the five basic functions defined below:

The functions *car* and *cdr* are selector functions. For a given s-expression which is not an *atom*, *car* selects its first component and *cdr* its second component. In both cases the argument is a pointer to an s-expression, and the result is a pointer to its selected component.

$$\textbf{function } \textit{car}(x \colon {\uparrow}\textit{sexpr}) \colon {\uparrow}\textit{sexpr}; \tag{29}$$
$$\textbf{begin } \textit{car} := x{\uparrow} \, . \, \textit{first} \textbf{ end}$$

$$\textbf{function } \textit{cdr}(x \colon {\uparrow}\textit{sexpr}) \colon {\uparrow}\textit{sexpr}; \tag{30}$$
$$\textbf{begin } \textit{cdr} := x{\uparrow} \, . \, \textit{second} \textbf{ end}$$

It is immediate from the above definitions that we get in trouble if we apply either of the above functions to an argument which, although it is of the type ${\uparrow}\textit{sexpr}$, happens to be a pointer to an atomic s-expression. In such a case the above two functions are undefined, and if used will result in an error which consists of accessing a nonexisting variable ($x{\uparrow} \, . \, \textit{first}$ in (29) and $x{\uparrow} \, . \, \textit{second}$ in (30)). This clearly points out the danger in using type unions. Secure programming in the above case requires testing of the current type of the argument. This test may be determined by a special function defined as follows:

$$\textbf{function } \textit{atom}(x \colon {\uparrow}\textit{sexpr}) \colon \textit{Boolean}; \tag{31}$$
$$\textbf{begin } \textit{atom} := x{\uparrow} \, . \, \textit{tag} = \textit{single} \textbf{ end}$$

An example which illustrates the precautions necessary when using the function *car* and *cdr* (and type unions in general) is illustrated below by the function *firstatom*, which delivers as its result the first atom of an s-expression.

$$\textbf{function } \textit{firstatom}(x \colon {\uparrow}\textit{sexpr}) \colon \textit{element}; \tag{32}$$
$$\textbf{begin while } \neg \textit{atom}(x) \textbf{ do } x := \textit{car}(x);$$
$$\textit{firstatom} := x{\uparrow} \, . \, a$$

$$\textbf{end}$$

The fourth basic function of pure Lisp (the first three are *car*, *cdr* and *atom*) is the function *eq*, defined as:

$$\textbf{function } \textit{eq}(x, y \colon {\uparrow}\textit{sexpr}) \colon \textit{Boolean}; \tag{33}$$
$$\textbf{begin } \textit{eq} := x{\uparrow} \, . \, a = y{\uparrow} \, . \, a \textbf{ end}$$

The function *eq* is intended to test equality of two atomic s-expressions. Thus the relational operator = which appears in its definition is just the usual one with which the scalar type *element* is equipped. Again, for the same reasons as for the function *car* and *cdr*, it is necessary to test whether the arguments of *eq*, although of the type ↑*sexpr*, point to elements which have the field *tag* equal to *single* (i.e. the element is an atom). An example of the correct use of the function *eq* will appear in the next section, which deals with recursive data structures and recursive procedures.

The last basic function of pure Lisp is of a constructive nature. Given two (pointers to) s-expressions, the function *cons* constructs a new s-expression out of the given ones, and returns as its value a pointer to the constructed s-expression. Recall that the **with** instruction lets us abbreviate *p*↑ . *tag* to *tag*, etc., in the following.

$$\begin{aligned}
&\textbf{function } cons(x,y\colon \uparrow\!sexpr)\colon \uparrow\!sexpr; \hspace{2cm}(34)\\
&\textbf{var } p\colon \uparrow\!sexpr;\\
&\textbf{begin } new(p);\ cons := p;\\
&\quad\textbf{with } p\!\uparrow \textbf{ do}\\
&\quad\textbf{begin } tag := pair;\\
&\qquad\quad first := x;\\
&\qquad\quad second := y\\
&\quad\textbf{end}\\
&\textbf{end}
\end{aligned}$$

Further examples of manipulation of s-expressions appear in the next section.

6.4 Recursive Algorithms and Recursive Data Structures

If the data structure upon which an algorithm should operate is recursive, then the use of recursive procedures and functions leads, as a rule, to elegant solutions. This point will be illustrated by several examples of recursive functions which operate upon the two recursive data structures defined so far: s-expressions and lists.

Consider first the function *equal*, which takes as its arguments two pointers to s-expressions, and returns as its result either *true* or *false* depending upon whether or not the arguments are equal s-expressions. The function *equal* makes use of the function *car*, *cdr*, *atom* and *eq* defined in the previous section.

$$\begin{aligned}
&\textbf{function } equal(x,y\colon \uparrow\!sexpr)\colon Boolean; \hspace{3cm}(1)\\
&\textbf{begin if } atom(x) \lor atom(y) \textbf{ then if } atom(x) \land atom(y) \textbf{ then } equal := eq(x,y)\\
&\hspace{4cm}\textbf{else } equal := false\\
&\quad\textbf{else if } equal\,(car(x),\,car(y)) \textbf{ then}\\
&\qquad equal := equal(cdr(x),\,cdr(y))\\
&\qquad\textbf{else } equal := false\\
&\textbf{end}
\end{aligned}$$

Apart from the recursive nature of the function equal, one other aspect should also be observed. Since the underlying type (*sexpr*) is not only recursive but also a union of types, all necessary checks of the current type of the arguments of the functions *eq*, *car* and *cdr* are made before these functions are called. The call $eq(x, y)$ gets executed only if both x and y in this call are atomic, and the calls $car(x)$, $car(y)$, $cdr(x)$ and $cdr(y)$ get executed only if their arguments x and y are not atomic s-expressions.

Consider now how lists whose elements are of the type defined as:

$$\textbf{type } element = \textbf{record } key\text{: } integer;\tag{2}$$
$$link\text{: } \uparrow element$$
$$\textbf{end}$$

can be manipulated using recursive functions. All lists in the rest of this section are of this type.

The function *copy* declared in (3) has as its argument a pointer to the head of a list, and returns as its value a pointer to the head of the newly constructed list, which is obtained by copying the list to which the argument of the function *copy* points.

(3)

```
function copy(x: ↑element): ↑element;
var p: ↑element;
begin if x = nil then copy := nil
    else begin new(p); copy := p;
        p↑ . key := x↑ . key;
        p↑ . link := copy(x↑ . link)
    end
end
```

Some of the functions that follow make use of the function *copy*.

The function *append* declared in (4) constructs a list which is obtained by appending a copy of the list to which y points at the end of a copy of the list to which x points. The result of this function is a pointer to the constructed list.

(4)

```
function append(x, y: ↑element): ↑element;
var p: ↑element;
begin if x = nil then append := copy(y)
        else begin new(p); append := p;
        p↑ . key := x↑ . key;
        p↑ . link := append(x↑ . link, y)
    end
end
```

Suppose now that the keys in a list to which x points are all distinct. Then the function *member* declared in (5) tests whether a is a member of this set of keys (i.e., whether an element with the key a occurs in the list x), and if so it delivers the value *true*, and if not, *false*.

function *member*(*a*: *key*; *x*: ↑*element*): *Boolean*;   (5)
begin if *x* = **nil then** *member* := *false*
    else if *x*↑ . *key* = *a* **then** *member* := *true*
        else *member* := *member*(*a*, *x*↑ . *link*)
end

Under the same assumption of distinctness of keys in a list the functions *union* (6) and *intersect* (7) are declared. The function *union* constructs a new list whose set of elements is the usual union of the sets of elements of lists *x* and *y*. The function *intersect* constructs a new list whose set of elements is the intersection of the sets of elements of the lists *x* and *y*. Furthermore, the order in which these elements appear in the lists *x* and *y* is preserved in the newly constructed list. Both functions return as their value a pointer to the constructed list.

function *union*(*x*, *y*: ↑*element*): ↑*element*;   (6)
var *p*: ↑*element*;
begin if *x* = **nil then** *union* := *copy*(*y*)
    else if *member*(*x*↑ . *key*, *y*) **then** *union* := *union*(*x*↑ . *link*, *y*)
        else begin *new*(*p*); *union* := *p*;
                p↑ . *key* := *x*↑ . *key*;
                p↑ . *link* := *union*(*x*↑ . *link*, *y*)
        end
end

function *intersect*(*x*, *y*: ↑*element*): ↑*element*;   (7)
var *p*: ↑*element*;
begin if *x* = **nil then** *intersect* := **nil**
    else if *member*(*x*↑ . *key*, *y*) **then**
        begin *new*(*p*); *intersect* := *p*;
            p↑ . *key* := *x*↑ . *key*;
            p↑ . *link* := *intersect*(*x*↑ . *link*, *y*)
        end
        else *intersect* := *intersect*(*x*↑ . *link*, *y*)
end

Observe that in (6) and (7) the fact that every recursive procedure call of *union* and *intersect* creates its private instance of the variable *p* plays an essential role.

We hope that the reader appreciates the elegance of the recursive algorithms defined in this section. But, once again, be aware of the fact that these recursive procedures and functions can be very inefficient because of the number of recursive calls which they give rise to when called. Even in the case of recursive data structures, many recursive algorithms can be expressed in a more efficient, repetitive way. For example, it is clear that the previously given function *firstatom* ((32) of Section 6.3) which delivers the first atom of an s-expression is more efficient than the following recursively defined function:

$$\textbf{function } firstatom(x: \uparrow sexpr): element; \qquad\qquad (8)$$
$$\textbf{begin if } atom(x) \textbf{ then } firstatom := x\uparrow . a$$
$$\qquad \textbf{else } firstatom := firstatom(car(x))$$
$$\textbf{end}$$

where the definitions of the type *sexpr* and functions *atom* and *car* given in Section 6.3 apply.

Similarly, although the function *copy* as declared in (3) is very attractive, it is possible to rewrite it into a more efficient, though not nearly as elegant, repetitive form, as follows:

$$\textbf{function } copy(x: \uparrow element): \uparrow element; \qquad\qquad (9)$$
$$\textbf{var } p, pred: \uparrow element;$$
$$\textbf{begin if } x = \textbf{nil then } copy := \textbf{nil}$$
$$\qquad \textbf{else begin } new(p); copy := p;$$
$$\qquad\qquad p\uparrow . key := x\uparrow . key;$$
$$\qquad\qquad pred := p; x := x\uparrow . link;$$
$$\qquad\qquad \textbf{while } x \neq \textbf{nil do}$$
$$\qquad\qquad \textbf{begin } new(p); pred\uparrow . link := p;$$
$$\qquad\qquad\qquad p\uparrow . key := x\uparrow . key;$$
$$\qquad\qquad\qquad pred := p; x := x\uparrow . link$$
$$\qquad\qquad \textbf{end}$$
$$\qquad\qquad pred\uparrow . link := \textbf{nil}$$
$$\qquad \textbf{end}$$
$$\textbf{end}$$

Although there may be better ways than (9) of defining *copy* repetitively it is unlikely that any such form is more satisfactory than (3) from the point of view of simplicity and conceptual clarity. We would encounter similar problems in expressing the functions *append*, *union* and *intersection* in repetitive form. In conclusion, recursive algorithms should be considered where appropriate, at least as a step in program development. After this step, further refinement steps may lead to a repetitive solution, where indicated by an analysis of efficiency.

Bibliographic Remarks

The recursive solution to the 8-queens problem presented in this chapter is from Dijkstra (1972). Some examples of the recursive data structures and recursive algorithms are adapted from McCarthy *et al.* (1962). Our exposition of pointers and list manipulations in Pascal is based on Jensen and Wirth (1974) and Wirth (1976). The proof rule for recursive procedures is due to Hoare (1971a). This rule was in fact proved by computational (fixed-point) induction in Manna and Vuillemin (1972). The *Quicksort* algorithm and its proof of correctness are from Foley and Hoare (1971).

The exercises in this chapter are based on Aho *et al.* (1974), Manna (1974), Weissman (1967), Knuth (1968) and Knuth (1973).

Exercises

1. Declare a recursive procedure with one variable parameter which is a pointer to an s-expression. A call of this procedure modifies the s-expression to which its argument points in such a way that it exchanges the first and the second components of each of its subexpressions. For example, if the original s-expression was of the form

$$((a,b),\, c)$$

then the resulting s-expression would be

$$(c,\, (b,a))$$

where *a*, *b* and *c* stand for s-expressions.

2. Declare a procedure which sorts a list of integers into *odd* and *even*, and has two results of the form:

$$(odd\ count,\ list\ of\ odd\ numbers)$$
$$(even\ count,\ list\ of\ even\ numbers).$$

3. Consider the following type definitions:

type *suite* = (*spade, heart, diamond, club*);
     rank = (*one, two, three, four, five, six, seven,*
               eight, nine, ten, jack, queen, king, ace);
     card = **record** *s*: *suite*;
             r: *rank*;
             p: ↑*card*
    end;
    element = **record** *sp*: ↑*card*;
               l: ↑*element*
    end

Declare a function with one parameter, a pointer to a list of cards (i.e., elements of the type *card* defined above), which returns as the result a pointer to a list of elements of type *element* defined above. The function performs the following:
i. The argument is regarded as a pointer to a list which represents a hand. The function separates these cards into four suits, constructing a list of cards for each of the four suits.
ii. Then it constructs a list of these four lists. This four element list has the elements of the type *element*, the component *sp* points to a list which represents a suit, and the component *l* to the next element of the four element list. The result of the function is a pointer to the four element list.

4. Given the type *node*, a *binary tree* over the type *node* is defined in the following way:
  i. An empty set of elements of the type *node* is a binary tree.
  ii. If T_1 and T_2 are binary trees over the type *node*, then so is the triple (n,T_1,T_2), where n is an element of the type *node*. T_1 and T_2 are called the left and the right subtrees of the tree (n,T_1,T_2).

A nonempty binary tree (n,T_1,T_2) is usually graphically represented as follows:

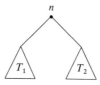

where this should be understood in a recursive manner, just as the definition of a binary tree. Using pointers, define the type of nodes of a binary tree associating an integer with each node. Write a program which reads a file of integers and constructs a binary tree out of them. Observe that you have to decide about a convention by which a sequence of integers represents a binary tree.

5. There exist three strategies of searching a binary tree visiting all of its nodes:
  a.   i. Visit the root
     ii. Search the left subtree
    iii. Search the right subtree
  b.   i. Search the left subtree
     ii. Visit the root
    iii. Search the right subtree
  c.   i. Search the left subtree
     ii. Search the right subtree
    iii. Visit the root

The above three operations are called *preorder*, *inorder* and *postorder* tree traversals. Write the algorithms which perform the above search operations upon a binary tree defined in the previous exercise. Assume that the programs are supposed to write (into the file *output*) integers associated with nodes of the tree.

6. In the previous two exercises binary trees were considered which had the property that an integer was associated with each of their nodes. If all of these integers are different in a given binary tree, then they are called *keys*. In general, the type of a key can be any totally ordered type. So the scalar types qualify immediately. A binary search tree is a binary tree such that every subtree (n,T_1,T_2) of it has the property that each key in the set of keys associated with the nodes of the left subtree T_1, is less than the key associated with n, and each key in the set of keys associated with the nodes of the right subtree T_2 is greater than the key associated with n. Write a program which reads a file of integers and builds a binary search tree associating these integers with the nodes of the tree.

7. Write an algorithm which deletes an arbitrary node from a binary search tree and restructures the tree in such a way that the obtained tree is a binary search tree.

8. Write recursive procedures which perform preorder, postorder and endorder traversals of a binary tree. Suppose that the operation to be perfomed upon each node is printing its contents (without link fields).

9. Write a recursive procedure which inserts a given record at the appropriate place into a given binary search tree. After this insertion the obtained tree must still be a binary search tree.

10. Write a recursive procedure which deletes a record determined by a given pointer from a given binary search tree. This deletion requires restructuring of the tree, but upon this modification the resulting tree must be a binary search tree.

11. Consider the following recursive function declaration:

$$\begin{aligned}
&\textbf{function } f(x: integer);\\
&\textbf{begin if } \neg odd(x) \textbf{ then } f := x \textbf{ div } 2\\
&\qquad\qquad \textbf{else } f := f(f(3 * x + 1))\\
&\textbf{end}
\end{aligned}$$

Prove that every execution process invoked by a call $f(x)$ where x is a natural number, terminates.

12. Design a recursive procedure which solves the following problem (Towers of Hanoi): Three pins and n discs of different sizes are given. All n discs are piled on one pin in such a way that no disc is above a disc smaller than itself, as in the following figure:

The desired procedure moves the pile of discs from one pin to another by a succession of moves which must satisfy the restriction that no disc can be above a disc smaller than itself on the same pin.

13. Given $n \times n$ matrices A and B, where

$$A = \begin{pmatrix} a_{11} & \cdots & a_{1n} \\ \vdots & & \\ a_{n1} & \cdots & a_{nn} \end{pmatrix} \qquad B = \begin{pmatrix} b_{11} & \cdots & b_{1n} \\ \vdots & & \\ b_{n1} & \cdots & b_{nn} \end{pmatrix}$$

the most straightforward algorithm for computing their product C where

$$C = \begin{pmatrix} c_{11} & \cdots & c_{1n} \\ \vdots & & \\ c_{n1} & \cdots & c_{nn} \end{pmatrix} \qquad c_{ij} = \sum_{k=1}^{n} a_{ik}b_{kj} \quad \text{for} \quad 1 \leqslant i, j \leqslant n$$

is performing n multiplications and n additions for each c_{ij}. An alternative, recursive procedure, may be obtained by dividing A, B and C into $n/2 \times n/2$ blocks like this

$$A = \begin{pmatrix} A_{11} & A_{12} \\ \hline A_{21} & A_{22} \end{pmatrix}$$

where A_{ij} are submatrices of A. It can be easily verified that

$$\left(\begin{array}{c|c} A_{11} & A_{12} \\ \hline A_{21} & A_{22} \end{array}\right)\left(\begin{array}{c|c} B_{11} & B_{12} \\ \hline B_{21} & B_{22} \end{array}\right) = \left(\begin{array}{c|c} A_{11}B_{11} + A_{12}B_{21} & A_{11}B_{12} + A_{12}B_{22} \\ \hline A_{21}B_{12} + A_{22}B_{21} & A_{21}B_{12} + A_{22}B_{22} \end{array}\right)$$

Design a recursive algorithm for matrix multiplication which is based on the above observations.

14. Design a recursive procedure for straight merge sort of arrays, using roughly the following strategy:

(a) A recursive call first sorts the first half of the array, unless this half consists of only one element, in which case we are done.

(b) The second recursive call sorts the second half of the array.

(c) Finally, the third action is a call of a procedure which merges the two sorted halves into a sorted array.

The above reasoning assumes that the number of array elements is a power of 2, but the reader is expected to give a solution for the general case.

15. Consider the following two declarations of recursive functions

function $f(x: integer)$;
begin if $(x = 0) \lor (x = 1)$ **then** $f := 1$
      else $f := f(x - 1) + f(x - 2)$
end

function $g(x: integer)$;
begin if $(x = 0) \lor (x = 1)$ **then** $g := 1$
      else $g := 2 * g(x - 2)$
end

Show that the following holds:

$$\forall x,y((x \geqslant y) \supset (f(x) \geqslant f(y) \geqslant 1))$$
$$\forall x(g(x) \leqslant f(x))$$

where x and y are integer expressions.

16. Consider the following two recursive functions which compute the factorial function:

function $f(x: integer)$;
begin if $x = 0$ **then** $f := 1$
      else $f := x * f(x - 1)$
end

function $g(x,y,z: integer)$;
begin if $x = y$ **then** $g := z$
      else $g := g(x, y + 1, (y + 1) * z)$
end

Prove that the following holds

$$\forall x((x \geq 0) \supset (f(x) = g(x,0,1))).$$

17. Write a piece of program which deletes a record from a list and appends it at the end of another list. (We can think of this second list as the list of available memory.)

18. Suppose that we want to manipulate lists whose elements are of the type *node*. Suppose that we are allowed to have a certain amount of memory for that. Representing the available memory as a list, write the procedures which accomplish the tasks of *new* and *dispose*.

19. Generalize the memory management approach from the previous exercise for the situation where we want to manipulate several lists of different types.

20. Graphical representations of two types of doubly linked lists are given below. Discuss the basic operations of search, deletion, and insertion for these structures and write the corresponding algorithms.

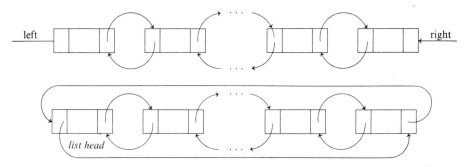

21. Use the experience gained in solving the 8-queens problem in solving the following problem: Generate a sequence of N characters chosen from the alphabet $\{1, 2, 3\}$ such that no two immediately adjacent subsequences are equal.

22. Modifying the global structure of the solution to the problem posed in the previous exercise, and retaining the original modules, find a solution to the following problem: Generate all sequences of N characters chosen from the alphabet $\{1, 2, 3\}$, which contain no two immediately adjacent equal subsequences.

23. Provide a top-down proof of correctness of the algorithm which generates a sequence of N characters, chosen from the alphabet $\{1, 2, 3\}$, such that no two immediately adjacent subsequences are equal.

24. Provide a proof of correctness for the algorithm which generates all appropriate sequences (see exercise 22). Recall that the solution to this generalized algorithm was supposed to be constructed by modifying the global structure of the original solution while retaining the modules. The proof of correctness obtained in the previous exercise should thus be adapted to the proof of correctness of the generalized algorithm in such a way that the correctness of particular modules established in the previous exercise is exploited.

7
Programming with and without Gotos

7.1 Goto Statements

So far, we have considered some well-known regular structuring concepts like conditionals, loops, procedures etc. There is, however, one device which allows the introduction of almost any statement composition scheme. This device is the **goto** statement. Its form is:

$$\textbf{goto } L \tag{1}$$

and the effect of its execution is that program execution is continued from the point of the program determined by L. L is called a *label*. In Pascal, it is a sequence of at most 4 digits. L: is used as a prefix of the statement to which control should be transferred.

A label must appear in a label declaration before it appears either in a **goto** statement or as a prefix of some statement. The form of a label declaration is **label** $L_1, \ldots, L_n$ where $L_1, \ldots, L_n$ are labels. The scope rules for labels are just like the scope rules for identifiers explained in Section 5.1. The following example illustrates some of them:

$$\begin{aligned}
&\textbf{label } 1; \{\text{block } A\} \\
&\quad \ldots \\
&\quad \textbf{procedure } B; \{\text{block } B\} \\
&\qquad \textbf{label } 3; \\
&\quad \textbf{begin} \\
&\quad 3: S1; \\
&\qquad \ldots \\
&\qquad \textbf{goto } 3; \{\text{this is OK}\} \\
&\qquad \ldots \\
&\qquad \textbf{goto } 1; \{\text{this is OK}\} \\
&\quad \textbf{end}; \{\text{block } B\}
\end{aligned} \tag{2}$$

    begin {block *A*}

    . . .

    1: *S2*;
    {a **goto** 3 in this block would be an error}
    end

The scope of a label *L* declared in a block *A* is the entire text of block *A*. One statement in the statement part of *A* may be prefixed with *L*:, and in that case **goto** *L* may occur, possibly more than once, in the whole of block *A*. Jumps (**gotos**) from outside a structured statement into that statement are conceptually unacceptable; they should be abolished under all circumstances to avoid mistakes caused by using variables outside their proper scope, etc. Much of our work in later sections will be seeing conditions under which the use of **gotos** is compatible with good programming methodology. To see the problems caused by careless use of **gotos** the reader should analyse carefully the following examples:

    for *j* := 2 **to** 15 **do**   (3)
       begin *S*1;
          4: *S2*
       end;

       . . .

    goto 4

                if *q* **then goto** 2;   (4)

                . . .

                if *b* **then** 2: *S*;

                        procedure *P*   (5)
                          begin . . .
                             4: *S*

                                . . .

                          end;
                          begin . . .

                                  goto 4
                          end

It is not hard to see that the above examples make little sense.

The **goto** statement is clearly a very powerful feature. In fact, it is too powerful. Its improper use leads to all sorts of structural irregularities, yielding programs which are obscure, hard to understand, hard to modify and hard to prove correct.

One essential reason that some programs are hard to understand is the difference between the textual, static program structure, and the dynamic structure of the computations it evokes at execution time. Use of regular structuring concepts like loops, conditionals etc, helps in achieving a struc-

ture for the program text which does reflect the dynamic structure of processes that occur at execution time. However, in the case of a badly placed
goto statement, there need exist little correspondence between the textual
and computational (static and dynamic) program structure. Because of all
this there is a current well justified trend in programming to avoid **goto**
statements wherever regular structuring methods would give a better solution. We discuss this in detail in subsequent sections, where we will also offer
a number of *structured*—and, thus, carefully constrained—uses of the **goto**
which are completely satisfactory.

Cleaning up Unstructured Algorithms Using Invariants

We now examine an algorithm for computing the greatest common divisor
of two numbers. We use it as an example of a poorly structured algorithm,
and demonstrate how we can use our knowledge of invariants to clean up
the structure of the algorithm.

Recall three basic properties of the function *gcd* which follow from its
definition:

$$gcd(u,v) = gcd(v,u) \tag{6}$$

$$gcd(u,v) = gcd(-u,v) \tag{7}$$

$$gcd(u,0) = |u| \tag{8}$$

The *gcd* algorithm given below is based solely on the operations of
subtraction, testing whether a number is even or odd, and halving. Because
halving involves shifting the binary representation of an even number to the
right the algorithm is called the *binary gcd algorithm*. This algorithm is
based on four further properties of positive integers u and v:

If u and v are both even, then $\tag{9}$

$gcd(u,v) = 2gcd(u \text{ } \mathbf{div} \text{ } 2, v \text{ } \mathbf{div} \text{ } 2)$

If u is even and v is odd, then $\tag{10}$

$gcd(u,v) = gcd(u \text{ } \mathbf{div} \text{ } 2, v)$

If $u > v$ then $gcd(u,v) = gcd(u - v, v)$ $\tag{11}$

If u and v are both odd, then $u - v$ is even and $\tag{12}$

$|u - v| < max(u,v)$

The algorithm (13) is written on the basis of the following statement
structuring rules: sequential composition, conditional composition, and
jumps. The improvement of its structure will be the subject of our further
elaborations.

begin $x := u$; $y := v$;   (13)
   $k := 1$;
 1 : **if** $even(x) \wedge even(y)$ **then**
   begin $x := x$ **div** 2; $y := y$ **div** 2;
      $k := k * 2$;
      goto 1
   end;
   if $odd(x)$ **then**
   begin $t := -y$; **goto** 3 **end**
   else $t := x$;
   {The sign of t indicates whether it is x or y}
 2 : $t := t$ **div** 2;
 3 : **if** $even(t)$ **then goto** 2;
   if $t > 0$ **then** $x := t$ **else** $y := -t$;
   {The sign of t is used to adjust x or y as appropriate}
   $t := x - y$;
   if $t \neq 0$ **then goto** 2 **else** $x := x * k$;
   {$gcd(u,v) = x$}
end

The structure of the algorithm (13) can be improved in a straightforward manner by discovering the **while-do** and **repeat-until** loops in it. This leads to the algorithm (14).

begin $x := u$; $y := v$;   (14)
   $k := 1$;
   while $even(x) \wedge even(y)$ **do**
   begin $x := x$ **div** 2; $y := y$ **div** 2;
      $k := k * 2$
   end; {$gcd(u,v) = k * gcd(x,y)$, $odd(x) \vee odd(y)$}
   if $odd(x)$ **then** $t := -y$ **else** $t := x$;
   repeat
         while $even(t)$ **do** $t := t$ **div** 2;
         if $t > 0$ **then** $x := t$ **else** $y := -t$;
         {$odd(x) \wedge odd(y)$}
         $t := x - y$
   until $t = 0$;
   $x := x * k$
   {$gcd(u,v) = x$}
end

The algorithm (14), although much clearer than the algorithm (13), and without any jumps, is still not too easy to understand. A clearer algorithm is obtained if one tries to derive it directly from the properties (9), (10), (11) and (12). Such an algorithm is presented in (15).

$$\textbf{begin } x := u;\, y := v; \tag{15}$$
$$k := 1;$$
$$\textbf{while } even(x) \wedge even(y) \textbf{ do}$$
$$\textbf{begin } x := x \textbf{ div } 2;\, y := y \textbf{ div } 2;$$
$$k := k * 2$$
$$\textbf{end}; \quad \{gcd(u,v) = k * gcd(x,y)\}$$
$$\textbf{repeat } \{odd(x) \vee odd(y)\}$$
$$\textbf{while } even(x) \textbf{ do } x := x \textbf{ div } 2;$$
$$\textbf{while } even(y) \textbf{ do } y := y \textbf{ div } 2;$$
$$\{odd(x) \wedge odd(y)\}$$
$$\textbf{if } x > y \textbf{ then } x := x - y \textbf{ else } y := y - x$$
$$\textbf{until } (x = 0) \vee (y = 0)$$
$$\textbf{if } x = 0 \textbf{ then } gcd := y * k \textbf{ else } gcd := x * k$$
$$\textbf{end } \{gcd = gcd(u,v)\}$$

The algorithm (15) is derived on the basis of the following considerations:

i. Because of the property (9) after the loop

$$\textbf{while } even(x) \wedge even(y) \textbf{ do} \tag{16}$$
$$\textbf{begin } x := x \textbf{ div } 2;\, y := y \textbf{ div } 2;$$
$$k := k * 2$$
$$\textbf{end}$$

$gcd(u,v) = k * gcd(x,y)$ holds. It is clear that this **while-do** statement must terminate, since x and y can only be divided by 2 a finite number of times.

ii. The loops:

$$\textbf{while } even(x) \textbf{ do } x := x \textbf{ div } 2; \tag{17}$$
$$\textbf{while } even(y) \textbf{ do } y := y \textbf{ div } 2$$

do not affect the value of $gcd(x,y)$. This follows from the property (10) and the fact that whenever the loops (17) are reached $odd(x) \vee odd(y)$ holds. This is certainly true the first time the loops (17) are reached, since that happens upon exit from the loop (16). Upon completion of execution of the loops (17) $odd(x) \wedge odd(y)$ holds, and after the statement **if** $x > y$ **then** $x := x - y$ **else** $y := y - x$ x will be odd and y will be even, or vice versa. This follows from (12). So whenever, later in the **repeat-until** loop in (15), the loops (17) are reached, either x or y will be odd.

iii. The step **if** $x > y$ **then** $x := x - y$ **else** $y := y - x$ is justified by (11) and (12) and of course (6). It follows from (11) and (6) that the statement **if** $x > y$ **then** $x := x - y$ **else** $y := y - x$ does not affect the value of $gcd(x,y)$. This statement reduces either x or y, but it leaves them non-negative, so that after some number of iterations the condition $(x = 0) \vee (y = 0)$ must be satisfied, and the **repeat-until** terminates.

A variation of the algorithm (15) is possible. It is based on the substitution of the statement **if** $x > y$ **then** $x := x - y$ **else** $y := y - x$ by the loops

$$\textbf{while } x > y \textbf{ do } x := x - y; \tag{18}$$
$$\textbf{while } y > x \textbf{ do } y := y - x.$$

This is again justified by (11) and by (6). And now on the basis of

$$gcd(u,u) = u$$

we can substitute in (15) the text $(x = 0) \vee (y = 0)$ by $x = y$, to obtain the following algorithm (19), which is not, however, as efficient as (15).

begin $x := u$; $y := v$;   (19)
       $k := 1$;
       while $even(x) \wedge even(y)$ **do**
       begin $x := x$ **div** 2; $y := y$ **div** 2;
           $k := k * 2$
       end; $\{gcd(u,v) = k * gcd(x,y)\}$
       repeat while $even(x)$ **do** $x := x$ **div** 2;
             while $even(y)$ **do** $y := y$ **div** 2; $\{odd(x) \wedge odd(y)\}$
             while $x > y$ **do** $x := x - y$;
             while $y > x$ **do** $y := y - x$
       until $x = y$;
       $\{gcd(u,v) = x * k\}$
       $gcd := x * k$
end

7.2 Proof Rules for Gotos

In the remaining sections we shall consider some special types of jumps, which occur frequently, do not cause program obscurity, and whose use is thus acceptable if regular structuring methods would not give a better solution. One should always try to solve the problem using the basic composition rules (sequencing, conditionals, repetition and recursion). If this does not give a good solution, then use of some of the special types of jumps is justified. The need to use the conventional way of setting labels and using **goto** statements should occur very seldom in high level language programming. However, for the sake of completeness and because of the fact that many a programmer will still use jumps in the conventional way, we present proof rules for dealing with conventional **goto** statements in program proving.

The important point to note about **goto**s is that they destroy the convention that we have used in our program specification (1) so far

$P \dashv$ (1)

S $\{P\}\ S\ \{Q\}$

$Q \dashv$

namely, that each statement has one entry and one exit. Consider, for example, a statement S which contains one or more **goto** L statements—but all for the same label L—but does *not* contain L: as a label. Then we call S an *L-statement* (so that if the label is 13:, we speak of a 13-*statement*), and may depict it in (2), where we have one precondition, but now must include *two* post-conditions—one for the normal exit, and one for all the exits via **goto** L that transfer control to the statement labelled L:

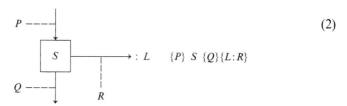

$$\{P\}\ S\ \{Q\}\{L:R\} \tag{2}$$

Thus the program specification $\{P\}\ S\ \{Q\}\ \{L:R\}$ for an *L*-statement means that if the computation state satisfies condition P on starting S, then on 'normal' exit from S, the computation state must satisfy Q, while on any exit from S via **goto** L, the computation state must satisfy R—i.e. Q holds on normal exit from S, while R holds after reaching the label L: on jumping from S by **goto** L.

The simplest example of such a specification is given in the proof rule (3)

$$\text{For every } P, \{P\}\ \textbf{goto}\ L\ \{\textit{false}\}\ \{L:P\}. \tag{3}$$

This just says that whatever condition P holds on entry to **goto** L, 'normal' exit is impossible, while P continues to hold on transfer to the statement labelled L:. For completeness, we note (4),

$$\text{If } S \text{ is } not \text{ an } L\text{-statement, then} \tag{4}$$
$$\{P\}\ S\ \{Q\}\quad \text{implies}\quad \{P\}\ S\ \{Q\}\ \{L: \textit{false}\}.$$

In other words, it is impossible to jump to the statement labelled L: by executing S, no matter what the precondition P.

To extend our analysis of proof rules for statements containing **goto**s, we turn now to a special case which can be treated without undesirable complexity when there is only one local label in a block. We then consider other uses of **goto**s in the remaining sections. The structure of a block with only one local label has the form

$$D;\ \textbf{begin}\ S_1;\ L:S_2\ \textbf{end} \tag{5}$$

where D is a sequence of declarations and S_1 and S_2 are sequences of statements. Jumps to L may occur both in S_1 and S_2. Let R be the condition which is to hold before every **goto** L statement occurs. In other words, R is the invariant attached to the points labelled with L. The insistence that every **goto** L (for a given label L) satisfies this same condition R is a crucial part of structuring statements that include gotos. Suppose that we want to prove

$\{P\}$ **begin** S_1; $L:S_2$ **end** $\{Q\}$. Then we have the situation shown in (6):

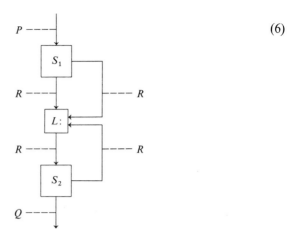

(6)

Clearly, the condition R holding after jump for any **goto** L should also hold both as the postcondition for S_1 and as the precondition for S_2. We thus have the proof rule:

$$\frac{\{P\}\,S_1\,\{R\}\,\{L:R\},\ \{R\}\,S_2\,\{Q\}\,\{L:R\}}{\{P\}\ \textbf{begin}\ S_1\,;\ L:S_2\ \textbf{end}\ \{Q\}}.\tag{7}$$

On taking S_2 empty, we obtain

$$\frac{\{P\}\,S_1\,\{R\}\,\{L:R\}}{\{P\}\ \textbf{begin}\ S_1\,;\ L:\ \textbf{end}\ \{R\}}.\tag{8}$$

On taking S_1 empty, we obtain

$$\frac{\{R\}\,S_2\,\{Q\}\,\{L:R\}}{\{R\}\ L:S_2\ \{Q\}}.\tag{9}$$

These are special cases of (7). For example, if S_1 is empty, we have $\{R\}\ S_1$ $\{R\}\ \{L:\ false\}$, but $false \supset R$, and so $\{R\}\ \{R\}\ \{L:R\}$ for any R.

Note that (9) is the traditional way to form a loop in older 'unstructured' programming languages. Thus (9) raises all the usual termination problems, as we shall see in the next example.

In order to illustrate the above proof rules, consider the problem of selecting the first n distinct numbers from the standard file *input*. The numbers are to be assigned in the order in which they are selected to the array variable a with indexes from 1 to n. A traditional way of expressing the solution would most likely have the following form, based on reading in each candidate for $a[i]$ and comparing it with $a[1], \ldots, a[i-1]$.

$$\begin{aligned}
&\textbf{for } i := 1 \textbf{ to } n \textbf{ do} \qquad\qquad\qquad\qquad (10)\\
&\textbf{begin } 1: read(r);\\
&\qquad\quad \textbf{for } j := 1 \textbf{ to } i-1 \textbf{ do}\\
&\qquad\quad \textbf{if } a[j] = r \textbf{ then goto } 1;\\
&\qquad\quad a[i] := r\\
&\textbf{end}
\end{aligned}$$

The logic behind the solution proposed in (10) is rather natural. In (10) the task of computing the value of the array a is broken into n identical steps of computing $a[i]$, for $i = 1, \ldots, n$. In addition, if we assume that the probability of two input values being equal is rather small, then the case of $a[j](j = 1, \ldots, i-1)$ being equal to the input value r is an exception. This exceptional situation leads to a break in the normal flow of operations and is thus naturally expressed by a jump.

Let

$$P([1 .. i])): \forall k,m((1 \leqslant k < m < i) \supset (a[k] \neq a[m])). \qquad (11)$$

Then $P([1 .. n])$, which is $\forall k,m((1 \leqslant k < m \leqslant n) \supset (a[k] \neq a[m])$ is the condition we must show to hold on exit from (10). According to the proof rule for the **for** statement, **for** $i := 1$ **to** n **do**, we have to prove

$$\begin{aligned}
&\{(1 \leqslant i \leqslant n) \wedge P([1 .. i]))\} \qquad\qquad\qquad (12)\\
&\textbf{begin } 1: read(r);\\
&\qquad\quad \textbf{for } j := 1 \textbf{ to } i-1 \textbf{ do}\\
&\qquad\quad \textbf{if } a[j] = r \textbf{ then goto } 1;\\
&\qquad\quad a[i] := r\\
&\textbf{end } \{P([1 .. i])\}
\end{aligned}$$

Now let

$$Q([1 .. j])) \text{ be } \forall k((1 \leqslant k < j) \supset (a[k] \neq r)). \qquad (13)$$

We first prove the following property for the body of the inner loop, which says to continue testing unless a j is found with $a[j] = r$.

$$\begin{aligned}
&\{(1 \leqslant i \leqslant n) \wedge P([1 .. i])) \wedge (1 \leqslant j \leqslant i-1) \wedge Q([1 .. j]))\} \qquad (14)\\
&\quad \textbf{if } a[j] = r \textbf{ then goto } 1\\
&\{(1 \leqslant i \leqslant n) \wedge P([1 .. i])) \wedge Q([1 .. j])\}\\
&\{1:(1 \leqslant i \leqslant n) \wedge P([1 .. i]))\}
\end{aligned}$$

(14) is proved observing that

$$(1 \leqslant i \leqslant n) \wedge P([1 \,.\, .\, i)) \wedge (1 \leqslant j \leqslant i - 1) \wedge Q([1 \,.\, .\, j)) \wedge (a[j] \neq r) \quad (15)$$
$$\supset (1 \leqslant i \leqslant n) \wedge P([1 \,.\, .\, i)) \wedge Q([1 \,.\, .\, j])$$

and

$$(1 \leqslant i \leqslant n) \wedge P([1 \,.\, .\, i)) \wedge (1 \leqslant j \leqslant i - 1) \wedge (a[j] = r) \quad (16)$$
$$\supset ((1 \leqslant i \leqslant n) \wedge P([1 \,.\, .\, i))).$$

So we may conclude

$$\{(1 \leqslant i \leqslant n) \wedge P([1 \,.\, .\, i)) \wedge Q([\ ])\} \quad (17)$$
for $j := 1$ **to** $i - 1$ **do**
if $a[j] = r$ **then goto** 1
$$\{(1 \leqslant i \leqslant n) \wedge P([1 \,.\, .\, i)) \wedge Q([1 \,.\, .\, i - 1])\}$$
$$\{1 : (1 \leqslant i \leqslant n) \wedge P([1 \,.\, .\, i))\}$$

But now

$$\{(1 \leqslant i \leqslant n) \wedge P([1 \,.\, .\, i)) \wedge Q([1 \,.\, .\, i - 1])\} \quad (18)$$
$$a[i] := r$$
$$\{P([1 \,.\, .\, i])\}$$

Note that $Q([\ ])$ is always *true* since $1 \leqslant k < 1$ is false for every k.

$$\{(1 \leqslant i \leqslant n) \wedge P([1 \,.\, .\, i))\} \quad (19)$$
begin *read(r)*;
        for $j := 1$ **to** $i - 1$ **do**
        if $a[j] = r$ **then goto** 1;
        $a[i] := r$
end
$$\{P([1 \,.\, .\, i])\}$$
$$\{1 : (1 \leqslant i \leqslant n) \wedge P([1 \,.\, .\, i))\}$$

where we have used the obvious proof rule

$$\frac{\{P\}\ S_1\ \{Q_1\}\ \{L : R\},\ \{Q_1\}\ S_2\ \{Q_2\}\ \{L : R\}}{\{P\}\ \textbf{begin}\ S_1 ; S_2\ \textbf{end}\ \{Q\}\ \{L : R\}}. \quad (20)$$

The desired conclusion (12) is now immediate from (19) using the proof rule (9).

Note, however, that our proof of (12) is not quite satisfactory. The proof rule (9) indeed tells us that when we exit from the loop in (12), the desired relations will hold—but it does *not* tell us that the loop caused by returning to 1: will terminate. A proof of termination requires the *additional* precondition that the input file contains at least n distinct entries.

7.3 Return Exits and the Algorithm Find

There do exist situations in which the **goto** statement is used in a very restrictive way. In these situations it causes an exit from a certain context of the program, to which return never occurs. These special types of the **goto** statement will be discussed in this, and in the subsequent two sections. It should be pointed óut immediately that if **gotos** are used in this restrictive way (for exiting), then they cause no problems in program readability and program proving.

The first type of **goto** statement to be discussed may be called a *return exit*. A return exit occurs upon recognition of the fact that the answer the algorithm is to produce has already been found. At that point the appropriate action is to jump right to the place where the desired answer is wanted, thus breaking away from the normal flow, and cutting across the regular hierarchical structure of nested loops, conditionals etc, built up to that point. The reader will recognize this as exactly the situation shown in (8) of Section 7.2.

The return exit will be illustrated by the algorithm *Find*. What is interesting about that example is that a return exit occurs in spite of the top-down program and proof development strategy.

The purpose of the algorithm *Find* is to find that element of an integer array A with index type $1 .. N$ whose value is fth in order of magnitude, and take it as the final value of $A[f]$. Furthermore, the elements of the array are to be rearranged in such a way that all the elements with subscripts lower than f have values $\leqslant A[f]$ and all the elements with subscripts greater than f have values $\geqslant A[f]$. This goal may be achieved in an obvious way, namely by sorting the array A. But if the array is large this method would take far longer than the one to be discussed here.

It is assumed that the array bounds are 1 and N, and that the given value of f satisfies the relation $1 \leqslant f \leqslant N$. With the assumption that this holds before the program is executed, we want to prove that

Found, which is $\forall p,q((1 \leqslant p \leqslant f \leqslant q \leqslant N) \supset (A[p] \leqslant A[f] \leqslant A[q]))$ (1)

will hold upon its execution for the final values of $A[i]$, $1 \leqslant i \leqslant N$. An additional requirement, not formally stated, is that the new array is the same as the original one up to permutation of its elements. This part of the correctness criterion will not be proved formally, as it will be clear from the proposed solution that it is satisfied.

In order to formulate the first version of the algorithm, consider a section of the array A, call it the middle part. Its extent is determined by the values of the variables m and n in such a way that m is the subscript of the leftmost element of the middle part and n is the subscript of the rightmost element of the middle part. The property on the basis of which the middle part is distinguished is defined as follows:

(i) $m \leqslant f \leqslant n$
(ii) $p < m \leqslant k$ implies $A[p] \leqslant A[k]$
(iii) $p \leqslant n < k$ implies $A[p] \leqslant A[k]$

This partition of the array A is illustrated by the figure (2), following

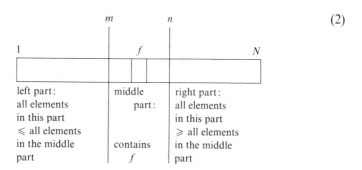

The algorithm starts with the whole array as the middle part and repeatedly reduces the middle part on condition that the above property of the middle part remains invariant throughout the process of repetition. The algorithm terminates when the middle part consists of only one element $A[f]$ and it should be intuitively clear that at that point the correctness criterion (1) will be satisfied. Thus the first version of the algorithm is

$$m := 1; n := N; \qquad\qquad\qquad (3)$$
while $m < n$ **do** reduce middle part

The invariant relation of the above loop may be restated as:

$$L(A,m,f) \text{ equals } (m \leqslant f) \wedge \forall p,q((1 \leqslant p < m \leqslant q \leqslant N) \supset (A[p] \leqslant A[q])) \quad (4)$$

$$R(A,n,f) \text{ equals } (f \leqslant n) \wedge \forall p,q((1 \leqslant p \leqslant n < q \leqslant N) \supset (A[p] \leqslant A[q])). \quad (5)$$

(4) will be called the *left-invariant* and (5) the *right-invariant*. We require that *reduce middle part* is refined in such a way that if $m < n$ and (4) and (5) hold before reduce middle part is executed, then (4) and (5) will again hold after it and either m increases or n decreases. Then we can prove that (3) is correct.

Indeed, we assume that before the assignments of the initial values to m and n are executed, the relation $1 \leqslant f \leqslant N$ must hold. This implies that the following two relations must hold at that point, too:

$$(1 \leqslant f) \wedge \forall p,q((1 \leqslant p < 1 \leqslant q \leqslant N) \supset (A[p] \leqslant A[q])) \qquad (6)$$

$$(f \leqslant N) \wedge \forall p,q((1 \leqslant p \leqslant N < q \leqslant N) \supset (A[p] \leqslant A[q])). \qquad (7)$$

The lefthand factors of each conjunction above follow from $1 \leqslant f \leqslant N$ and the quantified factors are true since $1 \leqslant p < 1 \leqslant q \leqslant N$ and $1 \leqslant p \leqslant N < q \leqslant N$ are always false. It follows now from (6) and (7) that after the assignments $m := 1; n := N$, the left-invariant (4) and the right-invariant (5) must hold.

On the basis of our assumption that *reduce middle part* is refined in such a way that the invariance of (4) and (5) is preserved, we conclude that (4) and (5) hold upon termination of the loop in (3). Termination is guaranteed by the requirement that m increases or n decreases each time round the loop, so that $m < n$ can only hold for a finite number of applications of *reduce middle part*. At termination, $m \geqslant n$ also holds. But then $m \leqslant f, f \leqslant n$ and

$m \geqslant n$ imply $m = n = f$. If $1 \leqslant p \leqslant f \leqslant q \leqslant N$ then either $p = f$ in which case $A[p] \leqslant A[f]$ is immediate, or $p < f$. In the latter case substituting f for both m and q in

$$\forall p,q((1 \leqslant p < m \leqslant q \leqslant N) \supset (A[p] \leqslant A[q]))$$

we get $A[p] \leqslant A[f]$. A similar argument based on the right-invariant gives $A[f] \leqslant A[q]$.

So we have proved that (3) is correct, provided that the body of the loop in (3) is correct. Our next task is to refine (3) preserving the criterion of correctness expressed by (4) and (5), and the reduction of $(n - m)$.

Remember the situation. There is a particular value v such that it is the fth value in order of magnitude of the array elements $A[i]$. But we do not know for which value of i. However, at the stage shown in (2), we are sure that it is not in $A[1 .. m - 1]$ or in $A[n + 1 .. N]$. So to achieve our goal of actually placing v as $A[f]$, with $A[i] \leqslant v$ for $i \leqslant f$ and $v \leqslant A[j]$ for $f \leqslant j$, we only have to rearrange the elements of $A[m .. n]$. In particular, then, we have to achieve the following goal

> Partition the elements from $A[m]$ to $A[n]$ in such a way that   (8)
> all the elements from $A[m]$ to $A[f]$ are less than or equal to
> all the elements from $A[f]$ to $A[n]$.

Now, an important element of top-down design is to recognize when an algorithm already developed (an abstract statement which has already been refined) can be used in solving a new problem. The alert reader may have been reminded by (8) of the procedure *Partition* which we developed in Section 5.3. There we showed that the procedure satisfied the following correctness criterion

> Given an array A of type **array** $[1 .. N]$ **of** *integer*, and given   (9)
> integers m,n such that $m < n$, then the statement

$$Partition(A,i,j,m,n)$$

> permutes the elements of A between m and n, leaving the others
> unchanged, and assigns to the integer variables i and j values
> which satisfy

$$(j < i) \wedge \forall p,q((m \leqslant p < i) \wedge (j < q \leqslant n)) \supset (A[p] \leqslant A[q])).$$

In other words, $Partition(A,i,j,m,n)$ does partition $A[m .. n]$ into two pieces, but does not guarantee that the 'crossover' occurs at f as specified in (8).

On exit from $Partition(A,i,j,m,n)$, we have $m \leqslant j < i \leqslant n$, and so f can appear in one of three ranges:

(i) $f \leqslant j$
(ii) $i \leqslant f$
(iii) $j < f < i$.

In each case, we have from (9) that $A[1], \ldots, A[m-1]$ and $A[n+1], \ldots, A[N]$ have been left undisturbed, while $A[m], \ldots, A[n]$ have been permuted in such a way that

$$(j < i) \wedge \forall p,q(((m \leqslant p < i) \wedge (j < q \leqslant n)) \supset (A[p] \leqslant A[q])). \quad (10)$$

The three cases (i), (ii) and (iii) for the position of f are shown in Figure (11).

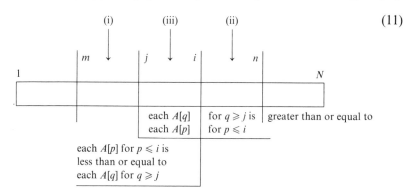

(11)

If i and j crossed above f (case (i)), we assign j as the new value of n, since the fth element in order of magnitude must be between m and j. If i and j crossed below f (case (ii)), we assign i as the new value of m, since in that case the desired element must be between i and n. If $j < f < i$ (case (iii)) we can prove (as seems clear from (11)) that the desired correctness criterion holds, and we exit the loop, jumping to the end of the program.

The above discussion suggests the following refinement of *reduce middle part*

$$\text{Partition}(A,i,j,m,n); \qquad\qquad\qquad (12)$$
if $f \leqslant j$ **then** $n := j$
else if $i \leqslant f$ **then** $m := i$
       else goto 13

Consider, then, what happens to **while** B **do** S when the body S of the loop is an L-statement. The only change in (13) from the usual annotation of a **while-do** loop with invariants is that there is an invariant R which is to hold whenever a **goto** L exit is executed.

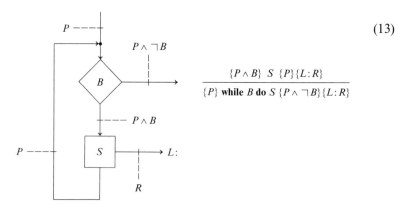

(13)

$$\frac{\{P \wedge B\}\ S\ \{P\}\{L:R\}}{\{P\}\ \textbf{while}\ B\ \textbf{do}\ S\ \{P \wedge \neg B\}\{L:R\}}$$

Thus—bearing in mind proof rule (8) of Section 7.2—we see that to check that, with the refinement given in (12), *reduce middle part* is indeed correct, we must verify that

$$\{L(A,m,f) \wedge R(A,n,f) \wedge (m < n)\} \tag{14}$$
reduce middle part
$$\{L(A,m,f) \wedge R(A,n,f)\}$$
$$\{13:\ Found\}$$

where *Found* is the correctness criterion of (1).

We start our proof of correctness by assuming, then, that before executing *Partition*(A,i,j,m,n) we have $(m < n)$ and the left invariant and right invariant hold:

$$(m \leqslant f) \wedge \forall p,q((1 \leqslant p < m \leqslant q \leqslant N) \supset (A[p] \leqslant A[q]))$$
$$\text{which is } L(A,m,f) \quad (15)$$

$$(f \leqslant n) \wedge \forall p,q((1 \leqslant p \leqslant n < q \leqslant N) \supset (A[p] \leqslant A[q]))$$
$$\text{which is } R(A,n,f) \quad (16)$$

(i) We first show that if $f \leqslant j$, then we have both

$$L(A,m,f) \quad \text{and} \quad R(A,j,f)$$

holding after *Partition*(A,i,j,m,n) where $L(A,m,f)$ is again given by (15), while $R(A,j,f)$ is given by

$$(f \leqslant j) \wedge \forall p,q((1 \leqslant p \leqslant j < q \leqslant N) \supset (A[p] \leqslant A[q])). \tag{17}$$

It is clear that $L(A,m,f)$ still holds, since the rearrangement of $A[m], \ldots, A[n]$ by *Partition*(A,i,j,m,n) does not affect the truth of (15).

Turning to (17), we see that $f \leqslant j$ by our assumption that case (i) holds. Let us pick p and q such that $1 \leqslant p \leqslant j < q \leqslant N$. We must show that $A[p] \leqslant A[q]$. There are three cases:

(a) If $p < m$, then $A[p]$ does not change during *Partition*(A,i,j,m,n), and the new $A[q]$ is one of the old $A[k]$'s for $k \geqslant m$. Thus $A[p] \leqslant A[q]$ by the fact that (15) held before *Partition*(A,i,j,m,n).

(b) Similarly, if $n < q$, then $A[q]$ does not change during *Partition*(A,i,j,m,n), and the new $A[p]$ is one of the old $A[k]$'s for $k \leqslant n$. Thus $A[p] \leqslant A[q]$ by the fact that (16) held before *Partition*(A,i,j,m,n).

(c) If, in the remaining case, we have $m \leqslant p < q \leqslant n$, so that both $A[p]$ and $A[q]$ lie in the region that *Partition*(A,i,j,m,n) rearranged, we must call upon (10). Now $p \leqslant j < q$ by assumption, and so we have both $m \leqslant p \leqslant j < i$ and $j < q \leqslant n$, so that (10) does indeed imply that $A[p] \leqslant A[q]$.

Thus we have completed our proof that $L(A,m,f)$ and $R(A,j,f)$ both hold if after *Partition*(A,i,j,m,n) we have $f \leqslant j$.

A similar proof yields:

(ii) If $i \leqslant f$ holds after *Partition*(A,i,j,m,n), then $L(A,i,f)$ and $R(A,n,f)$ hold.

(iii) We must show that if $j < f < i$, then *Found* holds after
Partition(A,i,j,m,n).

But by (10) we have, for all p and q, that

$$(m \leqslant p \leqslant f \leqslant q \leqslant n) \supset ((1 \leqslant p < i) \wedge (j < q \leqslant n)) \qquad (18)$$
$$\supset (A[p] \leqslant A[q]).$$

Again, the fact that *Partition*(A,i,j,m,n) affects A only by permuting
$A[m], \ldots , A[n]$ lets us deduce that

$$(1 \leqslant p < m \leqslant f \leqslant q \leqslant N) \supset (A[p] \leqslant A[q]) \qquad (19)$$

from $L[A,m,f]$, while

$$(1 \leqslant p \leqslant f \leqslant n < q \leqslant N) \supset (A[p] \leqslant A[q]) \qquad (20)$$

holds by $R(A,n,f)$. Combining (18), (19) and (20), we deduce that

$$\forall p,q((1 \leqslant p \leqslant f \leqslant q \leqslant N) \supset (A[p] \leqslant A[q])) \qquad (21)$$

which is precisely *Found*.

We have thus demonstrated that

$$\{L(A,m,f) \wedge R(A,n,f) \wedge (m < n)\} \qquad (22)$$
$$Partition(A,i,j,m,n)$$
$$\{((f \leqslant j) \wedge L(A,m,f) \wedge R(A,j,f))$$
$$\vee ((i \leqslant f) \wedge L(A,i,f) \wedge R(A,n,f))$$
$$\vee ((j < f < i) \wedge Found)\}.$$

But this implies that

$$\{L(A,m,f) \wedge R(A,n,f) \wedge (m < n)\} \qquad (23)$$
$$Partition(A,i,j,m,n);$$
$$\textbf{if } f \leqslant j \textbf{ then } n := j$$
$$\textbf{else if } i \leqslant f \textbf{ then } m := i$$
$$\qquad \textbf{else goto } 13$$
$$\{L(A,m,f) \wedge R(A,n,f)\} \ \{13: Found\}.$$

In other words, we have verified that our refinement of *reduce middle part* is
correct.

Since we already have the Pascal procedure *Partition* in our library, we
have thus completed the design procedure for *Find* and we thus obtain:

```
procedure Find(var: array A[1 .. N] of integer; f: integer);   (24)
var m,n,i,j: integer; label 13;
begin m := 1; n := N;
      while m < n do
      begin Partition(A,i,j,m,n);
            if f ≤ i then n := j
            else if j ≤ f then m := i
                 else begin goto 13
      end
 13: end
```

Moreover, our above analysis does indeed verify that the procedure *Find* is correct.

7.4 Failure Exits and the Algorithm Lookup

The function *Lookup* is designed to perform a search of a one-dimensional, sorted array A with the component type *integer* and index type the subrange $1 .. N$. The search is a *binary* one, repeatedly splitting the array in two, as in (20) of Section 3.4. It is assumed that no two elements of the array have the same value. Altogether, the array A satisfies the property *sorted*(A) which here means $\forall i,j((1 \leqslant i < j \leqslant N) \supset (A[i] < A[j]))$. The function *Lookup* is to discover that element of the array A whose value is equal to a given number x. It is assumed that x satisfies the relation:

$$A[1] \leqslant x < A[N]. \tag{1}$$

The value returned by the function is the index of that element of the array which equals x. But the trouble is that such an element may not exist and we do not know that it does not until we have searched the array.

$$
\begin{aligned}
&\textbf{function } Lookup(\textbf{var } A: \textbf{array } [1 .. N] \textbf{ of } integer; \qquad\qquad (2)\\
&\qquad\qquad\qquad x: integer): 1 .. N;\\
&\quad\textbf{var } i,m,n: 1 .. N; \textbf{ label } 11;\\
&\quad \{(1 < N) \wedge sorted(A) \wedge (A[1] \leqslant x < A[N])\}\\
&\quad\textbf{begin } m := 1; n := N;\\
&\qquad\quad \{(m < n) \wedge sorted(A) \wedge (A[m] \leqslant x < A[n])\}\\
&\qquad\quad\textbf{while } m + 1 < n \textbf{ do}\\
&\qquad\quad\textbf{begin } i := (m + n) \textbf{ div } 2;\\
&\qquad\qquad\quad\textbf{if } x < A[i] \textbf{ then } n := i\\
&\qquad\qquad\quad\textbf{else if } A[i] < x \textbf{ then } m := i\\
&\qquad\qquad\qquad\textbf{else begin } Lookup := i;\\
&\qquad\qquad\qquad\qquad\quad \{A[Lookup] = x\}\\
&\qquad\qquad\qquad\qquad\textbf{goto } 11\\
&\qquad\qquad\qquad\textbf{end}\\
&\qquad\quad\textbf{end};\\
&\qquad\quad \{(m + 1 = n) \wedge sorted(A) \wedge (A[m] \leqslant x < A[n])\}\\
&\qquad\quad\textbf{if } A[m] \neq x \textbf{ then } \{\neg\exists k((1 \leqslant k \leqslant N) \wedge (A[k] = x))\}\\
&\qquad\qquad\qquad\textbf{goto } 13\\
&\qquad\qquad\quad\textbf{else } Lookup := m;\\
&\quad 11: \textbf{end}\\
&\qquad \{A[Lookup] = x\} \ \{13: Failure\}\\
&\textbf{where}\\
&\qquad\qquad Failure = \neg\exists k((1 \leqslant k \leqslant N) \wedge (A[k] = x)). \qquad\qquad (3)
\end{aligned}
$$

There are two jumps in (2) used in two quite different situations. The jump **goto** 11 is a return exit. It is used to exit the function *Lookup* at the point where we discover the solution to the posed problem, i.e., when we find the desired element of the array *A*. The second jump (**goto** 13) is used at the point where we discover that the array *A* does not contain an element with the desired properties. Having discovered that, it does not make sense to simply exit the function *Lookup* in a normal way, since in that case some index value must be returned by the function. What is performed is a *failure exit* from the function body via the statement **goto** 13. Thus the use of *Lookup* in a block requires that the block contains a program part labelled 13 which specifies some appropriate action to be performed in this situation.

There are, of course, ways of avoiding this failure exit and the reader is invited to investigate some of them in exercise 6. The real question is whether these other ways are any better than the solution (2).

To refine our analysis, note that (2) has the form

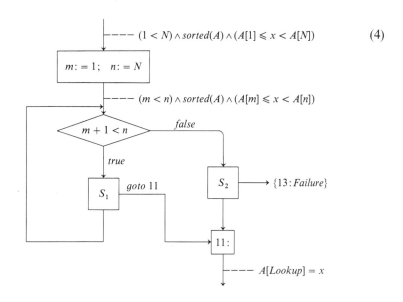

$$\qquad\qquad (1 < N) \wedge sorted(A) \wedge (A[1] \leqslant x < A[N]) \qquad\qquad (4)$$

Thus we wish to establish, amongst other things, that $(m < n) \wedge sorted(A) \wedge (A[m] \leqslant x < A[n])$ is an invariant of the loop, and that a **goto** 11 guarantees the postcondition $A[Lookup] = x$. In other words, we must establish that

$$\{((m < n) \wedge sorted(A) \wedge (A[m] \leqslant x < A[n]) \wedge (m + 1 < n)\} \qquad (5)$$
$$S_1$$
$$\{(m < n) \wedge sorted(A) \wedge (A[m] \leqslant x < A[n])\} \ \{11 : A[Lookup] = x\}$$

where we note that the precondition is equivalent to $\{(m + 1 < n) \wedge sorted(A) \wedge (A[m] \leqslant x < A[n])\}$.

Before establishing (5), we note that

$$(m < n) \wedge sorted(A) \wedge (A[m] \leqslant x < A[n]) \wedge \neg(m + 1 < n) \qquad (6)$$
$$\equiv (m + 1 = n) \wedge sorted(A) \wedge (A[m] \leqslant x < A[n])$$
$$\equiv sorted(A) \wedge (A[m] \leqslant x < A[m + 1])$$

and it is obvious that S_2 is correct, since

$$\{sorted(A) \wedge (A[m] \leqslant x < A[m + 1])\} \qquad (7)$$
if $A[m] \neq x$ **then goto** 13
else $Lookup := m$
$\{A[Lookup] = A[m] = x\} \ \{13: Failure\}$

It is also obvious that

$$\{(1 < N) \wedge sorted(A) \wedge (A[1] \leqslant x \leqslant A[N])\} \qquad (8)$$
$$m := 1; n := N$$
$$\{(m < n) \wedge sorted(A) \wedge (A[m] \leqslant x < A[n])\}$$

as required in (4). Thus all that remains to prove correctness of the specification (2) is to check that (5) is correct, namely

$$\{(m + 1 < n) \wedge sorted(A) \wedge (A[m] \leqslant x < A[n])\} \qquad (9)$$
begin $i := (m + n)$ **div** 2;
   if $x < A[i]$ **then** $n := i$
   else if $A[i] < x$ **then** $m := i$
      else begin $Lookup := i$;
             goto 11
      end
end
$\{(m < n) \wedge sorted(A) \wedge (A[m] \leqslant x < A[n])\} \ \{11: A[Lookup] = x\}$

Note, first, that $m + 1 < n$ implies $m < i = (m + n)$ **div** $2 < n$; and that $sorted(A)$ is preserved throughout the procedure. Then, with the given preconditions, if $x < A[i]$, then $A[m] \leqslant x < A[i]$ and so $n := i$ restores $(m < n) \wedge (A[m] \leqslant x < A[n])$. Again, if $A[i] < x$ then $A[i] \leqslant x < A[n]$ and so $m := i$ restores $(m < n) \wedge (A[m] \leqslant x < A[n])$. Finally, if $\neg(x < A[i]) \wedge \neg(A[i] < x)$, then we have $A[i] = x$ and so $A[Lookup] = x$ on transfer to 11: This completes our proof that (2) is correct.

7.5 Loops with Exits in the Middle

There exist reasonably frequent situations in which the design of an algorithm leads to a so-called loop with exits in the middle. We saw examples of such structures in (8) and (9) of Section 7.2. A loop with one exit in the middle can also be built up in the fashion shown in the following diagram:

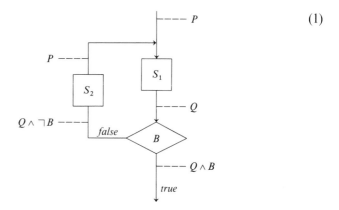

Expressing the computation described by (1) is easy with the **goto** statement.

One way of doing it is:

$$1: \textbf{begin } S1; \qquad\qquad\qquad\qquad (2)$$
$$\textbf{if } B \textbf{ then goto } 2;$$
$$S2;$$
$$\textbf{goto } 1;$$
$$2: \textbf{end}$$

Another way is:

$$\textbf{while } true \textbf{ do} \qquad\qquad\qquad\qquad (3)$$
$$\textbf{begin } S1;$$
$$\textbf{if } B \textbf{ then goto } 11;$$
$$S2;$$
$$\textbf{end}; 11:$$

In (3), 11 labels the empty statement. (3) makes clear that the algorithm consists of a loop in which the number of repetitions is controlled entirely within the loop body. When the condition B is satisfied, an exit from the loop occurs. Of course, we are assuming that in (2) both S_1 and S_2 are nonempty statements, since if S_2 is empty, (1) reduces to the **repeat-until** statement and if S_1 is empty, (1) reduces to the **while-do** statement.

Expressing (1) in terms of the basic repetitive and conditional composition rules does, however, lead to some undesirable complications, as can be seen from the following two representations of (1):

$$\textbf{begin } S1; \qquad\qquad\qquad\qquad (4)$$
$$\textbf{while } \neg B \textbf{ do}$$
$$\textbf{begin } S2; S1 \textbf{ end}$$
$$\textbf{end}$$

$$\begin{aligned}
&\textbf{begin } S1\\
&\quad \textbf{if } \neg B \textbf{ then}\\
&\quad \textbf{repeat } S2; S1 \textbf{ until } B\\
&\textbf{end}
\end{aligned} \qquad (5)$$

Both yield the same computation sequence as (1), but both require writing S_1 out twice, though only (5) requires B to be written twice. If the test B is simple, the form of (5) may be acceptable, but (4) would seem to be generally preferable.

The reader may check that, no matter which representation—(2), (3), (4) or (5) is used—the proof rules already available allow us to conclude that that statement S represented by (1) satisfies the proof rule

$$\frac{\{P\}\, S_1\, \{Q\},\ \{Q \wedge \neg B\}\, S_2\, \{P\}}{\{P\}\, S\, \{Q \wedge B\}}. \qquad (6)$$

It is very important to observe that the need for a loop with exits in the middle is often only the result of a certain approach chosen in the design of the desired algorithm, rather than a real necessity. The example that follows shows that sometimes an even better solution may be found if we stick to the basic composition rules.

(7)

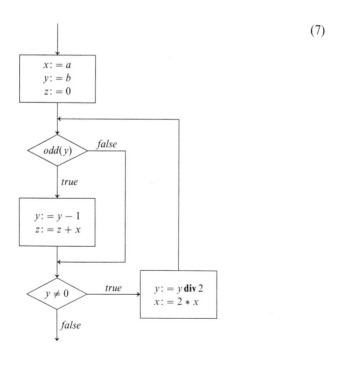

The algorithm in (7) multiplies two nonnegative integers a and b with the use of addition, doubling and halving only. The result is represented as the value of the variable z.

One way of avoiding the exit in the middle of the outer loop in (7) is by displacing the loop termination test, positioning it in front of the $odd(y)$ test to obtain the following program:

$$x := a; y := b; z := 0; \qquad\qquad\qquad\qquad (8)$$
$$\textbf{while } y \neq 0 \textbf{ do}$$
$$\qquad \textbf{begin if } odd(y) \textbf{ then}$$
$$\qquad\qquad \textbf{begin } y := y - 1; z := z + x \textbf{ end};$$
$$\qquad\qquad y := y \textbf{ div } 2;$$
$$\qquad\qquad x := 2 * x$$
$$\qquad \textbf{end}$$

Observe that if $y = 0$ before the $odd(y)$ test in (7) is executed, then $y := y - 1; z := z - x$ will be omitted, and the loop in (7) will then be exited. If $y = 0$ in (8), the loop in (8) will not be executed at all, i.e., it will be terminated. Thus in this case the effects of the two programs are equivalent. If $y \neq 0$ then the modified version (8) has an additional effect in the case $y = 1$. Indeed, if $y = 1$ before the body of the loop in (7) is executed, then the statements $y := y \textbf{ div } 2$, $x := 2 * x$ will not get executed. On the other hand, if $y = 1$ before the body of the loop in (8) is entered, the statements $y := y \textbf{ div } 2$; $x := 2 * x$ will be executed. This additional shift of x is undesirable since it may cause an overflow. Thus the **goto** free solution in (8) although quite attractive at first, now proves to be unacceptable.

An algorithm which meets all the desired criteria is obtained starting from the most obvious multiplication algorithm under the stated constraints, which is:

$$x := a; y := b; z := 0; \qquad\qquad\qquad\qquad (9)$$
$$\textbf{while } y \neq 0 \textbf{ do}$$
$$\textbf{begin } \{(y > 0) \wedge (x * y + z = a * b)\}$$
$$\qquad y := y - 1;$$
$$\qquad z := z + x$$
$$\textbf{end}$$

The algorithm in (9) is not efficient. In order to improve it, we observe that if we substitute a statement at the point of the program with the invariant $(y > 0) \wedge (x * y + z = a * b)$, and if that statement does not affect this invariant, then the result of the program in (9) will remain the same. The statement:

$$\textbf{while } \neg odd(y) \textbf{ do} \qquad\qquad\qquad\qquad (10)$$
$$\textbf{begin } y := y \textbf{ div } 2; x := 2 * x \textbf{ end}$$

certainly does not affect the relation $(y > 0) \wedge (x * y + z = a * b)$. So we obtain the following improvement of the algorithm (8). Note that it avoids the unnecessary additional shift that we saw in (8).

$$x := a; y := b; z := 0; \qquad (11)$$
$$\textbf{while } y \neq 0 \textbf{ do}$$
$$\textbf{begin } \{(y > 0) \wedge (x * y + z = a * b)\}$$
$$\qquad \textbf{while } \neg odd(y) \textbf{ do}$$
$$\qquad \textbf{begin } y := y \textbf{ div } 2; x := 2 * x \textbf{ end };$$
$$\qquad y := y - 1;$$
$$\qquad z := z + x$$
$$\textbf{end}$$

It would be wrong, however, to believe that a transformation of the type described above is always possible in such a satisfactory manner. In fact, in order to give the problem a fair treatment, we show one more example (a factoring into primes algorithm). Although we show how to eliminate some **goto**s the result will not be as satisfactory as in the previous example.

Every positive integer can be expressed in a unique way in the form

$$n = 1 * p_1 * p_2 * \cdots * p_t, p_1 \leqslant p_2 \leqslant \cdots \leqslant p_t \qquad (12)$$

where p_i $(i = 1, \ldots ,t)$ are primes. The apparently ridiculous factor 1 ensures that when $n = 1$ this equation holds for $t = 0$.

The most obvious algorithm for prime factorization follows from the following considerations. If $n > 1$, n is divided by successive primes $p = 2,3,5 \ldots$, until the smallest p is discovered for which $n \bmod p = 0$. This p is the smallest prime factor of n, and so the same process may be applied to $n \textbf{ div } p$ in order to discover further prime factors of n. If this process is successful, we eventually reduce n to 1, at which point the algorithm terminates. However, it is possible that n is either initially a prime or reduced to a prime later on and the fact is that we don't have to wait until we reach such a p in order to conclude that $n = p$. If at any point in the process of finding the next prime factor of n, we discover that $n \bmod p \neq 0$ and $n \textbf{ div } p \leqslant p$, then we can conclude that n is a prime, for if n was not a prime under these conditions, we would have by (12) that $n \geqslant p_1^2$. But the condition $p_1 > p$ implies

$$p_1^2 \geqslant (p + 1)^2 > p(p + 1) > p^2 + n \bmod p$$
$$\geqslant (n \textbf{ div } p) * p + n \bmod p = n,$$

so $p_1^2 < n$.

The algorithm (14) is based on the above considerations. It uses a sequence of auxiliary trial divisors

$$2 = d_0 < d_1 < d_2 < d_3 < \cdots \qquad (13)$$

which includes all prime numbers $\leqslant \sqrt{n}$. The sequence of ds must also include at least one value such that $d_k > \sqrt{n}$. An efficient way for generating ds is to use the sieve of Eratosthenes.

(14)

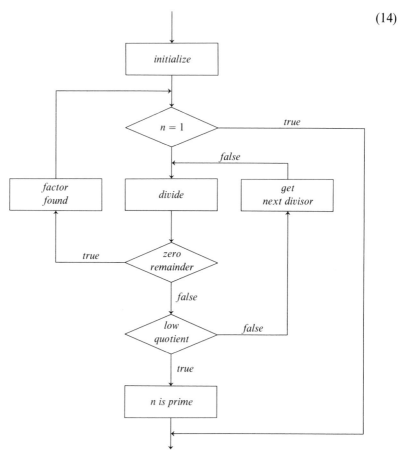

The various boxes in (14) may be refined as follows:

$$\begin{aligned}
&\{initialize\}\; t := 0;\, k := 0 \qquad\qquad\qquad (15)\\
&\{divide\}\; q := n \textbf{ div } d[k];\\
&\qquad\qquad r := n \textbf{ mod } d[k]\\
&\{low\; quotient\}\; q \leqslant d[k]\\
&\{factor\; found\}\; t := t + 1;\\
&\qquad\qquad p[t] :=d[k];\\
&\qquad\qquad n := q\\
&\{get\; next\; divisor\}\; k := k + 1\\
&\{zero\; remainder\}\; r = 0\\
&\{n\; is\; prime\}\; t := t + 1;\, p[t] := n
\end{aligned}$$

The structure of the algorithm (14) can be somewhat simplified by the following observation: If $n = 1$ then $n \textbf{ div } p = 0$ and $n \textbf{ mod } p = 1$, since $p \geqslant 2$, $n \textbf{ div } p = 0 \leqslant p$, so the condition *low quotient* is satisfied. Thus if $n = 1$ the conditions *zero remainder* and *low quotient* will be satisfied, and we can omit the test $n = 1$ preserving correctness of the algorithm and introducing one additional computation *divide* at the point when the prime factorization is found.

(16)

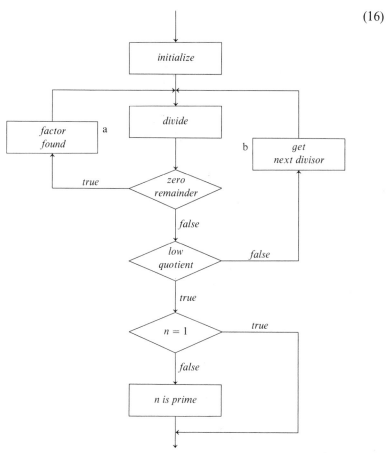

This version of the algorithm makes clear that we have the loop a nested inside the loop b, where both a and b have an exit in the middle. There is no question about it that these exits can be eliminated, but this does not seem to be possible without at least some undesirable effects such as reevaluation of conditions in loops. Here is one way of modifying the structure of (16) to obtain a **goto**-free solution.

$$
\begin{aligned}
&initialize; \hspace{5cm} (17)\\
&divide\ by\ 2;\\
&\textbf{while}\ zero\ remainder \lor high\ quotient\ \textbf{do}\\
&\textbf{begin if}\ zero\ remainder\ \textbf{then}\ factor\ found\\
&\hspace{1.5cm}\textbf{else}\ get\ next\ divisor;\\
&\hspace{1.5cm}divide\\
&\textbf{end};\\
&\textbf{if}\ n \neq 1\ \textbf{then}\ n\ is\ prime
\end{aligned}
$$

The abstract algorithm (17) refines to the following specific form:

$$\begin{aligned}
&\textbf{begin } t := 0;\, k := 0; \qquad\qquad\qquad\qquad\qquad\qquad\qquad (18)\\
&\quad q := n \textbf{ div } d[0];\\
&\quad r := n \textbf{ mod } d[0];\\
&\quad \textbf{while } (r = 0) \vee (q > d[k]) \textbf{ do } \{n \text{ is not a prime}\}\\
&\quad \textbf{begin if } r = 0 \textbf{ then } \{\textit{factor found}\}\\
&\qquad\quad \textbf{begin } t := t + 1;\\
&\qquad\qquad\quad p[t] := d[k];\\
&\qquad\qquad\quad n := q\\
&\qquad\quad \textbf{end}\\
&\qquad\quad \textbf{else } \{\textit{get next divisor}\}\ k := k + 1;\\
&\qquad\quad \{\textit{divide}\}\\
&\qquad\quad q := n \textbf{ div } d[k];\\
&\qquad\quad r := n \textbf{ mod } d[k]\\
&\quad \textbf{end };\\
&\quad \{(n \textbf{ mod } d[k] \neq 0) \vee (n \textbf{ div } d[k] \leqslant d[k])\}\\
&\quad \textbf{if } n = 1 \textbf{ then } \{n \text{ is prime}\}\\
&\quad \textbf{begin } t := t + 1;\\
&\qquad\quad p[t] := n\\
&\quad \textbf{end}\\
&\textbf{end}
\end{aligned}$$

Bibliographic Remarks

The first paper which explicitly stated the problems caused by the **goto** statement and attracted wide attention was Dijkstra (1968a). A detailed analysis of the **goto** issue was given in Knuth (1974). Some examples of abuses of the **goto** statement presented in this chapter are from Jensen and Wirth (1974). Some material on the design of the **goto**-free programs presented in this chapter is based on Wirth (1974). The unstructured version of the binary *gcd* algorithm is from Knuth (1969). The proof rules for return exits, error exits, and the special type of conventional jumps are from Arbib and Alagić (1978)—they replace those of Clint and Hoare (1972) which do not explicitly address the two-exit situation. Thus our proof of correctness is different from that of the function *Lookup* in Clint and Hoare (1972). Our development of the algorithm *Find* using *Partition* is new. The full algorithm differs little from that of Hoare (1971b), but the proof of correctness is completely new. The exercises in this chapter are derived from the following sources: Wirth (1974), Conway and Gries (1975), Knuth (1968), Knuth (1969).

Exercises

1. Design an alternative **goto** free solution to the problem of selecting the first n distinct numbers from the file *input* abandoning

for $i := 1$ **to** n **do**
$a[i] :=$ *the next suitable number*

as the first step in program development.

2. The **goto** statement in the traditional solution to the problem of selecting the first n distinct numbers from the file *input* can be eliminated almost mechanically as follows: An additional Boolean variable *ok*, which is set to *false* if $a(j) \neq r$ and to *true* otherwise, is introduced. The inner **for** statement is replaced with a more flexible **while-do** statement in which repetition stops when either $j \geq r$ or $a[j] \neq r$. Write up this solution, and show that it is both less efficient and less clear than not only the presented **goto**-free solution (and the solution from the previous exercise) but also the traditional solution with the **goto** statement.

3. The final solution for prime factorization presented in this chapter can be further improved using **repeat-until** and not **while-do** statements. Perform this modification.

4. An algorithm for searching a linear list and performing some operation f upon its nodes was presented in the chapter on data types (pointers). Write an algorithm which accomplishes the same task, but does not use an auxiliary variable which is set to *true* in the loop body if the end of the list is reached, and tested before every repetition.

5. The following loop is intended to read integers from the file *input* and print them as they are read until a number is read which is either negative, or ends with the number 3, or is a power of 2.

while $\neg eof$ **do**
begin *read*(a);
    if $(a < 0) \vee (a \bmod 10) = 3$
    then goto 11;
    $p := 1$;
    while $p < a$ **do** $p := p * 2$;
    if $p = a$ **then goto** 11;
    write(a)
end; 11:

Prove correctness.

6. (a) Rewrite program (2) of Section 7.4 to avoid use of a failure exit, but instead using *Lookup* = 0 to signal that no i exists with $A[i] = x$. (The disadvantage of this is that it confuses the type of an index with the type of an error message. Further, an explicit test for *Lookup* = 0 is still required in the same program.)

   (b) To avoid type confusion, one could try to return two values, one indicating whether the search succeeded, and the other indicating the result of the search (if it succeeded) and N otherwise. Pascal only allows a function to return a result of scalar type (or *real*) or pointer type. Define a Pascal function which returns a pointer to value of type **record** *success*: *Boolean*; *result*: 1 . . N **end** with the indicated properties.

(c) Use the idea of (b), but defining *Lookup* as a procedure.

7. Suppose that we want to design a function which performs a search of an ordered linear list in order to locate the record with a given key. Would a return exit be useful? Would an error exit be useful?

8. Design a procedure which sums and counts the integers from *a* to *b* which are divisible by 3 or 5. Analyze whether there is a need or justification for a return exit.

9. Suppose that *n* is an odd number and that it can be factored. Then *n* can be written as

$$n = u * v \text{ where } u \leqslant v. \tag{1}$$

If *n* is odd, then both *u* and *v* will be odd. Fermat's algorithm for finding the largest factor of *n* less than or equal to $\sqrt{n}$ is based on the observation that under the above assumptions there exist integers *x* and *y* such that

$$x = (u + v) \textbf{ div } 2, \qquad y = (v - u) \textbf{ div } 2 \tag{2}$$

$$n = x^2 - y^2, \qquad 0 \leqslant y < x \leqslant n. \tag{3}$$

The algorithm consists of a search for the values *x* and *y* which satisfy (2) and (3). *u* is then recaptured as $x - y$. In the algorithm (5) the variables *xx* and *yy*, rather than *x* and *y*, are used, where the following relations hold:

$$xx = 2x + 1 \tag{4}$$

$$yy = 2y + 1.$$

Observe that in (5), *root(n)* denotes the largest integer less than or equal to $\sqrt{n}$ (this quantity may be computed using the function *root* given in the chapter on procedures and functions).

```
begin xx := 2 * root(n) + 1;                                    (5)
      yy := 1;
      r := root(n)² − n;
      2: if r < 0 then goto 4;
      3: r := r − yy;
         yy := yy + 2;
         goto 2;
      4: if r = 0 then goto 5;
         r := r + xx;
         xx := xx + 2;
         goto 3;
         5: u := (xx − yy) div 2
end
```

Discover the invariants which explain the essence of the algorithm (5) and restructure the algorithm to obtain a **goto**-free one whose structure reflects directly the discovered invariants.

References

This list of references contains many publications on program design and proofs of correctness in addition to those cited in the text.

Aho, A. V., Hopcroft, J. E. and Ullman, J. D. (1974): *The Design and Analysis of Computer Algorithms*. Addison-Wesley.

Alagić, S. (1976): *Principles of Programming*. (In Serbo-Croatian). Svjetlost-Sarajevo, Yugoslavia.

Alagić, S. (1977): Cleaning up unstructured algorithms using invariants. *Informatica*, Journal of the Slovenian Computer Society, Ljubljana, Vol. *1*, No. 2.

Alagić, S, Arbib, M. A. and Taylor, R. W. (1974): Algebraic Models of Syntax, Semantics, and Data Structures. COINS Technical Report 74B-1: Computer and Information Science Department, University of Massachusetts at Amherst.

Alagić, S., Kulenovic, A. (1981): Relational Pascal database interface. *Computer Journal*, Vol. 24, No. 2, pp. 112–117.

Arbib, M. A. and Alagić, S. (1978): Proof rules for gotos (to appear).

Ashcroft, E. A., Clint, M. and Hoare, C. A. R. (1976): Remarks on "Program proving: Jumps and functions by M. Clint and C. A. R. Hoare". *Acta Informatica 6*, 317–318.

Bobrow, L. S. and Arbib, M. A. (1974): *Discrete Mathematics: Applied Algebra for Computer and Information Science*. Hemisphere Books.

Böhm, C. and Jacopini, G. (1966): Flow-diagrams, Turing machines and languages with only two formation rules. *Communications of the ACM 9*, 366–371.

Branquart, P., Levi, J., Sintzoff, M. and Wodon, P. L. (1972): The composition of semantics in Algol 68. *Communications of the ACM 14*, 697–708.

Clint, M. (1973): Program proving: Coroutines. *Acta Informatica 2*, 50–63.

Clint, M. and Hoare, C. A. R. (1972): Program proving: Jumps and functions. *Acta Informatica 1*, 214–224.

Conway, R. (1976): PL/CS—A highly-disciplined subset of PL/C. *ACM SIGPLAN Notices*, Dec. 1976.

Conway, R. and Gries, D. (1975): *An Introduction to Programming: A Structured Approach Using PL/I and PL/C-7*. Winthrop.

Conway, R., Gries, D. and Zimmerman, P. (1976): *A Primer on Pascal*. Winthrop.

Dahl, O. J. and Hoare, C. A. R. (1972): Hierarchical program structures. In: O. J. Dahl, E. W. Dijkstra, and C. A. R. Hoare: *Structured Programming*. Academic Press, 197–220.

Dahl, O. J., Myhrhang, B., Nygaard, K. (1967): The Simula 67 Common Base Language. Norwegian Computing Centre, Forskningsveien 1B, Oslo 3.

Dahl, O. J., Nygaard, K. (1966): Simula—an Algol based simulation language. *Communications of the ACM 9*, 671–678.

De Morgan, R. M., Hill, I. D. and Wichmann, B. A. (1976): Modified Report on the Algorithmic Language Algol 60. *Computer Journal 19*, No. 4. 364–379.

Dijkstra, E. W. (1962): *A Primer of Algol 60 Programming.* Academic Press.

Dijkstra, E. W. (1968a): Goto statement considered harmful. *Communications of the ACM 11*, 147–148, 538, 541.

Dijkstra, E. W. (1968b): A constructive approach to the problem of program correctness. *BIT 8*, 174–186.

Dijkstra, E. W. (1971): A short introduction into the art of programming. Dept. of Mathematics, Technological University, Eindhoven, EWD 316.

Dijkstra, E. W. (1972): Notes on structured programming. In: O. J. Dahl, E. W. Dijkstra and C. A. R. Hoare: *Structured Programming*, Academic Press, 1–82.

Dijkstra, E. W. (1972): The humble programmer. *Communications of the ACM, 15.*

Dijkstra, E. W. (1975): On guarded commands, nondeterminacy, and formal derivation of programs. *Communications of the ACM 18*, 453–457.

Dijkstra, E. W. (1976): *A Discipline of Programming.* Prentice-Hall.

Floyd, R. W. (1967): Assigning meanings to programs. In: Proc. Sym. in Applied Math., Vol. 19, *Mathematical Aspects of Computer Science* (J. T. Schwartz, ed.). Amer. Math. Soc. 19–32.

Foley, M. and Hoare, C. A. R. (1971): Proof of a recursive program: Quicksort. *Computer Journal 14*, 391–395.

Gries, D. (1971): *Compiler Construction for Digital Computers.* John Wiley.

Gries, D. (1973): Describing an algorithm by Hopcroft. *Acta Informatica 2*, 97–109.

Gries, D. (1977): On believing programs to be correct. *Communications of the ACM 20*, 49–50.

Gries, D. (1974): On structured programming—a reply to Smoliar. *Communications of the ACM 17*, 655–657.

Haberman, A. N. (1973): Critical comments on the programming language Pascal. *Acta Informatica 3*, 47–57.

Hoare, C. A. R. and Wirth, N. (1966): A contribution to the development of Algol. *Communications of the ACM 9*, 413–432.

Hoare, C. A. R. (1968): Record handling. In: F. Genuys (ed.): *Programming Languages.* NATO Advanced Study Institute. Academic Press.

Hoare, C. A. R. (1969): An axiomatic basis for computer programming. *Communications of the ACM 12*, 576–580, 583.

Hoare, C. A. R. (1971a): Procedures and parameters; an axiomatic approach. Symposium on Semantics of Algorithmic Languages (E. Engeler, ed.), *Lecture Notes in Mathematics 188*, Springer-Verlag.

Hoare, C. A. R. (1971b): Proof of a program: Find. *Communications of the ACM 14*, 39–45.

Hoare, C. A. R. (1972): Notes on data structuring. In: O. J. Dahl, E. W. Dijkstra and C. A. R. Hoare: *Structured Programming.* Academic Press. 83–174.

Hoare, C. A. R. (1972a): Proof of correctness of data representation. *Acta Informatica 1*, 271–281.

Hoare, C. A. R. (1972b): Proof of a structured program: 'The sieve of Eratosthenes.' *Computer Journal 15*, 321–325.

Hoare, C. A. R. (1972c): A note on the for statement. *BIT 12*, 334–341.

Hoare, C. A. R. (1972d): Towards a theory of parallel programming. In: *Operating Systems Techniques.* Academic Press, 61–71.

Hoare, C. A. R. (1977): Communicating Sequential Processes. Department of Computer Science, The Queen's University of Belfast.

Hoare, C. A. R. and Lauer, P. E. (1973): Consistent and complementary formal theories of the semantics of programming languages. *Acta Informatica 3*, 135–153.

Hoare, C. A. R. and Wirth, N. (1973): An axiomatic definition of the programming language Pascal. *Acta Informatica 2*, 335–355.

IFIP (1964): Report on Subset Algol 60. *Communications of the ACM 7*, 626–628.

Jensen, K. and Wirth, N. (1974): Pascal user manual. In: Pascal User Manual and Report. *Lecture Notes in Computer Science* Vol. 18, Springer-Verlag.

Katz, S. and Manna, Z. (1975): A closer look at termination. *Acta Informatica 5*, 333–352.

Katz, S. and Manna, Z. (1975): Logical analysis of algorithms. *Communications of the ACM 19*, 188–206.

Knuth, D. E. (1967): The remaining trouble spots in Algol 60. *Communications of the ACM 10*, 611–618.

Knuth, D. E. (1968): *The Art of Computer Programming*: Vol. 1/Fundamental Algorithms. Addison-Wesley.

Knuth, D. E. (1969): *The Art of Computer Programming*: Vol. 2/Seminumerical Algorithms. Addison-Wesley.

Knuth, D. E. (1973): *The Art of Computer Programming*: Vol. 3/Sorting and Searching. Addison-Wesley.

Knuth, D. E. (1974): Structured programming with goto statements. *Computing Surveys 6*, 261–301.

Kowaltowski, T. (1977): Axiomatic approach to side effects and general jumps. *Acta Informatica 7*, 357–360.

Lampson, B. W., Horning, J. J., London, R. L., Mitchell, J. G. and Popek, G. L. (1977): Report on the programming language Euclid. *ACM SIGPLAN Notices 12*, No. 2.

Lecarme, O., Desjardins, P. (1975): More comments on the programming language Pascal. *Acta Informatica 4*, 231–243.

Ledgard, H. F., Cave, W. C. (1976): Cobol under control. *Communications of the ACM 19*, 601–608.

Manna, Z. (1974): *Mathematical Theory of Computation*. McGraw-Hill.

Manna, Z. and Vuillemin, J. (1972): Fixpoint theory of computation. *Communications of the ACM 15*, 528–536.

Manna, Z., Ness, S. and Vuillemin, J. (1973): Inductive methods for proving properties of programs. *Communications of the ACM 16*, 491–502.

Marmier, E. (1975): Automatic Verification of Pascal Programs. Ph.D. Dissertation. Swiss Federal Institute of Technology, Zurich.

McCarthy, J., Abrahams, P. W., Edwards, D. J., Hart, T. P., Levin, M. I. (1962): *Lisp 1.5 Programmer's Manual*. MIT Press.

McCarthy, J. (1960): Recursive functions of symbolic expressions and their computation by machine. *Communications of the ACM*. April 1960.

McKeeman, W. M. (1975): On preventing programming languages from interfering with programming. *IEEE Transactions on Software Engineering*, Vol. SE-1, 19–26.

Naur, P. (ed.) (1963): Revised report on the algorithmic language Algol 60. *Communications of the ACM 6*, 1–20.

Owicki, S. and Gries, D. (1976): Verifying properties of parallel programs: An axiomatic approach. *Communications of the ACM 19*, 279–285.

Owicki, S., and Gries, D. (1976): An axiomatic proof technique for parallel programs I. *Acta Informatica 6*, 319–340.

Stanat, D. F. and McAllister, D. F. (1977): *Discrete Mathematics in Computer Science*. Prentice-Hall.

Tremblay, J. P. and Manohar, R. (1975): *Discrete Mathematical Structures with Applications to Computer Science*, McGraw-Hill.

van Wijngaarden, A. (ed.), Mailloux, B. J., Peck, J. E. L. and Koster, C. H. A. (1969): Report on the algorithmic language Algol 68. *Numerische Mathematik 14*, 79–218.

van Wijngaarden, A., Mailloux, B. J., Peck, J. E. L., Koster, C. H. A., Sintzoff, M., Lindsey, C. H., Meertens, L. G. L. T. and Fisher, R. G. (1975): Revised Report on the algorithmic language Algol 68. *Acta Informatica 5*, 1–236.

Weissman, C. (1967): *Lisp 1.5 Primer*. Dickenson Publishing Company.

Wirth, N. and Weber, H. (1966): Euler: A generalisation of Algol and its formal definition. Parts I and II. *Communications of the ACM 9*, 13–23, 89–99.

Wirth, N. (1971): Program development by stepwise refinement. *Communications of the ACM 14*, 221–227.

Wirth, N. (1971): The programming language Pascal. *Acta Informatica 1*, 35–63.

Wirth, N. (1972): *Systematic Programming: An Introduction*. Prentice-Hall.

Wirth, N. (1974a): The programming language Pascal (Revised report). In: K. Jensen and N. Wirth: Pascal: User Manual and Report, *Lecture Notes in Computer Science*, Vol. 18. Springer-Verlag.

Wirth, N. (1974b): On the composition of well structured programs. *Computing Surveys 6*, 247–259.

Wirth, N. (1976): *Algorithms + Data Structures = Programs*. Prentice-Hall.

Wirth, N. (1977a): Modula: A Language for Modular Multiprogramming. *Software Practice and Experience 7*, 3–35.

Wirth, N. (1977b): Design and Implementation of Modula. *Software Practice and Experience 7*, 67–84.

Wirth, N. (1977c): The Use of Modula. *Software Practice and Experience 7*, 37–65.

Wulf, W. A., Russell, D. B. and Haberman, A. N. (1971): BLISS: A language for systems programming *Communications of the ACM 14*, 780–790.

Glossary

Definitions of important concepts are arranged alphabetically. Words in italics within a definition are of three kinds: the word which introduced the entry; another word of the glossary best defined in the context of that entry; or a word defined elsewhere in the glossary whose definition may help the reader better appreciate the given entry.

actual parameter see *parameter*

algorithm a recipe which spells out explicitly and unambiguously the steps which must be carried out to go from given information to obtain a correct solution (where one exists) to a problem within a finite time.

alphabet the alphabet of a programming language is a finite set of symbols which can be combined according to certain *syntactic rules* to form programs of the given language.

antisymmetric see *partial order*

array An *array* has as its set of values the set of all *functions* $B \to A$ for some *scalar* or *subrange type* B and some type A. For example, we can take $B = 1 .. N$ for some integer $N \geqslant 1$. B is called the *index type* and A the *component type*. If x denotes a variable of this type, and i belongs to B, then $x[i]$ denotes the i-component of the variable x, and i is called the array *index*. The operation of going from x to some $x[i]$ is called *indexing* or *subscripting*.

assignment statement a statement which assigns a new value to a particular *variable*.

atom see *s-expression*

backtracking In the stepwise construction of a solution to a problem, it may happen that a trial solution cannot be extended in any way to yield a complete solution. In that case, *backtracking* is required, to discard part of the trial solution, and see if a trial solution reached at an earlier stage can be successfully extended to yield a complete solution.

base see *floating point*

block A *block* in Pascal is the body of a *procedure*, *function*, or *program*. A block consists of a *declaration part* and a *statement part*. The declaration part defines those objects referenced in the statement part which are not defined outside the block. These are called *local* objects—the ones defined in the environment are called *global* objects. The objects can be constants, types, variables, procedures, functions and labels. The statement part of a block has the structure of a *compound statement*. It describes the actions performed by the block.

Boolean expression   see *logical formula*

Boolean operators   these are operators which act upon the truth values (*false, true*) (also known as Boolean values and logical values) to return truth values. Examples include conjunction $\land$, disjunction $\lor$, negation $\lnot$, implication $\supset$, and equivalence $\equiv$. Each Boolean operator may be specified by a *truth table* which has one row for each possible sequence of values for the arguments of the operator, showing the value of the operator following that sequence of argument values.

call by reference   *variable substitution*

call by value   *value substitution*

cardinality   the cardinality $|A|$ of a set A is the number of elements in A.

cartesian product   the *cartesian product* $A \times B$ of two sets A and B is the set of all ordered pairs (a,b) with $a \in A$ and $b \in B$.

case statement   a form of *conditional statement* which permits selection of one of several actions on the basis of some tests.

circular list   see *list*

codomain   see *function*

comments   text appended to an algorithm (in Pascal we enclose them in curly brackets { }) which are not part of the algorithm, but are rather designed to help the human reader understand the algorithm. These comments can also be a basic ingredient in a proof of correctness for the algorithm. See also *correctness*.

compiler   a program designed to transform a program from one *programming language* into another. If the second language is the *machine language* of some computer, then the result of compiling a program P is a program in machine language which enables the original abstract algorithm embodied in P to be executed by the processor of the computer.

component   see *array*

composition method   A programming language provides both *simple statements* and *composition methods*—such as *sequential composition* and *repetitive composition*—which allow us to form *structured statements* from other statements, which may themselves be simple or compound.

compound statement   a statement obtained by *sequential composition*.

computation state   the *computation state* at any time in the execution of an algorithm comprises the value of all program variables at that time. The current instruction and current computation state between them determine how the computation state is to be changed, and to which instruction control is next to be transferred.

correctness   We say that the program specification $\{P\}\ S\ \{Q\}$ is *partially correct* if we show that whenever a *computation state* satisfies the condition P immediately before execution of S, then the computation state obtained immediately after the execution of S is completed will satisfy condition Q. If, in addition, it can be proved that execution of S always terminates when started in a computation state satisfying P, then we say that the program specification is *totally correct*.

conditional statement   a statement which combines several statements by specifying which one is to be executed on the outcome of some test.

constant   an object whose values does not change during the execution of a program.

constant definition   introduces an identifier as a synonym for a constant to aid program readability and program modification.

data type   each variable occurring in an algorithm must have a specified *data type*—a set of values including all possible values which the variable may take; together with the basic operations and tests defined upon those values.

declaration   introduces the *identifier* which is to denote a constant, variable, data type, procedure or function and specifies certain conditions of its use. The *scope* of the declaration is the entire *block* in whose *declaration part* it appears. (One complication, though: there may be strictly smaller scopes nested within the given scope in which other declarations redefine the indentifier.)

declaration part   see *block*

design   see *top-down design*

disjoint union   the disjoint union $A \amalg B$ of two sets A and B is obtained by relabelling A and B to distinguish copies of a given element that occur in both sets, and then taking the union.

domain   see *function*

dynamic structure   each algorithm has both a *static structure*—as represented, for example, by the text—independent of input data, and a *dynamic structure*—the process of computation expressed as a sequence of *computation states*—dependent on the values given to the input data.

dynamic variable   a variable introduced by a pointer reference rather than by a declaration.

edge   see *graph*

equivalence relation   see *partial order*

existential quantification   see *quantification*

exponent   see *floating point*

failure exit   a *failure exit* from an algorithm occurs when it is determined before the normal exit that no solution exists to the problem which the algorithm is designed to solve.

field   see *record*

field-identifier   see *record*

file   the value of a *file* variable is a sequence of values of a given type. In a *sequential file*, the read-write head moves one entry right after each reading operation and can only be repositioned by moving all the way to the left; writing can only occur to the right of the last entry of the entire file, and no entry can be erased save by erasing the entire contents of the file.

floating point   the representation of a number in the form $m * B^e$, where m, B and e are integers of limited size, m is called the *mantissa*, B the *base*, and e the *exponent*. Usually B is fixed, so that different numbers are represented by changing the choice of m and e.

formal parameter   see *parameter*

function   in set theory, a *function* (also called a *map* or *mapping*) $f : A \to B$ from a set A (the *domain*) to a set B (the *codomain*) is a rule which assigns an element $f(a)$ of B to each element a of A. Such an assignment is also called a *total function*. If, by contrast, $f(a)$ may not be specified for all a in A, we call f a *partial function*.

    In Pascal, a *function* is used to define an abstract expression. A *function declaration* is made up of two parts. The *heading* gives the function identifier and specifies the data types of the function arguments and result, while the *function body* gives the instructions required to produce the result.

function space   the *function space* $[A \to B]$ comprises all *functions* $f : A \to B$ from A to B. $[A \to B]$ is also denoted B^A. See *array*.

global see *block*

goto   a **goto** statement is of the form **goto** L, and the effect of its execution is that program execution is continued from the point of the program determined by L. L is called a *label*. In Pascal, it is a sequence of at most four digits. L: is used as a prefix of the statement to which control should be transferred.

graph   a *directed finite graph* is given by a set of *nodes* and a set of *edges* where each edge is associated with an ordered pair of nodes—we say that the edge is *directed* from the first node to the second. We say the second node is a *successor* of the first. See also *list* and *tree*.

greatest common divisor   if x and y are integers not both zero, their greatest common divisor, $gcd(x,y)$, is the largest integer that divides both of them (that is, without a remainder).

identifier   a string of letters and digits, of which the first is a letter, to denote an object.

index   see *array*

indexing   see *array*

induction   a useful technique for proving that some property $P(n)$ holds for all non-negative integers n is to prove that $P(0)$ is *true*, and then to prove that if $P(n)$ is *true* for any given n, then $P(n + 1)$ must also be *true*. This proof method is called *(mathematical) induction*.

instruction   a basic statement in *machine language*.

intersection   the *intersection* $A \cap B$ of two sets A and B contains all elements which belong both to A and B.

invariant property   this is a property P associated with a *repetitive statement* such that if P holds of the computation state initially, then P will hold of the computation state following each loop traversal.

iterative composition   *repetitive composition*

L-statement   a statement which includes **goto** L, but does not include the label L: for the same *label L*.

label   see **goto**

linear order   a *partial order* $\leqslant$ on a set A is a *linear order* if, for any pair a and a' of elements of A, either $a \leqslant a'$ or $a' \leqslant a$ must hold. If we write $a < b$ for $(a \leqslant b) \wedge (a \neq b)$ then for any a and a', we have $a < a'$ or $a = a'$ or $a' < a$.

list   a *linear list* is a connected *graph* in which every node but the last has one successor. A *circular list* or *ring* is a connected graph in which every node has one successor.

local   see *block*

logical formula   an expression which, when evaluated, yields either *true* or *false*. As such it may be built up using *Boolean operators* and *quantifiers*. If no quantifiers are involved, we refer to it as a *Boolean expression*.

logical operators   are *Boolean operators*

loop   see *repetitive statement*

loop invariant   *invariant property*

machine language   each computer has an associated programming language called the *machine language* with the properties that each program is made up of simple statements called *instructions*, and that each instruction is directly executable by hardware wired into the machine.

mantissa   see *floating point*

map = **mapping** = *function* (set-theoretic sense)

mathematical induction   see *induction*

memory area   one or more *memory units* assigned to hold a value of some *type*.

memory unit   an addressable unit of computer memory.

node   see *graph*

null word   the word $\langle\ \rangle$ of length zero. It is different from the blank ' ', a word of length one.

palindrome   a sequence of characters which reads the same forwards and backwards.

parameter   the *formal parameters* of a *procedure* are the identifiers specified in the procedure heading which denote the arguments and results of the procedure. The formal parameters of a *function* just denote the arguments. In a call of a procedure or function, the *actual parameters* are supplied in place of the formal parameters.

partial correctness   see *correctness*

partial function   see *function*

partial order   a *transitive* $((aRb \wedge bRc) \supset aRc)$, *reflexive* (aRa) and *antisymmetric* $((aRb \wedge bRa) \supset (a = b))$ relation on a set A. By contrast, an *equivalence relation* is transitive, reflexive, and *symmetric* $(aRb \supset bRa)$.

partition   a splitting of a set into a collection of disjoint (i.e., nonoverlapping) subsets.

pointer   a *pointer* of type $\uparrow T$ is a variable p whose value points to a variable of type T—or else is **nil** if no variable is being pointed to. We call p a *reference* to a variable of type T. p is also called a pointer variable.

postcondition   see *program specification*

powerset   the elements of the powerset PA of a set A are the subsets of A.

precondition   see *program specification*

prime   a nonnegative number p is prime if its only divisors are 1 and p itself (but 1 is not a prime).

procedure   *top-down design*, by its very nature, structures a Pascal program into procedures. In Pascal, a *procedure* is used to refine an abstract statement. A *procedure declaration* is made up of two parts. The *heading* gives the procedure identifier and specifies the data types of the arguments and results of the procedure, while the *procedure body* gives the instructions required to implement the abstract statement which the procedure refines. See also *block*.

program   an *algorithm* expressed in a *programming language*. See also *block*

program specification   a *program specification* for a one-entry, one-exit program S is of the form $\{P\}\ S\ \{Q\}$, and specifies that if a computation state satisfies the relation P, then the computation state obtained from it upon completion of executing S will satisfy the relation Q. For an *L-statement* S, the specification is expanded to the form $\{P\}\ S\ \{Q\}\ L\colon \{R\}$, where Q is the condition on 'normal' exit, R the condition on jumping to the label L. Two important tasks, then, are to prove for a given S that a specification is correct, and to find an S which meets a given specification. See *correctness*. We may regard the *precondition* P as specifying when S may be used; and the *postcondition* Q as specifying the outcome of using S (when the precondition is satisfied) on normal exit.

programming language   a specially chosen notation for the specification of *algorithms* to a level of detail suitable for mechanical interpretation (perhaps after a *compiler* has transformed it into machine language).

proof of correctness   see *correctness* and *proof rule*

proof rule   a *proof rule* associated with a simple statement allows us to formally prove that its execution affects the computation state in some specified way. A proof rule associated with a *composition method* allows us to prove that a *specification* for a statement structured by that method follows from the specifications of the consituent pieces.

quantification   given a *logical formula P*, we may build up new formulas by *existential quantification*—to yield ∃*x*(*P*), interpreted as "there exists a value of *x* for which *P* is true"—and by *universal quantification*—to yield ∀*x*(*P*), interpreted as "for all values of *x*, *P* is true".

record   a *record* type has as its set of values the cartesian product of the underlying sets of one or more data types, called the *component types*. If *s* is an identifier for the component type *A*, then *x . s* is the *A*-component of the variable *x*. The component types are called *fields* and each *s* is called a *field-identifier*.

recursion   we say a function or procedure or data type is *recursive*, or is defined by *recursion*, if it is used within its own definition. For example, we can define *n*!, *n* factorial, recursively by $0! = 1$ while $n! = n * (n - 1)!$ for $n > 0$.

reference   see *pointer*

reflexive   see *partial order*

relation   a *relation* on a set *A* is a subset of *A* × *A*. We often write *aRa′* —*a* is *R*-related to *a′*—rather than $(a,a′) \in R$.

repetitive statement   Pascal has two forms of repetitive statement. The first form, **while** *B* **do** *S*, specifies that while the condition *B* is *true*, the action specified by *S* should be repeated. In the second form, **repeat** *S* **until** *B*, the action specified by *S* is repeated until the condition *B* holds *true*. Both forms are called *loops*, and each execution of *S* is called 'passing once round the loop'.

return exit   a *return exit* occurs when the answer an algorithm is to produce has been found prior to the normal exit and a jump is made directly to the place where the desired answer is wanted.

ring   see *list*

scalar type   a *data type* whose underlying set of values is finite and is equipped with a *linear order*. A *subrange type* is then one whose set of values comprises an interval of the original scalar type.

scope   see *declaration*

semantic rules   see *syntactic rules*

serial composition   *sequential composition*

sequential   a process is *sequential* if it consists of steps performed one after another in sequence (i.e. execution of different steps cannot occur at the same time as it may in a parallel process).

sequential composition   combining statements by requiring that they be performed one after another in some specified order.

sequential file   see *file*

set   a collection of elements, usually defined by some rule. $a \in A$ denotes that *a* is an element of the set *A*.

set difference   the *set difference A—B* of *A* and *B* contains just those elements of *A* which do not belong to *B*.

set type   in Pascal, a *set type* has for its set of values the *powerset* of the set of values of a *scalar type*.

s-expression   a recursive data type used in Lisp. Given a data type—whose elements are called *atoms*—the set of *s-expressions* is defined recursively as the smallest set which contains the atoms, and is such that it contains (s_1,s_2) whenever s_1 and s_2 are themselves *s*-expressions.

shift   in computers which represent numbers in binary representation, a *shift right* converts *x* to *x* **div** 2, while a *shift* to the *left* converts *x* to $x * 2$ or causes an *overflow*.

simple statement   see *composition method*

sorted   a value of a file or array variable is *sorted* (on a key field) if the component values are of scalar type or are records containing a key field of scalar type; and if the components are arranged in non-decreasing order (of the key field)—e.g. $i \leqslant j$ implies $A[i] . key \leqslant A[j] . key$, etc.

specification   see *program specification*

statement   the formal specification of an action to be performed in an algorithm. See also *composition method*.

statement part   see *block*

static structure   see *dynamic structure*

static variable   a *variable* introduced by a *declaration*.

structured statement   see *composition method*

structured type   a data type built up from other types which may or may not themselves be structured. Ways of building such types include forming *arrays*, *files*, *records*, or *set types*.

subrange type   see *scalar type*

subscripting   see *array*

subset A is a subset of B, $A \subseteq B$, if every element of A is also an element of B.

successor   see *graph*

symmetric   see *partial order*

syntactic rules   *syntactic rules* of a *programming language* specify which sequences of symbols of the language's alphabet are 'grammatical'. Not all 'grammatical' sequences are meaningful—and *semantic rules* determine which meaning, if any, such a construct possesses. Note that *proof rules* are an important form of semantic rules.

textfile   a file whose components are printable characters is called a *textfile*. They are divided into lines. The input and output of most programs are textfiles.

top-down design   designing an algorithm to solve a problem by decomposing the overall problem into precisely specified subproblems and then verifying that if each subproblem is solved correctly and the solutions are fitted together in a specified way, then the original problem will be solved correctly. This process of refinement is repeated until a desired level of detail is reached.

total correctness   see *correctness*

total function   see *function*

transitive   see *partial order*

tree   a *tree* is a *graph* in which each node is the successor of at most one other node.

truth table   see *Boolean operators*

union   the union $A \cup B$ of two sets A and B contains all elements which belong to A or B or both.

universal quantification   see *quantification*

value substitution   in a procedure or function call, *value substitution* occurs when memory is set aside for a *formal parameter*, and then the value at the time of the call of the corresponding *actual parameter* (which can be an expression) is placed in that location. The formal parameter in value substitution is thus treated as a local variable, which is initialized to the value of the corresponding actual parameter upon procedure call.

variable   an object whose value may be changed during the course of execution of an algorithm. In running a *compiled* program, a variable is assigned a *memory area* which holds the current value of the variable. See also *data type*.

variable declaration   introduces the *identifier* which is to denote a variable, and specifies the *data type* of the variable. See *declaration*.

variable substitution   in a procedure or function call, *variable substitution* occurs when a *formal parameter* is made to refer to the memory area of the *actual parameter* (which must be a global variable). This is also known as *call by reference*. The formal parameter in variable substitution is thus identified with the actual parameter, a global variable, to which it corresponds, for the duration of the execution.

Appendixes

Appendix 1 | The Syntax of Pascal

The *syntax* of Pascal is a set of rules which determines which strings of symbols can be accepted by a Pascal compiler as a well-formed portion of a Pascal program. The *semantics* of Pascal determines what these symbol strings mean.

To give a simple example of how this works, consider the definition

$$\langle \text{unsigned number} \rangle ::= \langle \text{unsigned integer} \rangle | \langle \text{unsigned real} \rangle \qquad (1)$$

The $\langle \ \rangle$ notation indicates a set of possible strings; the $::=$ notation means 'is defined to be'; and the $|$ denotes 'or'. Thus the above definition is shorthand for "By definition, an 'unsigned number' is either an 'unsigned integer' or an 'unsigned real'." To fill this in, we need further definitions

$$\langle \text{unsigned integer} \rangle ::= \langle \text{digit} \rangle^{+} \qquad (2)$$

$$\langle \text{digit} \rangle ::= 0|1|2|3|4|5|6|7|8|9 \qquad (3)$$

The $^{+}$ says 'a sequence of at least one of these'. Since no $\langle \ \rangle$ appear on the right-hand side of (3), it says that a digit is precisely one of the ten familiar figures. And then (2) says that an unsigned integer is a string of one or more digits: 0 or 13 or 17569. The semantics is just the usual interpretation of a string of digits as an integer in decimal notation.

$$\langle \text{unsigned number} \rangle ::= \langle \text{unsigned integer} \rangle . \langle \text{digit} \rangle^{+} | \qquad (4)$$
$$\langle \text{unsigned integer} \rangle . \langle \text{digit} \rangle^{+} E \langle \text{scale factor} \rangle |$$
$$\langle \text{unsigned integer} \rangle E \langle \text{scale factor} \rangle$$

$$\langle\text{scale factor}\rangle ::= \langle\text{unsigned integer}\rangle\,|\,\langle\text{sign}\rangle\langle\text{unsigned integer}\rangle \quad (5)$$

$$\langle\text{sign}\rangle ::= +\,|\,- \quad (6)$$

The first line of (4) tells us that an 'unsigned real' may take the form $a \cdot b$ where a is a string which is an unsigned integer, where . is the period symbol, and b is a string of one or more digits. The third line of (4) tells us that an unsigned integer may also take the form aEb where a is an 'unsigned integer' and b is a 'scale factor'. Thus we see that examples of 'unsigned reals' include 0.31 and 2.6E4 and $9.1E - 4$ and $13E + 2$ and $13E2$ and $143E - 5$. The interpretation of a string of the form aEb is, in more familiar notation, just $a * 10^b$ (where $*$ means multiplication). Thus the above examples of 'unsigned reals' have the same meaning as the usual decimal notations 0.31, 26000, 0.00091, 1300, 1300 and 0.00143, respectively.

Note that, as opposed to the text, we use E rather than e here. Below, we shall use **not**, **and**, **or**, etc., for $\neg$, $\wedge$, $\vee$, respectively—since this is closer to the form that the reader is likely to employ in running programs.

The way of writing syntactic definitions shown in (1)–(6) is called Backus-Naur form (BNF, for short) in honor of its use by J. W. Backus and P. Naur in defining the syntax of Algol 60. The one exception is our use of the $^{+}$ notation. For example, (2) is really shorthand for the BNF definition

$$\langle\text{unsigned integer}\rangle ::= \langle\text{digit}\rangle\,|\,\langle\text{digit}\rangle\langle\text{unsigned integer}\rangle \quad (7)$$

This is a *recursive definition* (cf. Section 6.1)—an 'unsigned integer' is either a digit, or a digit followed by an 'unsigned integer', which in turn is a digit or a digit followed by an unsigned integer, etc., etc. Continuing in this way, it is clear that definitions (7) and (2) are indeed equivalent. We shall also use the notation { } for a sequence of at least zero of elements of the enclosed collection. Thus $\langle\text{digit}\rangle^{+} = \langle\text{digit}\rangle\{\langle\text{digit}\rangle\}$.

We just add the obvious definitions

$$\langle\text{letter}\rangle ::= a\,|\,b\,|\ldots|\,x\,|\,y\,|\,z\,|\,A\,|\,B\,|\ldots|\,X\,|\,Y\,|\,Z \quad (8)$$

$$\langle\text{letter or digit}\rangle ::= \langle\text{letter}\rangle\,|\,\langle\text{digit}\rangle \quad (9)$$

In some implementations, $\langle\text{letter}\rangle$ may contain only lower-case or only upper-case letters. The set $\langle\text{character}\rangle$ includes letters and digits and any other basic characters and will be implementation-dependent. We now introduce the syntax of Pascal section by section in the order in which it is introduced in the text—with occasional addition, for completeness, of syntactic constructions not discussed in the text.

Section 1.3

$$\langle\text{identifier}\rangle ::= \langle\text{letter}\rangle\{\langle\text{letter or digit}\rangle\} \quad (10)$$

Section 2.2

A constant is defined either as the identifier of a constant, as a number, or as a string of characters (placed in quotes to ensure that we do not interpret the string, rather than taking it for itself):

$$\langle \text{constant identifier} \rangle ::= \langle \text{identifier} \rangle \tag{11}$$

$$\langle \text{string} \rangle ::= \text{'} \langle \text{character} \rangle^{+} \text{'} \tag{12}$$

$$\langle \text{constant} \rangle ::= \langle \text{constant identifier} \rangle \,|\, \langle \text{unsigned number} \rangle \,| \tag{13}$$
$$\langle \text{sign} \rangle \langle \text{constant identifier} \rangle \,|\, \langle \text{sign} \rangle \langle \text{unsigned number} \rangle \,|$$
$$\langle \text{string} \rangle$$

$$\langle \text{unsigned constant} \rangle ::= \langle \text{constant identifier} \rangle \,|\, \langle \text{unsigned number} \rangle \,| \tag{14}$$
$$\langle \text{string} \rangle \,|\, \textbf{nil}$$

In (14), **nil** is *not* a string of three letters—it is a single symbol of the Pascal alphabet, and is used to denote the null reference.

A variable is either an entire variable—and is simply given by an identifier—or is a component variable or a referenced variable:

$$\langle \text{variable} \rangle ::= \langle \text{entire variable} \rangle \,|\, \langle \text{component variable} \rangle \,| \tag{15}$$
$$\langle \text{referenced variable} \rangle$$

$$\langle \text{entire variable} \rangle ::= \langle \text{variable identifier} \rangle \tag{16}$$

$$\langle \text{variable identifier} \rangle ::= \langle \text{identifier} \rangle \tag{17}$$

We delay the discussion of component variables until we meet structured data types in Chapter 3, and the discussion of referenced variables until we meet recursive data types in Chapter 6.

A function designator is a string like $\sin(x)$ or $\text{mult}(x3,13)$ where a function identifier is followed by one or more arguments, or may consist of a function identifier alone:

$$\langle \text{function designator} \rangle ::= \langle \text{function identifier} \rangle \,|\, \langle \text{function identifier} \rangle \tag{18}$$
$$(\langle \text{actual parameter} \rangle \{,\langle \text{actual parameter} \rangle\})$$

$$\langle \text{function identifier} \rangle ::= \langle \text{identifier} \rangle \tag{19}$$

$$\langle \text{actual parameter} \rangle ::= \langle \text{expression} \rangle \,|\, \langle \text{variable} \rangle \,| \tag{20}$$
$$\langle \text{procedure identifier} \rangle \,|\, \langle \text{function identifier} \rangle$$

$$\langle \text{procedure identifier} \rangle ::= \langle \text{identifier} \rangle \tag{21}$$

The assignment of 'meaning' to a function designator is made in a function declaration—we discuss this in Chapter 5, along with procedure declarations. Unfortunately, it will be awhile (until (32)) before we define 'expressions'—and we shall see that they use function designators in their construction. This is alright, since $\sin x + \cos y$ is a reasonable expression, and $\sin(\sin x + \cos y)$

is therefore a reasonable function designator. In any case, we may now define a 'factor' to be a constant, a variable, a function designator, the negation of a factor (a recursive definition again) or—still holding things open for the later definition of expressions—a string of the form [e1], [e1, . . . ,eN] (N expressions separated by commas), or [e1 . . e2] (two expressions separated by two dots) where e1, . . . ,eN are expressions:

$$\langle \text{factor} \rangle ::= \langle \text{variable} \rangle \,|\, \langle \text{unsigned constant} \rangle \,|\, (\langle \text{expression} \rangle) \,| \quad (22)$$
$$\langle \text{function designator} \rangle \,|\, \textbf{not} \langle \text{factor} \rangle \,|\, \langle \text{set} \rangle$$

$$\langle \text{set} \rangle ::= [\langle \text{element list} \rangle] \qquad\qquad (23)$$

$$\langle \text{element list} \rangle ::= \langle \text{element} \rangle \{, \langle \text{element} \rangle\} \,|\, \langle \text{empty} \rangle \qquad (24)$$

$$\langle \text{element} \rangle ::= \langle \text{expression} \rangle \,|\, \langle \text{expression} \rangle \,.\,.\, \langle \text{expression} \rangle \qquad (25)$$

$$\langle \text{empty} \rangle ::= \qquad\qquad\qquad (26)$$

The definition (22) goes rather against the Pascal philosophy of tight type control. The idea is that a factor can denote a variable or constant whose values are (one of) numbers, logical values or sets—but the syntax allows such type confusions as **not** f where f is a number. The **not** in (22) is a single Pascal symbol—when the factor a denotes a truth value then **not** a is to denote its negation. Clearly, (23) and (24) define a set explicitly by listing its elements (and, as (26) shows, the list may be empty). The situation in (25) says that the element of a set may be denoted by an expression, or by a pair of expressions. In the latter case, the element is itself a set—for example [2 . . 6] denotes the set whose elements are integers n satisfying the inequalities $2 \leqslant n \leqslant 6$.

'Terms' are built up from factors using the so-called 'multiplying operators' $*$, $/$, **mod**, **div** and **and**. Note that **mod**, **div** and **and** are single symbols of the Pascal alphabet. Note again the type-confusion—**and** denotes a logical operator, while the other four symbols denote numerical operators.

$$\langle \text{multiplying operator} \rangle ::= * \,|\, / \,|\, \textbf{div} \,|\, \textbf{mod} \,|\, \textbf{and} \qquad (27)$$

$$\langle \text{term} \rangle ::= \langle \text{factor} \rangle \,|\, \langle \text{term} \rangle \langle \text{multiplying operator} \rangle \langle \text{factor} \rangle \qquad (28)$$

A 'simple expression' is then built up from terms (with or without signs) by using the so-called 'adding operators' $+$, $-$ and **or**:

$$\langle \text{adding operator} \rangle ::= + \,|\, - \,|\, \textbf{or} \qquad\qquad (29)$$

$$\langle \text{simple expression} \rangle ::= \langle \text{term} \rangle \,|\, \langle \text{sign} \rangle \langle \text{term} \rangle \,| \qquad\qquad (30)$$
$$\langle \text{simple expression} \rangle \langle \text{adding operator} \rangle \langle \text{term} \rangle$$

Finally, an 'expression' is either a simple expression, or is built up from two simple expressions S_1 and S_2 to form $S_1 R S_2$ where R is one of the 'relational operators' $<$, $\leqslant$, $=$, $\neq$, $\geqslant$, $>$ and **in**:

$$\langle \text{relational operator} \rangle ::= < \,|\, \leqslant \,|\, = \,|\, \neq \,|\, \geqslant \,|\, > \,|\, \textbf{in} \qquad (31)$$

Here, the Pascal symbol **in** denotes set membership.

$$\langle\text{expression}\rangle ::= \langle\text{simple expression}\rangle\,|\,\langle\text{simple expression}\rangle \qquad (32)$$
$$\langle\text{relational operator}\rangle\langle\text{simple expression}\rangle$$

Section 2.3

Statements in Pascal may appear with or without labels, and may be simple or structured. We defer the discussion of labelled statements till we discuss **goto**s in Section 7.1; we take up structured statements in the next section:

$$\langle\text{statement}\rangle ::= \langle\text{unlabelled statement}\rangle\,| \qquad (33)$$
$$\langle\text{label}\rangle : \langle\text{unlabelled statement}\rangle$$

$$\langle\text{unlabelled statement}\rangle ::= \langle\text{simple statement}\rangle\,| \qquad (34)$$
$$\langle\text{structured statement}\rangle$$

$$\langle\text{simple statement}\rangle ::= \langle\text{assignment statement}\rangle\,| \qquad (35)$$
$$\langle\text{procedure statement}\rangle\,|$$
$$\langle\text{go to statement}\rangle\,|\,\langle\text{empty statement}\rangle$$

The empty statement is just that (recall (26)):

$$\langle\text{empty statement}\rangle ::= \langle\text{empty}\rangle \qquad (36)$$

We discuss procedures in Section 5.1 and **goto**s in Section 7.1. An assignment tells us to assign the value of an expression to a variable or function identifier (note the different roles of $::=$ and $:=$):

$$\langle\text{assignment statement}\rangle ::= \langle\text{variable}\rangle := \langle\text{expression}\rangle\,| \qquad (37)$$
$$\langle\text{function identifier}\rangle := \langle\text{expression}\rangle$$

The second form in (37) is used to return the value of a function as the value assigned to the function identifier.

Sections 2.4 and 2.5

We now see the ways in which structured statements can be built up in terms of others.

$$\langle\text{structured statement}\rangle ::= \langle\text{compound statement}\rangle\,| \qquad (38)$$
$$\langle\text{conditional statement}\rangle\,|$$
$$\langle\text{repetitive statement}\rangle\,|\,\langle\text{with statement}\rangle$$

The treatment of the 'with statement,' and of the 'for statement', see (46) below, must wait till Section 3.4. However, the other syntactic definitions are straightforward:

$$\langle\text{compound statement}\rangle ::= \textbf{begin}\langle\text{statement}\rangle\{;\langle\text{statement}\rangle\}\textbf{end} \qquad (39)$$

$$\langle\text{conditional statement}\rangle ::= \langle\text{if statement}\rangle | \langle\text{case statement}\rangle \quad (40)$$

$$\langle\text{if statement}\rangle ::= \textbf{if}\langle\text{expression}\rangle\textbf{then}\langle\text{statement}\rangle | \quad (41)$$
$$\textbf{if}\langle\text{expression}\rangle\textbf{then}\langle\text{statement}\rangle\textbf{else}\langle\text{statement}\rangle$$

$$\langle\text{case statement}\rangle ::= \textbf{case}\langle\text{expression}\rangle\textbf{of}\langle\text{case list element}\rangle \quad (42)$$
$$\{;\langle\text{case list element}\rangle\}\textbf{end}$$

$$\langle\text{case list element}\rangle ::= \langle\text{case label list}\rangle : \langle\text{statement}\rangle | \langle\text{empty}\rangle \quad (43)$$

$$\langle\text{case label list}\rangle ::= \langle\text{case label}\rangle\{,\langle\text{case label}\rangle\} \quad (44)$$

$$\langle\text{case label}\rangle ::= \text{constant} \quad (45)$$

$$\langle\text{repetitive statement}\rangle ::= \langle\text{while statement}\rangle | \langle\text{repeat statement}\rangle | \quad (46)$$
$$\langle\text{for statement}\rangle$$

$$\langle\text{while statement}\rangle ::= \textbf{while}\langle\text{expression}\rangle\textbf{do}\langle\text{statement}\rangle \quad (47)$$

$$\langle\text{repeat statement}\rangle ::= \textbf{repeat}\langle\text{statement}\rangle\{;\langle\text{statement}\rangle\} \quad (48)$$
$$\textbf{until}\langle\text{expression}\rangle$$

Section 3.3

A type definition takes the form **type** $t = T$ where the syntactic form of t is an identifier and T is defined by (50).

$$\langle\text{type definition}\rangle ::= \langle\text{identifier}\rangle = \langle\text{type}\rangle \quad (49)$$

$$\langle\text{type}\rangle ::= \langle\text{simple type}\rangle | \langle\text{structured type}\rangle | \langle\text{pointer type}\rangle \quad (50)$$

We look at structured types in Section 3.4, and pointer types in Section 6.3. Here we look at the simple types.

$$\langle\text{simple type}\rangle ::= \langle\text{scalar type}\rangle | \langle\text{subrange type}\rangle | \langle\text{type identifier}\rangle \quad (51)$$

$$\langle\text{type identifier}\rangle ::= \langle\text{identifier}\rangle \quad (52)$$

Note that the syntax does not spell out all the necessary restrictions. It is no good using a type identifier as a simple type as in (51) unless definitions elsewhere ensure that the identifier denotes a scalar type or subrange type. A scalar type is given by the ordered sequence of its elements:

$$\langle\text{scalar type}\rangle ::= (\langle\text{identifier}\rangle\{,\langle\text{identifier}\rangle\}) \quad (53)$$

$$\langle\text{subrange type}\rangle ::= \langle\text{constant}\rangle .. \langle\text{constant}\rangle \quad (54)$$

The definition (54) only makes sense if it is known which type the subrange comes from. This will hold of $c1 .. c2$ if $c1$ and $c2$ only belong to one previously defined type. (Incidentally, it seems strange that the designers of Pascal syntax use 'identifier' in (53) and 'constant' in (54).) Note that $Boolean = (false, true)$ can be explicitly defined using the syntax of (53).

A constant definition takes the form $i1 = c1$; telling us that the identifier $i1$ will denote the constant $c1$. A string of such definitions is preceded by the Pascal symbol **const**.

$$\langle\text{constant definition part}\rangle ::= \langle\text{empty}\rangle| \qquad\qquad (55)$$
$$\textbf{const}\langle\text{constant definition}\rangle\{;\langle\text{constant definition}\rangle\};$$

$$\langle\text{constant definition}\rangle ::= \langle\text{identifier}\rangle = \langle\text{constant}\rangle \qquad (56)$$

On the other hand, a variable declaration **var** $v:T$; tells us that the identifier v denotes a variable of type T.

$$\langle\text{variable declaration part}\rangle ::= \langle\text{empty}\rangle| \qquad\qquad (57)$$
$$\textbf{var}\langle\text{variable declaration}\rangle\{;\langle\text{variable declaration}\rangle\};$$

$$\langle\text{variable declaration}\rangle ::= \langle\text{identifier}\rangle\{,\langle\text{identifier}\rangle\}:\langle\text{type}\rangle \quad (58)$$

The $\langle\text{empty}\rangle$ options in (55) and (57) correspond to the situation in defining a block (see Section 5.1) where we do not wish to define any constants or declare any variables local to the block.

Section 3.4

$$\langle\text{structured type}\rangle ::= \langle\text{unpacked structured type}\rangle| \qquad (59)$$
$$\textbf{packed}\langle\text{unpacked structured type}\rangle$$

The prefix **packed** does not affect the meaning of the types—it tells the computer that for this data type, economy of storage space is more important than efficiency of access time. We do not use this option in this book.

$$\langle\text{unpacked structured type}\rangle ::= \langle\text{array type}\rangle|\langle\text{record type}\rangle| \quad (60)$$
$$\langle\text{set type}\rangle|\langle\text{file type}\rangle$$

We discuss 'set types' in Section 3.7. A typical array type looks like **array** $[T0,T1]$ **of** T. Recall 'simple type' from (51).

$$\langle\text{array type}\rangle ::= \textbf{array}[\langle\text{index type}\rangle\{,\langle\text{index type}\rangle\}]\textbf{of} \qquad (61)$$
$$\langle\text{component type}\rangle$$

$$\langle\text{index type}\rangle ::= \langle\text{simple type}\rangle \qquad\qquad (62)$$

$$\langle\text{component type}\rangle ::= \langle\text{type}\rangle \qquad\qquad (63)$$

Given a variable x of type **array** $[T0,T1]$ **of** T, we refer to a component of the array with an expression like $x[i,j]$.

$$\langle\text{component variable}\rangle ::= \langle\text{indexed variable}\rangle|\langle\text{field designator}\rangle| \quad (64)$$
$$\langle\text{file buffer}\rangle$$

We defer 'field designator' to the discussion of records (79), and 'file buffer' to the discussion of files (86).

$$\langle\text{indexed variable}\rangle ::= \langle\text{array variable}\rangle$$
$$[\langle\text{expression}\rangle\{,\langle\text{expression}\rangle\}] \qquad (65)$$

$$\langle\text{array variable}\rangle ::= \langle\text{variable}\rangle \qquad (66)$$

Clearly, the proper use of (65) goes beyond the syntactic description to require that the variable denote an array with the correct number of components. With the fact that the index type is scalar comes the ability to repeat some statement over a subrange of the index type, **for** $v := a$ **to** b **do** S or **for** $v := a$ **downto** b **do** S.

$$\langle\text{for statement}\rangle ::= \textbf{for}\langle\text{control variable}\rangle := \langle\text{for list}\rangle\textbf{do}\langle\text{statement}\rangle \qquad (67)$$

$$\langle\text{for list}\rangle ::= \langle\text{initial value}\rangle\textbf{to}\langle\text{final value}\rangle| \qquad (68)$$
$$\langle\text{initial value}\rangle\textbf{downto}\langle\text{final value}\rangle$$

$$\langle\text{control variable}\rangle ::= \langle\text{identifier}\rangle \qquad (69)$$

$$\langle\text{initial value}\rangle ::= \langle\text{expression}\rangle \qquad (70)$$

$$\langle\text{final value}\rangle ::= \langle\text{expression}\rangle \qquad (71)$$

Note again that the syntactic definition does not exhaust the checks that must be made for proper use of a for statement. For example, to use **for** $v := a$ **to** b **do** S, we must have that the expressions a and b evaluate to values—$a1$ and $b1$, say—of the same type T as the variable v.

A typical record type declaration looks like **type** $T =$ **record** $s_1 : T_1 ; s_2 : T_2$ **end**.

$$\langle\text{record type}\rangle ::= \textbf{record}\langle\text{field list}\rangle\textbf{end} \qquad (72)$$

$$\langle\text{field list}\rangle ::= \langle\text{fixed part}\rangle|\langle\text{fixed part}\rangle;\langle\text{variant part}\rangle| \qquad (73)$$
$$\langle\text{variant part}\rangle$$

$$\langle\text{fixed part}\rangle ::= \langle\text{record section}\rangle\{;\langle\text{record section}\rangle\} \qquad (74)$$

$$\langle\text{record section}\rangle ::= \langle\text{field identifier}\rangle\{,\langle\text{field identifier}\rangle\}:\langle\text{type}\rangle| \quad (75)$$
$$\langle\text{empty}\rangle$$

The variant part allows us, for example, to define a 'disjoint union' of types T_1 and T_2 by forming a new type T whose variables are tagged with a label c_j corresponding to the type of their current value: **record case** tag$:(c_1,c_2)$ **of** $c_1:(s_1:T_1); c_2:(s_2:T_2)$ **end** where the identifier tag is here declared to be of the scalar type (c_1,c_2).

$$\langle\text{variant part}\rangle ::= \textbf{case}\langle\text{tag field}\rangle\langle\text{type identifier}\rangle\textbf{of}\langle\text{variant}\rangle \qquad (76)$$
$$\{;\langle\text{variant}\rangle\}$$

$$\langle\text{tag field}\rangle ::= \langle\text{field identifier}\rangle:|\langle\text{empty}\rangle \qquad (77)$$

$$\langle\text{variant}\rangle ::= \langle\text{case label list}\rangle:(\langle\text{field list}\rangle)|\langle\text{empty}\rangle \qquad (78)$$

where we recall (44) ⟨case label list⟩ ::= ⟨case label⟩{,⟨case label⟩} and
(45) ⟨case label⟩ ::= constant. Given a record x, the component variable
in field s is denoted $x . s$.

$$⟨\text{field designator}⟩ ::= ⟨\text{record variable}⟩ . ⟨\text{field identifier}⟩ \qquad (79)$$

$$⟨\text{record variable}⟩ ::= ⟨\text{variable}⟩ \qquad (80)$$

$$⟨\text{field identifier}⟩ ::= ⟨\text{identifier}⟩ \qquad (81)$$

Clearly, (79) should not be used unless the variable is of record type and the
identifier denotes a field of that record type. If we wish to fix a record x as a
context and refer to the field identifiers s as shorthand for $s . x$, we use the
with statement.

$$⟨\text{with statement}⟩ ::= \textbf{with}⟨\text{record variable list}⟩\textbf{do}⟨\text{statement}⟩ \quad (82)$$

$$⟨\text{record variable list}⟩ ::= ⟨\text{record variable}⟩\{,⟨\text{record variable}⟩\} \quad (83)$$

When we declare **var** f: **file of** T that f is a file variable whose entries are
of type T, we automatically introduce a buffer $f\uparrow$ of type T.

$$⟨\text{file type}⟩ ::= \textbf{file of}⟨\text{type}⟩ \qquad (84)$$

$$⟨\text{file variable}⟩ ::= ⟨\text{variable}⟩ \qquad (85)$$

$$⟨\text{file buffer}⟩ ::= ⟨\text{file variable}⟩\uparrow \qquad (86)$$

For completeness, we also note

$$⟨\text{file identifier}⟩ ::= ⟨\text{identifier}⟩ \qquad (87)$$

Section 3.7

If $T1$ is a scalar or subrange type, then **type** $T2 = $ **set of** $T1$ introduces a new
type $T2$ whose values are the subsets of the set of values of $T1$—i.e. **set of**
corresponds to forming powersets.

$$⟨\text{set type}⟩ ::= \textbf{set of}⟨\text{base type}⟩ \qquad (88)$$

$$⟨\text{base type}⟩ ::= ⟨\text{simple type}⟩ \qquad (89)$$

where, (51), a simple type is a subrange or scalar type (or a type identifier).

Sections 5.1 and 5.2 and 7.1

Before giving the formal definition of a block, we note (Section 7.1) that
certain statements can be preceded by labels, and that **goto** statements can
transfer control to the statement preceded by the label in the go to statement.

$$\langle label \rangle ::= \langle unsigned\ integer \rangle \tag{90}$$

(In most implementations, a label is limited to be at most four digits long.)

$$\langle go\ to\ statement \rangle ::= \mathbf{goto}\langle label \rangle \tag{91}$$

A program is made up of an identifier which names the program, the names of the input and output files, and a block which defines the program's computation.

$$\langle program \rangle ::= \langle program\ heading \rangle \langle block \rangle \tag{92}$$

$$\langle program\ heading \rangle ::= \mathbf{program}\langle identifier \rangle (\langle file\ identifier \rangle \tag{93}$$
$$\{,\langle file\ identifier \rangle\});$$

A block is a sequence of declarations followed by a statement part which makes use of the notations defined in these declarations:

$$\langle block \rangle ::= \langle label\ declaration\ part \rangle \tag{94}$$
$$\langle constant\ definition\ part \rangle$$
$$\langle type\ definition\ part \rangle$$
$$\langle variable\ declaration\ part \rangle$$
$$\langle procedure\ and\ function\ declaration\ part \rangle$$
$$\langle statement\ part \rangle$$

$$\langle label\ declaration\ part \rangle ::= \langle empty \rangle\,|\,\mathbf{label}\langle label \rangle\{,\langle label \rangle\}; \tag{95}$$

We have already met the constant definition part (55), and the variable declaration part (57). In just the same way, we have

$$\langle type\ definition\ part \rangle ::= \langle empty \rangle\,| \tag{96}$$
$$\mathbf{type}\langle type\ definition \rangle\{;\langle type\ definition \rangle\};$$

The procedure and function declaration part is a sequence of zero or more procedure and function declarations:

$$\langle procedure\ and\ function\ declaration\ part \rangle ::= \tag{97}$$
$$\{\langle procedure\ or\ function\ declaration \rangle;\}$$

$$\langle procedure\ or\ function\ declaration \rangle ::= \langle procedure\ declaration \rangle\,| \tag{98}$$
$$\langle function\ declaration \rangle$$

The syntax of procedure declarations is as follows:

$$\langle procedure\ declaration \rangle ::= \langle procedure\ heading \rangle \langle block \rangle \tag{99}$$

$$\langle procedure\ heading \rangle ::= \tag{100}$$
$$\mathbf{procedure}\langle identifier \rangle;\,|\,\mathbf{procedure}\langle identifier \rangle$$
$$(\langle formal\ parameter\ section \rangle\{;\langle formal\ parameter\ section \rangle\});$$

$\langle$formal parameter section$\rangle$ ::= $\langle$parameter group$\rangle|$ (101)
                    var$\langle$parameter group$\rangle|$
                    function$\langle$parameter group$\rangle|$
                    procedure$\langle$identifier$\rangle$\{,$\langle$identifier$\rangle$\}

$\langle$parameter group$\rangle$ ::= $\langle$identifier$\rangle$\{,$\langle$identifier$\rangle$\}:$\langle$type identifier$\rangle$ (102)

The syntax of function declarations also makes use of the formal parameter section:

$\langle$function declaration$\rangle$ ::= $\langle$function heading$\rangle\langle$block$\rangle$ (103)

$\langle$function heading$\rangle$ ::= **function**$\langle$identifier$\rangle$:$\langle$result type$\rangle$;$|$ (104)
                    function$\langle$identifier$\rangle$($\langle$formal parameter section$\rangle$
                    \{;$\langle$formal parameter section$\rangle$\}):$\langle$result type$\rangle$;

$\langle$result type$\rangle$ ::= $\langle$type identifier$\rangle$.   (105)

Finally, we have

$\langle$statement part$\rangle$ ::= $\langle$compound statement$\rangle$ (106)

We saw in (35) that one form of a simple statement is a procedure statement, which is a call to a procedure with a specification of its actual parameters:

$\langle$procedure statement$\rangle$ ::= $\langle$procedure identifier$\rangle|$ (107)
                    $\langle$procedure identifier$\rangle$($\langle$actual parameter$\rangle$
                    \{,$\langle$actual parameter$\rangle$\})

where 'actual parameter' is given by (20).

Section 6.3

We conclude by giving the syntax for references:

$\langle$pointer type$\rangle$ ::= $\uparrow\langle$type identifier$\rangle$ (108)

$\langle$pointer variable$\rangle$ ::= $\langle$variable$\rangle$ (109)

$\langle$referenced variable$\rangle$ ::= $\langle$pointer variable$\rangle\uparrow$ (110)

For ease of reference, the above syntax can be summarized in the following diagrams, adapted from Jensen and Wirth [1974, pp. 116–118]. An acceptable instance of a syntactic construct is obtained by starting at the entry point of its diagram and following any path which leads to the exit.

IDENTIFIER

UNSIGNED INTEGER

UNSIGNED NUMBER

UNSIGNED CONSTANT

CONSTANT

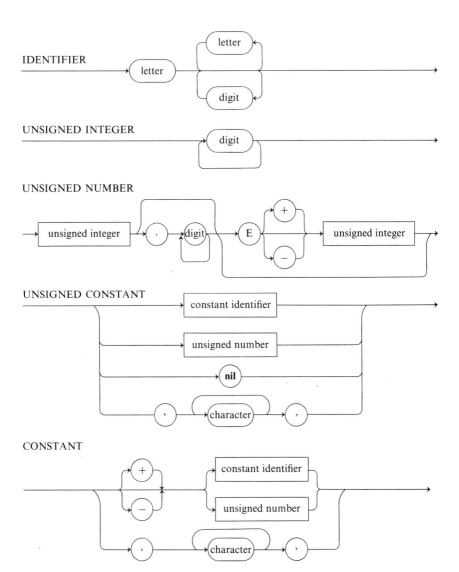

VARIABLE

FACTOR

TERM

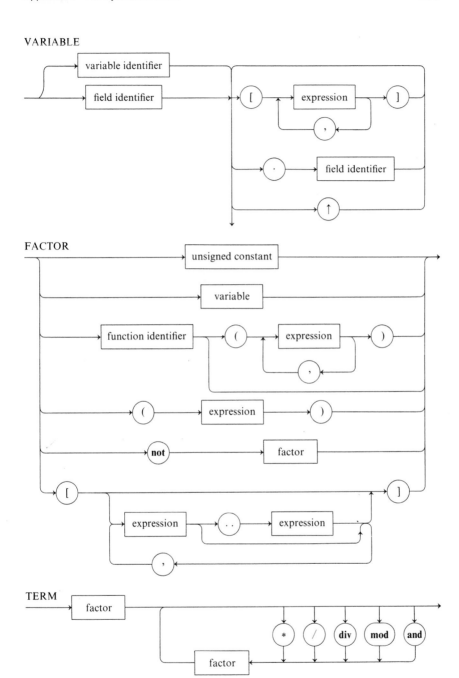

SIMPLE EXPRESSION

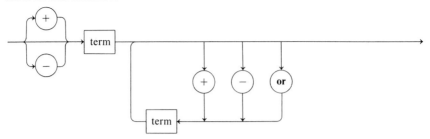

EXPRESSION

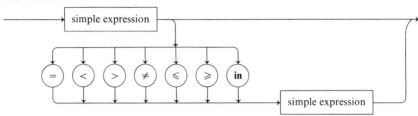

PARAMETER LIST

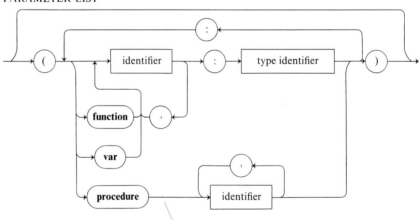

SIMPLE TYPE

TYPE

FIELD LIST

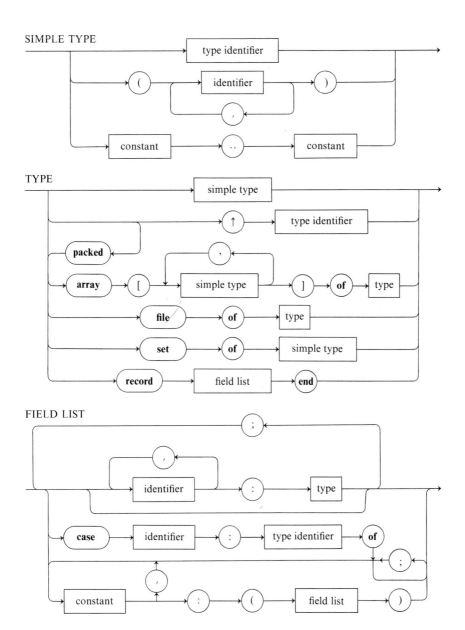

STATEMENT

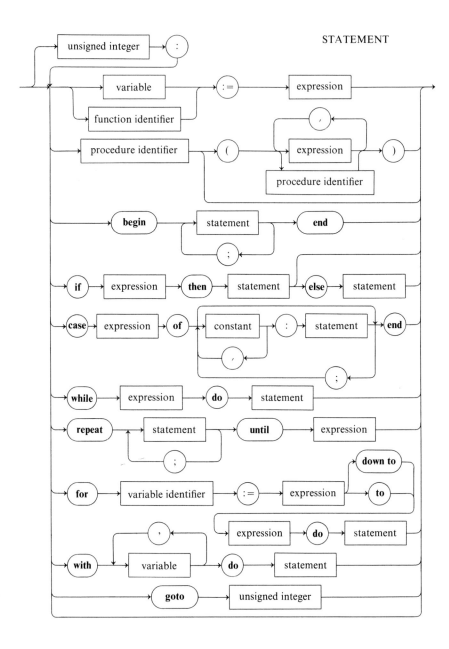

BLOCK

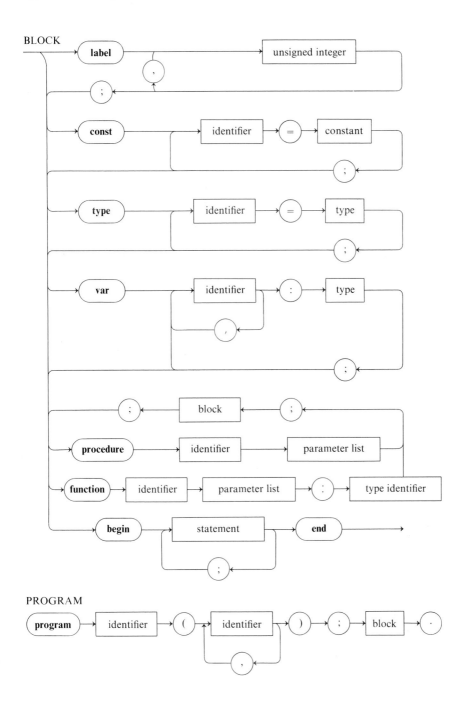

PROGRAM

Appendix 2   Proof Rules

Consequence Rules

$$\frac{\{P\}\ S\ \{R\},\ R \supset Q}{\{P\}\ S\ \{Q\}} \tag{1}$$

$$\frac{P \supset R,\ \{R\}\ S\ \{Q\}}{\{P\}\ S\ \{Q\}}$$

Null Rule

$$\{P\}\ \{P\} \tag{2}$$

Assignment Rule

Let x be a variable of type T, and e an expression whose type is either T or a subrange of T. P_e^x denotes a logical formula P in which the expression e is substituted for all free occurences of variable x.

$$\{P_e^x\}\ x := e\ \{P\} \tag{3}$$

Compound Rule

$$\frac{\{P_{i-1}\}\ S_i\ \{P_i\}\ \text{for}\ i = 1, \ldots ,n}{\{P_0\}\ \textbf{begin}\ S_1;S_2;\ldots;\ S_n\ \textbf{end}\ \{P_n\}} \tag{4}$$

Conditional Rules

$$\frac{\{P \wedge B\}\ S_1\ \{Q\},\ \{P \wedge \neg B\}\ S_2\ \{Q\}}{\{P\}\ \textbf{if}\ B\ \textbf{then}\ S_1\ \textbf{else}\ S_2\ \{Q\}} \tag{5}$$

$$\frac{\{P \wedge B\}\ S\ \{Q\},\ P \wedge \neg B \supset Q}{\{P\}\ \textbf{if}\ B\ \textbf{then}\ S\ \{Q\}} \tag{6}$$

Case Rule

$$\frac{\{P \wedge (x = k_i)\}\ S_i\ \{Q\}\ \text{for}\ i = 1,2, \ldots ,n}{\{P \wedge (x \in [k_1, \ldots ,k_n])\}\ \textbf{case}\ x\ \textbf{of}\ k_1 : S_1;\ \ldots;\ k_n : S_n\ \textbf{end}\ \{Q\}} \tag{7}$$

The above rule applies to those cases where multiple labels precede some of the statements S_i since $k_a, k_b, \ldots, k_m : S$ stands for $k_a : S; k_b : S; \ldots; k_m : S$.

While-do Rule

$$\frac{\{P \wedge B\}\ S\ \{P\}}{\{P\}\ \textbf{while}\ B\ \textbf{do}\ S\ \{P \wedge \neg B\}} \tag{8}$$

Repeat-until Rule

$$\frac{\{P\}\ S\ \{Q\},\ Q \wedge \neg B \supset P}{\{P\}\ \textbf{repeat}\ S\ \textbf{until}\ B\ \{Q \wedge B\}} \tag{9}$$

For Rules

Denote with:

$$[a\,..\,b] = \text{the set of } j \text{ such that } a \leqslant j \leqslant b$$
$$[a\,..\,i) = \text{the set of } j \text{ such that } a \leqslant j < i$$
$$(i\,..\,b] = \text{the set of } j \text{ such that } i < j \leqslant b$$
$$[\ ] = \text{the empty set}$$
$$P(s) = \text{an assertion about the interval } s$$

$$\frac{\{(a \leqslant i \leqslant b) \wedge P([a\,..\,i))\}\ S\ \{P([a\,..\,i])\}}{\{P([\ ])\}\ \textbf{for}\ i := a\ \textbf{to}\ b\ \textbf{do}\ S\ \{P([a\,..\,b])\}} \tag{10}$$

$$\frac{\{(a \leqslant i \leqslant b) \wedge P((i\,..\,b])\}\ S\ \{P([i\,..\,b])\}}{\{P([\ ])\}\ \textbf{for}\ i := b\ \textbf{downto}\ a\ \textbf{do}\ S\ \{P([a\,..\,b])\}} \tag{11}$$

With Rule

Let x be a variable of type **record** $s_1 : T_1;\ s_2 : T_2; \ldots; s_m : T_m$ **end**. $P^{x_1, x_2, \ldots, x_m}_{y_1, y_2, \ldots, y_m}$ denotes a logical formula P in which a simultaneous substitution of all occurences of x_i by the corresponding y_i is performed. All x_i are assumed to be distinct.

$$\frac{\{P^{x \cdot s_1, \ldots, x \cdot s_m}_{s_1, \ldots, s_m}\}\ S\ \{Q^{x \cdot s_1, \ldots, x \cdot s_m}_{s_1, \ldots, s_m}\}}{\{P\}\ \textbf{with}\ x\ \textbf{do}\ S\ \{Q\}} \tag{12}$$

Rules for Standard File Operators

Let f be a variable of type **file of** T_0. f_L and f_R are of type T so that $f = f_L f_R$, the concatenation of two sequences (files). $\langle\ \rangle$ denotes the empty sequence and $\langle x \rangle$ a singleton sequence. Functions $first: T \rightarrow T_0$ and $rest: T \rightarrow T$ are defined as follows:

$$first(\langle x \rangle f) = x \qquad rest(\langle x \rangle f) = f$$

where $first(\langle \ \rangle)$ is undefined and $rest(\langle \ \rangle)$ is undefined. The following holds:

$$eof(f) \equiv (f_R = \langle \ \rangle)$$

The proof rule (13) says that the operation $get(f)$ is applicable only if $eof(f)$ is *false*, i.e., $f_R \neq \langle \ \rangle$. In that case it corresponds to the following set of assignments performed simultaneously:

$$f_L := f_L first(f_R) \qquad f\uparrow := first(rest(f_R)) \qquad f_R := rest(f_R)$$

$$\{ \neg eof(f) \wedge P_{f_L first(f_R), first(rest(f_R)), rest(f_R)}^{f_L \quad f\uparrow \quad f_R} \} \ get(f) \ \{P\} \tag{13}$$

The proof rule (14) says that the operation $put(f)$ is applicable only if $eof(f)$ is *true*. In that case it leaves $eof(f)$ and $f_L = f$ unchanged, and corresponds to the assignment:

$$f := f\langle f\uparrow \rangle$$

$$\{ eof(f) \wedge P_{f\langle f\uparrow \rangle}^{f} \} \ put(f) \ \{P \wedge eof(f)\} \tag{14}$$

The effect of the operator $reset(f)$ is equivalent to the effect of the following three assignments executed simultaneously:

$$f_L := \langle \ \rangle \qquad f\uparrow := first(f) \qquad f_R := f_L f_R$$

$$\{P_{\langle \rangle, \langle \rangle}^{f_L, \ f_R}\} \ rewrite(f) \ \{P \wedge eof(f)\} \tag{15}$$

The proof rule (16) says that the effect of the operator $rewrite(f)$ is equivalent to the effect of the assignment:

$$f_L : \langle \ \rangle \text{ and } f_R := \langle \ \rangle$$

$$\{P_{\langle \rangle, \langle \rangle}^{f_L, \ f_R}\} \ rewrite(f) \ \{P \wedge eof(f)\} \tag{16}$$

In the above rules the assertion P must not contain f, f_L, f_R and $f\uparrow$, except in those cases where they occur explicitly in the list of substituents.

Proof Rule for Blocks

Let D be a sequence of declarations and S a compound statement. Let H be a set of assertions which describe the properties of the objects declared in D. For the definitions of constants in D the corresponding assertions in H are the equations which appear in these constant definitions. For a variable declaration **var** $x: T$ in D, the corresponding assertion is x **in** T. This means that T determines the operators which can be applied to x and the axioms associated with these operators. For the type definitions in D the corresponding assertions in H describe the properties of the newly introduced types. With these assumptions the following proof rule holds for the block $D; S$:

$$\frac{H \vdash \{P\} \ S \ \{Q\}}{\{P\} \ D; S \ \{Q\}} \tag{17}$$

In the above proof rule the logical formulas P and Q may not contain any identifiers declared in D. If, however, they do, the rule can be applied only after an alphabetic change of identifiers local to the block $D; S$.

Proof Rule for Functions

Let

function $f(L):T; \ S$

be a function declaration, where f is its identifier, L is the parameter specification list, T is the type of the result, and S is the function body. Let x be the list of parameters in L. Assume that no assignments to either variable parameters in x or nonlocal variables of f occur within S. Furthermore, suppose that f does not occur free in P and none of the variables in x occurs free in Q. Then:

$$\frac{\{P\} \ S \ \{Q\}}{\forall x(P \supset Q^f_{f(x)})} \tag{18}$$

The property $\forall x(P \supset Q^f_{f(x)})$ is then used when proving properties of expressions in which calls of the function f occur. In proving $\{P\} \ S \ \{Q\}$ in (18) we can use the assertions about the formal parameters of f which follow from the specifications in L, as well as the properties of the global variables which occur in S. Observe that if S does contain global variables, then they will appear in P and Q.

If the function f is recursive, then when proving $\{P\} \ S \ \{Q\}$ for (18) the property $\forall x(P \supset Q^f_{f(x)})$ may be assumed to hold for the calls of the function f which occur within S.

In applying the proof rule (18) it is essential to verify that if P holds before execution of S, S will terminate. Otherwise this rule may lead to incorrect conclusions.

Proof Rule for Procedures

Let

procedure $p(L); \ S$

be a procedure declaration, where p is its identifier, L is the parameter specification part and S is the procedure body. Let x be the list of formal parameters specified in L. Then:

$$\frac{\{P\}\ S\ \{Q\}}{\forall x(dis(x) \supset \{P\}\ p(x)\ \{Q\})} \tag{19}$$

In the proof rule (19) we have used $dis(x)$ to make explicit the requirement that the procedure call $p(x)$ satisfies the following conditions:

(i) All the actual variable parameters in x are distinct and none of them occurs in the actual value parameters in x.
(ii) None of the global variables in S which are subject to assignment when S is executed occur within the actual value parameters in x.

P and Q will, in general, include both the formal parameters x and the global variables of the procedure p, but none of the value parameters of x are allowed to occur free in Q. For a specific call $p(a)$ where the list of actual parameters a satisfies the above conditions, from (19) we obtain:

$$\{P_a^x\}\ p(a)\ \{Q_a^x\} \tag{2}$$

on the assumption that $dis(a)$ holds.

If the procedure p is recursive, then when proving $\{P\}\ S\ \{Q\}$ for (19) we may assume that the property $\{P\}\ p(x)\ \{Q\}$ holds for every call $p(x)$ which occurs within S if the actual parameters x of such a call obey the above stated discipline.

Proof Rules for Gotos

An *L-statement* is a statement which contains one or more occurrences of **goto** L, but no occurrence of the target L:, for the specified label L. For such a statement we use a program specification of the form

$$\{P\}\ S\ \{Q\}\ \{L:R\} \tag{21}$$

to indicate that with precondition P guarantees that execution of S will yield to satisfaction of Q upon 'normal' exit, and of R on a jump to L:. We have the following proof rules.

$$\text{For every } P,\ \{P\}\ \textbf{goto}\ L\ \{false\}\ \{L:P\} \tag{22}$$

$$\{P\}\ S\ \{Q\}\ \text{implies}\ \{P\}\ S\ \{Q\}\ \{L:false\} \tag{23}$$
if S does not contain **goto** L.

$$\frac{\{P\}\ S_1\ \{R\}\ \{L:R\},\ \{R\}\ S_2\ \{Q\}\ \{L:R\}}{\{P\}\ \textbf{begin}\ S_1;\ L:S_2\ \textbf{end}\ \{Q\}} \tag{24}$$

$$\frac{\{P\}\ S_1\ \{Q_1\}\ \{L:R\},\ \{Q_1\}\ S_2\ \{Q_2\}\ \{L:R\}}{\{P\}\ \textbf{begin}\ S_1;\ S_2\ \textbf{end}\ \{Q_2\}\ \{L:R\}} \tag{25}$$

$$\frac{\{P \wedge B\}\ S\ \{P\}\ \{L:R\}}{\{P\}\ \textbf{while}\ B\ \textbf{do}\ S\ \{P \wedge \neg B\}\ \{L:R\}} \tag{26}$$

Index of Algorithms

Author Index

Subject Index

Computer Science from Springer-Verlag

Compiler Construction
An Advanced Course
Second Edition
Edited by **F. L. Bauer** and **J. Eickel**
1976. xiv, 638p. 123 illus. 2 tables. paper
(Springer Study Edition)

This text consists of papers carefully prepared by a group of experts for a workshop on compiler construction held in Munich in 1974 and repeated in 1975. The second edition contains an addendum by A. P. Ershov to the contribution by F. L. Bauer, as well as a new paper by D. Gries on "Error Recovery and Correction—An Introduction to the Literature."

Software Engineering
An Advanced Course
Edited by **F. L. Bauer**
1977. xii, 545p. paper
(Springer Study Edition)

Proceedings of an Advanced Course on Software Engineering, organized by the Mathematical Institute of the Technical University of Munich and the Leibniz Computing Center of the Bavarian Academy of Sciences, March, 1972.

MICROCOMPUTER
Problem Solving Using PASCAL
By **K. L. Bowles**
1977. x, 563p. paper

This text introduces problem solving and structured programming using the PASCAL language, extended with built-in functions for graphics. Designed for a one-quarter/semester curriculum at the sophomore/junior level, this book serves a dual purpose: to teach students an organized approach to solving problems, and to introduce them to the computer and its applications, which may be of use later in their chosen professions.

PASCAL
User Manual and Report
Second Edition
By **K. Jensen** and **N. Wirth**
1978. viii, 167p. paper
(Springer Study Edition)

This book is divided into two parts: the User Manual and the Revised Report. The Manual is directed at those who have previously acquired some familiarity with computer programming, and who wish to become acquainted with PASCAL. Many examples demonstrate the various features of this language. Tables and syntax specifications are included in the appendix. The Report serves as a concise and ultimate reference for both programmers and implementors. By defining Standard PASCAL, the book provides a common base for various implementations of the language.

Texts and Monographs in Computer Science

Chess Skill in Man and Machine
Edited by **P. W. Frey**
1977. xi, 217p. 55 illus. cloth.

Design of Digital Computers
An Introduction
Second Revised Edition
By **H. W. Gschwind** and **E. J. McCluskey**
1975. ix, 548p. 375 illus. cloth.

The Origins of Digital Computers
Selected Papers
Second Edition
Edited by **B. Randell**
1975. xvi, 464p. 120 illus. cloth

Automata-Theoretic Aspects of Formal Power Series
By **A. Salomaa** and **M. Soittola**
1978. approx. 240p. cloth.

Adaptive Information Processing
An Introductory Survey
By **J. R. Sampson**
1976. x, 214p. 83 illus. cloth.